Salafism in Nigeria

Islam, Preaching, and Politics

The specter of Boko Haram dominates much media coverage and academic analysis of northern Nigeria. But, as Alexander Thurston argues here, beyond the sensational headlines this group generates, the dynamics of Muslim life in northern Nigeria remain poorly understood. Drawing on interviews with leading Salafis in Nigeria as well as on a rereading of the history of the global Salafi movement, this volume explores how a canon of classical and contemporary texts defines Salafism. Examining how these texts are interpreted and – crucially – who has the authority to do so, Thurston offers a systematic analysis of curricula taught in Saudi Arabia and how they shape religious scholars' approach to religion and education once they return to Africa.

Essential for scholars of religion and politics, this unique text explores how the canon of Salafism has been used and refined, from Nigeria's return to democracy to the jihadist movement Boko Haram.

Alexander Thurston is Visiting Assistant Professor of African Studies at Georgetown University's School of Foreign Service. He has conducted field research in Nigeria and Senegal and has published in *African Affairs*, the *Journal of the American Academy of Religion*, the *Journal of Religion in Africa*, and *Islamic Africa*, as well as with the Brookings Institution, the Center for Strategic and International Studies, and the Carnegie Endowment.

THE INTERNATIONAL AFRICAN LIBRARY

The International African Library is a major monograph series from the International African Institute. Theoretically informed ethnographies, and studies of social relations 'on the ground' which are sensitive to local cultural forms, have long been central to the Institute's publications programme. The IAL maintains this strength and extends it into new areas of contemporary concern, both practical and intellectual. It includes works focused on the linkages between local, national and global levels of society; writings on political economy and power; studies at the interface of the socio-cultural and the environmental; analyses of the roles of religion, cosmology and ritual in social organisation; and historical studies, especially those of a social, cultural or interdisciplinary character.

For a list of titles published in the series, please see the end of the book.

Salafism in Nigeria

Islam, Preaching, and Politics

Alexander Thurston

International African Institute, London
and
CAMBRIDGE
UNIVERSITY PRESS

CAMBRIDGE
UNIVERSITY PRESS

University Printing House, Cambridge CB2 8BS, United Kingdom

One Liberty Plaza, 20th Floor, New York, NY 10006, USA

477 Williamstown Road, Port Melbourne, VIC 3207, Australia

314-321, 3rd Floor, Plot 3, Splendor Forum, Jasola District Centre, New Delhi - 110025, India

79 Anson Road, #06-04/06, Singapore 079906

Cambridge University Press is part of the University of Cambridge.

It furthers the University's mission by disseminating knowledge in the pursuit of education, learning and research at the highest international levels of excellence.

www.cambridge.org
Information on this title: www.cambridge.org/9781316610190

First published 2016
First paperback edition 2018

A catalogue record for this publication is available from the British Library

Library of Congress Cataloging in Publication data
Thurston, Alexander, author.
Salafism in Nigeria : Islam, preaching, and politics / Alexander Thurston.
New York : Cambridge University Press, 2016. Series: The international African library ; 52
Includes bibliographical references and index.
LCCN 2016026912 ISBN 9781107157439 (hardback : alk. paper)
LCSH: Salafeiyah. Salafeiyah – Nigeria. Boko Haram. Salafeiyah – Saudi Arabia.
LCC BP195.S18 T48 2016 DDC 297.8/109669 – dc23
LC record available at https://lccn.loc.gov/2016026912

ISBN 978-1-107-15743-9 Hardback
ISBN 978-1-316-61019-0 Paperback

Contents

Acknowledgments — *page* vii
List of Maps — ix

Introduction: Defining Salafism, Analyzing Canons — 1

Part I: Salafism and Its Transmission

1 The Canon and Its Canonizers — 31
2 Africans and Saudi Arabia — 64
3 Nigerians in Medina — 92

Part II: The Canon in Action

4 Teaching the Canon — 117
5 The Canon in Religious Debates and Electronic Media — 140
6 The Canon in Politics — 168

Part III: Boko Haram and the Canon

7 Boko Haram from Salafism to Jihadism — 193
8 Reclaiming the Canon — 220
Conclusion — 240

Appendix 1: The Sermon of Necessity (Khuṭbat al-Ḥāja) — 247
Glossary of Persons — 249
Glossary of Arabic Terms — 254
Bibliography — 257
Index — 277

Acknowledgments

Many people helped me with the research and writing for this book. I have benefited tremendously from the generous mentorship and collegiality of Muhammad Sani Umar, Benjamin Soares, Rüdiger Seesemann, Robert Launay, Leonardo Villalon, Murray Last, Paul Lubeck, John Campbell, Terje Østebø, Brannon Ingram, John Voll, Jonathan Brown, Adam Higazi, Matt Page, Ibrahim Yahaya Ibrahim, Dan Eizenga, Mamadou Bodian, Brandon Kendhammer, Susan O'Brien, Marc-Antoine Pérouse de Montclos, and Carl LeVan. In Nigeria, the research assistance of Usman Aliyu was invaluable to me, as was his friendship. I was also welcomed and helped by Ibrahim Muhammad, Abubakar Mustapha, Uba Abdalla Adamu, Haruna Salihi, Mustapha Ismail, Munir Maitama, Hafizu Zailani, Adamu Sagagi, Ahmadu Bello Hassan, Carmen McCain, Jack Tocco, Hannah Hoechner, Abbe Katerega, and many others. Many people gave generously of their time for interviews, especially Abdulwahhab Abdullahi, Bashir Aliyu, Abdullahi Saleh Pakistan, Nazifi Inuwa, Lawi Atiku, Baba Uba Ringim, Kabiru Uba Ringim, and Bashir Tijjani Uthman. The faculty and staff at Bayero University Kano and at Aminu Kano College of Islamic and Legal Studies were generous with their time and assistance. Colleagues at Georgetown University, especially Scott Taylor, Lahra Smith, Jonathan Brown, and Paul Heck, provided a stimulating intellectual atmosphere and a friendly environment in which to teach and write. My thanks to all of you.

In 2015, as I was revising this book into its final form, the African Studies community lost two great scholars to cancer: Stephen Ellis and J. D. Y. Peel. I was privileged to correspond with each of them in their final months and was humbled that each of them took time to push a young scholar to sharpen his thinking: Professor Ellis encouraged me to revise a conference presentation, while Professor Peel, as series editor at the International African Library, gave me incisive comments that led me to rewrite this book's introduction. Both men embodied an ideal of thoughtful and generous mentorship, and I am grateful to have known them.

The research for this book was supported by fellowships from the Social Science Research Council, the Wenner-Gren Foundation, the African

Studies Program at Northwestern University, and Northwestern's Buffett Institute. Other versions of two chapters have previously appeared in print: Chapter 3 was published as "Ahlussunnah: A Preaching Network from Kano to Medina in Back" in *Shaping Global Islamic Discourses: The Role of al-Azhar, al-Medina and al-Mustafa*, edited by Masooda Bano and Keiko Sakurai; Chapter 5 was published as "The Salafi Ideal of Electronic Media as an Intellectual Meritocracy in Kano, Nigeria" in the December 2015 issue of the *Journal of the American Academy of Religion*. I am grateful to Edinburgh University Press and Oxford University Press, respectively, for permission to republish those chapters. My thinking for this book was decisively shaped by my attendance at the conference "Centres of Learning and Change," held at Oxford University in 2012 and organized by Masooda Bano and Keiko Sakurai; I thank the conference organizers as well as Mike Farquhar and Stéphane Lacroix, from whose input I benefited tremendously. My intellectual debts to several scholars I have not met – especially Thomas Hegghammer, Joas Wagemakers, and David Commins – should be clear, although I bear sole responsibility for any mistakes and misinterpretations. Finally, I thank Stephanie Kitchen of the International African Library and Maria Marsh of Cambridge University Press for their patient shepherding of this manuscript through the review and publication process, and I thank Miles Irving for designing the book's maps.

I also thank my family and friends for their love and support. My grandparents, Theodore and Yetta Ziolkowski, have inspired me through their embodiment of the life of the mind. My sister Lara is not only a keen observer of international affairs but also all that one could ask for in a friend and confidante. Friends, including Josh Nelson, Lance Steagall, Jason Rosenbaum, and Brett Sweeney, have always encouraged my scholarly pursuits and have helped me make that scholarship relevant to a wider audience. Ann Wainscott is the love of my life, and without our ongoing conversations on Islam and politics, as well as her daily companionship, this book would not have come together. The extended Wainscott family has also welcomed and supported me, and I am grateful to them for that. Finally, my parents, Bob Thurston and Gretchen Ziolkowski, have given me a life of possibilities while teaching me to affirm the inherent dignity of all people. I dedicate this book to them.

Maps

1. Present-Day Nigeria *page* x
2. Local Government Areas in Kano State, Nigeria xi
3. Present-Day Saudi Arabia xii

Map 1. Present-Day Nigeria

Map 2. Local Government Areas in Kano State, Nigeria

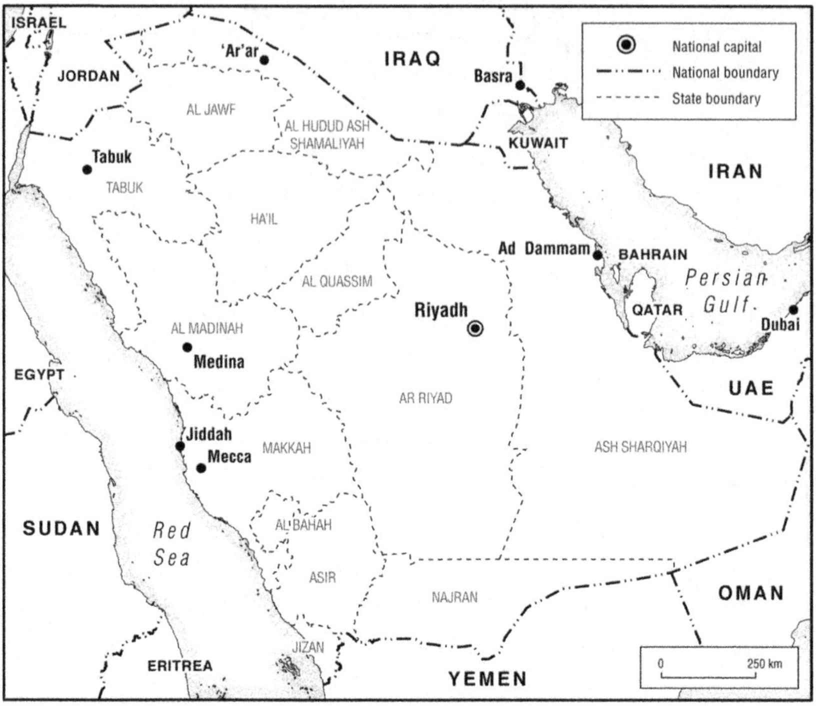

Map 3. Present-Day Saudi Arabia

Introduction

Defining Salafism, Analyzing Canons

This book examines the interaction between two important forces on the world stage: Nigeria, the most populous country in Africa, and Salafism, a loosely organized community of Muslim activists who claim that they alone incarnate the practices and beliefs of the earliest Muslims. In northern Nigeria, a majority-Muslim region, Salafis have become prominent as preachers, media stars, and allies of certain elected politicians. These Salafis challenge the religious dominance of hereditary Muslim rulers and Sufi shaykhs by advancing a largely textualist model of religious authority. This book provides insight into how Nigerian Muslims are negotiating their relationships with one another and with the contemporary Middle East – especially Saudi Arabia, where Salafism receives political and institutional support. At the same time, the trajectory of Salafism in northern Nigeria sheds light on the stages through which the global Salafi movement has passed. Salafis around the world, even in non-Arab lands, have come to invoke a set of Arabic texts and a group of twentieth-century Middle Eastern thinkers as standards of authority in local struggles over who gets to speak for Islam. Examining Salafism in Nigeria illustrates how references to core texts can reflect membership in religious communities – and how such references provide a key tool for understanding the many geographically dispersed, decentralized religious activist networks that are helping to shape the world today.

On the basis of fieldwork in Nigeria and a historical study of the formation of Salafism, I argue that Salafism is embodied in and transmitted through a canon, a communally negotiated set of texts that is governed by rules of interpretation and appropriation. Salafis invoke the canon to spread Salafism but also to police the boundaries of Salafism. The idea of a Salafi canon is implicit, although underdeveloped, in some previous work on Salafism;[1] here I make it the explicit theoretical frame for analysis, examining how the canon formed and how it is disseminated.

[1] Richard Gauvain mentions a "modern Salafi legal canon," and David Commins has described a "reconstruction of Salafism's patrimony" by scholars in Saudi Arabia starting in the 1970s. What I describe here incorporates both of these notions but asserts an even broader reading of Salafism as a set of texts that provides mechanisms for Salafizing the

This understanding of Salafism challenges widespread Western depictions of Salafism as a one-dimensional and "literalist" school of interpreting the Qur'an and the Sunna (the authoritative tradition of the Prophet Muḥammad, as preserved in reports of his words and deeds, reports known as *aḥādīth* in the plural and *ḥadīth* in the singular). Salafis do not simply consult scriptures and then derive practice. Indeed, individual Muslims who "return to the Qur'an" outside of established scholarly frameworks often generate unusual and divergent interpretations of Islam.[2] Salafism, in contrast, "is a system of startling coherence and uniformity."[3] Its canon attempts to unify the Salafi community in the present, as well as to align earlier texts with a twentieth-century understanding of Salafism, and vice versa. Today global Salafism is characterized by tension over who gets to define the boundaries of this canon.

This book offers a case study of Salafism in Nigeria and a broader framework for understanding how contemporary religious activists engage textual traditions. Many canons, open-ended and contested but nevertheless influential, operate in different religious communities today. In a world marked by the "fragmentation of sacred authority,"[4] attention to canons helps identify the shifting sources of claims to religious leadership: each body of texts transmits a particular set of rules and standards.

Intra-Muslim struggles, in Africa as elsewhere, are not just contests pitting one worldview or group against another, but also battles to determine which body of texts a community will consider authoritative. Conflicts over canons are struggles over "basic, usually unarticulated, differences in how such groups define what it means to know."[5] In northern Nigeria, Salafis have sought to partly supplant, and partly co-opt, a rival canon based on Sunni Islam's Mālikī legal school and on Sufism, a form of Islamic mysticism. Salafis have also worked to replace a classical, teacher-centric mode of knowledge transmission with a set of allegedly transparent methods for accessing foundational Islamic texts. The Salafi

past and present – not just in the legal sphere but also in terms of religious authority, Muslim politics, and communal identity. See Gauvain, *Salafi Ritual Purity: In the Presence of God* (New York: Routledge, 2013), 227; and David Commins, "From Wahhabi to Salafi" in *Saudi Arabia in Transition Saudi Arabia in Transition: Insights on Social, Political, Economic and Religious Change*, edited by Bernard Haykel, Thomas Hegghammer, and Stéphane Lacroix, 151–66 (Cambridge: Cambridge University Press, 2015), 164.

2 For two examples, see Muḥammad Shaḥrūr, *Al-Kitāb wa-l-Qur'ān: Qirāa Mu'āṣira* (Damascus: Al-Ahālī li-l-Ṭibā'a wa-l-Nashr wa-l-Tawzī', 1990); and Sayyid Quṭb, *Fī Ẓilāl al-Qur'ān* (Beirut: Dār al-Shurūq, 1973–4).

3 Gauvain, *Salafi Ritual Purity*, 11.

4 Dale Eickelman and James Piscatori, *Muslim Politics*, second edition (Princeton: Princeton University Press, 2004), 70.

5 Rudolph T. Ware III, *The Walking Qur'an: Islamic Education, Embodied Knowledge, and History in West Africa* (Chapel Hill: University of North Carolina Press, 2014), 15.

canon represents both a field of debate within the Salafi community and a tool deployed in debates with other communities.

Although African Muslims have sometimes been crudely stereotyped as inherently "syncretist," the study of Islam in Africa – especially when scholars of other regions are willing to take seriously the theological commitments of African Muslims – has a major role to play in theory-building projects about contemporary Muslim activism worldwide.[6] Africa is the site of new renegotiations of "Muslim politics" that do not fit into the frameworks familiar from Middle Eastern Studies.[7] Few African countries have equivalents to the Egyptian Muslim Brotherhood; when scholars of the Middle East treat that organization as the archetype of Muslim political activism, they risk missing a much broader spectrum of activist postures. Even specialists on the Middle East now "warn . . . against overgeneralizing based on the Egyptian case."[8] Scholars of Islam need to more carefully delineate the theologies and ideologies of activist groups. In the Middle East, the rise of Salafi political parties in post-2011 Egypt and Tunisia has challenged assumptions that the Middle East is gripped by a two-sided struggle between authoritarian regimes and a catch-all category of actors called "Islamists."[9] Salafis' creed and worldview, which are much more tightly defined than the rather generic and flexible outlook of the Brotherhood, mean that Salafi activism proceeds from a different intellectual foundation than the Brotherhood's.[10] There is a need to consider Salafism on its own terms, and not just in relation to Islamism. The wide range of regime types that exist in Africa and the growing variety of Muslim communities there permit rich observations about how Salafism can generate varied activist postures in different contexts.

6 For critiques of the idea of an inherently and unusually "syncretist" kind of "African Islam," see Roman Loimeier, *Muslim Societies in Africa: A Historical Anthropology* (Bloomington: University of Indiana Press, 2013); and Ware, *The Walking Qur'an*. For a critique of the marginalization of the study of Islam in Africa, see Benjamin Soares, "The Historiography of Islam in West Africa: An Anthropologist's View," *The Journal of African History* 55:1 (March 2014): 27–36.

7 René Otayek and Benjamin Soares, "Introduction: Islam and Muslim Politics in Africa" in *Islam and Muslim Politics in Africa*, edited by Benjamin Soares and René Otayek, 1–24 (New York: Palgrave Macmillan, 2007).

8 Marc Lynch, "Introduction" in *Rethinking Islamist Politics*, Project on Middle East Political Science Briefing 24, 3–6 (11 February 2014), 4.

9 See Stéphane Lacroix, "Sheikhs and Politicians: Inside the New Egyptian Salafism," Brookings Institution, June 2012. Available at: www.brookings.edu/~/media/research/files/papers/2012/6/07-egyptian-salafism-lacroix/stephane-lacroix-policy-briefing-english.pdf; accessed March 2015; and Jonathan A. C. Brown, "Salafis and Sufis in Egypt," Carnegie Endowment for International Peace, December 2011. Available at: http://carnegieendowment.org/files/salafis_sufis.pdf; accessed September 2015.

10 Noah Salomon, "The Salafi Critique of Islamism: Doctrine, Difference and the Problem of Islamic Political Action in Contemporary Sudan" in *Global Salafism: Islam's New Religious Movement*, edited by Roel Meijer, 143–68 (New York: Columbia University Press, 2009).

Nigeria's politics, encompassing a federalist system, the implementation of Islamic law (*sharīʿa*) in northern states, a vibrant media, and ongoing processes of democratization, allows for an examination of how multiple kinds of Muslim activists compete within a partially open society. As in other African societies, religious activism in Nigeria is an important form of "politics from below."[11] Important conflicts can begin with seemingly minor struggles over control of mosques, with alleged blasphemies uttered by preachers, or with intra-Salafi competition for audiences. As they grow, these disputes can shape electoral outcomes, fuel intercommunal violence, and shift the balance of power among constituencies. Islamic Studies has taken a strong interest in questions of micropolitics and ethical self-fashioning at the level of the individual,[12] but there is a need to connect micropolitics to other forms of mobilization by believers. Studying the deployment of canons helps us connect what happens in the mosque with what happens in the public sphere. Nigeria's Boko Haram movement, a fringe offshoot of the Salafi preaching circles discussed in this book, is only one example of why it is important to understand interconnections between preaching and politics.

Salafism in Nigeria tells how a group of Nigerians from modest origins became some of the most controversial Muslim voices in Africa. After examining the formation of Salafism's canon over more than a millennium, I turn to twentieth-century Nigeria and Saudi Arabia, tracing the paths of Shaykh Jaʿfar Maḥmūd Ādam (1961/2–2007), Dr. Muḥammad Sani ʿUmar Rijiyar Lemo (b. 1970),[13] Shaykh Abdulwahhab Abdullah (b. 1953), and another half-dozen Muslim scholars. As young preachers in the 1980s, they won scholarships to Saudi Arabia's Islamic University of Medina. There they studied a canon of texts that pulled together writings from ninth-century Baghdad, medieval Syria, nineteenth-century Yemen and India, and the twentieth-century Middle East. I chart the Nigerians' return home in the 1990s and 2000s, analyzing how they taught the canon – and how they brought it into politics. I conclude by examining the rise of the jihadi movement Boko Haram, showing the centrality of the canon in conflicts between this group and other Salafis. The graduates of Medina are now competing with Boko Haram to define Islam and its textual bases. That struggle – perhaps even more than the fight between Boko Haram and the Nigerian state – will shape Nigeria's religious trajectory for years to come.

11 Jean-Francois Bayart, "Le politique par le bas en Afrique noire: Questions de méthode," *Politique Africaine* 1 (1981): 53–82.

12 Saba Mahmood, *Politics of Piety: The Islamic Revival and the Feminist Subject* (Princeton: Princeton University Press, 2005).

13 For the sake of clarity, I refer to him as "Rijiyar Lemo" throughout the book, partly to distinguish him from the Nigerian scholar Dr. Muhammad Sani Umar, formerly of Northwestern University and now of Ahmadu Bello University, Zaria.

Defining Salafism through Creed and Canon

Before discussing the Salafi canon, it will be useful to discuss the Salafi creed. Salafis are just as keen to explain what they reject as they are to state what they believe, and Salafism can be described through five binary oppositions: Sunni Islam and not Shīʿism; literalism in contrast to speculative theology (*ʿilm al-kalām*) or philosophy (*falsafa*); direct consultation of foundational texts rather than allegiance to established legal schools; an impulse to "purify" others and a rejection of Sufism, especially organized, "ecstatic" Sufism;[14] and finally, an insistence on producing "evidence." This insistence means, in theory and often in practice, that Salafis refuse to defer to authority based on spiritual, intellectual, or biological genealogies[15] or to accept that the most precious knowledge is secret, elusive, or even unattainable.[16] Let us investigate each binary.

First, Salafis are Sunni Muslims, or even "über-Sunnis" who claim that the earliest Muslims (*al-salaf al-ṣāliḥ*, the "pious predecessors") constituted a unified, orthodox, exemplary moral community. Salafis call Shīʿī Muslims apostates for rejecting certain Companions of the Prophet Muḥammad, including three of the four "Rightly Guided Caliphs." Salafis assert that their own particular beliefs are completely contiguous with those of Islam itself. Indeed, many Salafis would reject the term "Salafism," preferring to describe themselves simply as the only genuine Muslims or to use various names that connote claims to authenticity and rigor in interpreting Islam. One twentieth-century Salafi scholar writes:

> In the contemporary world, those who follow the Salafi approach, believe in it, and call [people] to it, have multiplied. They are known in the Indian subcontinent as "salafis" and "*ahl al-ḥadīth*" (the people of *ḥadīth*). In some Arab and non-Arab countries they are known as "*anṣār al-sunna al-muḥammadiyya*" (defenders of the Muḥammadan model, an organization founded in 1926) – such as Egypt, Sudan, Somalia, and Thailand. They are known in the Levant as "salafis." All of them call for a return to Islam in its correct conception as a creed (*ʿaqīda*) and as a set of legal provisions (*aḥkām*). [They call] for speculative

14 Jonathan A. C. Brown, "Is Islam Easy to Understand or Not? Salafis, the Democratization of Interpretation, and the Need for the Ulema," *Journal of Islamic Studies* 26:2 (2015): 117–44.

15 William Graham has analyzed the "*isnād* paradigm" in which Islamic knowledge has meaning in the context of a "chain of personal transmission" that links the possessor of knowledge back to the source of that knowledge. William Graham, "Traditionalism in Islam: An Essay in Interpretation," *Journal of Interdisciplinary History* 23:3 (Winter 1993): 495–522. See also Rüdiger Seesemann, "On the Cultural History of Islamic Knowledge and Its Contemporary Relevance," Religious Studies Faculty Colloquium, Northwestern University, 17 February 2010.

16 Noah Salomon, "Evidence, Secrets, Truth: Debating Islamic Knowledge in Contemporary Sudan," *Journal of the American Academy of Religion* 81:3 (September 2013): 820–51.

> theology (*ʿilm al-kalām*) – which came between people and the correct creed, which the first group [of Muslims] followed – to be abandoned. They reject the educational approach at all levels, and replace it with the Salafi approach whose source is the Book of Allah and the Sunna of the Messenger of Allah, may Allah bless him and grant him peace, which was all the *salaf* knew.[17]

In this book I retain "Salafism" as the most neutral term I have found for describing the movement. For me, the label acknowledges that these activists have a particular ideological construction of the *salaf*, but I do not endorse their view of themselves as the only true Muslims. It is important to note that many other Muslims would vigorously dispute Salafis' understandings of the early community and its legacy. For example, Sufi Muslims argue that their path represents the truest legacy of the Prophet's generation, for whom Sufism was "a reality without a name."[18]

A second binary opposition involves theology. Salafis hold a highly detailed creed and prefer to speak of "creed" (*ʿaqīda*) rather than speculative theology (*ʿilm al-kalām*). They believe that the Qurʾan is uncreated and has existed eternally with God. They say that descriptions of Allah's attributes in the foundational texts of Islam should be understood literally, albeit without "*tamthīl* (likening them to human characteristics) and *takyīf* (probing their modality, i.e., asking how)."[19] If the Qurʾan says that God has a "hand" (as in, for example, 36:83) or a "throne" (as in 7:54), then Salafis say that Muslims must accept the existence of a literal hand and a literal throne.[20] Such stances mean that Salafis oppose many widespread theological schools, including the Ashʿariyya, which allows a role for metaphorical interpretation of God's attributes. Salafis also reject the study of philosophy, including Greek philosophy and Islamic philosophy, believing that philosophy's influence warps the integrity of Muslims' creeds; Salafis today hail various figures in their canon not just for articulating the "sound" creed but also for fighting to roll back the effects of medieval Muslims' engagement with philosophy.

Third, Salafis emphasize *aḥādīth* over all other potential sources of law, save the Qurʾan. For Salafis, *aḥādīth* and the Sunna, understood as a totalizing model of behavior exemplified by the Prophet, constitute a manual that should ground all actions and beliefs in textual evidence. The

[17] Muḥammad Amān al-Jāmī, *Majmūʾ Rasāʾil al-Jāmī fī al-ʿAqīda wa-l-Sunna* (Medina: Dār Ibn Rajab, 1993), 81.

[18] Martin Lings, *What Is Sufism?* (Berkeley: University of California Press, 1975), 45.

[19] Muḥammad Ṣāliḥ al-ʿUthaymīn, *ʿAqīdat Ahl al-Sunna wa-l-Jamāʿa* (Al-Riyāḍ: Muʾassasat al-Shaykh Muḥammad Ṣāliḥ al-ʿUthaymīn al-Khayriyya, 2009); see also Jon Hoover, *Ibn Taymiyya's Theodicy of Perpetual Optimism* (Leiden: Brill, 2007).

[20] For one account of how such claims can divide Muslim communities, see Rüdiger Seesemann, "The Quotidian Dimension of Islamic Reformism in Wadai (Chad)" in *L'islam politique au sud du Sahara: Identités, discours, et enjeux*, edited by Muriel Gomez-Perez, 327–46 (Paris: Karthala, 2005).

most prominent Nigerian graduate of Medina, Jaʿfar Ādam, explained in one lecture,

> Every religious matter... must be well established in Allah's Book [i.e., the Qurʾan] and what has been verified in the *aḥādīth* of Allah's Prophet – may Allah bless him and grant him peace – on the basis of the understanding and exegesis of the pious forefathers (Hausa: *magabata nagari*, a rendering of the Arabic *al-salaf al-ṣāliḥ*).[21]

This stance means that Salafis reject the established Sunni schools of law (*madhāhib*, singular *madhhab*), and claim to derive practice directly from the Qurʾan and the Sunna. This rejection of legal schools distinguishes Salafis from the Wahhābī movement that is dominant in present-day Saudi Arabia; Wahhābīs embrace the Salafi creed but follow the Ḥanbalī school of law. Saudi Arabia witnessed a "Salafi turn" over the second half of the twentieth century, with scholars downplaying their affiliation to Ḥanbalism.[22] In Africa, the rejection of legal schools also distinguishes Salafis today from many earlier African anti-Sufi movements that held a Salafi creed but preserved affiliations to particular legal schools.

Fourth, Salafis channel their beliefs into a "muscular discourse that is directed at reforming other non-Salafi Muslims, and which amounts to an activist worldview in which one sees oneself as pure and the other as in need or purification in both belief and practice."[23] Salafis emphasize the idea of God's absolute uniqueness (*al-tawḥīd*) and hold a particularly broad understanding of what constitutes polytheism. Many Salafis charge that Sufi orders, with their hierarchical structures and specialized techniques for transmitting mystical knowledge, have introduced blameworthy innovations (*bidiʿ*, singular *bidʿa*) into Islam and have even lapsed into polytheistic worship of shaykhs.[24] In contemporary Nigeria, Salafis have oscillated between strident denunciations of Sufism and an

21 Jaʿfar Maḥmūd Ādam, untitled lecture, 16 August 2006, Kano.

22 Commins, "From Wahhabi to Salafi"; on some Saudi Arabian scholars' turn away from the legal schools, see Frank Vogel, *Islamic Law and Legal System: Studies of Saudi Arabia* (Leiden: Brill, 2000), 78. Given this evidence, I disagree with Nabil Mouline that the term "Hanbali-Wahhabism" is more "objective" than the term "Salafism." Salafis who disavow all legal schools are not Ḥanbalī (unless one understands "Ḥanbalī" to refer to creed instead of to law). Additionally, the Salafi canon includes works that are explicitly anti-Wahhābī. See Nabil Mouline, *The Clerics of Islam: Religious Authority and Political Power in Saudi Arabia*, translated by Ethan S. Rundell (New Haven and London: Yale University Press, 2014), 9–10.

23 Bernard Haykel, "On the Nature of Salafi Thought and Action" in *Global Salafism: Islam's New Religious Movement*, edited by Roel Meijer (New York: Columbia University Press, 2009), 33–57; 37.

24 Some late nineteenth- and early twentieth-century thinkers in the Salafi canon endorsed "sober" Sufism, especially as a private discipline outside the context of Sufi orders. David Commins, *Islamic Reform: Politics and Social Change in Late Ottoman Syria* (New York: Oxford University Press, 1990), 80–1.

approach that privileges the dissemination of Salafi thought over anti-Sufi polemics.

Fifth, Salafis charge themselves with the duty of undertaking the intellectual and moral renewal of the Muslim community. This posture includes an insistence that all Muslim practice be based on textual "evidence," rather than on the inherited teachings of scholarly lineages. Such a posture has profound consequences for attitudes toward knowledge: Salafis reject the idea that the most meaningful knowledge is that which is transmitted from person to person, claiming instead that knowledge is found in the correct interpretation of Islam's foundational texts. These texts are held to be transparent and clear, requiring no intermediaries. Salafis also believe that expert scholars in the contemporary period can reassess *aḥādīth*, scrutinizing their chains of transmission and even their content to generate new rankings of the reports – meaning that some long-cherished reports become viewed as "weak" and hence less actionable and that unusual interpretations of worship and law, based on new assessments of "sound" reports, can come to the fore in Salafi practice.

These binary oppositions capture part of the Salafi worldview. To define contemporary Salafis solely through their beliefs, however, risks missing two important facets of this movement, or "approach" (*manhaj*) in Salafi terms. First, the movement has complex and recent historical origins, representing an intersection of several currents of thought from the Arabian Peninsula, the wider Middle East, the Indian subcontinent, and North and sub-Saharan Africa. If scholars uncritically accept the Salafi claim that their stances today are little different from those of the earliest Muslims or of various theologians from the classical and medieval periods, we miss intellectual and political developments that shaped contemporary Salafism. It is possible to identify different stages in different communities' acceptance of Salafism's core ideas and to place figures along a continuum according to their conformity to a rather strict definition of Salafism. I use the term "proto-Salafi" to describe figures who held some but not all of the ideas contained in the Salafi intellectual package today,[25] and I use the term "fully Salafi" to describe those who are anti-Ashʿarī, anti-*madhhab*, and genealogically affiliated to a recognizably Salafi canon.

Furthermore, as Henri Lauzière has shown, even the meaning of the word and concept "Salafism" or *salafiyya* changed over the course of the twentieth century, moving from a narrow theological term to a name designating an activist movement.[26] The contemporary Salafi project of

[25] See also Brown, "Is Islam Easy to Understand or Not?" 118, footnote 3.

[26] Henri Lauzière, *The Making of Salafism: Islamic Reform in the Twentieth Century* (New York: Columbia University Press, 2015). Lauzière's "conceptual history" approach is

renewal was inherited from promoters of Islamic revival who appeared in the late nineteenth and early twentieth centuries. The project, however, was transformed by later Salafis from the goal of Islamizing modernity and modernizing Islam into a mission of purifying Muslim societies from the inside. Despite the different orientations in these projects, common threads link them, especially a willingness to break with intellectual traditions. For both revivalists and their Salafi heirs, "returning to the sources" of Islam meant claiming intellectual freedom. In the context of West Africa, where the terms "Salafism" and "Wahhābism" have often been misapplied, it is important to recognize that Salafism is not just opposition to Sufism. Salafism is a complex intellectual tradition.

Second, as noted earlier, the Salafi movement has a more developed internal textual tradition than is often assumed. Salafism has jettisoned much of the Sunni scholastic corpus.[27] Yet Salafism has a distinctive "intellectual posture" and distinctive "intellectual traditions,"[28] including a large body of texts other than scripture. Additionally, when Salafi scholars claim that Islam's foundational texts are "easy to understand," they are making a rhetorical move to "undermin[e] the rigid authority of the *madhhabs*."[29] Salafi scholars do not seek to hand over interpretation of texts to uneducated persons but rather to train audiences in Salafi methods of interpretation. Salafi scholars themselves work from texts other than Qurʾan and *aḥādīth*: they read the Qurʾan together with exegeses they consider authoritative, and they read *aḥādīth* as part of carefully assembled collections, including collections reedited or reassessed by recent Salafi scholars.

Beyond exegeses and *aḥādīth* collections, Salafis' interpretive practices are heavily conditioned by a set of identifiable texts that have accumulated and interacted over centuries. These texts have clear relationships to one another, evident in citations, common vocabularies, and a shared set of theological and legal concerns. Salafis apply a "canonizing discourse,"[30] which unifies and retroactively Salafizes texts while policing and explaining any divergences that authors exhibit with regard to the Salafi creed. The process of canonization reached a new stage in the late twentieth century with the unofficial but widespread designation of three scholars – an Albanian, Shaykh Muḥammad Nāṣir al-Dīn al-Albānī (1914–99), and two Saudi Arabians, Shaykhs ʿAbd al-ʿAzīz ibn Bāz (1910–99)

pathbreaking, but the notion of a canon allows me to capture intellectual processes than cannot be described through a conceptual history of one term. As seen earlier, not all Salafis even use the term "salafī" to describe themselves and their project.

27 Haykel, "On the Nature of Salafi Thought and Action," 36.

28 Thomas Hegghammer, "Jihadi-Salafis or Revolutionaries? On Religion and Politics in the Study of Militant Islamism" in *Global Salafism*, ed. Meijer, 244–66; 250.

29 Brown, "Is Islam Easy to Understand or Not?," 144.

30 El Shamsy, *Canonization of Islamic Law*, 224.

and Muḥammad ibn Ṣāliḥ al-ʿUthaymīn (1925–2001) – as standards by which Salafis would measure the authority of other thinkers.

Salafis' use of texts ranging over centuries does not, in their eyes, conflict with their claim to reincarnate early Muslim practice. Rather, they take comfort in the idea that "pure" Muslims existed in various historical circumstances. For Salafis, these Muslims' lives, memorialized in texts, prove that it is possible to revive the early community's example in any time and place.

Today, the canon is distinguished by clear features. For example, prominent Salafis from Nigeria to Indonesia use the Prophet Muḥammad's *Khuṭbat al-Ḥāja* (Sermon of Necessity) as an opening doxology to introduce their formal religious lectures. The Sermon was repurposed and revived by al-Albānī in the early 1950s and spread as a marker of Salafi discourses in the following decades.[31] The contemporary Salafi movement, in Nigeria and elsewhere, is at its heart an educational movement dedicated to spreading the canon as the basis for identity, interpretation, and action.

Defining Salafism through its canon invites a rethinking of internal divisions within the Salafi movement. One influential typology classifies Salafis into three groups: quietists or "purists," who hold themselves aloof from politics; "politicos" or activists, who comment on political affairs and challenge political authorities nonviolently; and "jihadis" who declare contemporary Muslim rulers apostates and seek to impose the Salafi creed and a Salafi social order through violence.[32] More recent scholarship has challenged this typology, showing that "quietists" participate in politics[33] and that defining jihadis through their supposed theological commitments is a fraught endeavor.[34] Attention to the canon further blurs the boundaries that allegedly divide these three tendencies. Many figures molded in the "quietist" tradition act strikingly like "politicos," including in northern Nigeria. Many jihadis pay partial homage to the major – and now canonized – "quietist" scholars.[35] Some of the

[31] Muḥammad Nāṣir al-Dīn al-Albānī, *Khuṭbat al-Ḥāja allatī Kāna Rasūl Allāh – Ṣalla Allāh ʿalayhi wa-Sallam – Yuʿallimuhā Aṣḥābahu* (Al-Riyāḍ: Maktabat al-Maʿārif li-l-Nashr wa-l-Tawzīʿ, 2000 [1953]). For an Indonesian example, see Jaʿfar ʿUmar Thalib, "Waspada Bahaya Syiah dan JIL," YouTube, 28 December 2013. Available at: www.youtube.com/watch?v=aI09_TGb8UE; accessed December 2014.

[32] Quintan Wiktorowicz, "Anatomy of the Salafi Movement," *Studies in Conflict & Terrorism* 29 (2006): 207–39.

[33] Jacob Olidort, "The Politics of 'Quietist' Salafism," Brookings Institution (February 2015). Available at: www.brookings.edu/~/media/research/files/papers/2015/02/salafism-quietist-politics-olidort/brookings-analysis-paper_jacob-olidort-inside_final_web.pdf; accessed March 2015; and Salomon, "Salafi Critique of Islamism."

[34] Hegghammer, "Jihadi-Salafis."

[35] The Salafi-jihadi thinker Abū Muḥammad al-Maqdisī, in an undated interview, describes attending lessons with Ibn Bāz and states that upon meeting al-Albānī, he "kissed his hand (*qabbaltu yadahu*)" despite their political differences. Available

most prominent jihadis behave, methodologically and discursively, like quietists.[36] Tellingly, one finds the Sermon of Necessity in books by "quietists," activist sermons by "politicos," and even in the Friday Sermon that proclaimed the Islamic State's Caliphate. The canon continues to provide a platform for unity in a highly fragmented Salafi community.

Theorizing Canons in the Contemporary World

Recent works in religious studies have emphasized themes of religion in motion – whether by defining religions as "confluences of organic-cultural flows"[37] or by calling attention to the "portable practices" and "transposable messages" that allow religious traditions to cross different kinds of boundaries.[38] Canons relate to both of these themes: their formation represents the outcome of particular kinds of confluences, and their transmission provides a mechanism through which practices and messages are disseminated and transformed. Moreover, as religious studies increasingly finds itself obsessed with the question of whether various analytical categories are viable – including the category of "religion" itself – attention to canons can help ensure that the categories we use to describe religious movements are grounded in rich, empirically observable discursive formations.

Multiple layers of meaning are contained in the idea of a canon. The Greek word *kanṓn* means "measuring rod" or "standard." Even in antiquity, "canon" carried a dual sense of "rule" and "list," which together suggest the idea of the "normative-prescriptive list."[39] Since antiquity, the word "canon" has been heavily associated with Roman Catholicism. In that context, canon has multiple senses, including the canonization of texts, as in the closed set of scriptures included in the New and Old Testaments; the canonization of saints, in the sense of regulating admission to a fixed group of revered figures; canon law, or regulations for the church and its members; and the notion of church officials as "canons"

at: www.youtube.com/watch?v=sFh4R_F5BrE; accessed January 2015. Another Salafi-jihadi scholar, Abū Qatāda al-Filasṭīnī, praises the scholarship of Ibn Bāz and al-Albānī while rejecting their politics in the interview, "Ḥiwār maʿa al-Shaykh Abī Qatāda min Dākhil al-Sujūn al-Brīṭāniyya – 1429h," Minbar al-Tawḥīd wa-l-Jihād, 2008. Available at: www.tawhed.ws/r?i=1502091r; accessed May 2015.

36 Joas Wagemakers, *A Quietist Jihadi: The Ideology and Influence of Abu Muhammad al-Maqdisi* (Cambridge: Cambridge University Press, 2012), 10.

37 Thomas Tweed, *Crossing and Dwelling: A Theory of Religion* (Cambridge, MA: Harvard University Press, 2006), 54.

38 Thomas Csordas, "Introduction: Modalities of Transnational Transcendence" in *Transnational Transcendence: Essays on Religion and Globalization*, edited by Thomas Csordas, 1–30 (Berkeley: University of California Press, 2009).

39 Einar Thomassen, "Some Notes on the Development of Christian Ideas about a Canon" in *Canon and Canonicity: The Formation and Use of Scripture*, edited by Einar Thomassen, 9–28 (Copenhagen: Museum Tusculanum Press, 2010), 10.

subject to canon law. All of these notions of canon reflect the authorizing powers of the Catholic Church, as a religiopolitical body. The Church uses canonization to designate who or what belongs or does not belong to a given normative list, whether of texts, persons, or rules. Canonization is a fundamentally political act of simultaneous inclusion and exclusion. The Catholic Church even developed an anticanon: its *Index Librorum Prohibitorum* (List of Prohibited Books) appeared in twenty editions between 1559 and 1966, when it was abolished. At times, the *Index* blacklisted upward of 550 books considered heretical and dangerous to papal authority.[40] The equally contentious struggles over whether to canonize certain figures as saints – Joan of Arc was not canonized until 1920, nearly five centuries after being condemned to burn as a heretic in 1431 – further reflect how canonization is a process of drawing and policing the boundaries of a community.

Despite the heavily Catholic connotations of the term canonization, and the lingering implication that canonization is a process managed by a singular, central authority, the idea of canons and canonization has passed through literary studies and into, among other fields,[41] Islamic studies. Along the way, the term has acquired a looser meaning as a more organic and open-ended process through which communities reassess their boundaries. Canonization, in other words, is a framework for examining the relationship among texts, communities, and boundaries.

Outside the context of Catholicism, canonization has come to refer mostly to bodies of texts, but we lose much if we forget the other senses of the word. The canonization of texts implies some canonization of authors as well – not necessarily as "saints," whatever that word may mean for a particular community, but as intellectual and moral authorities. For example, the classicist and Conservative former London mayor Boris Johnson, in a 2011 essay titled "The Ten Greatest Ancient Greeks," discussed a "mind-bogglingly brilliant speech" by Pericles that "says everything you need to know about politics and good government."[42] For Johnson, "Pericles" – not just his writings, but also the man – stood for an embodied ideal of political morality.

For their part, Salafis are allergic to the idea of "sainthood" in Islam, but Salafis do defer to figures in their canon; many Salafis do not cite

40 Paul Grendler, "Printing and Censorship" in *The Cambridge History of Renaissance Philosophy*, edited by C. B. Schmitt, Quentin Skinner, Eckhard Kessler, and Jill Kraye, 25–54 (Cambridge: Cambridge University Press, 1988), 45.

41 For one example of usage outside literary studies, see Michalis Psalidopoulos, ed., *The Canon in the History of Economics: Critical Essays* (London and New York: Routledge, 2000).

42 Boris Johnson and York Membery, "Homer to Plato: Boris Johnson on the Ten Greatest Ancient Greeks," *Daily Mail*, 25 June 2011. Available at: www.dailymail.co.uk/home/moslive/article-2007229/Homer-Plato-Boris-Johnson-greatest-ancient-Greeks.html; accessed March 2014.

aḥādīth without mentioning whether al-Albānī has "authenticated" them. There are no "canons," in the sense of priests, among Salafis – but there are canonizers, many of whom have worked within institutions such as the Islamic University of Medina. Such institutions have been hubs for canonization, showing how the process requires at least some centralizing efforts, even outside the Roman Catholic context. The Salafi canon is not regulated by formal bodies, but it is no accident that the canon took its clearest shape in Saudi Arabia, the country with the most hierarchical and institutionalized religious field in the Sunni Muslim world.

Islam, and particularly Sunni Islam, famously has no central spiritual authority. Different institutions have attempted to lead the Sunni world and provide it with unified intellectual direction over the course of its history, from the Caliphate to Egypt's Al-Azhar University. Yet Sunnis lack any institution as strong as the papacy. As theories of canonization have passed into Islamic Studies, then, it is notable that they have been applied to the two types of institutions where the most wide-ranging agreement about authority can be found in the Sunni world: first, the canonical collections of *aḥādīth*, considered the second-most sacred texts in Sunni Islam after the Qurʾan,[43] and second, the major Sunni legal schools, which most Sunnis consider authoritative.[44] Existing studies, in other words, have concentrated on how enduring institutions emerged out of the dynamic intellectual world of the early Muslim centuries. The development of canons represented a bid to fix structures of authority in classical Islam. Canons served political purposes, and legal canons in particular were united more by shared ideals and methods than by rigid lists of texts.

Canonization may be "a universal feature of literate societies,"[45] but the canonizing impulse waxes and wanes. Canons are most likely to form when confluences of events produce uncertainty about the sources of moral authority. That the Catholic Church's *Index Librorum Prohibitorum* first appeared in 1559 was no accident – it responded not just to the Protestant Reformation but also to "the sheer volume of printed subversion" that exploded amid the growth of "print capitalism" in post-Gutenberg Europe.[46] To add another example, in eighteenth-century England, "the swelling of the book trade, the passing of aristocratic authority, the rise in literacy, the prominence of women writers and

[43] Jonathan A. C. Brown, *The Canonization of al-Bukhārī and Muslim: The Formation and Function of the Sunnī Ḥadīth Canon* (Leiden: Brill, 2007).

[44] Brannon Wheeler, *Applying the Canon in Islam: The Authorization and Maintenance of Interpretive Reasoning in Ḥanafī Scholarship* (Albany: State University of New York Press, 1996); and Ahmed El Shamsy, *The Canonization of Islamic Law: A Social and Intellectual History* (Cambridge: Cambridge University Press, 2013).

[45] Thomassen, "Some Notes," 10.

[46] Benedict Anderson, *Imagined Communities: Reflections on the Origin and Spread of Nationalism*, revised edition (London and New York: Verso, 1991), 40.

readers, the professionalization of criticism, together provoked over the course of the century a recourse to older works as national heritage."[47] Amid uncertainty, communities seek to construct a heroic past to structure a moral community in the present and reassert confidence "that the great thing existed and was therefore possible, and so may be possible again."[48]

In the Muslim world, the past two hundred years and more have seen profound uncertainty; Muslim scholars have responded by reinventing tradition in myriad ways, including by attacking, reassembling, or reimagining the very institutions mentioned earlier, the *aḥādīth* collections and the schools of law. The Salafi canon is one manifestation of the impulse to create a new and unified center of authority. Even as a minority strand within contemporary Islam, Salafism seeks to speak for the whole.

When believers fashion canons, they make claims to continuity with the past, but they do not always surrender their prerogative to add to a canon. A twenty-first-century Colorado pastor seeks, she says, to "be deeply rooted in tradition in order to innovate with integrity."[49] Similarly, Nigerian Salafis work both to establish continuity with a Salafized history and to use their canon as a template that helps them confront new situations – ranging from a perceived crisis of marriage in urban northern Nigeria to the challenge of navigating Nigerian politics. Canons form out of a need to address change, but once formed, they become vehicles for structured improvisation. The Salafi canon has certain fixed elements and thinkers – the Damascene Shaykh Aḥmad ibn Taymiyya (1263–1328) above all – but is open to constant renegotiation. The canon is the field wherein broader questions of authority are resolved. The power to decide who is in and who is out, or how to Salafize those who are included, is the power to determine what Salafism means; there have even been attempts to generate a Salafi anticanon.[50] The stakes are high, particularly when the struggle involves questions about the legitimacy of violent struggle against fellow Muslims.

The Canon in Action

In July 2009, Boko Haram launched an armed uprising in which more than 1,100 people died. Three months before, when tensions were

[47] Jonathan Kramnick, *Making the English Canon: Print-Capitalism and the Cultural Past, 1700–1770* (Cambridge: Cambridge University Press, 1998), 1.

[48] Friedrich Nietzsche, *The Use and Abuse of History*, translated by Adrian Collins (New York: Cosimo, 2010), 13–14.

[49] Interview with Nadia Bolz-Weber from the podcast *On Being*, 23 October 2014. Available at: www.onbeing.org/program/nadia-bolz-weber-seeing-the-underside-and-seeing-god-tattoos-tradition-and-grace/5896; accessed October 2014.

[50] See Mashhūr ibn Ḥasan Āl Salmān, *Kutub Ḥadhdhara minhā al-ʿUlamāʾ* (Al-Riyāḍ: Dār al-Ṣamīʿī, 1995).

already simmering, the Nigerian Salafi scholar Dr. Muḥammad Sani ʿUmar Rijiyar Lemo traveled to Maiduguri, the impoverished northeastern city where Boko Haram had taken root. He went there at personal risk: two years before, Rijiyar Lemo's close friend Jaʿfar Ādam, the most famous Nigerian Salafi preacher of their generation, had been assassinated while leading morning prayers at a mosque on the eve of Nigeria's 2007 elections. The gunmen's identity remains unknown, but suspicion has long rested on Boko Haram, whose leader had become estranged from Ādam, his former teacher.[51] Salafis like Ādam and Rijiyar Lemo had been speaking against Boko Haram for years, first in private but increasingly in public.

In his two-day lecture series in Maiduguri, Rijiyar Lemo delivered what seemed at first to be an impartial historical overview of the twentieth century's "jihad groups," which he broadly defined as including Egypt's Muslim Brotherhood, Afghanistan's anti-Soviet mujahedeen, Palestine's Hamas, and others. Just below the surface of the lecture, however, was a discourse that sought to delegitimize Boko Haram. Rijiyar Lemo attacked Boko Haram indirectly by differentiating between "defensive jihads" of the type found in Afghanistan, where Muslim lands were under attack by an outside force, and the aggressive jihads undertaken by militants who took up arms even when no outsider was occupying their lands.[52] Rijiyar Lemo approved of defensive jihad but criticized aggressive jihadis. He saw them not only as ineffective but as intellectually deficient. He told his audience: "Abū Muḥammad al-Maqdisī is not a scholar – not like Shaykh al-Albānī or ʿUthaymīn or Ibn Bāz."[53] To those with knowledge of the Salafi canon, this was a serious critique of the intellectual credentials of al-Maqdisī, one of the most important thinkers in the global jihadi movement and a direct influence on Boko Haram.

Rijiyar Lemo's statement leads us to the question of canonical authority in contemporary Salafism. Abū Muḥammad al-Maqdisī (b. 1959) is a Palestinian-Jordanian jihadi thinker and an inspiration to many violent Muslim groups, including Boko Haram. The other three thinkers named are the scholars who, individually and as a trio, epitomize canonical authority for many Salafis around the world. Al-Albānī, born in Albania but raised in Syria, earned a global reputation as a critical

[51] Andrea Brigaglia, "Jaʿfar Mahmood Adam, Mohammed Yusuf and al-Muntada Islamic Trust: Reflections on the Genesis of the Boko Haram Phenomenon in Nigeria," *Annual Review of Islam in Africa* 11 (2012): 35–44.

[52] Definitions of jihad are contested among Muslims, but the understanding here is that defensive jihad falls on the entire Muslim community in the face of an external non-Muslim oppressor. Aggressive jihad is an effort to take territory when no Muslim lands are at risk. For a study of shifting meanings of jihad, see Ayesha Jalal, *Partisans of Allah: Jihad in South Asia* (Cambridge, MA: Harvard University Press, 2010).

[53] Muḥammad Sani ʿUmar Rijiyar Lemo, "Kungiyoyin Jihadi (2)," Maiduguri, April 2009.

evaluator of classical collections of *ḥadīth*.[54] His scholarship provided subsequent Salafis with a standard for determining the strength of *ḥadīth*, and therefore for deciding which texts are actionable according to Salafi stipulations.[55] Ibn Bāz and Ibn ʿUthaymīn were the two most famous Saudi Arabian scholars of the late twentieth century. They served as members of the Committee of Senior Scholars (*Hayʾat Kibār al-ʿUlamāʾ*), the Kingdom's top religious body. Ibn Bāz played a "papal role" within Saudi Arabia and for Salafis elsewhere.[56] Ibn ʿUthaymīn published widely on the fundamentals of the Salafi creed, writing in a clear and accessible style.[57] Together, the Albanian and the two Saudis embodied a certain Salafi ideal of scholarship, creedal purity, and political sobriety.

The three scholars are invoked in Salafi literature around the world. Take, for example, a 2001 book titled *Riyāḍ al-Janna fī al-Ḥathth ʿalā al-Tamassuk bi-l-Sunna* (The Gardens of Paradise in Impelling Adherence to the Prophet's Normative Model of Conduct), which assembled lectures, writings, and *fatāwā* (legal opinions) by these three authors. The book presented these texts as keys to understanding how to actualize the authentic Islamic scriptural tradition. The compiler explained, "In every time and place, Allah Most High sends for His religion whom He wills from among the people of knowledge, who are committed to the path of the pious predecessors (*al-salaf al-ṣāliḥ*) in explaining the texts and understanding the creed and the method." The compiler identified the three canonical authors as the foremost contemporary representatives of this creed and method.[58] He emphasized the idea that contemporary Salafis approach the early Muslim experience through the intermediary of later intellectual authorities.

Let us return to Rijiyar Lemo's lecture of 2009, which applied a *kanṓn*, a measuring rod, and found that al-Maqdisī fell short of the ideal represented by these pillars of Salafi identity. Through his critique, Rijiyar Lemo indicated that Boko Haram had left the Salafi mainstream. Worse, he implied that Boko Haram's reading of texts was done through shoddy intermediaries, rather than with the help of the best scholars. Because

54 Stéphane Lacroix, "Between Revolution and Apoliticism: Nasir al-Din al-Albani and his Impact on the Shaping of Contemporary Salafism" in *Global Salafism*, 58–80; and Jacob Olidort, "The Politics of 'Quietist' Salafism," Brookings Institution (February 2015). Available at: www.brookings.edu/~/media/research/files/papers/2015/02/salafism-quietist-politics-olidort/brookings-analysis-paper_jacob-olidort-inside_final_web.pdf; accessed March 2015.

55 Brown, *Canonization*, 321–34.

56 Stéphane Lacroix, *Awakening Islam: The Politics of Religious Dissent in Contemporary Saudi Arabia*, translated by George Holoch (Cambridge, MA: Harvard University Press, 2011), 90.

57 See Muḥammad al-ʿUthaymīn, *ʿAqīdat Ahl al-Sunna wa-l-Jamāʿa*, Fourth Edition (Al-Riyāḍ: Al-Maktab al-Taʿāwunī li-l-Daʿwa wa-l-Irshād wa-Tawʿiyat al-Jāliyyāt, 2001/2).

58 Muḥammad ibn Riyāḍ al-Aḥmad al-Salafī Atharī, *Riyāḍ al-Janna fī al-Ḥathth ʿalā al-Tamassuk bi-l-Sunna* (Beirut: Dār al-Kutub al-ʿIlmīyya, 2001), 5.

citing textual evidence is the central practice Salafis use to justify their positions on different issues, when Rijiyar Lemo challenged Boko Haram's evidence, he was challenging their legitimacy as Salafis. Such debates over who counts as a Salafi, and where to define the boundaries of the canon, are dividing Salafi communities around the world. Non-jihadi Salafis are working fiercely to ensure that the interpretations of al-Albānī, Ibn Bāz, and Ibn ʿUthaymīn win out. The present study explains why and how these three men – an Albanian and two Saudi Arabians – came to have such symbolic resonance in a remote corner of Nigeria.

The Content of the Canon

As a set of theological propositions, Salafism has long historical roots, yet I favor a relatively recent start date for the Salafi phenomenon as an empirically observable and consistent set of discourses. Salafism crystallized in two phases. In the first, from 1880 to 1950, intensifying translocal encounters brought like-minded, *ḥadīth*-oriented scholars from across the Muslim world into closer contact. The constituent ideas of Salafism were largely present in different localities before the twentieth century, but it was not until this period that major thinkers emerged who combined these ideas into a framework that claimed universal applicability.

The 1960s marked a new phase in Salafism's development. Some of the key institutions of contemporary Salafism emerged, allowing for the worldwide and systematic transmission of Salafi thought. These institutions include, above all, the Islamic University of Medina, founded in 1961. Luminaries of the Salafi movement, including Ibn Bāz and al-Albānī, served at the Islamic University as administrators and instructors. The university attracted faculty from around the Muslim world even as Egypt's al-Azhar, a millennium-old center of Islamic learning, was brought more tightly under the control of a military government through a major legal reform in the same year of the Islamic University's founding. The Islamic University was a critical institution in the transmission of Salafism to Nigeria. The 1960s was also the period when figures like al-Albānī began to consolidate their scholastic and religious reputations in the Muslim world. Al-Albānī began publishing his *Silsilat al-Aḥādīth al-Ḍaʿīfa wa-l-Mawḍūʿa wa-Atharuhā al-Sayyiʾ fī al-Umma* (The Series of Weak and Forged Hadith Reports, and Their Negative Effect on the Muslim Community) in 1959.[59] The institutions, works, and individuals who came to represent Salafism in the 1960s would have a decisive influence on the trajectory of Salafism in Nigeria a generation later.

[59] Muḥammad Nāṣir al-Dīn al-Albānī, *Silsilat al-Aḥādīth al-Ḍaʿīfa wa-l-Mawḍūʿa wa-Atharuhā al-Sayyiʾ fī al-Umma* (Riyāḍ: Maktabat al-Maʿārif, 1992 [1959]).

The Salafi canon can be seen as a river into which three major streams flowed. One stream came from Sunni Islam's Ḥanbalī legal and theological school, or rather from ideas that spilled beyond its banks. The thought of major Ḥanbalī thinkers, especially Ibn Taymiyya, forms the classical canon of Salafism. Their writings provide three of Salafism's core themes: scriptural literalism, an exclusive and über-Sunni identity that intensely valorizes the Prophet's Companions, and a template for how Muslims who perceive themselves to be the only true believers can exist and act as a pure vanguard. One outgrowth of this Ḥanbalī stream was the Wahhābī movement, founded in present-day Saudi Arabia by the Ḥanbalī reformer Shaykh Muḥammad ibn ʿAbd al-Wahhāb (1703–92). The oft-heard equation of Wahhābism with Salafism is partly correct, but it misses several factors: first, the complexity of Ḥanbalī influences on contemporary Salafism; second, Salafism's rejection of established legal schools; and third, the other streams that differentiate Salafism from Wahhābism.

Another stream flowed through Yemen and India in the eighteenth and nineteenth centuries, with branches running into Iraq and what became Saudi Arabia. An outgrowth of earlier networks of scholars interested in the study of *ḥadīth*,[60] thinkers in this second stream rejected jurisprudential schools and used *ijtihād*, or personal legal and intellectual effort, to derive correct Islamic practice from the Qurʾan and the Sunna. These Yemeni and Indian thinkers looked partly to authorities such as Ibn Taymiyya, but they distanced themselves from the movement of Ibn ʿAbd al-Wahhāb and did not consider themselves Ḥanbalī as a matter of legal affiliation.

The third stream was the Islamic revivalism and modernism of the late nineteenth and early twentieth centuries, when prominent Muslim reformers became gripped by the question of how to explain and answer the challenges that European scientific, political, economic, and military dominance posed for Muslim lands.[61] Major modernist thinkers include figures like Shaykh Muḥammad Rashīd Riḍā (1865–1935), who is often described as the "conservative," scripturalist side of a movement that included more "liberal" figures who explored forms of theological rationalism that later Salafis would abhor.[62] Both Western scholars and

[60] See Basheer Nafi, "Taṣawwuf and Reform in Pre-Modern Islamic Culture: In Search of Ibrāhīm al-Kūrānī," *Die Welt des Islams* 42:3 (2002): 307–55; and John Voll, "ʿAbdallah ibn Salim al-Basri and 18th Century Hadith Scholarship," *Die Welt des Islams* 42:3 (2002): 356–72.

[61] Charles Kurzman, "Introduction: The Modernist Islamic Movement" in *Modernist Islam, 1840–1940: A Sourcebook*, edited by Charles Kurzman, 3–27 (Oxford: Oxford University Press, 2002).

[62] Abdullah Saeed, "Salafiya, Modernism, and Revival" in *The Oxford Handbook of Islam and Politics*, edited by John Esposito and Emad el-Din Shahin, 27–41 (New York: Oxford University Press, 2013); and Richard C. Martin, Mark R. Woodward, and Dwi

Muslim thinkers have often referred to the modernists as "Salafiyya," an appellation that has contributed to conceptual confusion surrounding the meaning of the contemporary term Salafi. Scholars should not, however, make a hasty and totalizing division between the turn-of-the-century "Salafiyya" and more recent Salafis: the two phenomena are intertwined. For this reason, I refer to certain "Salafiyya" scholars as "proto-Salafis" because they were incorporated later into the canon.

This third stream has left an imprint in the religious terrain of contemporary Salafism, particularly because of the revivalists' discourses about returning to the sources of Islam. Some revivalists, such as Riḍā, also became important defenders of the Wahhābī project at a time when its image outside Saudi Arabia was mostly negative. Although theological tensions existed between Riḍā and the Wahhābīs of his time,[63] Riḍā and his disciples contributed to the "Salafi turn" of Wahhābīs, who took on a more global perspective in the twentieth century.[64] Yet Salafism has moved away from the revivalists' concern with how to be modern and toward a concern with how to purify creed and action; Salafism has, in other words, redefined the notion of revival.

To shape identities, a canon must be a living thing. As such, it has the power to cause ruptures. Nigerian Salafi preachers like Rijiyar Lemo and Ādam arrived in Medina in the 1980s and 1990s already opposed to Sufism and in favor of literal readings of scriptures. But during their studies, they came to see anti-Sufi activists back home as rigid and parochial. In Medina, Salafis came into contact with texts that suggested more nuanced positions on many issues, including relations with Sufis. Nigerian graduates of Medina came home not just as anti-Sufis but as Salafis – as scholar-activists who looked to figures like al-Albānī as vital authorities. Starting in the 1990s, graduates including Rijiyar Lemo and Ādam dedicated themselves to teaching canonical texts. In the process, they created a mass audience of young Nigerians who cared not just about refuting the Sufi next door but also about understanding the words of ninth-century *ḥadīth* compilers, medieval Damascene theologians, and a twentieth-century Albanian iconoclast.

The Setting: Northern Nigeria

On the Atlantic coast of West Africa sits Nigeria, an increasingly important actor on the world stage and a significant corner of the Muslim world. Nigeria is home to more than 180 million people; the most reliable

S. Atmaja, *Defenders of Reason in Islam: Muʿtazilism from Medieval School to Modern Symbol* (London: Oneworld, 1997).

63 Henri Lauzière, *The Making of Salafism: Islamic Reform in the Twentieth Century* (New York: Columbia University Press, 2015), Chapter 2.

64 Commins, "From Wahhabi to Salafi," 152.

estimates suggest that around fifty percent of them are Muslims. These figures make Nigeria the globe's sixth most populous Muslim country.[65] It is, in John Paden's formulation, a "pivotal state in the Muslim world" because of its large population, economic resources, and political importance. Yet compared with other pivotal Muslim states, Paden argues, Nigeria is "the least well-known."[66]

Nigeria's Muslim community offers a mosaic of religious, political, and cultural styles. This study concentrates on Muslim-majority northern Nigeria, but the southwestern part of the country is home to millions of Muslims as well.[67] The north is home to a thousand-year-old tradition of Muslim scholarship and politics. This tradition has contributed to local and regional canons,[68] which Salafis have sometimes challenged and sometimes co-opted.

In the north, patterns of Muslim authority continue to be strongly influenced by hereditary rule and Sufi orders. The northwest's Muslim hereditary rulers are heirs to the Sokoto Caliphate, a polity established by Shaykh ʿUthmān dan Fodio (1754–1817), who initiated a jihad in 1804 against Hausa rulers he saw as apostate Muslims.[69] The Caliphate endured until the British conquest of 1897–1903, after which the descendants of dan Fodio and his lieutenants largely remained in power as pillars of Indirect Rule in colonial Northern Nigeria. Dan Fodio, and most of those rulers who followed him, belonged to Sufi orders, particularly the Qadiriyya.

In the northeast, Kanuri, Arab, Fulani, and other Muslims are heirs to the vestiges of a thousand-year-old Muslim empire, Kanem-Bornu, which once sent so many students to Egypt that the University of Al-Azhar named a dormitory for them.[70] The descendants of a

65 Pew Research Center, "The Future of the Global Muslim Population," 2010.

66 John Paden, *Faith and Politics in Nigeria: Nigeria as a Pivotal State in the Muslim World* (Washington, DC: United States Institute of Peace, 2007), 3.

67 David Laitin, *Hegemony and Culture: Politics and Religious Change among the Yoruba* (Chicago: University of Chicago Press, 1986); J. D. Y. Peel, *Religious Encounter and the Making of the Yoruba* (Bloomington: Indiana University Press, 2000); Ami Shah, "The Urban Living Room: Space and Identity amongst Migrant Communities in Ibadan, Nigeria, and Ahmedabad, India," Ph.D. dissertation, University of Oxford, 2007; and Benjamin Soares, "An Islamic social movement in Contemporary West Africa: NASFAT of Nigeria" in *Movers and Shakers: Social Movements in Africa*, edited by Stephen Ellis and Ineke van Kessel (Leiden: Brill, 2009), 178–96.

68 Bruce Hall and Charles Stewart, "The Historic 'Core Curriculum' and the Book Market in Islamic West Africa" in *The Trans-Saharan Book Trade: Manuscript Culture, Arabic Literacy and Intellectual History in Muslim Africa*, edited by Graziano Krätli and Ghislaine Lydon, 109–74 (Leiden: Brill, 2011); and Hamid Bobboyi, "Scholars and Scholarship in the Relations between the Maghrib and the Central Bilad al-Sudan during the Pre-Colonial Period" in *Reclaiming the Human Sciences and Humanities through African Perspectives*, Volume 1, edited by Helen Lauer and Kofi Anyidoho, 746–760 (Accra: Sub-Saharan Publishers, 2012).

69 Murray Last, *The Sokoto Caliphate* (London: Longmans, Green and Co. Ltd., 1967).

70 S. A. S. Galadanci, *Ḥarakat al-Lugha al-ʿArabiyya wa-Ādābuhā fī Nayjīriyā*, second edition (Cairo: Dār al-Maʿārif, 1993).

scholar named Shaykh Muḥammad al-Amīn al-Kānimī (1776–1837), who helped save Kanem-Bornu from conquest by dan Fodio's forces, continue to rule from Maiduguri, a precolonial market turned colonial provincial capital and, later, a postcolonial metropolis. Sufi orders have considerable strength in the northeast, but anti-Sufi forces have gained considerable ground there since the 1980s. By the 2000s, Maiduguri was a hub of Salafi activity, as the site of an annual *tafsīr* (Qurʾanic exegesis) by Ādam and as the incubator of Boko Haram.

The late colonial period saw the emergence of new kinds of Muslim elites, including Western-educated Muslim intellectuals and politicians.[71] In the lead-up to independence in 1960, hereditary Muslim rulers protected their status from political challenges, but in a way that involved partial subservience to political authorities.[72] In the postcolonial period, the hereditary rulers have lost some of their influence and credibility. Many northerners perceive them as beholden to corrupt politicians.[73] Alongside the political fragmentation of Northern Nigeria into states after a military government reorganized the country in 1967, a "fragmentation of sacred authority" has occurred, as new voices have challenged the dominance of hereditary rulers and Sufi shaykhs.[74] Various Muslim activist movements have arisen, most notably the anti-Sufi movement Jamāʿat Izālat al-Bidʿa wa-Iqāmat al-Sunna (the Society for the Removal of Heretical Innovation and the Establishment of the Prophetic Model, hereafter Izala, founded in 1978).[75] The Salafi graduates of Medina emerged from Izala but distanced themselves from it. In contrast to Izala, Salafis engage more strongly with the canon as they attempt to transcend the boundaries of a specific organization and project absolute continuity with the Prophet and his Companions.

The Salafi challenge to both hereditary rulers and Sufi shaykhs has been formidable, especially in Kano, the north's most populous city and the home of many leading Salafi preachers, including Ādam and Rijiyar Lemo. However, calling the hereditary rulers "traditional" would be a mistake. Their ranks include figures like Sanusi Lamido Sanusi (b. 1961), an internationally acclaimed central banker who became emir of Kano in 2014. Sufi styles of leadership are also changing, reflecting

71 Muhammad Sani Umar, *Islam and Colonialism: Intellectual Responses of Muslims of Northern Nigeria to British Colonial Rule* (Leiden: Brill, 2006).

72 Mahmood Yakubu, *An Aristocracy in Political Crisis* (Aldershot, UK: Avebury, 1996), 231.

73 Salisu Suleiman, "Northern Traditional Institutions and the Crises of Legitimacy," *Nigerians Talk*, 24 September 2012. Available at: nigerianstalk.org/2012/09/24/northern-traditional-institutions-and-the-crises-of-legitimacy-salisu-suleiman/; accessed January 2015.

74 Eickelman and Piscatori, *Muslim Politics*.

75 See Kane, *Muslim Modernity*; Loimeier, *Islamic Reform and Political Change*; Ben Amara, "The Izala Movement in Nigeria"; and Elisha Renne, "Educating Muslim Women and the Izala Movement in Zaria City, Nigeria," *Islamic Africa* 3:1 (2012): 55–86.

longer-term organizational and doctrinal shifts within the Sufi orders.[76] Sufis are neither parochial nor backward: today, one of northern Nigeria's few billionaires is the son of a leading Sufi shaykh in Kano.[77] Salafi-Sufi struggles should not be read reductively as a contest between the new and the old but rather as a battle to define the theological basis and social expressions of Muslim authority in a rapidly changing society.

The fragmentation of sacred authority has also involved a proliferation of small sects, which contributes to Salafis' sense that ordinary Nigerian Muslims face the lure of heresy from multiple directions. Two important clusters of sects are Shīʿī Muslims and "Qurʾan-only" Muslims. The former cluster includes a range of figures, from the politically confrontational "Muslim Brothers" of Ibrahim al-Zakzaky (b. 1953) to more quietist scholars, some of them educated in centers of Shīʿī learning like Qum, Iran. The latter cluster includes groups that uphold doctrine that discard *aḥādīth* and adhere only to the Qurʾan, sometimes evolving quite unusual interpretations of Islam. The most famous Nigerian Qurʾan-only sect was called Maitatsine (He Who Curses) after the nickname given to its founder, the Cameroon-born Muḥammad Marwa (d. 1980).[78] When the Maitatsine group rose up in the 1980s, it was brutally crushed by authorities, but Qurʾan-only groups still exist in Nigeria; the best known today is called Kala Kato (Hausa for "a mere man said it," referring to the *aḥādīth*).[79] Salafis regard these groups as theological and even physical dangers. One Nigerian Salafi told me that the number of Shīʿa in Nigeria was often underestimated because of those who operate "underground," and that the Shīʿa sought "to kill [the real] Muslims."[80] The Salafi emphasis on refuting "sects (*firaq*)," a theme in the curriculum of the Islamic University of Medina, primes Salafis to see even small groups as potentially large problems.

In Nigeria, religious life unfolds amid what one former head of state called "do-or-die" politics.[81] As an amalgamation of diverse peoples and cultures, Nigeria has struggled to balance federalist aspirations against regionalism and ethnic self-assertion. The worst episode of interregional conflict was the civil war from 1967–70, which claimed more than one

[76] Paden, *Religion and Political Culture in Kano*.

[77] This is Abdulsamad Rabiu (b. 1960), son of Shaykh Isyaku Rabiu (b. 1928). See Kerry Dolan, "Meet Africa's Newest Billionaire, Abdulsamad Rabiu," *Forbes*, 13 November 2013. Available at: www.forbes.com/sites/kerryadolan/2013/11/13/meet-africas-newest-billionaire-abdulsamad-rabiu/; accessed January 2015.

[78] Paul Lubeck, "Islamic Protest under Semi-Industrial Capitalism: ʿYan Tatsine Explained," *Africa* 55:4 (1985): 369–89.

[79] "Islamic Actors and Interfaith Relations in Northern Nigeria," Nigeria Research Network Policy Paper 1 (March 2013), 8. Available at: www3.qeh.ox.ac.uk/pdf/nrn/nrn-pp01.pdf; accessed October 2015.

[80] Field notes, November 2011.

[81] President Olusegun Obasanjo (served 1999–2007) made this comment in advance of the 2007 general election.

million lives. Centrifugal forces have appeared in other contexts, such as periodic waves in which new states split from old ones. Other signs of division appeared with recent rebellions in the Niger Delta (2006–9) and Boko Haram's uprising in the northeast. In the north, the implementation of *sharīʿa* at the state level since 1999 has been a marker of regional differentiation and a means of drawing boundaries around the Muslim community.[82] The *sharīʿa* project has exacerbated power struggles among Muslims, as Salafis, Sufis, politicians, and hereditary rulers compete to define public morality.[83]

Despite the country's divisions, the central government remains a prize that many elites have sought to purchase with money and blood.[84] The early postcolonial period (1960–99) witnessed six successful military coups. Several attempted democratic transitions ended in tragedy: Moshood Abiola, the winner of the country's most credible election, held in 1993, never entered the presidential villa at Aso Rock as the country's leader but rather died a political prisoner. Even after Nigeria returned to civilian control in 1999, elections have been occasions for widespread rigging and violence, with 2007 marking a low in credibility and 2011 a high in post-election killings. The relatively peaceful election in 2015 of Muhammadu Buhari, a former military ruler who stood in the opposition until he became the first candidate to defeat an incumbent in Nigerian history, marks a break with the past. However, Buhari's initial difficulties in maintaining party discipline and fighting corruption show that Nigerian politics remains turbulent.

Amid ferocious competition for power at the national level, episodes of religious violence have occurred in many localities in the north. In the country's Middle Belt,[85] a stunning diversity of ethnic and religious groups sometimes ignites into a conflagration of intercommunal murder. Authorities are often unable or unwilling to overturn a culture of impunity for the killers.

Religious life in Nigeria proceeds amid glaring economic disparities. Nigeria is a rich country, but many Nigerians are poor. In good times, the country exports two million or more barrels of oil per day, placing

[82] Murray Last, "The Search for Security in Muslim Northern Nigeria," *Africa* 78:1 (February 2008): 41–63.

[83] Alex Thurston, "Muslim Politics and Sharīʿa in Kano, Nigeria," *African Affairs* 114:454 (January 2015): 28–51; and Susan O'Brien, "La charia contestée: Démocratie, débat et diversité musulmane dans les 'états Charia' du Nigeria," *Politique Africaine* 106 (2007): 46–68.

[84] Daniel Jordan Smith, *A Culture of Corruption: Everyday Deception and Popular Discontent in Nigeria* (Princeton: Princeton University Press, 2008).

[85] Adam Higazi, "The Jos Crisis: A Recurrent Nigerian Tragedy," Friedrich Ebert Stiftung, Discussion Paper 2 (January 2011). Available at: http://library.fes.de/pdf-files/bueros/nigeria/07812.pdf; accessed January 2015; and Moses Ochonu, *Colonialism by Proxy: Hausa Imperial Agents and Middle Belt Consciousness in Nigeria* (Bloomington: Indiana University Press, 2014).

it among the top twelve oil producers in the world for 2013. Its gross domestic product (GDP) grew at a rate of over 6 percent every year from 2006 to 2013,[86] with growth of more than 8 percent in the nonoil sector.[87] In early 2014, Nigeria released "rebased" figures of its 2013 GDP that showed its economy as the largest in Africa, standing at nearly $510 billion. Yet 61 percent of Nigerians live on less than one dollar a day.[88] Inequality is worsening: from 1986 to 2010, the share of Nigeria's wealth held by its richest 20 percent of citizens increased from 45 to 54 percent.[89]

Disparities also divide the country's regions from one another. Of Nigeria's six "geopolitical zones," a convention used in Nigeria to discuss political geography, the two zones furthest north – the North West and the North East – had the highest poverty rates, respectively 77.7 and 76.3 percent, in 2010, whereas the South West, the least poor zone, had a poverty rate of 59.1 percent.[90] Crushing poverty, combined with birth rates that exceed seven children per woman in parts of the north, has made it difficult for many Nigerians to provide for their families. Although demographics alone do not determine the shape of religious life in northern Nigeria, the economic and demographic background informs the social bases of religious movements and provides a context that many religious entrepreneurs seek to address.

Religious life in northern Nigeria is also shaped by media and globalization. Electronic media are interwoven with daily life, especially in urban areas.[91] Global media connect the region to the rest of the world, especially the Muslim world. Radio brings world events to northern Nigerian Muslims in Hausa, the lingua franca of their region.[92] The BBC, Voice of America, Radio France International, Deutsche Welle, and China Radio International all maintain Hausa broadcast services. Through both legitimate and stolen satellite television hookups, Al Jazeera television serves

86 The World Bank, "GDP Growth (Annual %) – Nigeria." Available at: http://data.worldbank.org/indicator/NY.GDP.MKTP.KD.ZG/countries/NG?display=graph; accessed March 2014.

87 Central Bank of Nigeria, *Annual Report 2011*. Available at: www.cenbank.org/Out/2012/publications/reports/rsd/arp-2011/Chapter%206%20-%20Real%20Sector%20Developments.pdf; accessed March 2014.

88 BBC News, "Nigerians Living in Poverty Rise to Nearly 61%," 13 February 2012. Available at: www.bbc.co.uk/news/world-africa-17015873; accessed March 2014.

89 World Bank Poverty and Inequality Database 2014.

90 "93.9% Nigerians Poor – NBS," *Vanguard*, 13 February 2012. Available at: http://www.vanguardngr.com/2012/02/93-9-nigerians-considered-themselves-to-be-poor-nbs/; accessed March 2014.

91 Brian Larkin, *Signal and Noise: Media, Infrastructure, and Urban Culture in Nigeria* (Durham: Duke University Press, 2008).

92 Muhammad Sani Umar, "Education and Islamic Trends in Northern Nigeria: 1970s–1990s," *Africa Today* 48:2 (Summer 2001): 127–50.

those northern Nigerians who understand Arabic, while CNN World and other channels serve English speakers. The Internet, especially through rapidly proliferating smartphones, connects some fifty million northern Nigerians to the wider world.[93] Nigerians flock to Facebook, Twitter, and forums like Nairaland. Far from being geopolitically or religiously remote, northern Nigeria is deeply interconnected with many other parts of the world.

This confluence of factors makes northern Nigeria an important case study for analyzing the transmission of Salafism. Political turbulence, religious contention, and global interconnectedness are not only defining characteristics of Nigeria but also central themes in this study. Nigeria's dislocations, both local and global, have created opportunities for Salafis to present their canon as a foundation for religious coherence and a basis for activism in a chaotic world.

The Structure of the Argument

This study examines how the deployment of the Salafi canon has been a central mechanism for defining, transmitting, and contesting Salafism worldwide. Part I, "Salafism and Its Transmission," examines the formation of the canon and its dissemination to Nigeria. Chapter 1, "The Canon and Canonizers," describes how the Salafi canon formed and discusses the canonizers who helped to shape it. The chapter argues that the Salafi view of history reflects a process of canonization that emphasizes and reframes some elements of Salafis' intellectual genealogies while strategically downplaying the diverse origins of Salafi thought. Chapter 2, "Africans and Saudi Arabia," shows how Salafis in Saudi Arabia prioritized outreach to Africa soon after the founding of the Islamic University of Medina in 1961. This outreach initially stumbled but became more sophisticated by the 1980s. African Salafis in Saudi Arabia helped theorize ways to co-opt African Muslim history, and Saudi Arabia's local partners in Africa formed networks that helped recruit students. Chapter 3, "Nigerians in Medina," traces the intellectual trajectories of Nigerian Salafis who studied in Medina between the 1980s and the 2000s. The Islamic University provided a transformational experience for these Nigerians, moving them into full participation in the Salafi worldview. They returned home committed to teaching the canon and using its authority to delegitimize rivals.

[93] "Nigeria Has 48m Active Internet Users – NITDA," *Vanguard*, October 7, 2014. Available at: http://www.vanguardngr.com/2014/10/nigeria-48m-active-internet-users-nitda/; accessed January 2015.

Part II, "The Canon in Action," discusses how the Nigerian graduates of Medina have deployed the canon in education, media, and politics. Chapter 4, "Teaching the Canon," analyzes how Nigerian Salafi leaders transmit the canon to their students. As teachers, Nigerian Salafis aim to equip their students with scriptural and canonical texts that will let them articulate and defend the Salafi creed. They offer canonical works as guides to understanding how to live and behave in the contemporary world. Chapter 5, "The Canon in Religious Debates and Electronic Media," explores how the canon appears in religious debates between Nigerian Salafis and their local Muslim rivals, including young Sufi shaykhs and progressive Muslim intellectuals. For all sides, electronic media have become a key site for intellectual struggle, which affects the terms of the debate: Salafis extend their idea of unambiguous proof-texts to other media, and their critics partly accept the assumption that textual evidence should be the agreed-on standard of truth. Chapter 6, "The Canon in Politics," examines how Nigerian Salafis draw on Qurʾanic verses, *ḥadīth* reports, and the canon to address local and global political controversies. In political discourse, Nigerian Salafis use a stripped-down, scripturally focused version of the canon to argue for the need to Islamize Nigerian society.

Part III, "Boko Haram and the Canon," shows how the canon has been central to struggles between Boko Haram and the graduates of Medina. Chapter 7, "Boko Haram from Salafism to Jihadism," places Boko Haram's engagement with Salafism in a global comparative context, including by analyzing the overlapping intellectual genealogies of Boko Haram and the Islamic State in Iraq and al-Shām (ISIS). Boko Haram's founder Muḥammad Yūsuf (1970–2009) remained anchored in the Salafi canon, but the canon is less present in the statements of his successor Abubakar Shekau, whose behavior and messages resemble those of ISIS's founders. Chapter 8, "Reclaiming the Canon," explores how Salafis outside of Boko Haram have invoked the Salafi canon in a bid to discredit Boko Haram's leaders. The chapter relates trends in Nigeria to global, intra-Salafi struggles to control the canon.

In the past century, Salafism emerged as a clearly defined worldview that synthesized earlier Islamic intellectual and religious traditions even as it reevaluated and rejected long-standing scholarly assumptions and precedents in Sunni Islam. In the past half-century, Salafism developed institutional channels for refining its worldview and disseminating its teachings globally, including to places like northern Nigeria. In the past two decades, Salafism has become an object of scrutiny from Western and Muslim policymakers, many of whom are alarmed by increasing Salafi involvement in politics and suspicious of perceived links between Salafi theology and jihadi violence. Amid these changes and controversies, it is vital for non-Salafis to understand the Salafi worldview. This worldview has been articulated and transmitted through a canon, one that incorporates works ranging from the earliest scriptures to the most recent polemics. From analyzing how Salafis learn, transmit, and contest the canon, we can better understand changes in Muslim religious authority around the world.

Part I

Salafism and Its Transmission

1 The Canon and Its Canonizers

When contemporary Salafis seek examples of moral purity, they look above all to the Prophet Muḥammad, the other prophets, and the Companions of the Prophet Muḥammad. But Salafis also treat certain other Muslims as moral authorities. These figures are not selected haphazardly. They represent traditions that contributed core ideas to the Salafi worldview: interpretations of Sunni identity, attitudes about how to derive legal rulings, and ideologies about reviving the spirit of the early Muslim community. Such ideas, and the figures who articulated and represented them, find expression in a "normative-prescriptive list," a canon.

The canon includes many figures who would not have understood themselves as contemporary Salafis understand them. In contrast to most Western scholarly accounts of Salafism, I argue that Salafism is not simply a set of ideas that has existed across the centuries; put differently, contemporary Salafism is not simply a rearticulation of positions held by figures like Shaykh Aḥmad Ibn Taymiyya (1263–1328), who championed exclusivist Sunni Islam in the wake of the collapse of the ʿAbbasid Caliphate (750–1258). Rather, canonization allows contemporary Salafis to retroactively portray earlier figures as part of a cohesive community. Canonization elides disagreements among these figures and strips away elements of their identities that might make contemporary Salafis uneasy. For example, Salafi processes of canonization overlook or explain away Ibn Taymiyya's partial embrace of rationalist methods in theology,[1] his possible sympathies for Sufism,[2] his openness to the ideal that damnation was impermanent,[3] and even his lifelong bachelorhood.[4] Salafis in Nigeria pass over this latter idiosyncrasy in silence even as they make marriage a central topic of their preaching. In other words, the canon reconstructs

[1] See Yossef Rapoport and Shahab Ahmed, eds., *Ibn Taymiyya and His Times* (Oxford: Oxford University Press, 2010).

[2] George Makdisi, "Ibn Taymiyya: A Sufi of the Qadiriya Order," *American Journal of Arabic Studies* 1 (1973): 118–29.

[3] Muḥammad ibn Ismāʿīl al-Amīr al-Ṣanʿānī, *Rafʿ al-Astār li-Ibṭāl Adilla al-Qāʾilīn bi-Fanāʾ al-Nār*, edited by Muḥammad Nāṣir al-Dīn al-Albānī (Beirut: Maktab al-Islāmī, 1984).

[4] Donald Little, "Did Ibn Taymiyya Have a Screw Loose?" *Studia Islamica* 41 (1975): 93–111.

the past and mediates between that past and the present. The capacity to present a coherent and idealized past gives Salafism much of its appeal: the canon provides its adherents with theological confidence and political meaning.

The Salafi "intellectual posture"[5] cannot be understood without reference to this canon. Immersion in the canon is what distinguishes Salafis from other Muslims, including other Muslims who reject Sufism. A Muslim who condemns Sufis but preserves an attachment to a legal school or to Ashʿarī theology or who has no connection to the world of contemporary Salafi scholarship is not fully Salafi. Without understanding this distinction, the formation of Salafism in the twentieth century – and its differentiation from closely related but nevertheless distinct movements, such as Wahhābīs, who maintain an affiliation to the Ḥanbalī school of law – cannot be adequately studied, including in sub-Saharan Africa.

My approach to delineating the boundaries of Salafism is deliberately narrow; Salafism cannot be a meaningful analytical category if it refers to any and all Muslims who seem puritanical. The category acquires meaning only through a strict set of recognizable, empirical criteria that appear in behavior and discourse. The canon provides a clear mechanism for tracing the appearance of such criteria, which in turn enables a study of the remarkable discursive uniformity among Salafis from Nigeria to Indonesia.

This chapter investigates how the canon formed and who formed it. I focus on three traditions that contributed to contemporary Salafism: first, the Hanbalī school as a theological (more than a legal) movement, and particularly its emphasis on a literalist creed rooted in an idealized reading of the early Muslim community's experience; second, a set of Yemeni and Indian thinkers who favored absolute *ijtihād* (direct engagement with Qurʾanic verses and *ḥadīth* reports to derive legal rulings, rather than interpretation performed through the framework of an established legal school); and third, the revivalist currents in the Middle East in the late nineteenth and early twentieth centuries. By revivalism, I mean thinkers who spoke explicitly about "reawakening" Islam and Muslims, specifically in the context of their effort to find an authentically Islamic basis from which to respond to European scientific, military, economic, and political domination of Muslim lands.

As this chapter traces the formation of the canon, it also shows the breadth of the curriculum that Nigerian students encountered at the Islamic University of Medina. African graduates of Arab universities are

[5] Thomas Hegghammer, "Jihadi-Salafis or Revolutionaries? On Religion and Politics in the Study of Militant Islamism" in *Global Salafism: Islam's New Religious Movement*, edited by Roel Meijer, 244–66 (New York: Columbia University Press, 2009), 250.

frequently stereotyped as narrow "Wahhābīs" who lack knowledge of any scholars beyond Ibn Taymiyya and Shaykh Muḥammad ibn ʿAbd al-Wahhāb (1703–92), a religious reformer whose *daʿwa* (call to renewed Islamic faith) transformed the religious and political trajectory of present-day Saudi Arabia. Yet the curriculum in Medina was global. As a consequence, Nigerian Salafis have been able to draw on a globally diverse but theologically coherent set of references when they present Salafi ideas to their audiences. Nigerian Salafis use the canon to transform the way their audiences see Muslim history and geopolitics; the canon's wide historical and geographic scope supports this effort.

Canonizers

Salafis use various methods to reframe works they include in their canon. Like other canonizers, secular and religious, they edit texts by compiling and comparing different versions of these texts that exist in manuscript form – a process visible, for example, when William Shakespeare's contemporary editors note differences between various folio versions of his plays. When establishing authoritative versions of texts, Salafis handle *aḥādīth* with particular care. Salafis cite and grade the *aḥādīth* used by canonical authors – even if this means pointing out that canonical authors sometimes (usually inadvertently) used weak or forged reports. Canonizers also scrutinize the creeds of their subjects, sometimes noting authors' deviations from perceived orthodoxy and sometimes remaining strategically silent about incongruities. Finally, Salafis fit canonical authors into the moral narrative of Salafi history, emphasizing – as many Muslim biographers do – authors' perceived moral qualities in addition to their intellectual accomplishments. Salafis show how canonical figures actualized the ideals of the early Muslim community.

Salafi techniques of canonization reflect both classical inheritances and contemporary institutional arrangements. Salafi canonizers build on long-standing genres within Islamic scholarship, particularly commentary and biographical dictionaries. Yet canonizers' techniques also reflect the role of Saudi Arabian universities in canonization. Many projects of canonization grow out of academic writings at these universities, such as M.A. theses and Ph.D. dissertations. The canon that emerges from the application of these methods is vast, but canonizers impose some uniformity through a shared set of techniques that appear in forewords and footnotes – textual glosses that enclose and discipline the core text. Academic conventions are central to Salafis' canonization efforts.

Canonizers include a number of scholars, especially individuals who completed advanced degrees at Saudi Arabian universities. Canonization is a massive communal undertaking. Yet from the perspective of Nigerian graduates of the Islamic University of Medina, canonical authority has largely run through the university and figures associated with it. One such figure is Shaykh Muḥammad Nāṣir al-Dīn al-Albānī, the Albanian/Syrian *ḥadīth* evaluator. As one biographer of the Nigerian Salafi Shaykh Jaʿfar Maḥmūd Ādam wrote, "Hardly would a new book by Shaykh Nāṣir al-Dīn al-Albānī come out than [Ādam] would rush to look for it, purchase it, and study it."[6] Al-Albānī merits attention as a canonizer for three reasons: he personally canonized numerous texts, he embodied the intersection of the three intellectual streams described earlier, and he influenced numerous other canonizers, who continue to refer to his authority as both a commentator on texts and a verifier of *ḥadīth* reports. Al-Albānī's canonizing projects reached back to points all along the intellectual genealogies that fed into Salafism. He taught, edited, and commented on works by classical *ḥadīth* collectors,[7] by figures in the Yemeni-Indian genealogy discussed later in the chapter,[8] and by representatives of the revivalist movement from the turn of the twentieth century.[9]

Canonizers did not consider the canonized to be intellectually infallible. Indeed, canonizers attributed their penchant for reexamining cherished ideas to the canonical figures themselves, asserting intellectual independence as a core value contained within the canon. In one early work, al-Albānī disagreed with several classical authorities on the soundness of a particular *ḥadīth*. He commented that even though he respected these authorities, he could disagree "because they, may Allah have mercy on them, taught us freedom of opinion and frankness in speech, so much so that they forbade us from blindly emulating them (*taqlīdihim*)."[10] Canonization upholds canonized figures as moral and intellectual authorities but does not present them as perfect.

The Salafi canonizer often appears, whether in his own rendering or in biographical depictions, as the lone figure working in solitude in a library, inhabiting a world of texts. Al-Albānī in particular is often described as the ultimate autodidact. Yet this solitary work depended on the efforts of people who collected and safeguarded texts. Canonizers' legitimacy also relied on the authority present in specific intellectual lineages. In this way, canonization is a largely institutionalized process. In one passage,

6 Muḥammad al-Thānī ʿUmar Mūsā Rijiyar Lemo, *Ayyāmī maʿa Dāʿiyat al-Jīl wa-Mufassir al-Tanzīl* (Kano: Dar al-Ḥikma li-al-Kitāb al-Islāmī, 2011), 57.

7 Muḥammad Nāṣir al-Dīn al-Albānī, *Ḍaʿīf al-Adab al-Mufrad li-l-Imām al-Bukhārī* (al-Jubayl, Saudi Arabia: Dār al-Ṣiddīq, 1994).

8 See note 3 above.

9 Muḥammad Rashīd Riḍā, *Ḥuqūq al-Nisāʾ fī al-Islām*, edited by Muḥammad Nāṣir al-Dīn al-Albānī (Beirut: al-Maktab al-Islāmī, 1984).

10 Muḥammad Nāṣir al-Dīn al-Albānī, *Khuṭbat al-Ḥāja allatī Kāna Rasūl Allāh – Ṣalla Allāh ʿalayhi wa-Sallam – Yuʿallimuhā Aṣḥābahu* (Al-Riyāḍ: Maktabat al-Maʿārif li-al-Nashr wa-l-Tawzīʿ, 2000 [1953]), 39.

Al-Albānī described how he found a late nineteenth-century revivalist text during a visit to Medina in 1978:

> During the period of my stay there I frequented the library of the Islamic University – according to my custom whenever I travel there – to study the gems among the photocopies (*nafāʾis al-muṣawwarāt*) gathered there of rare *ḥadīth* manuscripts and other manuscripts held in different libraries in the countries of the world. This [collection] is due to the ardor and the efforts of His Excellence the Shaykh ʿAbd al-Muḥsin al-ʿAbbād, the current vice president of the University, and before him His Excellency, the Most Erudite Shaykh ʿAbd al-ʿAzīz ibn ʿAbd Allāh ibn Bāz, Secretary General of the Administration for Scholarly Researches and Islamic Legal Rulings in the Kingdom of Saudi Arabia, may Allah reward them well for knowledge and Islam – and for the support they and others gave to proceeding in this great and important project, which has eased the difficult, and brought the far-off near, for scholars conducting research, and for industrious students, so that they may investigate and disseminate the traces of our predecessors, and the as-yet unpublished writings of our scholars. Allah is All-Hearing, Ever-Responding.[11]

As seen in this example, the canon represents the intersection of the institutional (in the form of resources), the genealogical (in the form of personal links that connect canonizers to Salafi authorities), and the textual (in the form of texts authorized by the Salafi community). It should not surprise us, then, that al-Albānī donated his own personal library to the Islamic University of Medina,[12] thereby continuing the canonization process.

The Classical Canon and Its Ḥanbalī Roots

How do Salafis understand the genesis and evolution of their canon? For one answer, I turn to Dr. Muḥammad Amān al-Jāmī (1931–96). His ideas were highly influential at the Islamic University of Medina in the 1980s and 1990s when Nigerian Salafis were studying there.

Born in the Harar region of Ethiopia, al-Jāmī spent his adult life in Saudi Arabia. He studied with the foremost Wahhābī and Salafi teachers of the mid-twentieth century, including the Grand Mufti of Saudi Arabia Shaykh Muḥammad ibn Ibrāhīm Āl al-Shaykh (1893–1969) and Shaykh ʿAbd al-ʿAzīz ibn Bāz, respectively the founding president and vice president of the Islamic University of Medina. Al-Jāmī became a pillar of the Salafi establishment in Saudi Arabia. His circle, strongly influenced by the teachings of al-Albānī, became dominant at Medina in

11 Nuʿman Khayr al-Dīn al-Ālūsī, *Al-Āyāt al-Bayyināt fī ʿAdam Samāʿ al-Amwāt ʿind al-Ḥanafiyya al-Sādāt* (1888), edited by Muḥammad Nāṣir al-Dīn al-Albānī (Riyadh: Maktabat al-Maʿārif li-al-Nashr wa-l-Tawzīʿ, 2005), 17–18.

12 See his will, available at: http://www.alalbany.net; accessed March 2015.

the 1980s and 1990s, where al-Jāmī chaired the Faculty of Ḥadīth. The "Jāmīs" espoused loyalty to the Saudi state, which gave them substantial backing.[13] If there is a voice that expresses Saudi-approved Salafism in its late-twentieth-century strand, the type that Nigerian students at the Islamic University of Medina were most likely to encounter, it is al-Jāmī's.

Examining al-Jāmī's narration of Salafi history clarifies the outlines of the classical Salafi canon – the core works that Salafis consider essential to defining creed. For contemporary Salafis, the classical canon exemplifies how true Muslims have actualized the creed in difficult circumstances. Al-Jāmī's essay "Al-ʿAqīda al-Islāmiyya wa-Tārīkhuhā" ("The Islamic Creed and Its History") presents Islamic history and Salafi history as identical.

Save only the prophets and the early Muslim community, no figures have ranked more prominently in the Salafi worldview than three later Muslims: Imam Aḥmad bin Ḥanbal (780–855), an important figure in the articulation of Sunni creed and identity during a transitional phase for Islamic creed and law; Ibn Taymiyya; and Ibn ʿAbd al-Wahhāb. Al-Jāmī's "The Islamic Creed and Its History" gives prominent places to these three men.

All three belonged to the Ḥanbalī school, named after Ibn Ḥanbal. Ḥanbalism is often described as one of four legal schools in Sunni Islam, but the school's "leaders were often unwilling to acknowledge the same kind of taqlid [emulation of jurisprudential authorities] as provided the institutional security of the other schools . . . each major teacher felt free to start afresh, according to the needs of his own time for reform in a puritan direction."[14] Ibn Ḥanbal himself did not seem to conceive of himself as a jurist, but rather as a pious Muslim attempting to uphold the importance of *ḥadīth* and defend what he considered the pure creed of Islam.[15] In the context of Salafism, Ḥanbalism is better understood as a theological and interpretive tradition, rather than as a legal school.

Core theological ideas from Ḥanbalism that Salafis took up include the insistence that the Qurʾan was not a created object; the rejection of both anthropomorphic and metaphorical understandings of Allah's attributes; the notion that the path toward ultimate truth could proceed only through the early community's understanding of Islam; and a hostility toward a

13 Stéphane Lacroix, *Awakening Islam: The Politics of Dissent in Contemporary Saudi Arabia*, translated by George Holoch (Cambridge, MA, and London: Harvard University Press, 2011), 211–17; and Lacroix, "Between Revolution and Apoliticism: Nasir al-Din al-Albani and His Impact on the Shaping of Contemporary Salafism" in *Global Salafism*, edited by Roel Meijer, 58–80.

14 Marshall Hodgson, *The Venture of Islam*, Volume 3 (Chicago: University of Chicago Press, 1974), 160.

15 Knut S. Vikør, *Between God and the Sultan: A History of Islamic Law* (Oxford and New York: Oxford University Press, 2005), 101.

number of schools that proliferated in the first few centuries of Islam, such as the Muʿtazila (who advocated rationalist theology) and the Shīʿa (who contested the order and manner of succession to the Prophet among his Companions). As they canonized Ibn Ḥanbal, Ibn Taymiyya, and Ibn ʿAbd al-Wahhāb, twentieth-century Salafis like al-Jāmī focused on these figures' contributions not just to defining creed but to defending it: in the Salafi memory, these shaykhs are important partly for their hypervigilance against perceived heresy.

In addition to elements of creed that Ḥanbalism bequeathed to Salafis, Ḥanbalism had a political legacy that has informed Salafism. As Henri Laoust writes,

> Hanbalism has always found a climate favorable to its blooming during periods of troubles. Each time that Islam has felt itself to be threatened, both in its political security and in its doctrines, a Hanbali reaction has been shaped by the attachment to the ancient Sunna.[16]

Ḥanbalism's political aspects reinforce the sense that it is a totalizing movement rather than a school of law narrowly conceived. Ḥanbalism's legacy for Salafism has been its emphasis on *ijtihād* (a scholar's direct engagement with Qurʾanic verses and *ḥadīth re*ports to derive legal rulings), its passion for defending a certain vision of Sunni identity, and its political legacy as a force for both resistance and purification. Nigerian Salafis, operating in a context in which most Muslims belong to the Mālikī jurisprudential school of Sunni Islam, have disavowed Ḥanbalism as a legal identity even as they invoke Ibn Ḥanbal as "the imam of *ahl al-sunna*," a title by which he is known throughout the Salafi world.

Ibn Ḥanbal

Al-Jāmī's essay portrays Ibn Ḥanbal as a figure who upheld the tenets of Sunni identity at a time when the Muslim community had begun to fragment. Al-Jāmī writes that despite a proliferation of heretical sects,[17] Muslims preserved a strong degree of unity from the time of the Prophet's immediate successors through the Umayyad Caliphate (661–750) and the first six ʿAbbāsid rulers. This unity, al-Jāmī continues, collapsed only with the ʿAbbāsid Caliph al-Maʾmūn (r. 813–33). Under al-Maʾmūn and several of his successors, a *Miḥna* or inquisition attempted to enforce the doctrine that the Qurʾan was a created object. This notion was anathema to some early Sunnis, notably Ibn Ḥanbal, and it remains anathema

[16] Henri Laoust, *Essai sur les doctrines sociales et politiques de Taḳī-d-Dīn Aḥmad b. Taimīya, Canoniste ḥanbalite né à Ḥarrān en 661/1262, mort à Damas en 728/1328* (Cairo: Imprimerie de l'Institut Français d'Archéologie Orientale, 1939), 18.

[17] Such as the Shīʿa and the Khawārij.

to contemporary Salafis; for proponents of an uncreated Qur'an, the Qur'an has always existed alongside Allah as His speech. The belief that the Qur'an is uncreated is now mainstream, but during the *Miḥna* official orthodoxy held that it was a created thing. From the Salafi viewpoint, the period from al-Ma'mūn's *Miḥna* to the present has been one in which championing true monotheism requires extraordinary acts of intellectual and physical courage.

Ibn Ḥanbal was born in 780, likely in Baghdad. Although he was descended from soldiers and politicians, from the age of fifteen, he pursued knowledge of *ḥadīth*, traveling throughout Iraq, the Ḥijāz, Yemen, and Syria. Ibn Ḥanbal's best-known work is his *Al-Musnad* (literally "supported," a technical term in *ḥadīth* studies meaning a report with an unbroken chain of transmission or *isnād*), a massive collection of *ḥadīth* reports he gathered and evaluated.[18]

Ibn Ḥanbal spent much of his life in Baghdad, the capital of the 'Abbāsid Caliphate. He lived during a formative period for Sunni Muslim identities. The notion of "*ahl al-sunna*" – people upholding the Prophet's normative model – emerged roughly a century before Ibn Ḥanbal's birth, during the early Muslim community's second civil war (683–93). The early *ahl al-sunna* distinguished themselves from other sects, including the early Shī'a. These sects all took different positions on the question of who was suited to rule the Muslim community and who counted as an infidel. In this debate, *ahl al-sunna* endorsed the caliphs who had succeeded the Prophet Muḥammad.[19]

Ahl al-sunna partly overlapped with *ahl al-ḥadīth* (the people of *ḥadīth*), who preferred to resolve all religious questions through reference to Qur'an and *aḥādīth*, minimizing the role for human interpretation.[20] *Ahl al-ḥadīth*'s legacy has profoundly informed the Salafi methodology, to the extent that some forerunners of the Salafi movement, as well as some Salafis themselves, use this term to refer to themselves. Ibn Ḥanbal "was a rallying figure for the Traditionists, those who wanted to build only on *ḥadīth* and who had become a religio-political party supported by the majority of the people of Baghdad and normally in opposition to the caliph."[21]

During Ibn Ḥanbal's lifetime, the Mu'tazilī school of rationalist theology was ascendant. The Mu'tazila emerged in the eighth century in Basra and became a driving force behind the *Miḥna*. In al-Jāmī's telling,

[18] Christopher Melchert, *Ahmad ibn Hanbal* (London: Oneworld, 2006); and Scott Lucas, *Constructive Critics, Ḥadīth Literature, and the Articulation of Sunnī Islam: The Legacy of the Generation of Ibn Sa'd, Ibn Ma'īn, and Ibn Ḥanbal* (Leiden: Brill, 2004).

[19] Muhammad Qasim Zaman, *Religion and Politics under the Early 'Abbāsids: The Emergence of the Proto-Sunnī Elite* (Leiden: Brill, 1997), 49–50.

[20] Jonathan A. C. Brown, *The Canonization of Al-Bukhārī and Muslim: The Formation and Function of the Sunnī Hadīth Canon* (Leiden: Brill, 2007).

[21] Vikør, *Between God and the Sultan*, 102.

An extremist group of the Muʿtazila gained influence... over the Caliph al-Maʾmūn... until they made him deviate from the Salafi approach the Caliphs before him had followed – the Umayyads and the ʿAbbāsids – and they caused him to fall into a false belief (*bāṭil min al-ʿaqīda*). They led him to believe in the creation of the Qurʾan, and in denying the attributes of Allah, and dealing with all the divine requirements by relying on reason and following empty opinions with complete insolence, turning away from the texts of the Book and the Sunna, even scorning them, and claiming that they brought no intellectual benefit, and even opposing them. This was a heretical innovation that was not known among the caliphs before him.[22]

Ibn Ḥanbal rejected the notion of a created Qurʾan. In his *Kitāb al-Sunna* (The Book of the Sunna), he says, "Whoever says that the Qurʾān is a created object is, for us, an unbeliever (*kāfir*)."[23]

Ibn Ḥanbal hoped to avoid involvement in political disputes. He "stood for unhesitating obedience to the ruler, except in disobedience to God. Yet... what he asked most of all was to be left alone."[24] Defending creed trumped political quietism, and his response to the *Miḥna* has left a legacy that helps structure Salafis' views on the proper relationship between temporal authority and Muslims. As al-Jāmī puts it, under the *Miḥna*, some *ʿulamāʾ* bowed to pressure from the state while others resisted it. Of those who resisted, al-Jāmī writes,

At their forefront was the Imam Aḥmad ibn Ḥanbal, may Allah Most High have mercy on him, who stood by his word, and maintained his creed. Torture and maltreatment did not influence him, and the disorder (*fitna*) did not sway his heart. He paid no attention to the authority and power of the Caliph.[25]

For Salafis, the *Miḥna* represents an episode in which divine mandates trumped temporal authority. In Ibn Ḥanbal's meld of political quietism and outspoken theological defiance, Salafis find continuities with both the uncompromising preaching of the Qurʾanic prophets and the later struggles of Ibn Taymiyya, Ibn ʿAbd al-Wahhāb, and other canonical figures. Like Ibn Ḥanbal, a number of canonical figures have experienced the tension between "apoliticism and revolution."[26] A key component of the Salafi identity is the feeling that one is in a minority facing a world, and a state, gone awry.

In "The Islamic Creed and Its History," al-Jāmī highlights Ibn Ḥanbal's opposition to speculative theology and philosophy. Here Salafism's "canonizing discourse" makes the past – in this case the eighth

22 Muḥammad Amān al-Jāmī, *Majmūʿ Rasāʾil al-Jāmī fī al-ʿAqīda wa-l-Sunna* (Medina: Dār Ibn Rajab, 1993), 36–7.
23 Aḥmad ibn Ḥanbal, *Kitāb al-Sunna* (Mecca: al-Maṭbaʿ al-Salafiyya, 1930/1), 4.
24 Michael Cook, *Commanding Right and Forbidding Wrong in Islamic Thought* (Cambridge: Cambridge University Press, 2001), 113.
25 Al-Jāmī, *Majmūʿ Rasāʾil*, 37.
26 Lacroix, "Between Revolution and Apoliticism."

century – relevant to the present. Al-Jāmī quotes Ibn Ḥanbal's remark, "Do not keep company with those who engage in speculative theology (*ahl al-kalām*), even if they defend the sunna (*dhubbū ʿan al-sunna*)."[27] Al-Jāmī writes,

> In this age, when negligence and apathy have appeared regarding keeping company with heretics (*ahl al-bidʿa*) and being friendly with them, it is incumbent on students to re-examine their tolerant stance, which indicates weak zeal and apathy in forbidding wrong, while employing the counsel (*naṣīḥa*) of the Imam of *ahl al-sunna* and the preventer of heresy (*qāmiʿ al-bidʿa*), Imam Aḥmad ibn Ḥanbal, may Allah be satisfied with him; and . . . to beware the heretic among speculative theologians and the Sufis, and among the Shīʿa (*rawāfiḍ*, literally "rejecters," i.e. of the order of succession to the Prophet), and others; fearing that they might be influenced by their heresy, which might corrupt their creed.[28]

For al-Jāmī, Ibn Ḥanbal's advice is timeless because it provides guidance for how to live in the world after the age of the Companions, an age characterized by a proliferation of sects within the Muslim community. From the Imam's time until his own, al-Jāmī suggests, defending the pure Islamic creed required uncompromising champions and constant vigilance.

The canonization of Ibn Ḥanbal has involved not only holding him up as an exemplary figure but also teaching and defending his works. Defenders arose not just among followers of the Ḥanbalī legal school but also with figures outside the school, such as al-Albānī and the Nigerian Salafis. For example, al-Albānī wrote a short book refuting the charge that authorship of the *ḥadīth* collection *Al-Musnad* had been falsely attributed to Ibn Ḥanbal.[29] Nigerian Salafis have presented Ibn Ḥanbal not as a legal authority but as a champion of the true creed.

Ibn Taymiyya

For Salafis, Ibn Taymiyya is another figure who upheld the true Islamic creed in a time of turmoil. Salafis assert that he epitomizes intellectual virtuosity in the service of Islam. In "The Islamic Creed and Its History," al-Jāmī titles his section on Ibn Taymiyya "Breaking the Stagnation" (*Kasr al-Jumūd*). Al-Jāmī writes that after the time of the Caliph al-Maʾmūn, philosophy suffused Islamic society, posing intellectual dangers to Muslims. Ibn Taymiyya undid the damage:

> In that critical period a Salafi scholar appeared who studied these new forms of knowledge (*ʿulūm jadīda*) – or new conventions to be precise – just as others were

[27] Al-Jāmī, *Majmūʿ Rasāʾil*, 39.
[28] Al-Jāmī, *Majmūʿ Rasāʾil*, 42–3.
[29] Muḥammad Nāṣir al-Dīn al-Albānī, *Al-Dhabb al-Aḥmad ʿan Musnad al-Imām Aḥmad* (Al-Jubayl, Saudi Arabia: Dār al-Ṣiddīq, 1999).

studying them. But he studied them in complete silence, until he delved into all these speculative theological and philosophical conventions, with his complete mastery of Islamic sciences as creed and law, and the sciences of Qur'an and *ḥadīth* in particular, and the branches of the Arabic language too, and this was Taqī al-Dīn ibn Taymiyya, of Ḥarrān, of Damascus.[30]

Ibn Taymiyya's proficiency in the intellectual disciplines of heretics, al-Jāmī continues, allowed the Shaykh to combat them:

The Shaykh of Islam used these conventions to defend Islam and its creed in the language of the people who were attacking the creed, in a style they recognised. He came upon the people suddenly, as a soldier armed with the weapon of his age, trained in all the weapons used in the field, and he excelled in using them to the extent necessary. The Shaykh of Islam worked to renew the approach of the *salaf*, and to inspire the movement for calling people to Islam.[31]

In al-Jāmī's account, Ibn Tamiyya merits canonization for his ability to defend Islam through mastery of the numerous and sophisticated intellectual challenges that confronted the true faith. Here as elsewhere, al-Jāmī projects the Salafi identity back through time, drawing a straight line from the prophets to the *salaf* to Ibn Ḥanbal to Ibn Taymiyya.

Taqī al-Dīn Aḥmad ibn Taymiyya was born in 1263 in Ḥarrān, in present-day Turkey near its border with Syria. He came from a lineage of Ḥanbalī scholars. Amid the Mongols' invasion of the Muslim heartlands, his family fled to Damascus, which was emerging as a center of Ḥanbalī scholarship.[32] Ibn Taymiyya spent the majority of his life there, punctuated by extended – and sometimes involuntary – sojourns in Egypt.

Ibn Taymiyya's intellectual formation occurred in this Ḥanbalī milieu, although the shaykh would come to consider himself an absolute *mujtahid*, someone capable of deriving legal rulings directly from scriptural sources. As a young man, he studied Ibn Ḥanbal's *Al-Musnad* as well as the *ḥadīth* collections of other major compilers.[33] Ibn Taymiyya was influenced by Ibn Ḥanbal's works on creed and drew heavily on Ibn Ḥanbal's polemics against the Muʿtazila and other schools. Yet Ibn Taymiyya was not an uncritical partisan of the Ḥanbalī school. He "would ceaselessly research the thought of primitive Hanbalism, with the hope of smashing the school's immobilized codification, into which the work of later Hanbalites tended to congeal."[34]

30 Al-Jāmī, *Majmūʿ Rasā'il*, 48.
31 Ibid., 49.
32 Cook, *Commanding Right.*
33 Laoust, *Essai.*
34 Laoust, *Essai*, 77.

Ibn Taymiyya lived in an era when the last vestiges of the ʿAbbāsid Caliphate were crumbling. Mongol armies pushed into ʿAbbāsid territories, capturing Baghdad in 1258, followed by Aleppo and Damascus in 1260. Alongside, and often at war with, Mongol territories were ʿAbbāsid successor states, such as the Mamlūk Sultanate based in Cairo. Ibn Taymiyya was profoundly marked by the Mamlūk state's confrontation with the Mongols and the Crusaders: "His youth had been exalted by the triumphs of Islam over the Franks. His adult years would often pass under anxiety about a Mongol invasion, which he had already, as a child, tragically experienced."[35]

Ibn Taymiyya's entry into public life and public controversy came when he wrote *Al-Fatwā al-Ḥamawiyya al-Kubrā* (The Great Edict of Ḥamāh [a town in Syria]) in 1299. Ibn Taymiyya argued against positions held by the Muʿtazila, the Ashʿariyya, and others on the allegorical nature of Allah's attributes. The creed elicited a popular counter-reaction and accusations of anthropomorphism.[36] Because of this and other polemical exchanges, Ibn Taymiyya would spend many of the ensuing years caught up in controversies with religious rivals and temporal authorities. He was imprisoned repeatedly in Cairo and Damascus, dying in the latter city's citadel in 1328.

One example of the canonization of Ibn Taymiyya comes from a Saudi Arabian scholar who edited Ibn Taymiyya's *Al-Fatwā al-Ḥamawiyya al-Kubrā* as part of his master's degree work.[37] The canonizer outlined four reasons that pushed him to publish a new edition of the book. First was its "scholarly value," especially its treatment of "the unity of the names and attributes (*tawḥīd al-asmāʾ wa-l-ṣifāt*),"[38] one of three major forms of divine unity that Salafis routinely invoke. Second, the canonizer wrote, "This book is considered one of the strongest reactions to the Ashʿarī [theological] school" and it "treats a deviation in creed that is deeply embedded in the Islamic *umma* in the present time." Third, it has an "easy style (*uslūb sahl*)" and "is considered one of the foundational Salafi books (*ummahāt al-kutub al-salafiyya*), which is indispensable to the seeker of knowledge." Finally, the canonizer perceived a need for critical scholarly treatment of the text, particularly by verifying and citing *aḥādīth* and compiling the different versions of the text.[39] In addition to

35 Laoust, *Essai*, 63–4.
36 Laoust, *Essai*, 112.
37 This is Dr. Ḥamad ibn ʿAbd al-Muḥsin al-Tuwayjirī (b. 1964/5), who studied and worked at Imām Muḥammad ibn Saʿūd Islamic University. For his background, see "Tarjamat al-Duktūr Ḥamad ibn ʿAbd al-Muḥsin al-Tuwayjirī," undated. Available at: http://www.taimiah.org/index.aspx/function=author&Id=2; accessed September 2014.
38 Ḥamad ibn ʿAbd al- Muḥsin al-Tuwayjirī, "Editor's Introduction" in Taqī al-Dīn Ibn Taymiyya, *Al-Fatwā al-Ḥamawiyya al-Kubrā* (Riyadh: Dār al-Ṣamīʿī, 2004), 10.
39 Ibid., 11.

describing his editorial engagement with *Al-Fatwā al-Ḥamawiyya*, he included a biography of Ibn Taymiyya that detailed his "moral qualities."[40] The canonizer carefully framed his subject, situating his usefulness for contemporary Salafis in particular ways.

Ibn Taymiyya's legacy included scholars who studied directly with him, especially Ibn Qayyim al-Jawziyya (1292–1350) and Ismāʿīl ibn Kathīr (1301–73). Ibn al-Qayyim influenced Muhammad ibn ʿAbd al-Wahhāb, as well as several other figures discussed in this chapter. Ibn al-Qayyim has been incorporated into the Salafi canon due to his writings, but also because his life mirrored his master's in certain ways that make him, like Ibn Taymiyya, a touchstone for Salafi notions of principled opposition to oppression. Ibn Kathīr, meanwhile, has become a part of the Salafi canon due to his *tafsīr* (exegesis) of the Qurʾān and his historical work *Al-Bidāya wa-l-Nihāya* (The Beginning and the End).

Ibn Taymiyya's position within the Salafi canon is central, but the meaning of his legacy is disputed within the Salafi community, particularly when it comes to assessing his position on the sensitive and consequential question of *takfīr*, or declaring other Muslims to be unbelievers. In Ibn Taymiyya's works, especially his denunciations of Mongol converts to Islam as unbelievers, some Salafis and non-Salafis have perceived justifications for applying *takfīr* against a range of targets in the present, from ordinary Muslims to allegedly apostate Muslim rulers.[41] Other Salafis, working to police the boundaries of the canon, have sought to refute such interpretations of the shaykh's ideas. One contemporary canonizer, in his book *The Approach of Ibn Taymiyya to the Issue of Takfīr*, positions the shaykh as part of the "middle course" (*al-wāsiṭiyya*) that "*ahl al-sunna wa-l-jamāʿa*" follow. This course avoids the extremes of the *murjiʾa*,[42] or those who defer judgment on questions of *takfīr*, and "the rest of the heterodox (*ahl al-bidʿa*) . . . most of whom have anathematized anyone who disagrees with them." The author warned that "the issue of *takfīr*, like other legal issues, is not permitted to the ignorant (*al-jāhil*) to discuss"[43] and that some contemporary practitioners of *takfīr* "have begun to take from the words of Ibn Taymiyya things whose meanings they do not understand, or they understand [the meanings] but do not understand their intent."[44] The correct way to understand

40 Ibid., 23–7.

41 Emmanuel Sivan, *Radical Islam: Medieval Theology and Modern Politics*, second edition (New Haven: Yale University Press, 1990); Paul Heck, "'Jihad' Revisited," *Journal of Religious Ethics* 32:1 (Spring 2004): 95–128; 116–19.

42 For more on this politicized label and its transposition from its early Islamic context to contemporary intra-Salafi debates, see Daniel Lav, *Radical Islam and the Revival of Medieval Theology* (Cambridge: Cambridge University Press, 2012).

43 ʿAbd al-Majīd ibn ʿAbd Allāh al-Mashʿabī, Manhaj Ibn Taymiyya fī Masʾalat al-Takfīr (Al-Riyāḍ: Maktabat Aḍwāʾ al-Salaf, 1997), 3–4.

44 Al-Mashʿabī, *Manhaj Ibn Taymiyya*, 5–6.

Ibn Taymiyya's approach, the author continued, was to conceptualize *takfīr* as a specialized legal act that had to proceed according to strict engagement with criteria outlined in the Qur'an and the Sunna. The author devoted part of his book to specifying which groups Ibn Taymiyya had anathematized and on what basis. Among northern Nigerian Salafis, respect for Ibn Taymiyya runs high and suspicion of non-Salafi Muslims runs deep, but many of the leading graduates of Medina emphasize *ta'līm* (literally "instruction," but in this case the moral reformation of other Muslims through discursive persuasion) over *takfīr*.

Muḥammad ibn 'Abd al-Wahhāb

Another central figure in the Salafi canon is the Ḥanbalī shaykh Muḥammad ibn 'Abd al-Wahhāb, the eighteenth-century Arabian reformer. Through his attacks on other Muslims' creeds and practices, Ibn 'Abd al-Wahhāb caused a controversy during his lifetime that has not faded with the passing years. The label "Wahhābī" has been thrown at Muslim reformers and purists by their political and theological opponents from Mali to India, but contemporary Salafis do not consider themselves mere followers of Ibn 'Abd al-Wahhāb. He is a central, but not the sole, figure in the canon.

In the Salafi canon, Ibn 'Abd al-Wahhāb holds a prominent place due to his uncompromising championing of his brand of *tawḥīd* (the absolute unity of Allah). Al-Jāmī writes,

> In the twelfth century hijrī, the *dā'iya* (preacher), the *mujāhid* (striver), the Imam Muḥammad ibn 'Abd al-Wahhāb noticed that a violent storm was raging over the Islamic creed and its law, in order to change its characteristics, and move things out of place, and throw them wherever they fell. Many concepts were changed because of this. The matter became obscure for people in many domains and numerous issues. Many heretical innovations occurred in Islam that had nothing to do with Islam. And so the young *dā'iya* saw that he had to make himself ready to engage in *tajdīd* (renewal of Islam) and in restoring matters to the proper place they had been in before the storm.[45]

In political terms, if Ibn Ḥanbal provides Salafis with a model of uncompromising quietism, Ibn 'Abd al-Wahhāb provides them with a model of uncompromising activism. As with Ibn Ḥanbal and Ibn Taymiyya, al-Jāmī presents Ibn 'Abd al-Wahhāb as a hero who appeared to save the Muslim community at a critical juncture.

Muḥammad ibn 'Abd al-Wahhāb was born in 1703 in al-'Uyayna, in the Najd region of present-day Saudi Arabia. Like Ibn Taymiyya, Ibn

[45] Al-Jāmī, *Majmū' Rasā'il*, 63.

ʿAbd al-Wahhāb was the descendant of Ḥanbalī scholars.[46] Yet during his studies in Mecca, Medina, Basra, and possibly elsewhere, Ibn ʿAbd al-Wahhāb developed an understanding of *tawḥīd* and its requirements that broke with his family tradition.

A central preoccupation in Ibn ʿAbd al-Wahhāb's intellectual formation was his engagement with scripture and *ḥadīth.* It is noteworthy that some of his teachers of *ḥadīth* came from beyond the Ḥanbalī school. During his studies in Medina, he joined a cosmopolitan intellectual circle that had, for roughly a century, been pursuing a "revival of *ḥadīth* scholarship." The Medina circle was strongly interested in the works of Ibn Ḥanbal and Ibn Taymiyya. Many of these Medinan scholars belonged to the Naqshbandiyya Sufi order, but in the field of jurisprudence, "*madhhabī* (legal) affiliation was becoming an insignificant criterion in defining the nature of their intellectual association and interconnection."[47] Although Ibn ʿAbd al-Wahhāb broke with his Medinan teachers by attacking Sufism and anathematizing other Muslims, he built some of his ideas on the foundations that the Medinan shaykhs laid in the area of *ḥadīth* scholarship.

Although he began preaching as a young man, it was following his father's death in 1740 that Ibn ʿAbd al-Wahhāb initiated his enduring and public call for a reinvigorated *tawḥīd.* In the town of Dirʿiyya, he found an ally in the ruler, Muḥammad ibn Saʿūd (d. 1767). In 1744, the two men swore loyalty to each other and recognized each other's respective sway, the former in politics and the latter in religious doctrine.[48] As Ibn Saʿūd began a series of military conquests, Ibn ʿAbd al-Wahhāb corresponded with *ʿulamāʾ* throughout Najd. Scholars in conquered areas faced pressure to endorse his teachings or leave. Dirʿiyya became the foremost center for religious learning in Najd, as older centers of learning lost importance.[49] The two men's families have continued to uphold the alliance, as two Saudi emirates rose and fell only to be followed by a third, the present Saudi state.

Canonizers have revered but also reevaluated the work of Ibn ʿAbd al-Wahhāb. His *Kitāb al-Tawḥīd* (The Book of the Unity of God) is a core text, yet Salafis have not shied away from repackaging and critiquing it. Salafis' concern with assessing the reliability of *ḥadīth* reports magnifies their tendency to critically examine such canonical texts. One canonizer's introduction to an annotated edition of *Kitāb al-Tawḥīd* reads, "I wanted

46 David Commins, *The Wahhabi Mission and Saudi Arabia* (London: I.B. Tauris, 2006), 17.

47 Basheer Nafi, "A Teacher of Ibn ʿAbd al-Wahhāb: Muḥammad Ḥayāt al-Sindī and the Revival of Aṣḥāb al-Ḥadīth's Methodology," *Islamic Law and Society* 13:2 (2006): 208–241; 214–15.

48 Natana Delong-Bas, *Wahhabi Islam: From Revival and Reform to Global Jihad* (London: I.B. Tauris, 2007).

49 Commins, *Wahhabi Mission.*

to put the different texts of this book in order, and correct the errors that had entered into it in previous editions, and cite (*takhrīj*) its *ḥadīth* reports and non-prophetic sayings."[50] The editor, through this process of citation, identified and indicated "nineteen mistakes" (*awhām*) in the book.[51] Even a work central to the Salafi canon remains an object of critical reframing.

This edition of *Kitāb al-Tawḥīd* exemplifies how the canonical, the genealogical, and the institutional can interact through canonization. The Salafi compiler of that edition was a scholar in the lineage of the Yemeni Salafi shaykh Muqbil ibn Hādī al-Wādiʿī (1933–2001). Al-Wādiʿī belonged to the same generation as al-Jāmī and was, like al-Jāmī, strongly influenced by al-Albānī. The edition contained forewords by two of al-Wādiʿī's senior students and was published by the press associated with al-Wādiʿī's school Dār al-Ḥadīth. These forewords connected the text, genealogically, to al-Wādiʿī and through him to his teachers, including al-Albānī. Canonization enfolds classical texts within a repertoire of editorial methods and genealogical authorizations.

The Yemeni-Indian Strand

In his canonizing essay "The Islamic Creed and Its History," al-Jāmī gave pride of place to classical Ḥanbalī figures and their legacy in the twentieth century. He pointed to Saudi Arabia as the embodiment of Salafism in his own time: "In the contemporary world there has existed no Islamic *daʿwa* upon whose approach (*manhaj*) an Islamic state has been built, except the *daʿwa* of Imam Muḥammad ibn ʿAbd al-Wahhāb.'[52]

Yet Salafis have canonized figures beyond the Ḥanbalī-Wahhābī lineage. Salafis present their community as a global tendency, comprising movements with diverse names sharing a common creed.[53] Who, then, counts as a Salafi? Whose intellectual genealogies are legitimate from a Salafi point of view?

One major non-Ḥanbalī contribution to the canon has come from an intellectual genealogy that ran through Yemen and India in the eighteenth and nineteenth centuries. The central figures in this genealogy were not Ḥanbalīs in a legal sense, and they openly rejected Wahhābism. Yet twentieth-century Salafis such as al-Albānī approvingly cited their work and considered it part of the broader project of reviving the early Muslim community's ethos and approach.

50 ʿAlī ʿAbd al-Raḥmān Radmān al-Ḥabīshī, "Muqaddimat al-Muḥaqqiq" in Muhammad ibn ʿAbd al-Wahhāb, *Kitāb al-Tawḥīd* (Dammāj, Yemen: Maktabat al-Imām al-Wādiʿī, 2009), 12; on *takhrīj*, see Brown, *Canonization*, 211–17.

51 Al-Ḥabīshī, "Muqadimma," 30.

52 Al-Jāmī, *Majmūʿ Rasāʾil*, 78.

53 Al-Jāmī, *Majmūʿ Rasāʾil*, 81.

In the context of the canon, these Yemeni and Indian figures could even be used to discipline Ibn Taymiyya: Al-Albānī painstakingly edited and published a manuscript by a Yemeni intellectual, Shaykh Muḥammad ibn Ismāʿīl al-Amīr al-Ṣanʿānī (1688–1769), who had argued against the idea that Hell might be temporary, a position that Ibn Taymiyya had perhaps held. Al-Albānī wrote a long introduction to the work. He treated Ibn Taymiyya with the utmost respect but admitted the possibility that Ibn Taymiyya had, from a Salafi point of view, erred. Al-Albānī ultimately sided with Ibn al-Amīr. Bracing himself for vigorous objections from Ibn Taymiyya's other contemporary disciples, al-Albānī pointed out how Ibn al-Amīr used language of which contemporary Salafis would approve. Al-Albānī referred to Ibn al-Amīr's approach as "free of legal partisanship and having no Ashʿarī or Muʿtazilī attachment (*min ghayr al-ʿaṣabiyya al-madhhabiyya wa-lā mutābiʿat ashʿariyya aw muʿtaziliyya*)." Al-Albānī also noted that he had reached a similar conclusion about the issue of Hell's permanence – and Ibn Taymiyya's error or ambiguity on the issue – in his own work. It was not simply that the Yemeni scholar had produced strong textual evidence, but also that al-Albānī found his creed and methods compatible with those of contemporary Salafism.[54]

The Yemeni-Indian genealogy offered a major contribution to the formation of Salafism. Two key figures in this genealogy are shaykhs Muḥammad ibn ʿAlī al-Shawkānī (1760–1834) of Ṣanʿāʾ in Yemen and Ṣiddīq Ḥasan Khān al-Qannūjī (1832–90), who lived in Bhopal in India. These figures were incorporated into the curriculum that Nigerians studied, formally and informally, in Medina. Nigerian Salafis directly cite both al-Shawkānī and Khān.[55]

Al-Shawkānī was the most prominent Muslim scholar and judge in Yemen in his time. Born in the village of Hijrat Shawkān, he spent his adult life in Ṣanʿāʾ, where he served as chief judge of the Qāsimī imamate from 1795 until his death. The shaykh underwent a personal transition in religious allegiances, reflecting broader changes in Yemeni society. He "rejected unequivocally the Zaydī-Hādawī school he was born into [a branch of the Shīʿa] and saw himself more properly as the intellectual heir of the Sunnī Traditionists of highland Yemen, scholars who argued that the Sunnī canonical *ḥadīth* collections were unconditionally authoritative in matters of religion."[56] Most important from the perspective of al-Shawkānī's inclusion in the Salafi canon, he embraced the principle of

54 Al-Ṣanʿānī, *Rafʿ al-Astār*, 7.

55 Rijiyar Lemo, *Ayyāmī*.

56 Bernard Haykel, *Revival and Reform in Islam: The Legacy of Muhammad al-Shawkānī* (Cambridge and New York: Cambridge University Press, 2003), 10. Knut Vikør questions the extent of al-Shawkānī's conversion, given that al-Shawkānī remained in the employ of a Zaydī imam; see *Between God and the Sultan: A History of Islamic Law* (New York: Oxford University Press, 2006), 123, footnote 21.

absolute *ijtihād* and regarded himself as absolutely qualified to perform it, basing legal rulings on foundational texts alone and rejecting other legal sources such as scholarly consensus and analogy.[57] In keeping with its anti-*madhhab*ism (rejection of established legal schools), the Salafi canon has enthusiastically embraced al-Shawkānī's legal manual *Nayl al-Awṭār fī Sharḥ Muntaqā al-Akhbār* (Attaining the Alms in Commenting on the Choicest Traditions). Twentieth-century Salafis canonized not only al-Shawkānī's legal works but also works by his teachers in the Yemeni Traditionist lineage – the earlier-mentioned Ibn al-Amīr, for example, had taught al-Shawkānī's primary teacher. Even in the case of al-Shawkānī, however, later Salafi canonizers seem to have strategically overlooked elements of his thought – his approach to Qurʾanic exegesis, for example, gave less weight to Prophetic Companions' and Successors' interpretations than contemporary Salafis do. He was also franker than his canonizers in acknowledging the problems that differences of opinion within the early Muslim community might pose for those attempting to reconstruct an authentic, original Islam.[58]

The Yemeni Sunni tradition to which al-Shawkānī belonged was not a Yemeni equivalent of the Wahhābī project. The Yemeni Traditionists held mixed attitudes toward Wahhābīs. The two circles drew on some of the same intellectual sources, such as Ibn Taymiyya, and they shared attitudes favoring scriptural literalism and disavowing popular Sufism. Yet "a doctrinal polemic raged between the Wahhābīs and the Yemeni Traditionists, in which the latter accused the Wahhābīs of extremism."[59] Ibn al-Amīr, who strongly influenced al-Shawkānī's views on *ijtihād*, initially approved of his contemporary Ibn ʿAbd al-Wahhāb, but later changed course, dismissing the shaykh and his writings.[60] Al-Shawkānī followed a similar pattern, expressing early praise for Ibn ʿAbd al-Wahhāb but subsequently viewing the Wahhābīs as extremists who threatened Yemen.[61]

Although Yemen abuts Saudi Arabia, al-Shawkānī influenced the Salafi canon in large part through the Indian *ahl-e ḥadīth* movement, and particularly through Ṣiddīq Ḥasan Khān, who became a major transmitter of al-Shawkānī's work. Khān was born in Bareilly, which sits in present-day Uttar Pradesh State, northern India. Khān's birthplace and family traditions connected him to one of the two major intellectual traditions

57 Haykel, *Revival and Reform*, 92–5.

58 Johanna Pink, "Where Does Modernity Begin? Muḥammad al-Shawkānī and the Tradition of *Tafsīr*" in *Tafsīr and Islamic Intellectual History: Exploring the Boundaries of a Tradition*, edited by Andreas Görke and Johanna Pink, 323–60 (Oxford: Oxford University Press, 2014).

59 Haykel, *Revival and Reform*, 128.

60 Michael Cook, "On the Origins of Wahhabism," *Journal of the Royal Asiatic Society*, Third Series, 2:2 (July 1992): 191–202; 200.

61 Haykel, *Revival and Reform*, 128–9.

that influenced his thought (the other being al-Shawkānī). This was the tradition represented by Shāh Walī Allāh (1703–62), a renowned scholar, *ḥadīth* master, and Sufi.[62] Like al-Shawkānī, however, Walī Allāh rejected the use of weak *ḥadīth* reports, thereby anticipating an issue that would become a touchstone for twentieth-century revivalists and Salafis alike.[63] As a youth, Khān studied logic, philosophy, jurisprudence, and *ḥadīth* with *ʿulamāʾ* in northern India. By 1859, Khān had established himself in the city of Bhopal semi-permanently.[64] In 1871, he married Jahan Begum (1838–1901), Bhopal's ruler. He helped rule Bhopal until 1885, when British colonial authorities deposed him.

In Bhopal, Khān encountered the Yemeni circles that connected him to al-Shawkānī and the legacy of Ibn Taymiyya. As one biographer of Khān writes, "In the 1860's *ʿulamāʾ*, full of the ideas of Ibn Taimīyyah and al-Shawkānī, were found in the courts of the Indian princely states, especially Hyderabad and Bhopal."[65] Khān's pilgrimage in 1868–9 deepened his contact with the works of al-Shawkānī and Ibn Taymiyya. During the eight-month journey, he passed through Yemen, where he visited Yemeni scholars who had spent time in Bhopal.[66] He studied *ḥadīth* and transcribed scholarly works, for example those of Ibn al-Amīr. He purchased Ibn Taymiyya's *Iqtiḍāʾ al-Ṣirāṭ al-Mustaqīm li-Mukhālafat Aṣḥāb al-Jaḥīm* (The Necessity of the Straight Path for Opposing the People of Hell), as well as al-Shawkānī's *Irshād al-Fuḥūl ila Taḥqīq al-Ḥaqq min ʿIlm al-Uṣūl* (Guiding the Masters to Verify the Truth through Knowledge of the Foundations), *Nayl al-Awṭār*, and *Fatḥ al-Qadīr* (God's Triumph); the last of these was al-Shawkānī's exegesis of the Qurʾan. After performing *ḥajj*, visiting Medina, and returning to Mecca for *ʿumra*, he traveled back to Bhopal, where he began championing the need for a *ḥadīth-bas*ed revival and attacking *taqlīd* and Ḥanafism.[67]

Khān's marriage to Jahan Begum helped him secure the institutional and financial support he needed to propagate his ideas. Working with a team of copyeditors, transcribers, reviewers, and publishers, Khān abridged, translated, and synthesized texts by Ibn Taymiyya, Walī Allāh,

[62] Saeedullah, *The Life and Works of Muhammad Siddiq Hasan Khan, Nawab of Bhopal* (Lahore: Published by Sh. Muhammad Ashraf, printed at Ashraf Press, 1973), 31.

[63] Jonathan A.C. Brown, *Misquoting Muhammad: The Challenge and Choices of Interpreting the Prophet's Legacy* (London: Oneworld, 2014), 254.

[64] Saeedullah, *Life and Works*, 34–9.

[65] Saeedullah, *Life and Works*, 13. One such Yemeni scholar was Shaykh Ḥusayn ibn Muḥsin al-Anṣārī (1829–1909). Al-Anṣārī studied with al-Shawkānī's son Aḥmad, and his father had studied with al-Shawkānī himself. Al-Anṣārī went to visit his brother Zayn al-ʿĀbidīn in Bhopal during the 1860s and spent much of the rest of his life there, interrupted by sojourns in Yemen. See Muḥammad Ziyād al-Takla, "Ḥusayn ibn Muḥsin al-Anṣārī al-Yamānī," al-Alukah, 2009. Available at: http://www.alukah.net/culture/0/7590; accessed September 2014.

[66] The two scholars mentioned in the previous note.

[67] Saeedullah, *Life and Works*, 14; 42–44.

al-Shawkānī, and others. He published these texts in multiple places – Istanbul, Egypt, and India – and in multiple languages – namely Persian, Arabic, and Urdu. Khān's travels, activism, and publishing represented a cosmopolitan project of uniting the umma through scripturalism. Khān used the spaces of mobility opened by the Ottoman and British Empires but also reacted against imperial efforts to divide the Muslim world along national identities and borders.[68]

What the Indian and Yemeni traditions shared was an emphasis on the right of the individual scholar to practice *ijtihād* by going back to the foundational texts of Islam. Shāh Walī Allāh had called for intellectual and spiritual elites to embrace a renewed *ijtihād*. Khān built on this legacy, yet in some respects he diverged from Walī Allāh. Walī Allāh belonged to the Naqshbandiyya Sufi order and defended Sufi ideas such as *waḥdat al-wujūd* (literally "monism of being," or the notion that all things are merely manifestations of God and that nothing exists apart from Him – a notion anathema to contemporary Salafis, who abhor any perceived blurring of the line between Creator and created).[69] Khān approvingly cited some Sufi intellectuals. Yet he condemned many practices associated with Sufism, such as visiting saints' tombs, and he opposed public discussion or teaching of *waḥdat al-wujūd*. Additionally, while Walī Allāh endorsed the preeminence of the Ḥanafī school among the Indian masses, and reserved the privilege of *ijtihād* for elites, Khān publicly attacked the school's founder Abū Ḥanīfa and promoted a broader *ijtihād*. Finally, Walī Allāh sought unity between Sunni and Shīʿī Muslims,[70] while Khān sought to prevent Shīʿa from celebrating their rituals.[71] Khān and like-minded Indian *ʿulamāʾ* of his day placed a premium on the notions of *tawḥīd*, *ijtihād*, and eradicating *bidʿa* (heretical innovations).[72]

Khān's *al-Tāj al-Mukallal min Jawāhir Maʾāthir al-Ṭirāz al-Ākhir wa-l-Awwal* (The Tower Adorned with Jewels of the Achievements of the Recent and Original Model) provides insight into his views on *ijtihād* and his understanding of a canon of *mujtahids*. Khān's canon is not the Salafi canon per se, but rather a precursor to it, a proto-Salafi corpus. *Al-Tāj al-Mukallal* is a biographical dictionary with the purpose of defending *ijtihād*, as Khān explained in the introduction:

This is a commemoration of a blessed group of people with knowledge of the exalted prophetic *ḥadīth*, who worked with the Prophet's tradition (*al-athar*

68 Seema Alavi, "Siddiq Hasan Khan (1832–1890) and the Creation of a Muslim Cosmopolitanism in the 19th Century," *Journal of the Economic and Social History of the Orient* 54 (2011): 1–38.
69 Barbara Metcalf, *Islamic Revival in British India: Deoband, 1860–1900* (Princeton: Princeton University Press, 1982).
70 Metcalf, *Islamic Revival.*
71 Saeedullah, *Life and Works.*
72 Saeedullah, *Life and Works*, 125.

> *al- muṣṭafawī*), and their glorious deeds, which are needed by students [trying to] understand what the *salaf* of this *umma* practiced (*mā kāna ʿalayhi salaf hādhihi al-umma*), and their successors the imams who worked with evidence (*al-dalīl*), rejected emulation (*taqlīd*) [of legal schools], and refused idle talk.[73]

Khān went on to refute the views of those who claimed that *ijtihād* had ended after the classical period. He wrote that Allah "has guaranteed the preservation of His authentic religion. The meaning of that is not its preservation in the bellies of scrolls and notebooks (*buṭūn al-ṣuḥuf wa-l-dafātir*), but rather the provision of those who will explain it to people in every time and at every need."[74]

Who comprised this blessed group? *Al-Tāj al-Mukallal* contains 543 names, starting with Ibn Ḥanbal and ending with Khān. The dictionary contains figures from the classical Ḥanbalī tradition such as Ibn Taymiyya, but also figures whom later Salafis would compartmentalize, such as the Andalusian philosopher and jurist Ibn Rushd (1126–98), whose works on comparative jurisprudence are acceptable to Salafis but whose embrace of philosophy is not.[75] The dictionary devotes prominent entries to representatives of the Yemeni tradition, such as Ibn al-Amīr and al-Shawkānī. Khān's canon was mostly, but not entirely, made up of figures whom later Salafis would claim for their canon.

Like the Yemeni scholars who inspired him, Khān disavowed any allegiance to Wahhābism. In 1884, Khān published *An Interpreter of Wahabiism* to allay British authorities' concerns about Wahhābism in India and refute his opponents' use of this label to describe *ahl-e ḥadīth*. In the book, Khān used the criterion of allegiance to a legal school to differentiate his movement from Wahhābism. "In my opinion," he wrote, "the Mohamedans of the world may be divided into two classes. The *Ahl-e-Sunnat* and *Jamaat*, also called *Ahl-e-Hadis*, and the *Mukallids* [i.e., those who practice emulation of a school] of particular forms of faith."[76] Explaining Wahhābism as a Ḥanbalī sect, he noted, "The truth is, that the Wahābis are a set of *Mukallids* of a particular religion."[77] Notably, it was Khān's attitude toward legal affiliation, and not the voices of those

[73] Ṣiddīq Ḥasan Khān, *Al-Tāj al-Mukallal min Jawāhir Maʾāthir al-Ṭirāz al-Ākhir wa-l-Awwal*, second edition (Beirut: Dār Iqrāʾ, 1983), 19.

[74] Khān, *Al-Tāj al-Mukallal*, 21.

[75] Ibn Rushd's *Bidāyat al-Mujtahid* (The Beginning of the Independent Legal Scholar), a work that compares the four Sunni schools of law, has been taught at the Islamic University. Mike Farquhar, "The Islamic University of Medina since 1961: The Politics of Religious Mission and the Making of a Modern Salafi Pedagogy" in *Shaping Global Islamic Discourses: The Role of al-Azhar, al-Medina, and al-Mustafa*, edited by Masooda Bano and Keiko Sakurai, 21–40 (Edinburgh: Edinburgh University Press, 2015), 32.

[76] Ṣiddīq Ḥasan Khān, *An Interpreter of Wahabiism* (Bhopal: Siddiq Hasan Khan, 1884), 89.

[77] Khān, *An Interpreter*, 33.

Wahhābīs who adhered to Ḥanbalism as a legal school, that would ultimately become the dominant tendency in the twentieth-century global Salafi approach to law.

Despite Khān's disavowal of Wahhābism, India's *ahl-e ḥadīth* ('*ḥadīth* folk') movement, of which Khān was a leading figure, was considered sufficiently pure by nineteenth-century Wahhābī *ʿulamāʾ* that they sent some of their sons to study there.[78] These Saudi *ʿulamāʾ* included Shaykh Saʿd ibn Ḥamad ibn ʿAtīq (1850/1–1930), the son of a major Wahhābī scholar. Ibn ʿAtīq traveled to India in 1883–4 and remained there nine years, studying *ḥadīth* collections with Khān, Yemeni scholars resident in India, and others. When Ibn ʿAtīq returned to Saudi Arabia, he completed his studies and then became a judge, including in Riyāḍ, where he also served as imam of the Great Mosque and as a close advisor to King ʿAbd al-ʿAzīz. Ibn ʿAtīq's pupils included Shaykh ʿAbd al-ʿAzīz ibn Bāz, one of the foremost canonical authorities in contemporary Salafism.[79]

For contemporary Salafis, accepting the Yemeni-Indian genealogy has entailed legitimizing some thinkers, such as Khān, who were not theologically identical to later Salafis. Canonizing these figures meant, as canonization had for Ibn Taymiyya and others, ignoring or forgiving certain departures from later Salafi creed. One Salafi biographer of Khān placed him in the intellectual lineage of Aḥmad ibn Ḥanbal and Ibn Taymiyya, but noted discrepancies. Khān's writings, the biographer wrote, were "a true picture (*ṣūra ṣādiqa*) of the return to what the pious predecessors and imams of the umma practiced, except for a few issues in which he leaned toward the Ashʿarīs."[80] Some thinkers are incorporated into the Salafi canon with caveats attached.

As Chapter 2 discusses, India's *ahl-e ḥadīth* would play a significant role in establishing some of Saudi Arabia's Islamic educational institutions in the early twentieth century. Before turning to the Salafi intellectual landscape of the twentieth century, however, it is important to examine one of the most complicated but influential strands in the canon – the revivalists, modernists, and proto-Salafis who flourished in Cairo, Damascus, and elsewhere around the turn of the twentieth century.

78 Nabil Mouline, *The Clerics of Islam: Religious Authority and Political Power in Saudi Arabia*, translated by Ethan Rundell (New Haven: Yale University Press, 2014).

79 ʿAbd Allāh ibn ʿAbd al-Raḥmān ibn Ṣāliḥ āl Bassām, *ʿUlamāʾ Najd khilāl Thamāniyat Qurūn*, *Volume* 2, second edition (Al-Riyāḍ: Dār al-ʿāṣima li-l-Nashr wa-l-Tawzīʿ, 1998), 220–7; and Muḥammad Ziyād al-Takla, "Al-ʿAllāma Saʿd ibn Ḥamad ibn ʿAtīq," Alukah, 24 May 2007. Available at: http://www.alukah.net/culture/0/800; accessed September 2014.

80 Akhtar Jamāl Luqmān, *Al-Sayyid Ṣiddīq Ḥasan al-Qannūjī: Ārāʾuhu al-Iʿtiqādiyya wa-Mawqifuhu min ʿAqīdat al-Salaf* (al-Riyāḍ: Dār al-Hijra, 1996), 8.

Islamic Revival in the Late Nineteenth and Early Twentieth Centuries

The nineteenth century saw intellectual ferment among Muslim thinkers in the Middle East. The diverse tendencies these thinkers represented cannot be easily summarized, but they shared an interest in questioning received modes of Islamic thought and reinvigorating the Muslim community. Basheer Nafi has pointed to four major themes in their discourses: "*tawhid* [divine unity]; return to the Qur'an and Sunna, the ultimate source of legitimacy in Islam; assertion of the role of reason; and the call for renewed *ijtihad*." The thinkers in this period have often been called "modernists," meaning that they were strongly interested in Islamizing what they perceived as a Eurocentric modernity – a complex of institutional and scientific achievements that they admired but whose moral foundation they questioned. This project of Islamizing modernity also sought to "modernize" Islam, or to place the Muslim world on an equal footing to Europe in scientific and political terms. Nafi writes that Muslim revivalists viewed their project of "reviving" Islam "through the prism of modernity; for modernity, however it was perceived, was the internalised, powerful influence against which the project of Islamic reconstruction and revival was envisioned."[81] Despite their interest in modernity, however, these figures should not be viewed solely as modernists. Some revivalists were forerunners – and in some cases, literally fathers and grandfathers – of the Syrian and Egyptian circles that later Salafis like al-Jāmī counted as part of the global Salafi movement.

Scholars of Islam have written extensively on the "Islamic modernist" triumvirate of Shaykhs Jamāl al-Dīn al-Afghānī (1838–97), Muḥammad ʿAbduh (1849–1905), and Muḥammad Rashīd Riḍā (1865–1935). The relationship between these figures and the Salafi movement is complex, particularly in the case of Riḍā, who had sympathies for both camps. This confusion stems in part from the appellation "Salafiyya" that some Western scholars have bestowed on this movement. Appearances of the word "Salafiyya" in revivalist discourses, however, do not automatically mean that turn-of-the-twentieth-century figures belong to the Salafi canon. Indeed, Al-Afghānī's emphasis on articulating a Muslim modernity, and ʿAbduh's sympathy for the Muʿtazila, place them outside the standards of orthodoxy that later Salafis would define.

The revivalists are nevertheless important to the canon. Some revivalists helped connect the streams that fed into the canon. For example, Shaykh Nuʿman Khayr al-Dīn al-Ālūsī of Baghdad (1836–99) wrote a

[81] Basheer Nafi, "The Rise of Islamic Reformist Thought and Its Challenge to Traditional Islam" in *Islamic Thought in the Twentieth Century*, edited by Suha Taji-Farouki and Basheer Nafi (London and New York: I.B. Tauris, 2004), 40.

treatise defending Ibn Taymiyya against charges of heresy. He was influenced by India's *ahl-e ḥadīth* and arranged for one of his sons to study with Ṣiddīq Ḥasan Khān.[82] Khān read al-Ālūsī's book and praised it, and the two corresponded about how to respond to popular Sufism.[83] The Iraqi scholar has been welcomed posthumously into the canon, in part because he embodies the intersection of Ibn Taymiyya's legacy, the Yemeni-Indian *ijtihād* enthusiasts, and the late-nineteenth-century revivalists.

Al-Ālūsī's *Jalā' al-'Aynayn fī Muḥākamat al-Aḥmadayn* (Clearing the Eyes in the Trial of the Two Aḥmads, completed 1880) illustrates how the genealogical and intellectual streams that would form the Salafi canon were beginning to converge by the late nineteenth century. The text strove to rehabilitate Ibn Taymiyya. Al-Ālūsī vigorously defended the thirteenth-century shaykh (one of the two Aḥmads referenced in the title) against charges by Shaykh Aḥmad ibn Ḥajar al-Haytamī (1503–66), a Shāfi'ī scholar and the other titular Aḥmad. Al-Ālūsī explained that al-Haytamī had attributed to Ibn Taymiyya "some beliefs contradicting *ahl al-sunna* (*nasaba ilayhi ba'ḍ al-'aqā'id al-mukhālafa li-ahl al-sunna*)," such as opposing the Caliphs 'Umar and 'Alī.[84] Had Ibn Taymiyya's opponents successfully demonstrated that the shaykh had criticized or rejected key Companions of the Prophet, they would have overturned Ibn Taymiyya's claim to represent the authentic and coherent legacy of the early community. Al-Ālūsī worked to refute these charges.

His approach further illuminates the contours of the proto-Salafi canon that emerged outside present-day Saudi Arabia. Al-Ālūsī explained why he wrote the book:

> So I drew up this sketch, clarifying in it – if Allah Most High wills – what each of these two shaykhs said, and transmitting the comments that are made upon [their words] in the speech of truth-seekers (*al-muḥaqqiqīn*), and past and contemporary scholarly luminaries (*wa-l-jahābidha al-mutaqaddimīn wa-l-muta'akhkhirīn*), who are peers and associates of these two Imams, so that the pious onlooker may know the truth.[85]

In his "Chapter Exonerating the Shaykh from What Has Been Attributed to Him, and Contemporary Truth-Seekers' Praise for Him," al-Ālūsī listed some of these luminaries. They included students of Ibn Taymiyya, as well as Ḥanbalī scholars from Baghdad and Damascus. Yet al-Ālūsī also included Shāfi'ī and Ḥanafī scholars. Finally, he included the Yemeni-Indian intellectual lineage discussed in the previous section: Walī Allāh, al-Shawkānī, and Khān. Ibn Taymiyya, in other words, had left a legacy of

[82] David Commins, *Islamic Reform: Politics and Social Change in Late Ottoman Syria* (New York and Oxford: Oxford University Press, 1990), 25.
[83] Khān, *Al-Tāj al-Mukallal*, 514.
[84] Nu'man Khayr al-Dīn al-Ālūsī, *Jalā' al-'Aynayn fī Muḥākamat al-Aḥmadayn* (Cairo: Maṭba'at al-Madanī, 1980), 14.
[85] Al-Ālūsī, *Jalā' al-'Aynayn*, 15.

defenders who came from diverse lands and schools. Like Khān, al-Ālūsī was constructing a global genealogy of purist Sunni Muslims.

The figures in al-Ālūsī's proto-canon were united by more than just praise of Ibn Taymiyya: some of them also endorsed and, for al-Ālūsī, embodied the principle of *ijtihād*. Al-Ālūsī viewed *ijtihād* as an indispensable legal technique. He defined it as "the jurisprudent's (*faqīh*'s) utmost exertion to acquire an opinion in a judgment." Going further, he wrote, "The *faqīh* and the *mujtahid* are two synonymous expressions. [The *mujtahid-faqīh*] is the mature, the judicious, in other words possessing the faculty through which he obtains different forms of knowledge. . . . This faculty is reason."[86] For Ālūsī, figures like Ibn Taymiyya, al-Shawkānī, and Khān were all absolute *mujtahids* – that is, figures who had the authority to make rulings outside the framework of the four Sunni legal schools.

Intellectually, al-Ālūsī was not alone in the Arab world. A circle of Damascene *ʿulamāʾ* played a major role within the emerging revivalist trend in both its modernist and conservative formations. The circle included Shaykhs ʿAbd al-Razzāq al-Bīṭār (1837–1916), Ṭāhir al-Jazāʾirī (1852–1920), and Jamāl al-Dīn al-Qāsimī (1866–1914). Al-Ālūsī's *Jalāʾ al-ʿAynayn* influenced this circle, helping to spark their interest in Ibn Taymiyya and in *ijtihād*.[87] Damascene *ʿulamāʾ* also had more direct access to Ibn Taymiyya's thought due to the intellectual legacy he left among the city's Ḥanbalī scholars and the voluminous writings he left, many of them in unpublished form, in the city where he spent most of his life. Al-Jazāʾirī's involvement in cataloguing rare manuscripts at al-Ẓāhiriyya Library led to his immersion in and dissemination of Ibn Taymiyya's thought (and also helped set the stage, in terms of intellectual infrastructure, for al-Albānī's work at al-Ẓāhiriyya two generations later). Ibn Taymiyya's ideas furnished the revivalists with intellectual ammunition that they used to attack official *ʿulamāʾ* and popular Sufism, although many of these revivalists, unlike later Salafis, preserved strong sympathies for elite, intellectual Sufism.[88] The Syrian revivalists also discovered Khān and al-Shawkānī – Jamāl al-Dīn al-Qāsimī wrote a Qurʾanic exegesis that was influenced by Khān's *Fatḥ al-Bayān fī Maqāṣid al-Qurʾān* (The Triumph of Explaining the Meanings of the Qurʾan), which was itself based on al-Shawkānī's *Fatḥ al-Qadīr*.[89] By the turn of the twentieth century, the constituent elements of the emerging Salafi synthesis were interacting and producing new written corpuses.

86 Al-Ālūsī, *Jalāʾ al-ʿAynayn*, 190.
87 Commins, *Islamic Reform*, 38–40.
88 Itzchak Weismann, "Between Ṣūfī Reformism and Modernist Rationalism: A Reappraisal of the Origins of the Salafiyya from the Damascene Angle," *Die Welt des Islams* 41:2 (July 2001): 206–37.
89 Pink, "Where Does Modernity Begin?"

Another partisan of Ibn Taymiyya and defender of *ijtihād* was Muḥammad Rashīd Riḍā, who was born in Tripoli in Ottoman Syria (present-day Lebanon) and lived there until 1897. Riḍā's anti-Sufi attitudes began to form before he left Tripoli for Cairo, and he was familiar with Ibn Taymiyya through al-Ālūsī. In Egypt, he engaged more thoroughly with the works of Ibn Taymiyya and his students.[90] Riḍā experimentally combined ideas in ways that prefigured contemporary Salafism: he rejected the legal schools and popular Sufism, and he insisted on the need to reexamine *ḥadīth*. Riḍā also, like some other revivalists, became a supporter of the Saudi state and a sympathetic voice raised in defense of Wahhābism. He used the platform of his journal *al-Manār* (The Lighthouse) to argue for the religious and political legitimacy of the Wahhābī project.[91]

The revivalists have been incorporated selectively and with reservations into the Salafi canon. Al-Albānī, for example, published an annotated version of Riḍā's *Ḥuqūq al-Nisā' fī al-Islām* (The Rights of Women in Islam) in 1984 but critiqued some of Riḍā's scriptural sources and intellectual conclusions.[92] Other revivalists have been lauded: al-Jāmī describes Ṭāhir al-Jazā'irī as both a hero of the resistance to French colonialism and an authority on creed, praising books such as his *Al-Jawāhir al-Kalāmiyya fī Iyḍāḥ al-'Aqīda al-Islāmiyya* (The Theological Jewels in Clarifying the Islamic Creed).[93] Nevertheless, of the authorities in the broad canon, Nigerian Salafis have cited the revivalists the least, suggesting that study of revivalists was not emphasized in Medina.

Twentieth-century Salafis largely discarded the modernist concerns of their revivalist predecessors. Figures like al-Albānī were interested in purifying Muslim societies as a goal in and of itself, rather than as part of project to Islamize European-style modernity and in so doing compete with the West. Al-Albānī and his peers also subordinated human reason to divine revelation, and their version of *ijtihād* departs from the reason-oriented version that some revivalists embraced. Moreover, whereas the revivalists treated *ijtihād* as a way of reimagining core assumptions about Islam's place in a European-dominated world, later Salafis saw *ijtihād* more narrowly as a method for determining correct practice.

To understand and historicize the transition from revivalism to Salafism, it is important both to distinguish between the two movements' orientations but also to acknowledge the considerable overlap that has remained in terms of creed, method, and genealogy – even if Salafis today

[90] Albert Hourani, *Emergence of the Modern Middle East* (Berkeley: University of California Press, 1981), 98.

[91] Muḥammad Rashīd Riḍā, *Al-Wahhābiyyūn wa-l-Ḥijāz* (Cairo, 1925).

[92] Muḥammad Rashīd Riḍā, *Ḥuqūq al-Nisā' fī al-Islām*, edited by Muḥammad Nāṣir al-Dīn al-Albānī (Beirut: al-Maktab al-Islāmī, 1984).

[93] Al-Jāmī, *Majmū' Rasā'il*, 325.

are often keen to downplay the role that Muslim scholars' engagement with European modernity played in the emergence of Salafism. As the next section describes, the revivalists and modernists set the stage for the emergence of Salafism through their partnerships with the Wahhābī scholars of the young Saudi state.

An Emerging Salafi Worldview

The Salafi movement emerged in two major groups. The first, largely comprising Syrians and Egyptians, grew out of the revivalist currents described earlier. The second group included Wahhābīs in Saudi Arabia who absorbed Indian influences and/or became sympathetic to the revivalist project, particularly its rejection of legal schools. From the 1920s, as the nascent Saudi state began to cultivate international Muslim connections, these groups began to interact intensively with one another.

The Syrian and Egyptian Salafis were influenced by, and in some cases descended from, the revivalist generation of Riḍā. For example, the Syrian Salafi Shaykh Muḥammad Bahjat al-Bīṭār (1894–1976) was the grandson of Shaykh ʿAbd al-Razzāq al-Bīṭār (1837–1916), whom Riḍā had credited with helping to launch the "Salafi" revival in Damascus. The younger al-Bīṭār's study circle in Damascus influenced al-Albānī.[94] Al-Bīṭār edited and composed works on Ibn Taymiyya and others in the canon. In Egypt, three representatives of the emerging Salafi movement were Shaykhs Muḥammad Ḥāmid al-Fiqqī (1892–1959), ʿAbd al-Ẓāhir Abū al-Samaḥ (1881–1952), and Aḥmad Shākir (1892–1958), all graduates of al-Azhar and either students or associates of Riḍā.[95]

Several events in 1926 marked the emergence of this Salafi trend and its interaction with the young Kingdom of Saudi Arabia. In Cairo, al-Fiqqī founded *Jamāʿat Anṣār al-Sunna al-Muḥammadiyya* (The Society of the Defenders of the Prophet's Model), one of the world's first institutionalized Salafi organizations. A decade later, the society began to publish a journal titled *Al-Hady al-Nabawī* (Prophetic Guidance). The journal became a venue for writings by Egyptian and Syrian thinkers such as Shākir and Abū al-Samaḥ.[96] This circle began to promote a "defined ethos and movement with the moniker 'Salafism.'"[97] Also in 1926, following an international conference in Mecca, several non-Saudi

[94] Lacroix, "Between Revolution and Apoliticism."

[95] Richard Gauvain, *Salafi Ritual Purity: In the Presence of God* (New York: Routledge, 2012).

[96] Fatḥī Amīn 'Uthmān, "Tarjamat Samāḥat al-Shaykh Muḥammad Ḥāmid al-Fiqqī," Jamāʿat Anṣār al-Sunna al-Muḥammadiyya, 15 September 2010. Available at: www.ansaralsonna.com/web/play-1622.html; accessed September 2014.

[97] Jonathan A. C. Brown, "From Quietism to Parliamentary Giant: Salafism in Egypt and the Nour Party of Alexandria," unpublished paper, 5.

Salafis were integrated into the Kingdom's religious and scholastic establishment. King ʿAbd al-ʿAzīz invited al-Bīṭār to direct the Educational Institute (*al-Maʿhad al-ʿIlmī*) in Mecca, and he asked Abū al-Samaḥ to become the third Imam of the Grand Mosque there.[98] These men met some skepticism and resistance from Wahhābī scholars,[99] but they contributed to forming a global Salafi identity even inside Wahhābī-dominated Saudi Arabia. Their publishing efforts also put newly edited and printed versions of works in the emerging canon into wider circulation. Al-Fiqqī edited and republished numerous works, especially by Ibn Taymiyya and Ibn al-Qayyim, and he published his own pro-Wahhābī book in 1936.[100]

At the same time that these institutional patterns were forming, new methodologies were emerging. These methodologies epitomized Salafism's combination of reverence for *ḥadīth* with a willingness to critically evaluate *ḥadīth* collections. Shākir spent decades reworking classical compilations of *ḥadīth*, especially Ibn Ḥanbal's *Al-Musnad.*[101] In his introduction to the edited *Al-Musnad*, Shākir wrote that as a young man he found among his father's books the various canonical collections of *ḥadīth*, of which *Al-Musnad* was one. Shākir commented,

> I found it an ocean with no shore, and a light to be illuminated by, but necks will be broken over it, for it is organised on the basis of the Companions' traditions [i.e., organised by transmitter rather than by topic]. Gathered in it are the *aḥādīth* of each Companion, consecutively without organisation. Almost no one can benefit from it except he who memorizes it, as the first ancient ones used to memorize. That was impossible, including for me. So I became infatuated and preoccupied with it. I saw that the best way it could serve the sciences of *ḥadīth* was for a man to agree to bring this great *Musnad* closer to the people, so that its benefit would spread, and so that there would be an imam for people. I wished to be that man.[102]

The archetype of the solitary canonizer – the figure immersed in texts as he attempts to revitalize early Islamic thought for a twentieth-century audience – appears powerfully in this passage. Also present is the ambition of using critical scholarship to revive the authentic Sunna. Yet such

98 Government of Saudi Arabia, "Al-Imāma wa-l-Aʾimma fī al-Masjid al-Ḥarām." Available at: www.alharamain.gov.sa//index.cfm?do=cms.conarticle&contentid=5809&categoryid=993; accessed September 2014.

99 Mouline, *The Clerics of Islam*, 109–13.

100 Muḥammad Ḥāmid al-Fiqqī, *Athar al-Daʿwa al-Wahhābiyya fī al-Iṣlāḥ al-Dīnī wa-l-ʿUmrānī fī Jazīrat al-ʿArab wa-Ghayrihā*, edited by Aḥmad al-Tuwayjirī (Al-Riyāḍ: Dār al-Sunna li-l-Nashr, 2006/2007 [1936]).

101 Ebrahim Moosa, "Shaykh Aḥmad Shākir and the Adoption of a Scientifically-Based Lunar Calendar," *Islamic Law and Society* 5:1 (1998): 57–89; 58.

102 Aḥmad Shākir, "Introduction" in Aḥmad Ibn Ḥanbal, *Al-Musnad*, Volume 1 (Cairo: Dār al-Maʿarif, 1949), 4.

canonizing, or recanonizing, efforts were only possible because of a web of personal, intellectual, and institutional arrangements.

The canon comes into view in Shākir's project. Shākir commented that as he researched commentaries on *Al-Musnad*, he discovered only three men who truly knew the text: Ibn Taymiyya and two of his students. Shākir set out to write a set of linguistic and scholarly indexes for *Al-Musnad*. These indexes disciplined the text, numbering every *ḥadīth* and then listing the number under every topic for which the *ḥadīth* is relevant. Shākir also evaluated the *aḥādīth* in *Al-Musnad*, noting the presence of weak narrators – thereby suggesting which reports were, from Shākir's standpoint, actionable and which were not. Both methodologically and genealogically, Shākir's work demonstrated the techniques and framing devices that would come to characterize the Salafi canon. The Saudi-Wahhābī establishment embraced Shākir's work, including his critiques of Westernization; Shaykh Muḥammad ibn Ibrāhīm Āl al-Shaykh (1893–1969), who served as Saudi Arabia's grand mufti, wrote an introduction to Shākir's *Ḥukm al-Jāhiliyya* (The Rule of Pre-Islamic Ignorance).[103]

Changing approaches to *ḥadīth* criticism influenced the work of al-Albānī. As his surname indicates, the famous *ḥadīth* evaluator was born in Albania. His father, a watchmaker, studied Islamic sciences in Istanbul. The family moved to Damascus after Ahmet Zogu, a secularizing dictator, became president of Albania in 1925. Al-Albānī attended a primary school there and studied the Qur'an, Ḥanafī jurisprudence and other subjects with his father. Al-Albānī also studied jurisprudence, rhetoric, and other topics with several shaykhs in Damascus.[104]

Al-Albānī's turn to Salafism began with reading Rashīd Riḍā's writing in *Al-Manār* and particularly a critical treatment of al-Ghazālī's *Iḥyā' 'Ulūm al-Dīn* (The Revival of the Religious Sciences), a crowning text in classical intellectual Sufism. For al-Albānī, the significance of this criticism was its attack on the textual basis of long-accepted frameworks for understanding Islam. From this inspiration, al-Albānī proceeded to study *Al-Mughnī 'an Ḥaml al-Asfār fī al-Asfār*, in which Shaykh 'Abd al-Raḥīm ibn Ḥusayn al-'Irāqī (1325–1403) cited and graded the *aḥādīth* present in the *Iḥyā'*. Evaluating these *aḥādīth* was not a mere scholastic exercise: for al-Albānī as for Shākir, weak *aḥādīth* – reports whose chains of transmission contained gaps or demonstrable inconsistencies and whose texts contradicted those of firmly established reports – corrupted the Muslim community in creed and worship.

[103] Aḥmad Shākir, *Ḥukm al-Jāhiliyya* (Cairo: Maktabat al-Sunna, 1992).
[104] "Sīrat al-Shaykh al-Mujaddid al-Albānī wa-Nash'atihi al-'Ilmiyya," Turāth al-Albānī website, undated. Available at: www.alalbany.net/5374; accessed September 2014.

Seeking further sources on *ḥadīth* criticism, al-Albānī spent long hours in Damascus' Ẓāhiriyya Library.[105] In the 1950s, he began to publish articles on *ḥadīth* criticism in the journal *Al-Tamaddun al-Islāmī* (Islamic Civilization), which was run by Syrian Salafis.[106] These writings formed the nucleus of his first multivolume work of *ḥadīth* criticism, *Silsilat al-Aḥādīth al-Ḍaʿīfa wa-l-Mawḍūʿa wa-Atharuhā al-Sayyiʾ fī al-Umma* (The Series of Weak and Fabricated Reports and Their Negative Effect on the Muslim Community), which began to appear in 1959. On the strength of his expertise in *ḥadīth*, al-Albānī taught at the Islamic University of Medina from 1961 to 1963. This sojourn helped extend his influence and his method to younger generations of Saudi Arabian scholars – and to Salafis worldwide. His later residence in Syria and Jordan, and his visits to Egypt and other countries, would ensure that many late-twentieth-century audiences encountered him directly.

In terms of intellectual influences, al-Albānī reached back to all three strands included in the canon. He edited and commented on works by Ibn Taymiyya and other Hanbalī authorities. He also engaged the Yemeni-Indian tradition and, as noted earlier, works by Riḍā.

Al-Albānī became both canonizer and canonized. One 2002 edition of Khān's *Al-Rawḍa al-Nadiyya* (The Dewy Meadow, itself a commentary on al-Shawkānī's *Al-Durar al-Bahiyya*, The Glittering Jewels) shows the complexity of the canonization process. The editor writes that he initially attempted to edit al-Shawkānī's own commentary on *Al-Durar al-Bahiyya* but then turned to Khān's commentary in response to its popularity among students. The editor incorporated al-Albānī's commentary on *Al-Rawḍa al-Nadiyya* as well as commentary from Aḥmad Shākir. The editor also cited and verified all of the *aḥādīth* in the original text.[107] Contemporary Salafi processes of canonization, in other words, take as their objects the different streams of the canon and then filter them through the methods of al-Albānī and Shākir.

Al-Albānī found peers in key members of the Saudi-Wahhābī establishment, in particular Shaykhs ʿAbd al-ʿAzīz ibn Bāz and Muḥammad ibn Ṣāliḥ al-ʿUthaymīn. The three men worked together as colleagues and participated in a coordinated defense of the canon, for example, when Ibn Bāz asked al-Albānī to defend the authenticity of Ibn Ḥanbal's *Al-Musnad*.[108] Their collaboration reinforced their emerging association in the Salafi mind as a triumvirate of creedal purity.

[105] "Sīrat al-Shaykh." See also Muḥammad Nāṣir al-Dīn al-Albānī, *Fihris Makhṭūṭāt Dār al-Kutub al-Ẓāhiriyya: Al-Muntakhab min Makhṭūṭāt al-Ḥadīth* (Damascus: Majmaʿ al-Lugha al-ʿArabiyya bi-Dimashq, 1970).

[106] Thomas Pierret, *Religion and State in Syria: The Sunni Ulama from Coup to Revolution* (Cambridge and New York: Cambridge University Press, 2013), 107.

[107] Ṣiddīq Ḥasan Khān, *Al-Rawḍa al-Nadiyya*, edited by Ḥilmī ibn Muḥammad Ismāʿīl al-Rushdī (Alexandria: Dār al-ʿAqīda, 2002).

[108] Al-Albānī, *Al-Dhabb al-Aḥmad.*

Ibn Bāz and Ibn ʿUthaymīn were sympathetic to al-Albānī's views even when these contradicted aspects of Wahhābism. Although often educated entirely within the Kingdom, Saudi scholars of their generation were exposed to a range of influences from the wider world, particularly the streams of scripturalist and revivalist thought that fed into the Salafi canon. As noted earlier, Ibn Bāz studied with Saʿd ibn ʿAtīq, one of the Wahhābī scholars who studied in India in the late nineteenth century. Ibn ʿUthaymīn spoke of being broadly influenced by Rashīd Riḍā's methods.[109] Moreover, both Ibn Bāz and Ibn ʿUthaymīn participated in Saudi Arabia's emerging system of institutionalized higher education. Universities, including the Islamic University of Medina, became settings in which these Saudi scholars interacted with people and ideas from beyond the Kingdom's borders, which confronted them with the challenge of integrating multiple influences into a Salafi worldview that moved beyond Wahhābī parochialism.

In one major example of their embrace of a global Salafi identity over a Wahhābī-Ḥanbalī identity, Ibn Bāz and Ibn ʿUthaymīn were sympathetic to the rejection of the four Sunni legal schools.[110] They anchored this position in the canon, especially the writings of classical Ḥanbalī authorities such as Ibn Taymiyya's student Ibn al-Qayyim – bypassing, as it were, the question of Ibn ʿAbd al-Wahhāb's legal affiliation. Ibn Bāz wrote in one essay,

> It is not necessary to emulate one of the four imams, nor another, whatever his knowledge. Because the truth is in following the Qurʾan and the Sunna, not in emulating an individual person. Rather, in brief, emulation (*al-taqlīd*) is permissible out of necessity, [emulation] of he who is known for knowledge, virtue, and soundness of creed (*istiqāmat al-ʿaqīda*), just as the eminent Ibn al-Qayyim explained, may Allah have mercy upon him, in his book *Iʿlām al-Muwaqqiʿīn* (Informing the Signatories).[111]

In keeping with their Salafi identity, both Ibn Bāz and Ibn ʿUthaymīn were prominent canonizers. Ibn ʿUthaymīn published numerous commentaries on canonical works by Ibn Taymiyya and Ibn ʿAbd al-Wahhāb, such as Ibn Taymiyya's *Al-Fatwā al-Ḥamawiyya al-Kubrā*. These luminaries helped set the tone within Saudi universities, where numerous scholars and students edited, corrected, and canonized texts and thinkers from beyond the Kingdom, thereby helping to construct the Salafi canon. The

109 Muḥammad ibn Ṣāliḥ al-ʿUthaymīn, "Riḥlat al-Shaykh fī Ṭalab al-ʿIlm," broadcast on Holy Qur'an Radio, 1982/3. Available at: http://ar.islamway.net/lesson/55381/%D8%B1%D8%AD%D9%84%D8%A9-%D8%A7%D9%84%D8%B4%D9%8A%D8%AE-%D9%81%D9%8A-%D8%B7%D9%84%D8%A8-%D8%A7%D9%84%D8%B9%D9%84%D9%85; accessed October 2014.

110 Frank Vogel, *Islamic Law and Legal System: Studies of Saudi Arabia* (Leiden: Brill, 2000).

111 ʿAbd al-ʿAzīz Ibn Bāz, *Al-Shaykh Ibn Bāz wa-Mawāqifuhu al-Thābita*, edited by Aḥmad ibn ʿAbd Allāh al-Farīḥ (Kuwait: Maktabat al-Rushd, 2000), 287.

canonical authority of al-Albānī, Ibn Bāz, and Ibn ʿUthaymīn, backed by the authority of the broader canon, would strongly influence Nigerian students' conceptions of creed, method, worship, and identity.

As Chapter 3 discusses, the most intensive canonization of al-Albānī, Ibn Bāz, and Ibn ʿUthaymīn coincided with northern Nigerian Salafis' time in Medina in the 1980s and 1990s. In those decades, the canonical scholars were in the final bloom of their careers, still active as teachers and authors. At the same time, some of their senior students were establishing themselves as new authorities in the same tradition – and playing prominent roles at the Islamic University.

Finally, the three scholars' opposition to political revolution made them appealing to the Saudi regime (even as al-Albānī continued to experience problems with other Arab governments). During the 1990s, Islamists posed challenges within and outside the Kingdom. Canonization responded to this challenge, taking such forms as a collection of the three men's legal opinions on the Algerian jihad of the 1990s, where they rejected the ideas of revolt against Muslim rulers and anathematizing and killing Muslim civilians. Ibn ʿUthaymīn read the collection over personally, so that it bears the canonical authorities' personal approval.[112] By the time of their deaths in 1999–2001, their place as Salafi religious authorities was cemented, although it would not go unchallenged by Salafi-jihadi groups, including in northern Nigeria.

Conclusion

The Salafi canon unifies a diverse set of thinkers who lived across Islamic history. To achieve this unity, Salafi canonizers reframe thinkers and texts, reducing potential inconsistencies and harmonizing conflicts. The composite picture blends scriptural literalism, opposition to emulating established legal schools, and an ethos that seeks to revive the idealized purity of the early community.

The canon furnishes a sense of history that depicts a recurring struggle between a true Muslim vanguard and a host of heretics and enemies. Salafism's "canonizing discourse" provides tools for evaluating texts and for deciding whom to include, and whom to exclude, in the narrative of the true Islamic creed and its historical trajectory.

Salafis aspire to actualize the model they see in the careers of the Prophet Muhammad and his Companions. Nevertheless, they look to the lives of other Muslims for demonstrations that it is possible to uphold an exclusivist Sunni creed after the time of the early Muslim community, even in the face of profound political and religious resistance. Salafism

[112] ʿAbd al-Mālik Ramaḍānī al-Jazāʾirī, compiler, *Fatāwā al-ʿUlamāʾ al-Akābir fīmā Uhdira min Dimāʾ fī al-Jazāʾir* (ʿAjmān: Maktabat al-Furqān, 2001/2).

states that it wishes to return to a seventh-century ideal, but the Salafi canon relies heavily on what it portrays as instantiations of that ideal in other centuries.

The Salafi canon, in all its layers, profoundly shaped the curriculum and the intellectual environment that Nigerian students encountered at the Islamic University of Medina. Students at Medina would read works by a range of authors, including authors outside the Ḥanbalī legal school as well as authors who had denounced Wahhābism. The international character of the environment at the Islamic University will become clearer in the next chapter, which discusses the contributions of African Salafis to life in Medina and to Saudi Arabia's outreach to Africa.

2 Africans and Saudi Arabia

The Salafi canon took shape in the Middle East and the Indian subcontinent, and it exists primarily in Arabic. Yet it radiates beyond the Arab world, including to Africa, where there is widespread Arabic literacy among Muslim scholars. From Senegal to Sudan,[1] the canon informs debates about the nature of Islamic authority, sometimes from the margins of the debate and sometimes at its center.

In some Muslim communities, the lack of a broad and indigenous Islamic written tradition facilitates the spread of Salafism,[2] but in much of Africa, well-developed Islamic textual traditions hold sway. In northwest Africa, a Mālikī-Sufi canon remains dominant. Where the Salafi canon has made some headway, its dissemination owed much to the institutional and intellectual backing it received, both locally and from abroad. This chapter argues that the spread of the canon to Africa was enabled by two developments: the increasing sophistication of Saudi Arabia's institutional outreach to Africa starting in the 1960s (enabled partly by the contributions of Africans resident in the Kingdom), and the emergence of local African partners who, over time, built networks from which Saudi Arabia could recruit potential Salafis. As these developments intersected, material and intellectual forces reinforced one another.

Salafism should not be seen as a crude Middle Eastern "export" to Africa. Recent studies have examined the localization of Salafism in Ghana, Burkina Faso, and Ethiopia, calling attention to ways in which preachers shaped their discourses to address the concerns of local audiences and ways in which Salafism became implicated in local struggles.[3]

1 For a Senegalese example, see Muḥammad Aḥmad Lo, *Taqdīs al-Ashkhāṣ fī al-Fikr al-Ṣūfī*, new edition (Al-Dammām: Dār Ibn al-Qayyim li-l-Nashr wa-l-Tawzīʿ, 2002; Cairo: Dār Ibn ʿAffān, 2002). See also John Hunwick, compiler and editor, *Arabic Literature of Africa, Volume 4: The Writings of Western Sudanic Africa* (Leiden: Brill, 2003), 489–90; for a Sudanese example, see ʿUthmān ʿAbd Allāh Ḥabūb, *Al-Imāma al-ʿUẓmā: Wājibāt wa-Ḥuqūq* (Al-Riyāḍ: Maktabat al-Rushd, 2012). Both texts begin with the Sermon of Necessity, reference al-Albānī and/or Shākir's "authentication" of Prophetic traditions, and contain other markers of the Salafi canon.

2 Terje Østebø, *Localising Salafism: Religious Change among Oromo Muslims in Bale, Ethiopia* (Leiden: Brill, 2012), xx.

3 Ousman Kobo, *Unveiling Modernity in West African Islamic Reforms, 1950–2000* (Leiden: Brill, 2012); Abdulai Iddrisu, *Contesting Islam in Africa: Homegrown Wahhabism and*

Building on these studies, I emphasize not just localization, but also dialogical exchanges between localities. Compared with previous studies of Salafism in Africa, however, I pay greater attention to the internal dynamics of Saudi Arabia and the wider Middle East.

Saudi Arabia, in popular discourse, is often seen as a quasi-medieval kingdom that uses its oil wealth to disseminate an unchanging "Wahhābism." Yet as Stéphane Lacroix has argued, "It is necessary to effect a kind of Copernican revolution in the accepted approach: although Saudi Arabia is often considered solely as a power that exports Islam, it also has to be seen as the recipient of influences emanating from most currents of nineteenth- and twentieth-century revivalism."[4] In a similar vein, Chanfi Ahmed has examined the role of West African scholars in contributing to the development of Salafism inside Saudi Arabia – a trend that affected some communities back in Africa.[5] The Islamic University of Medina itself, as Mike Farquhar has shown, was "shaped by an unequal reciprocity between the Wahhabi institution, on the one hand, and the staff and students from all over the world, on the other."[6] These works point to the need to assess ongoing interactions between localities, and the power relations that shape those interactions. If neither Saudi Arabia nor Africa is static, then African Salafism is constantly reshaped through recurring encounters.

Saudi Arabia's material resources have allowed it to finance mosques, schools, and organizations across Africa. Analysts' focus on material forces, however, has occluded the role of intellectual forces in spreading Salafism in Africa. Some analysts wrongly assume that the intellectual materials of contemporary Salafism are static and simplistic – that Salafism, intellectually, consists of a few texts by Ibn Taymiyya and Ibn ʿAbd al-Wahhāb, grafted onto a one-dimensional understanding of the Qurʾan and the Sunna. On closer examination, it becomes clear that the breadth of the Salafi canon offers rich intellectual resources that help preachers win audiences. By examining the texts and ideas that Saudi Arabia incorporates into its outreach to Africa, we can increase our

Muslim Identity in Northern Ghana, 1920–2010 (Durham, NC: Carolina Academic Press, 2013); and Østebø, *Localising Salafism*. Even in Saudi Arabia's neighbor Yemen, localization obtains: see Laurent Bonnefoy, *Salafism in Yemen: Transnationalism and Religious Identity* (New York: Columbia University Press, 2011).

4 Stéphane Lacroix, *Awakening Islam: The Politics of Religious Dissent in Contemporary Saudi Arabia*, translated by George Holoch (Cambridge, MA: Harvard University Press, 2011), 1.

5 Chanfi Ahmed, *West African ʿulamāʾ and Salafism in Mecca and Medina: Jawāb al-Ifrīqī – The Response of the African* (Leiden: Brill, 2015).

6 Mike Farquhar, "The Islamic University of Medina since 1961: The Politics of Religious Mission and the Making of a Modern Salafi Pedagogy" in *Shaping Global Islamic Discourses: The Role of al-Azhar, al-Medina, and al-Mustafa*, edited by Masooda Bano and Keiko Sakurai, 21–40 (Edinburgh: Edinburgh University Press, 2015), 22.

understanding of Saudi Arabia's role in shaping the trajectory of Islamic discourses around the world.

In northern Nigeria, Saudi Arabian institutions found local partners and began offering resources quickly in the early 1960s. During this period, three major developments helped strengthen Saudi-Northern Nigerian ties: Nigeria achieved its independence, Northern Nigeria was still a formal administrative unit (as it had been in colonial times), and the Islamic University of Medina was founded. Yet Saudi Arabia's initial outreach was not enough to spread Salafism or its canon, at least not at first. Confounding the expectations of both sympathetic northern Nigerian officials and Saudi elites, the Islamic University alienated most members of the first cohort of northern Nigerian students sent to attend it. Meanwhile, Saudi Arabia's local northern Nigerian partners – the regional Premier Ahmadu Bello (1910–66) and his religious advisor Shaykh Abubakar Gumi (1924–92) – were only partly conversant with the Salafi canon, which was still taking shape in the 1960s. In short, although Saudi Arabia patronized anti-Sufi activities in northern Nigeria starting in the 1960s, it was not necessarily spreading what might be called "full" Salafism until significantly later.

Existing works on Salafism in Africa sometimes present a static picture of Salafism overly based on examples from the 1930s to the 1990s. That picture can give an outdated version of how structures of authority work within contemporary Salafism. If we take figures like Gumi as the ideal type of the African Salafi, we risk missing major trends that have occurred since the early postcolonial decades, when the careers of Gumi's generation of scholars flourished. Gumi's generation was not committed to rejecting the Sunni legal schools or to systematically purging Sunni Islam of "weak" *aḥādīth*, maneuvers that have become hallmarks of contemporary Salafism; Gumi was, in core ways, not fully Salafi in his legal outlook or his textual methodologies. Gumi's somewhat parochial intellectual outlook, and his lack of deep engagement with the canon, are important for understanding the conflicts that occurred between his successors and the graduates of Medina in the 1990s. The Medina graduates, born in the 1960s and 1970s, also sought to make more far-reaching changes in their audiences' understandings of Islam. With greater command of a more unified canon, the Medina graduates had intellectual resources that Gumi lacked.

The trajectory of Saudi outreach to Nigeria has importance for understanding the broader relationship of Saudi Arabia to the non-Arab Muslim world in the second half of the twentieth century. From the 1960s to the 1980s, Saudi Arabia's outreach to Africa generally and Nigeria specifically became more sophisticated in both intellectual and logistical terms. Chanfi Ahmed has analyzed early stages in this process, showing how African Salafis in Saudi Arabia helped build new institutions of learning inside the Kingdom. Here I highlight another role these African Salafis had: they not only participated in Saudi Arabian outreach to Africa, they also helped to theorize how to tailor the Kingdom's approach to *da'wa* to the context of Africa. Localization of the Salafi message occurred not just on the African terrain, but also inside Saudi Arabia itself.

Two core elements of this outreach were an effort to delegitimize Sufi orders and a project of co-opting African Islamic history. These elements aligned with the aims and worldviews of certain African Muslim elites whose contact with colonial education predisposed them to embrace anti-Sufism. Logistically, Saudi Arabia intensified its outreach to Africa by sending teams of scholars – including prominent African Salafis – to conduct educational and recruiting tours in Africa. In Nigeria, these intellectual and logistical efforts helped to produce a cadre of students who were well positioned to immerse themselves in the Salafi canon in Medina and to find it not alienating but religiously and intellectually transformative. Nigeria eventually became one of the Islamic University's most prominent recruiting sites.

The Islamic University of Medina and Its Global Outreach

The previous chapter discussed the Ethiopia-born Dr. Muḥammad Amān al-Jāmī, whose influence was strongly felt at the Islamic University of Medina during the 1980s and 1990s, when major Nigerian Salafis were studying there. I showed how al-Jāmī's essay "The Islamic Creed and Its History" presented the core Salafi canon as it was embedded in his telling of Islamic history. Notably, his essay closed by affirming the bright prospects he saw for Salafism's spread in the late twentieth century. He emphasized the role of Saudi Arabian universities in disseminating Salafism in the contemporary world:

> The Islamic University in the Prophet's City and Muḥammad ibn Sa'ūd Islamic University in Riyāḍ have a distinguished position, virtuous work, and praiseworthy activity in the spread of the Salafi creed (*'aqīda*).... That is represented in the students coming from those countries to these two universities, graduating from them every year in different numbers, to return to their countries, warn their peoples, and spread to them the pure Salafi creed.[7]

Al-Jāmī's mention of these universities points to the changing structure of Salafi thought and outreach in the second half of the twentieth century. By the 1920s, a trend toward the institutionalization of Salafism had begun in the Arab world with the founding of new Islamic associations such as Egypt's Jamā'at Anṣār al-Sunna al-Muḥammadiyya and new

[7] Muḥammad Amān al-Jāmī, *Majmū' Rasā'il al-Jāmī fī al-'Aqīda wa-l-Sunna* (Medina: Dār Ibn Rajab, 1993), 81–2.

schools inside Saudi Arabia. Several decades later, Salafism became even more institutionalized through structures like the Islamic University of Medina and the Muslim World League, both founded in Saudi Arabia in the early 1960s. These structures allowed Salafis in Saudi Arabia to systematically cultivate relationships with sympathetic Muslims from outside the Kingdom. By sending people and resources abroad, these new institutions helped to develop Salafi infrastructures elsewhere, especially mosques and schools, and to extend Salafi networks. The new institutions also drew in representatives of the wider Muslim world, allowing non-Saudi Muslims to serve on committees or to teach and study at the Islamic University of Medina.

The Islamic University was founded by King Saʿūd's royal decree in 1961. It joined a cohort of other young educational institutions. Saudi Arabia had established a Directorate of Education in 1925, which began to set up schools throughout the country.[8] Various tertiary institutions emerged beginning in the 1950s, such as the Riyāḍ Educational Institute, the College of *Sharīʿa*, and the University of Riyāḍ. But the Islamic University of Medina was distinctive in its global focus. It conceived of the entire Muslim umma, "in the eastern portions of the world and its western ones," as its target audience.[9] King Saʿūd, at the university's founding, said, "This University will contain students from all the corners of the world . . . from our African and Asian brothers who yearn to know Islam from its fountainheads."[10]

Saudi Arabia invested in new global Muslim institutions as a tool for advancing the Kingdom's perceived foreign policy interests, especially amid competition with Egypt. With the end of the Second World War, Saudi Arabia's global prominence increased, symbolized by the meeting of U.S. President Franklin Delano Roosevelt and King ʿAbd al-ʿAzīz in February 1945. As the Kingdom's role changed in a decolonizing Middle East, Saudi leaders felt threatened by the rise of newly independent, revolutionary Arab regimes, particularly that of Gamal ʿAbd al-Nāṣir in Egypt. An "Arab Cold War," which included a Saudi-Egyptian proxy war in North Yemen from 1962 to 1967,[11] coincided with a generational transition in the Kingdom. Power passed from King ʿAbd al-ʿAzīz to his sons, with Prince (later King) Fayṣal (1906–75) playing a prominent role. Prince Fayṣal had considerable international experience – he began

[8] "Nashʾat al-Wizāra," Saudi Arabian Ministry of Education and Instruction, 16 April 2014. Available at: www.moe.gov.sa/Arabic/Ministry/Pages/MinistryStart.aspx; accessed November 2014.

[9] King Saʿūd, decree 11, 3/25/1381 hijri. Available at: www.kingsaud.net/art/inside/light_green/index.html; accessed August 2014.

[10] "Al-Jāmiʿa al-Islāmiyya bi-l-Madīna – Ahdāf al-Jāmiʿa," King Saud memorial website, undated. Available at: www.kingsaud.net/art/inside/light_green/index1.html; accessed August 2014.

[11] North Yemen's civil war lasted from 1962 to 1970, but Egyptian forces withdrew in 1967.

representing his father overseas beginning in the 1920s, and served as the Kingdom's first foreign minister from 1930 until his death.[12] Fayṣal's grasp of geopolitics played a role in his backing for new global Muslim institutions: the Islamic University of Medina was meant, in large part, to counter the influence of Egypt's Al-Azhar University, which ʿAbd al-Nāṣir brought under greater state control in 1961. ʿAbd al-Nāṣir made sub-Saharan Africa a zone of strategic outreach, giving support to African revolutionary and liberation movements. Al-Azhar sent delegations of teachers to other African countries and helped to establish Islamic cultural centers and schools throughout the continent, including in Nigeria. Such moves ensured that Saudi-Egyptian rivalry would involve competing claims to Islamic leadership.

Following Egypt's defeat by Israel in 1967, Saudi Arabia increased its efforts to project leadership in Arab and Muslim lands. The Kingdom became the major backer of the Organization of the Islamic Conference, founded at an international conference in Rabat, Morocco, in 1969. From the start, the organization favored Africa; its first secretary-general was President Sekou Touré of Guinea. Saudi leaders also reached out directly to African countries with large Muslim communities. In 1972, King Fayṣal traveled to Uganda, Chad, Niger, Senegal, and Mauritania, all of which broke relations with Israel in 1972–3, as did many other African countries. The 1973 Arab-Israeli war and rising oil wealth provided impetus and means for Saudi Arabia and other Arab states to expand their outreach to Africa throughout the 1970s. This outreach took diverse forms, including diplomatic engagement, cultural exchange, and humanitarian aid. In the 1970s, as Saudi Arabia's oil revenues rose and as the monarchy sought to deepen its Islamic image to meet both Iranian and domestic religious challenges, the university received major boosts in funding – although funding would later fall in the 1980s amid recession.[13]

Saudi religious and political authorities made developing the Islamic University a priority. Senior religious authorities ran the university: its first president was the Grand Mufti Shaykh Muḥammad ibn Ibrāhīm Āl al-Shaykh. The university's first vice president was Shaykh ʿAbd al-ʿAzīz ibn Bāz. He later served as its president from 1970 to 1975, until he became chairman of the Permanent Commission for Research and Issuing Legal Rulings, a senior religious position. The head of the university has always been a Saudi national.[14]

The younger scholars who taught at Medina in its early days reflected the growing rationalization of education in Saudi Arabia, as well as the integration of African scholars into Salafi circles. For example, one of

[12] With the exception of one brief interlude.
[13] Farquhar, "The Islamic University," 23–4.
[14] Farquhar, "The Islamic University," 24.

the university's first teachers was the Saudi Arabian Shaykh ʿAbd al-Muḥsin al-ʿAbbād (b. 1934). Later, he taught several major Nigerian Salafi preachers who studied at the university between the 1980s and 2000s and also supervised several of their theses. Al-ʿAbbād attended the Educational Institute in Riyāḍ, studying there with Ibn Bāz as well as with two of the African Salafis discussed later. Al-ʿAbbād graduated from the institute shortly before the Islamic University's founding and was selected by Muḥammad ibn Ibrāhīm to teach there.[15] This trend – of Medina's faculty emerging from schools established earlier in the Kingdom's short history – would appear in the careers of African Salafi teachers at Medina as well.

Many of the scholars who taught at the Islamic University had a life-long association with the university and with Medina. Al-ʿAbbād served as the university's vice president from 1973 to 1979, and continued teaching there afterward. Beginning in 1985, he taught classical *ḥadīth* collections at the Prophet's Mosque in Medina. Some Nigerian students attended his lessons there. The long tenures of some faculty meant that the university had intellectual continuity over time. By the 1980s, faculty and administrators could draw on substantial experience as they taught international students.

The Islamic University cultivated a global Muslim leadership. Its Advisory Council (*al-majlis al-istishārī*), which met for the first time in 1962, drew from the Arab world, the Indian subcontinent, and sub-Saharan Africa. The council included major Salafi thinkers such as Ibn Bāz and al-Albānī, and younger thinkers like al-ʿAbbād. The council also included two members from sub-Saharan Africa: the Mauritanian-born Shaykh Muḥammad al-Amīn al-Shinqīṭī (1907–73) and Shaykh Abubakar Gumi of Nigeria.[16] The council included figures who were not theologically Salafi,[17] reflecting an opening toward the wider Muslim world that Wahhābī scholars had begun in the 1950s.[18]

The Islamic University cultivated a global pool of teachers, many of them non-Wahhābī Salafis. As the previous chapter discussed, al-Albānī taught at the university from 1961–3. Even though he was dismissed, he was replaced by another non-Saudi, a Pakistani from the *ahl-e ḥadīth* movement.[19] This international cadre of teachers meant that students at

[15] For his full biography, see ʿAbd al-Muḥsin al-ʿAbbād, *Kutub wa-Rasāʾil ʿAbd al-Muḥsin ibn Ḥamad al-ʿAbbād al-Badr* (al-Riyāḍ: Dār al-Tawḥīd li-l-Nashr, 2006).

[16] Aḥmad ibn ʿAṭīyya al-Ghāmidī, *Al-Kitāb al-Wathāʾiqī ʿan al-Jāmiʿa al-Islāmīyya bi-l-Madīna al-Munawwara (Medina*: al-Mamlaka al-ʿArabīyya al-Saʿūdīyya, Wizārat al-Taʿlīm al-ʿĀlī, al-Jāmiʿa al-Islāmīyya bi-l-Madīna al-Munawwara, 1998).

[17] Al-Ghāmidī, *Al-Kitāb al-Wathāʾiqī.*

[18] Thomas Hegghammer, *Jihad in Saudi Arabia: Violence and Pan-Islamism since 1979* (Cambridge: Cambridge University Press, 2010), 18.

[19] Mariam Abou Zahab, "Salafism in Pakistan: The Ahl-e Hadith Movement" in *Global Salafism: Islam's New Religious Movement*, edited by Roel Meijer (New York: Columbia University Press, 2009), 126–42.

Medina – including some of its most famous graduates – often worked with non-Saudi teachers. The Yemeni Shaykh Muqbil al-Wādiʿī (1933–2001), who would go on to become the preeminent Salafi in Yemen, wrote one paper under the supervision of an African Salafi and the aforementioned Pakistani scholar.[20]

As with the council, the university's faculty included non-Salafis, especially members of the Muslim Brotherhood who had fled regime crackdowns in Egypt.[21] However, Brothers teaching at Saudi universities tended to congregate in departments covering Islamic culture and contemporary thought, whereas Salafis dominated the teaching of creed.[22] When Brotherhood-linked dissent rose inside the Kingdom during the 1980s and early 1990s, the monarchy steadily increased the proportion of Saudis teaching at the Islamic University.[23] The Brotherhood has held little appeal, as a model, for Nigerian graduates of Medina. Nigerians would inevitably have come into contact with Brotherhood-linked teachers there, but they are mistrustful of formalized associations, and they view the Brotherhood's methods as a distraction from the core task of purifying Muslims' creeds and practices.

Activities in Medina accelerated the formation and institutionalization of a Salafi canon. The Islamic University did not, on its own, initiate the revival of works by authors like Ibn Taymiyya or Muḥammad al-Shawkānī – Egyptian presses were printing the latter's works in the 1950s, for example.[24] Yet Saudi Arabian schools and libraries made a profound impact by employing canonizers,[25] publishing books, and collecting manuscripts. As the theses and books produced at the university accumulated, it became a major force not just in spreading the canon but creating it. The teaching curriculum at the university, meanwhile, came to include books not just by Ibn Taymiyya and Ibn ʿAbd al-Wahhāb, but also by Ṣiddīq Ḥasan Khān and Rashīd Riḍā. In the field of law, the university – under pressure from foreign teachers, scholars, and members of the advisory council – moved from an initial reliance on the Ḥanbalī school to a greater emphasis on teaching comparative jurisprudence.[26] In other words, by the 1980s the University looked more like a global Salafi institution than a narrowly Wahhābī-Ḥanbalī one. Nigerian students who

[20] Usama Hasan, "Sheikh Muqbil Examined by Sheikh Abdul Ghaffar Hasan," Unity, 28 July 2012. Available at: http://unity1.wordpress.com/2012/07/28/sheikh-muqbil-examined-by-sheikh-abdul-ghaffar-hasan/; accessed October 2014.

[21] Lacroix, *Awakening Islam*, 43.

[22] Lacroix, *Awakening Islam*, 48.

[23] Farquhar, "The Islamic University," 25.

[24] Muḥammad ibn ʿAlī al-Shawkānī, *Nayl al-Awṭār* (Egypt: Muṣṭafā al-Bābī al-ḥalabī, 1952).

[25] The Yemeni canoniser ʿAbd al-Raḥmān Yaḥyā al-Muʿallimī (1896–1966) worked in the library of the Great Mosque in Mecca, and edited and published works such as al-Shawkānī's *Al-Fawāʾid al-Majmūʿa fī al-Aḥādīth al-Mawḍūʿa* (Cairo: Maktabat al-Sunna al-Muḥammadiyya, 1960).

[26] Farquhar, "The Islamic University," 32–5.

arrived during the 1980s encountered a less parochial curriculum than their antecedents in the 1960s experienced.

Other Saudi institutions with global reach were important counterparts to the Islamic University. The Muslim World League, founded 1962, constructed mosques and schools around the world and distributed works by Ibn Taymiyya and Ibn ʿAbd al-Wahhāb.[27] The Organization of the Islamic Conference (later the Organization of Islamic Cooperation) provided a framework for states with Muslim majorities (or substantial Muslim minorities) to cooperate in domains such as education. Nigeria would, amid domestic controversy, join it in 1986. The World Assembly of Muslim Youth, founded in 1972, promoted educational and scouting activities for Muslim children. Not all of these institutions were Salafi in terms of their leadership and activities, but their efforts helped provide the financial and logistical support for Salafi outreach to Africa and elsewhere.

African Salafis in Saudi Arabia

Chanfi Ahmed has shown that West African Salafis in Saudi Arabia played a powerful role in shaping contemporary Salafism and its institutions, including the Islamic University. These West Africans included Muḥammad al-Amīn al-Shinqīṭī, ʿAbd al-Raḥmān al-Ifrīqī (1908–57), Ḥammād al-Anṣārī (1925–97), and ʿUmar Fallāta (1926–98).[28] East African Salafis were important as well, as the influence of the Ethiopia-born al-Jāmī demonstrates. The history of Africans' contributions to Salafism challenges narratives that depict Africans as passive recipients of Saudi influences.

African Salafi scholars such as al-Shinqīṭī, of present-day Mauritania, worked in the new institutions of Salafi learning as teachers and administrators. At the Educational Institute in Riyāḍ and the Islamic University of Medina, African Salafis taught future Salafi luminaries, including Shaykh Muḥammad ibn al-ʿUthaymīn.[29] At the Islamic University, African Salafis influenced a younger generation of Saudi Salafis. Al-Shinqīṭī's pupils included Dr. Rabīʿ al-Madkhalī (b. 1931), an important defender of al-Albānī's legacy inside Saudi Arabia and an influential teacher in Medina at the time that Nigerian Salafis were studying there

27 Gilles Kepel, *Jihad: The Trail of Political Islam*, translated by Anthony F. Roberts (Cambridge, MA: Harvard University Press, 2003), 52; and Reinhard Schulze, *Islamischer Internationalismus im 20. Jahrhundert: Untersuchungen zur Geschichte der Islamischen Weltliga* (Leiden: Brill, 1990).

28 Ahmed, *West African ʿulamāʾ and Salafism.*

29 "ʿAn al-Shaykh," Muʾassasat al-Shaykh Muḥammad ibn Ṣāliḥ al-ʿUthaymīn al-Khayriyya, 2004. Available at: www.ibnothaimeen.com/all/Shaikh.shtml; accessed September 2014.

in the 1980s and 1990s.[30] In 1998, the university's director wrote that al-Shinqīṭī was

> one of those who contributed to the founding of the Islamic University, and one of those who made praiseworthy efforts in emphasizing the basic goal for the sake of which this blessed University was founded. And that [goal] is establishing the creed of the pious predecessors, purging it of defects, and spreading it among Muslims.[31]

Together with scholars from the Indian subcontinent, African Salafis helped shape prominent Salafi institutions and taught an influential cohort of global Salafi authorities – helping to make the university, over time, a truly global space.

Figures like al-Shinqīṭī were unquestionably Salafi. They broke with West African Islamic intellectual traditions and became immersed in the Salafi canon. One biographer of al-Shinqīṭī writes that he "had a Salafi creed before he came to the Kingdom,"[32] and goes on to speculate that he "did not study the creed of the *salaf* with anyone, but rather obtained it on his own." Al-Shinqīṭī arrived in the Kingdom with questions about the integrity of Wahhābism, given Wahhābism's poor reputation in the Muslim world at the time, but these concerns were allayed during his early contacts with Wahhābī scholars.[33] Meanwhile, he engaged the Salafi canon in ways that went beyond just Wahhābī texts, using works such as al-Shawkānī's *Nayl al-Awṭār* in his teaching.[34] He abandoned the Mālikī school: in his *Aḍwāʾ al-Bayān fī Tafsīr al-Qurʾān bi-l-Qurʾān* (The Lights of Explanation in Performing Exegesis of the Qurʾan by Means of the Qurʾan), al-Shinqīṭī stated that emulation (*taqlīd*) of a specific scholar was "among the heresies (*bidiʿ*) of the fourth [Islamic] century," and therefore unknown among the early Muslim community.[35] African arrivals, in other words, were adopting a posture that looked more like global Salafism than parochial Wahhābism. With local partners in Africa, however, Salafis would initially find a lower common denominator than

30 Roel Meijer, "Politicizing *al-jarh wa-l-taʿdil*: Rabi b. Hadi al-Madkhali and the transnational battle for religious authority" in *The Transmission and Dynamics of the Textual Sources of Islam: Essays in Honour of Harald Motzki*, edited by Nicolet Boekhoff-van der Voort, Kees Versteegh, and Joas Wagemakers, 375–99 (Leiden: Brill, 2011).

31 Abd al-ʿAzīz ibn Ṣāliḥ ibn Ibrāhīm al-Ṭawiyān, *Juhūd al-Shaykh Muḥammad al-Amīn al-Shinqīṭī fī Taqrīr ʿAqīdat al-Salaf* (Medina: The Islamic University, 1998), i–ii.

32 Al-Ṭawiyān, *Juhūd al-Shaykh*, 64. Al-Shinqīṭī was trained in the Mālikī school and does not seem to have moved beyond Mālikism until he came to Saudi Arabia.

33 Al-Ṭawiyān, *Juhūd al-Shaykh*, 66.

34 ʿAṭiyya Sālim, "Introduction" in Muḥammad al-Amīn al-Shinqīṭī, *Riḥlat al-Ḥajj ilā Bayt Allāh al-Ḥarām* (Cairo: Dār Ibn Taymiyya, undated).

35 Muḥammad al-Amīn al-Shinqīṭī, *Al-Qawl al-Sadīd fī Kashf Ḥaqīqa al-Taqlīd* (Benares: Idārat al-Buḥūth al-Islāmiyya wa-l-Daʿwa wa-l-Iftāʾ, 1983), 9.

Salafism – namely, anti-Sufism and a shared willingness to retell Islamic Africa's history.

Theorizing Salafi Outreach in Africa

African Salafis in Saudi Arabia did not just affect the course of Salafism's institutionalization inside the Kingdom. They also played leading roles in outreach to Africa. Ahmed has shown that African Salafis were important participants in a logistical sense, joining and leading outreach missions from the Islamic University to Africa. Here I show that African Salafis were also important participants in an intellectual sense; figures like al-Jāmī theorized and elaborated the intellectual basis and core arguments of Salafi outreach to Africa.

Amid Saudi-Egyptian competition for Islamic leadership in the 1960s, Africa stood out to Saudi Arabia as a promising zone for outreach, including because the Saudi Arabian religious establishment hoped to "'save' the African Muslims from the influence of Sufism."[36] Early in the Islamic University's history, senior staff such as General Secretary Shaykh Muḥammad al-ʿUbūdī (b. 1930) identified Africa as a target for outreach. He understood that Africa was internally heterogeneous and that simplistic outreach strategies could fail. In a talk on Africa in the late 1960s, he noted, "Africa is a wide and vast continent. . . . Conditions in its countries are widely diverse, and the circumstances that obtain in its regions are different." Yet he also averred that the present time was particularly suitable for "a wide Islamic campaign for outreach (*daʿwa*) and guidance (*irshād*)" because "the Christian religion, which is the principal competitor, has been linked in the minds of many Africans with European colonialism."[37] In the 1960s, Salafis at Medina were beginning to study both the religious landscape and the political character of African societies to facilitate effective outreach.

History was one tool in devising more sophisticated strategies in Africa. African Salafis like al-Jāmī produced narratives of African history that fit the Salafi worldview and informed Salafi outreach. In al-Jāmī's essay, "The Course of the Islamic *Daʿwa* in Africa across History" (*Sīrat al-Daʿwa al-Islāmiyya fī Ifrīqiyā ʿabr al-Tārīkh*), he depicted three periods of Islam's spread in Africa. First, a group of Companions sought refuge in Abyssinia while the Prophet was being persecuted in Mecca. Second, he said, there was a period when Islam was spread by people who, in his eyes, did not understand the faith. Those who spread Islam were, according to him, unschooled Muslim traders and devious Sufis. The

36 Ahmed, *West African ʿulamāʾ*, 142.
37 Muḥammad al-ʿUbūdī, "Dhikrayātī fī Ifrīqīyā," *Journal of the Islamic University of Medina* 1 (1966).

latter, al-Jāmī stated, "called [people] to everything except Islam in its correct conception."[38] Sufis' goals included "subjugating the masses and using them for their private interests," "arousing in the people a dislike of the *'ulamā'* of *sharī'a* and students of knowledge of the Book and the Sunna," and spreading teachings such as Ibn 'Arabi's "monism of being (*waḥdat al-wujūd*),"[39] an idea Salafis detest. Al-Jāmī argued against the viewpoint that Sufis deserve credit for the Islamization of Africa. He concluded that Sufis merely "called people to worship their shaykhs."[40] Al-Jāmī's version of Islamic Africa's history systematically maligned African Sufis while strategically omitting the vast tradition of scholarship and erudition among African Muslim scholars who had been trained in the classical system of Islamic education – many of whom were Sufis.[41]

After presenting this Salafized version of Africa's Islamic history, al-Jāmī turned to the present – what for him constituted the third phase, the "period of correction" (*dawr al-taṣḥīḥ*). He saw an opportunity for preachers to spread the correct creed in Africa. Yet he compared the current state of Salafi outreach unfavorably with Christian missionary work in Africa, writing critically of "the chaos (*al-fawḍā*) and aimlessness (*al-takhabbuṭ*) that reign over the ranks of those who belong to the Islamic *da'wa* and the lack of seriousness in their work."[42] This negative assessment underscores the contrast between Salafis' optimism about their prospects in Africa and their awareness that their strategies were unsophisticated. In contrast to the conventional wisdom of a well-organized and shadowy Saudi foreign policy that targeted a vulnerable and impoverished Africa, we see here how initial Salafi outreach faltered, even from the perspective of its proponents.

Al-Jāmī did speak positively of Saudi institutions. These organizations could prepare knowledgeable preachers who would spread the creed. He assigned a major role to Salafi institutions like the Islamic University in "correcting" African Muslims' beliefs and practices. He wrote,

> The Islamic universities, and at their head this university of ours, have begun to graduate a large number of the continent's sons at a time that is considered – truly – the best time, and the most auspicious, the most blessed, the most suitable for the Islamic project (*al-'amal al-islāmī*) on the continent. It is the time in which

38 Al-Jāmī, *Majmū' Rasā'il*, 316.
39 Al-Jāmī, *Majmū' Rasā'il*, 317–18.
40 Al-Jāmī, *Majmū' Rasā'il*, 318.
41 Examples could be multiplied of Muslim scholars in precolonial sub-Saharan Africa who dedicated their lives to pursuing and disseminating various forms of Islamic knowledge, including Sufism. In West Africa, notable figures include Shaykh Aḥmad Baba of Timbuktu (1556–1627), as well as the famous trio of scholars from present-day northern Nigeria: Shaykh 'Uthmān dan Fodio (1754–1817), his brother 'Abd Allāh (1766–1828), and his son Muḥammad Bello (1781–1837).
42 Al-Jāmī, *Majmū' Rasā'il*, 327.

the peoples of the continent are trying to free themselves of the vestiges of both Western and Eastern colonialism.[43]

Al-Jāmī went on to describe the potential for brotherhood among African, Arab, and other Muslim peoples. African graduates of Medina could actualize this brotherhood by teaching their peoples orthodoxy. He urged them to seize the opportunity.

Salafis in Medina did more than theorize – they also helped project the university's influence into Africa. This was part of a global effort, but Africa received special attention. University leaders advocated concrete steps for strengthening outreach in Africa, including funding African Muslim organizations, providing study grants to African students, conducting charity, and distributing books.[44]

From 1964 on, as Saudi Arabia sought information about the conditions of African Muslims and worked to build partnerships with local Muslims, the Islamic University and the Muslim World League sent delegations to Africa. Many delegations contained prominent African Salafis. The first delegation comprised al-ʿUbūdī and two African members. They traveled to Africa in 1964 to "get in touch with Muslims' leaders and *ʿulamāʾ*," "deliver religious lectures and speeches," "organize statistical charts of Muslim populations in each country," and identify promising local individuals, schools, and organizations. The delegation's nearly four-month journey took them to nine countries in East and Central Africa.[45] This and other delegations were empowered to distribute considerable amounts of money and assign scholarships to the Islamic University.[46]

As more delegations were dispatched, African Salafis like al-Shinqīṭī sometimes headed them. A biographer writes:

> There was an idea to send delegations to the Islamic countries and especially Africa. He – may Allah have mercy on him – was at the head of a delegation of the University to ten African countries that began with Sudan and ended with Mauritania, the home country of the Shaykh, may Allah have mercy on him.[47]

For his part, al-Jāmī traveled to Africa as part of university delegations in 1965/6, 1966/7, and 1975. He visited at least fifteen countries in West and Central Africa, including Nigeria. He characterized these trips positively, writing that he noticed progress over time. He credits several groups with this success: African students and pilgrims, preachers

43 Al-Jāmī, *Majmūʿ Rasāʾil*, 331.
44 Al-ʿUbūdī, "Dhikrayātī fī Ifrīqīyā."
45 Muḥammad al-ʿUbūdī, "Fī Ifrīqīyā al-Khaḍrā," *Journal of the Islamic University of Medina* 2 (1967).
46 Ahmed, *West African ʿulamāʾ*, 146–51.
47 Sālim, "Introduction," 25.

sent by the Directorate for Scholarly Researches (*Idārat al-Buḥūth al-ʿIlmiyya*), eminent Saudi religious personages, and delegations from Medina.[48]

In addition to delegations, global Salafi institutions produced literature that targeted African Muslim audiences, especially by criticizing African Sufi orders. In this way, theory and practice came together, as Salafis sought to renarrate African history and attack Sufism. During the 1970s and 1980s, the Islamic University and the Muslim World League published several major polemics against the Tijaniyya Sufi order written by African Salafis and reformist African Muslims. For example, Abubakar Gumi's participation in the League facilitated his contact with a Lebanese associate who published his 1972 *Al-ʿAqīda al-Saḥīḥa bi-Muwāfaqat al-Sharīʿa* (The Correct Creed Is in Accordance with the Law).[49] In 1981, on Gumi's recommendation, the Islamic University sponsored the publication in Beirut of *Al-Shaykh Ibrāhīm Inyās al-Sinighālī: Ḥayātuhu wa-Ārāʾuhu wa-Taʿlīmuhu* (Shaykh Ibrahim Niasse the Senegalese: His Life, His Views, and His Teaching), written by a Nigerian who had left the Tijaniyya. Gumi wrote the book's foreword.[50] Another anti-Tijani polemic was authored by a Ghanaian and titled *Risāla al-Dāʿī ilā al-Sunna wa-l-Zājir ʿan al-Bidʿa* (The Epistle of the One Who Calls People to the Sunna and Rebukes Heresy). The University published it in 1982 with a preface by Ibn Bāz.[51] Such criticisms of the Tijaniyya, including by Africans like the earlier-mentioned al-Ifrīqī,[52] were not new. But by supporting these works, the University directly challenged Sufis, its major competitors for the allegiance of African Muslims. The university and the Kingdom's authorities could give these works a stamp of canonical approval.

Despite global institutions' efforts and the work of individual African and Saudi Salafis, outreach between the 1960s and the 1980s hit a number of roadblocks. Students recruited to Medina did not necessarily have the experience their recruiters hoped. These problems occurred with Nigeria, whose trajectory illustrates the increasing sophistication of Salafi outreach from Saudi Arabia, and how Salafi institutions were able to achieve greater successes by the 1980s.

48 Al-Jāmī, *Majmūʿ Rasāʾil*, 328–30.
49 Abubakar Gumi with Ismaila Tsiga, *Where I Stand* (Ibadan: Spectrum Books, 1992), 140.
50 Muḥammad Dahiru Maigari *Al-Shaykh Ibrāhīm Inyās al-Sinighālī: Ḥayātuhu wa-Ārāʾuhu wa-Taʿlīmuhu* (Beirut: Dār al-ʿArabiyya, 1981); see also John O. Hunwick and R. S. O'Fahey, eds., *Arabic Literature of Africa, Volume 2: Writings of Central Sudanic Africa* (Leiden: Brill, 1995), 555–6.
51 Kobo, *Unveiling Modernity*, 225.
52 ʿAbd al-Raḥmān al-Ifrīqī, *Al-Anwār al-Raḥmāniyya li-Hidāyat al-Firqa al-Tijāniyya*, 1937.

Nigeria as a Zone of Salafi Outreach

For Salafi leaders in the mid-twentieth century, Nigeria represented an appealing zone for outreach. Northern and western Nigeria had some of the largest Muslim communities in sub-Saharan Africa, and leaders in both regions were receptive to outreach from foreign Muslims. Nigeria's importance to Saudi Arabia would only grow over time, as Nigeria became a mid-sized player in the global oil market, joining the Organization of Petroleum Exporting Countries in 1971. Nigerian pilgrims came to Saudi Arabia in ever-increasing numbers through the 1970s, reaching a peak of more than 100,000 in 1977, from a mere 2,500 in 1956.[53] Because of its economic, political, and cultural importance, Nigeria presented major incentives for Salafi outreach. Nigeria was valuable not only for its own sake, but also, along with Mauritania and Sudan, as countries Saudi Arabia perceived as "a springboard to enter sub-Saharan Africa."[54]

In the 1960s, Saudi outreach to northern Nigeria focused on elite cooperation. As Nigeria headed toward independence in 1960, an almost exclusively Muslim elite ruled its Northern Region. Northern Nigeria's elected leaders came partly from the region's hereditary Muslim ruling families. Ahmadu Bello, premier of the Northern Region from 1954 to 1966, was a member of the royal family of Sokoto. Yet Northern elites of Bello's generation had also been educated in colonial schools and, often, in England or the Arab world as well. These elites were often willing to challenge hereditary rulers and classical scholars, and their international experiences helped them to cultivate broad ties, especially within the Arab world. In the Western Region, dominated by the Yoruba, there were large Muslim associations such as the Ansar-Ud-Deen Society, and many Yoruba Muslims were beginning to study at al-Azhar and elsewhere in the Arab world.[55]

Ahmadu Bello was a particularly appealing partner for Saudi Arabia, more because of his internationally minded outlook than for his theological views. Bello was not a Salafi, nor was he a scholar. He remained immersed in many of the traditions of his Qadiriyya-affiliated royal lineage, and his efforts to reform Islamic practice and authority in northern Nigeria drew on Sufi styles. He branded his platform for unifying Northern Muslims "Usmaniyya," after his ancestor Shaykh ʿUthmān dan Fodio, the Qadiri scholar who led an early nineteenth-century jihad

[53] A. Y. Aliyu et al., *Hajj Research Project Nigeria*, Volumes 1–4 (Zaria: Ahmadu Bello University, 1983).

[54] Ahmed, *West African ʿulamāʾ*, 149.

[55] For examples, see John O. Hunwick and R. S. O'Fahey, eds., *Arabic Literature of Africa, Volume 2: Writings of Central Sudanic Africa* (Leiden: Brill, 1995).

and remained, for many Nigerians, a potent symbol of righteousness throughout the twentieth century.

Bello was keenly interested in strengthening ties with the Muslim and Arab world. He cultivated relationships in Saudi Arabia and also with Egypt's ʿAbd al-Nāṣir. Bello became the founding vice president of the Muslim World League, with Gumi as his representative.[56] In 1963, when Bello reopened the Sultan Bello Mosque (named for one of his ancestors), he invited the chief imam of Medina, Shaykh ʿAbd al-ʿAzīz ibn Ṣāliḥ, to give remarks at the ceremony.[57] Donations from Saudi Arabia and Kuwait helped Bello pursue some of his projects, such as *Jamāʿat Naṣr al-Islam* (The Society for the Victory of Islam), an organization designed to foster Northern Nigerian Muslim unity.[58] Bello's conversion campaigns, in which he proselytized to non-Muslims in Northern Nigeria, won Salafi approval; al-Jāmī and a delegation from the Islamic University attended one of Bello's conversion tours in 1965.[59]

Nigeria's precolonial past held precedents that African Salafi theorists like al-Jāmī found appealing. In his essay "The Course of the Islamic *Daʿwa* in Africa across History," al-Jāmī praised several "local preachers (*duʿāt maḥalliyyūn*)" for upholding true Islam in the past. The first figure al-Jāmī mentioned was dan Fodio. Al-Jāmī wrote that dan Fodio "called people to the true Islam (*daʿā al-nās ilā al-Islām al-ṣaḥīḥ*)."[60]

It is not difficult to see why dan Fodio excited theorists like al-Jāmī. On the surface, dan Fodio's message sounded similar to Ibn ʿAbd al-Wahhāb's opposition to perceived heresy. In the most famous work memorializing the jihad, dan Fodio's son, heir, and biographer wrote:

> There existed in this country different types of unbelief, deviation, and disobedience, shocking matters and repulsive conditions. They covered this country and filled it, such that in this country one could hardly find those whose faith was strong and who devoted themselves to God, except the rare few.... Among them were unbelievers who worshipped stones and *jinn*, and made clear that they were unbelievers, neither praying nor fasting nor giving alms.... Among them were people averring monotheism, praying, fasting, and giving alms without fulfilling (necessary) conditions... while they mixed these practices with the practices of the unbelief that they inherited from their fathers and forefathers.... And when [dan Fodio] began calling people to Allah, and advising them to worship Him according to the religion of Allah, destroying the customs of apostasy, eradicating Satanic innovations, and reviving the Sunna of the Prophet Muḥammad... the

56 Gumi, *Where I Stand*, 103–5.

57 "Speeches Delivered at the Historic Opening Ceremony of the Rebuilt £ 100,000 Sultan Bello Mosque on Friday, 5th July 1963 at Sokoto" (Zaria, Nigeria: Gaskiya Corporation, 1963).

58 Gumi, *Where I Stand*, 106–7.

59 Al-Jāmī, *Majmūʿ Rasāʾil*, 324.

60 Al-Jāmī, *Majmūʿ Rasāʾil*, 323–4.

fortunate ones rushed to his side, and the happy, rightly guided ones went to him, and people began to enter the religion of Allah in crowds [a reference to Qur'an 110:2].[61]

This passage resembles sympathetic accounts of the Wahhābī movement in eighteenth- and nineteenth-century Arabia. Dan Fodio and Ibn ʿAbd al-Wahhāb both denounced what they saw as paganism and called for strict adherence to scripture. Yet the two men had fundamental theological and intellectual differences. Dan Fodio and many of his followers belonged to the Qadiriyya Sufi order and lived in a world imbued with Sufi notions of esoteric knowledge and experience, while Ibn ʿAbd al-Wahhāb excoriated what he saw as Sufi excesses. Dan Fodio was an adherent of the Mālikī school of law, while Ibn ʿAbd al-Wahhāb followed the Ḥanbalī school. The intellectual tradition from which dan Fodio drew was substantially different from the tradition on which Ibn ʿAbd al-Wahhāb relied: the two men cited different authorities, placing them in different and sometimes opposed intellectual camps.[62]

Dan Fodio had enough in common with other scripture-centered agendas of reform, however, that Salafis worked to fold him into their projects. For al-Jāmī to reconcile his vision of Islam's African history with his championing of dan Fodio's legacy, he had to Salafize dan Fodio, effacing his Sufi allegiances and removing him from the webs of intellectual exchange in which he had existed. Such efforts to rewrite Nigeria's Islamic past did not immediately resonate with northern Nigerians, however.

Initial attempts to send Northern Nigerian students to Medina proved unsuccessful. In 1962, the Saudi Arabian government awarded scholarships to eighteen Northerners. At the Islamic University, many students rejected both the methods and the content of their instruction. Ultimately, all but two of the eighteen students dropped out of the program.[63] In one letter to the Northern Nigerian Regional government, students complained,

[61] Muḥammad Bello, *Infāq al-Maysūr fī Tārīkh Bilād al-Takrūr* (Cairo: Egyptian Ministry of Endowments, 1964 [1812/3]), 58–60.

[62] For a debate on whether dan Fodio, Ibn ʿAbd al-Wahhāb, Shāh Wālī Allāh, and al-Shawkānī form part of a broader, global eighteenth-century Islamic revival, see John Voll, "Linking Groups in the Networks of Eighteenth-Century Scholars" in *Eighteenth-Century Revival and Reform in Islam*, edited by Nehemiah Levtzion and John Voll (Syracuse: Syracuse University Press, 1987), 69–92; Ahmad Dallal, "The Origins and Objectives of Islamic Revivalist Thought, 1750–1850," *Journal of the American Oriental Society* 113:3 (July-September 1993), 341–59; and Bernard Haykel, *Revival and Reform in Islam: The Legacy of Muhammad Al-Shawkani* (Cambridge: Cambridge University Press, 2003).

[63] S. A. S. Galadanci, *Ḥarakat al-Lugha al-ʿArabiyya wa-Ādābuhā fī Nayjīriyā*, second edition (Cairo: Dār al-Maʿārif, 1993), 214.

> This University does not suit us. Since we came here we don't learn anything new. We are still learning the Arabic alphabets [sic] which we already knew. The only knew [sic] thing we learn in our class is, how to call people to their new Islamic Mission. We even prefer going back to Nigeria and continuing with our home study better to [sic] this University if we can't get any transfer. We cannot live here and waste our time for nothing.[64]

Others, asking for a transfer, wrote,

> We are requesting that our place of study be changed to somewhere appropriate, and that we study without being separated from our creed, respecting our rulers and religious leaders, without our good traditional customs, which Islam does not forbid, being attacked.[65]

Students felt strong enough in their own base of Islamic knowledge to challenge, at least privately, the claims to religious authenticity that they heard from teachers in Saudi Arabia. Northerners with a background in Sufism and the classical northwest African canon felt deeply uncomfortable in Medina. Northern leaders recognized the problem: when Abubakar Gumi visited Medina in 1964, he said that any student at the university must be "keen to improve his standard of education no matter how difficult the conditions under which he may have to live," and "should also be aware of the Saudi attitude towards 'Tariqqah' [Sufi orders]."[66]

This quotation calls attention to Gumi's particular role in the trajectory of Salafism in Nigeria. He merits special examination as a case of Saudi Arabia's efforts to partner with African Muslims during the early phase of its outreach. Ahmadu Bello was killed in Nigeria's first coup of 1966, but Gumi lived until 1992. He remained an influential religious and political figure in northern Nigeria, retaining region-wide appeal even after the breakup of the Northern Region into separate states. The following section argues that Gumi was critical to the development of Salafism in Nigeria – but that he himself was not fully Salafi, especially because of his lack of immersion in the Salafi canon. Gumi's case reflects larger patterns in the early phase of Saudi outreach to Africa. The Kingdom's institutions could promote anti-Sufism, but it took longer to promote the full Salafi identity as encapsulated within and symbolized by the canon.

From Colonial Education to Anti-Sufi Reformism: Shaykh Abubakar Gumi

Abubakar Gumi, the son of an Islamic scholar and judge, was born in present-day Zamfara State, Nigeria. He studied in colonial schools from

64 National Archives Kaduna (NAK) GENS 425, "Saudi Arabian Study Grants," 111.
65 "Saudi Arabian Study Grants," 166.
66 "Saudi Arabian Study Grants," 198.

an early age, first in the Middle School in Sokoto and subsequently at the Northern Provinces Law School in Kano, later renamed the School for Arabic Studies. At the school, Muslim elites read a condensed version of the classical Mālikī curriculum in a setting that encouraged a level of discussion and debate that would have been unusual in classical study circles. After he graduated, Gumi recalled,

> I did not welcome to study with the leading scholars around, because I had now become used to an approach quite different from theirs. Most of my former teachers had background in both the European and traditional Islamic schools and that made them to be different.... The city scholars had a less flexible background.[67]

Gumi reproached classical scholars for practices that deviated from what he had read in Mālikī texts at the School for Arabic Studies. Posted to the town of Maru in 1949 as a court scribe, Gumi came into conflict with the imam of the central mosque there due to the latter's (in Gumi's telling) preference for conducting ablutions with sand instead of water. When the imam rejected Gumi's textual citations, Gumi and his students refused to allow the imam to lead them in prayer.[68] Colonial schooling had shaped a reformist and critical outlook in Gumi, but his core textual references remained Islamic scriptures and Mālikī jurisprudence. At this time, he had little or no exposure to the Salafi canon, especially in its Yemeni, Indian, or late-nineteenth-century revivalist manifestations. This was largely due to timing – Middle Eastern presses had only begun to systematically produce Salafi canonical literature in the early twentieth century, and most of those texts had not reached Nigeria in large numbers, if at all.

The role of Gumi's colonial schooling in his anti-Sufism points to important dynamics in Muslim anti-Sufi reformist movements, of which Salafi movements are merely one subset. Significantly, Gumi's account of his early career suggests that he developed notions of textually inspired reform before he left Nigeria. These notions reflected his experiences in elite colonial schools and his mobility as an employee of the colonial administration, rather than Saudi Arabian influence. Scholars of West Africa have called attention to the influence of colonial pedagogies, epistemologies, and notions of modernity on Muslim reformist movements, particularly those that emerged between the 1930s and the 1980s.[69] Colonial education shaped not only the scholars who led reformist movements, but also the Western-educated lay elites who became important constituents within those organizations. Drawing on evidence from

67 Gumi, *Where I Stand*, 64.
68 Gumi, *Where I Stand.*
69 Rudolph Ware, *The Walking Qur'an: Islamic Education, Embodied Knowledge, and History in West Africa* (Chapel Hill: University of North Carolina Press, 2014).

Ghana and Burkina Faso, Ousman Kobo has shown that "colonial education . . . nurtured new elites who ambivalently shared the colonialists' negative attitude toward African traditions and local Islamic practices, even as they claimed to resist European cultural assimilation and wanted to be seen as defenders of indigenous traditions."[70] Some of these elites made ideal partners for Saudi Arabia.

Gumi became an open opponent of Sufism in stages. Between the late 1940s and the late 1960s, Gumi challenged practices associated with Sufis and classical scholars but did not publicize his anti-Sufi views. Around the late 1940s, he reportedly came into contact with Saʿīd ibn Hayatu, a descendant of dan Fodio and a leader in the "Mahdiyya," a set of millenarian anticolonial movements; Gumi married one of Hayatu's daughters and, under the family's influence, renounced his affiliation to the Qadiriyya order.[71] In the 1960s, Gumi became a key religious adviser to Ahmadu Bello as well as Grand Qadi (Judge) of the Northern Region. Gumi's rise within the judiciary was "a watershed in the development of anti-Sufism in Nigeria."[72] As Grand Qadi, he had opportunities to publicly question Sufi teachings. In 1964, he wrote to the Senegalese Sufi Shaykh Ibrāhīm Niasse (1900–75), the foremost leader of the Tijaniyya in West Africa, and asked for a *fatwā* (legal opinion). Gumi was concerned by reports that Sufi disciples who reached advanced spiritual states in retreats (*khalawāt*) were describing themselves and other entities as manifestations of Allah. Gumi asked Niasse to address the legal status of this act. Although Gumi addressed Niasse in polite language, Gumi made the high stakes of the question clear:

> If [this process] is legally correct, what is the interpretation of the meaning of "Lord of the Worlds" [*rabb al-ʿālamīn*, a name for Allah, that appears for example in Qurʾan 1:2] for the one who arrives at this extent [*ḥadd*], and what is the difference between it and incarnation [*ḥulūl*], or the saying of the Christians, "the Trinity." Issue a ruling for us, may Allah have mercy on you, and support the judgment with Qurʾanic proofs and sound Prophetic *aḥādīth*.[73]

Core assumptions of a textualist attitude appeared here: Gumi, who had perceived a discrepancy between what he read in texts and what he saw in practice, arrogated to himself the right to question a prominent Sufi authority. Although structured by his reading of Mālikī texts, this attitude

[70] Kobo, *Unveiling Modernity*, 13.
[71] Loimeier, *Islamic Reform*, 150.
[72] Muhammad Sani Umar, "Changing Islamic Identity in Nigeria from the 1960s to the 1980s: From Sufism to Anti-Sufism," in *Muslim Identity and Social Change in Sub-Saharan Africa*, edited by Louis Brenner, 154–78 (Bloomington: University of Indiana Press, 1993), 160.
[73] Quoted in Ibrahim Niasse, Ijābat al-Fatwā fī Tahāfut al-Ṣūfiyya (Kano: Northern Maktabat Printing Press, 1964), Northwestern University Library Paden Collection 286, 1.

indicated a kind of proto-Salafism: an anti-esotericism and an insistence that in theological debates, any argument other than textual proof was inadmissible.

Following the fall of the First Republic in the first coup of 1966, Gumi became more outspoken about his anti-Sufi views, possibly because the death of Bello obviated the necessity for Gumi to maintain political correctness on religious matters. He aired his anti-Sufism through his Ramadan *tafsīr* (Qur'anic exegesis) sessions, which were broadcast on the radio starting in 1967. In his memoir *Where I Stand* (dictated to an associate circa 1992, the year of his death), Gumi depicts the process of airing these views as the slow unfolding of a strategy. He first primed his audience for anti-Sufism by laying "the necessary intellectual foundations" and then introduced potentially controversial statements. Around 1971, Gumi recalls, "I improved on my previous comments, disagreeing openly with the popular scholars, where I could sufficiently explain the disagreements to my audiences for their easy comprehension."[74] It appears that the altered political landscape after the fall of Bello's government in 1966 allowed northern intellectuals to articulate their positions more strongly than before, when professional and political imperatives encouraged strategic silence on points that might have undermined Bello's efforts at Northern unity.

Gumi had lifelong connections to Saudi Arabia. From at least 1965 to 1974, he served on the Islamic University of Medina's Advisory Council, and from at least 1978 to 1987, he served on the university's Highest Council (al-majlis al-aʿlā).[75] The Muslim World League, with which Gumi was affiliated from its founding in 1962, sponsored his 1979 Hausa translation of the Qur'an. In 1989, Gumi won the King Faisal Award for service to Islam. Yet Gumi's writings show little engagement with the Salafi canon, especially its contemporary components. This posture contrasts markedly with the discourses of the graduates of Medina who returned home in the 1990s and 2000s.

"What I teach is simple," Gumi said in *Where I Stand*. "Let us go back to what the books say."[76] But which books? In his anti-Sufi tract *Al-ʿAqīda al-Ṣaḥīḥa bi-Muwāfaqat al-Sharīʿa*, Gumi referred frequently to scripture, and occasionally to classical Arab exegetes such as Ibn Kathīr (1301–73), a figure in the classical Salafi canon. Yet Gumi did not refer to any twentieth-century Muslim thinkers in *Al-ʿAqīda*, nor did he grapple extensively with evaluating the soundness of *aḥādīth*, a hallmark of contemporary Salafi methodology. It is almost certain that Gumi was familiar with Ibn ʿAbd al-Wahhāb's *Kitāb al-Tawḥīd* (The Book of the

74 Gumi, Where I Stand, 132.
75 Al-Ghāmidī, *Al-Kitāb al-Wathā'iqī, 149*–85.
76 Gumi, *Where I Stand*, 200.

Unity of God), a core text in the Salafi canon. However, familiarity did not mean engagement: neither *Al-ʿAqīda* nor *Where I Stand* cites Ibn ʿAbd al-Wahhāb, or any other Salafi canonical figure from the last three centuries. His written *tafsīr*, *Radd al-Adhhān ilā Maʿānī al-Qurʾān* (Bringing Minds Back to the Meanings of the Qurʾan), "seems to be a mere reproduction of the *Tafsīr al-Jalālayn*," the most widespread *tafsīr* in West Africa. Gumi "purged" that text of passages friendly to Sufis and of "purported Biblical material (*isrāʾīliyyāt*)," a genre of extra-Qurʾanic stories that Salafis reject. Meanwhile, Gumi added thematic passages from Sayyid Quṭb's *Fī Ẓilāl al-Qurʾān* (In the Shade of the Qurʾan),[77] a text that many Salafis have held at arm's length, preferring the exegesis of, above all, Ibn Kathīr. Gumi's use of *Tafsīr al-Jalālayn* reinforces the sense that the textual basis of his worldview remained the classical texts of northwest Islamic Africa, rather than the Salafi canon then taking definitive shape in the Middle East. For Gumi, certain broad themes of the Salafi worldview – anti-Sufism, and a claim to be returning to an authentic and anti-esoteric early Islam – overlaid an intellectual training that was still largely West African in character.

Other core elements of Salafism were missing from Gumi's thought, especially anti-*madhhab*ism, or rejection of legal schools. Gumi remained anchored in the Mālikī world of northwest Africa to a greater extent than his Nigerian Salafi successors. In *Where I Stand*, Gumi listed four authors whom he admired "more than anyone else on the African continent." Three of them were major figures in Mālikī jurisprudence: Ibn Abī Zayd al-Qayrawānī (d. 996), Qadi ʿIyāḍ (1083–1149), and Khalīl ibn Isḥāq al-Jundī (d. ca. 1365). The fourth was ʿUthmān dan Fodio.

Like al-Jāmī, Nigeria's Abubakar Gumi was keen to retell the history of dan Fodio's career. Gumi cast dan Fodio as a reformer: in the Sokoto Caliphate, Gumi wrote, "There was . . . a good attempt by the early leaders to put into practice the correct ideals of the religion."[78] Gumi dismissed dan Fodio's adherence to the Qadiriyya, asserting that dan Fodio "withdrew from [Sufism] when he realized its futility as an acceptable philosophy in Islam. Sufism advocates withdrawal from the society and as such, one could not possibly adopt it to build an Islamic State."[79] Tellingly, while Gumi recast dan Fodio as a reformed Sufi, he did not recast him as a reformed Mālikī. It is unclear whether or not Gumi abandoned his formal adherence to the Mālikī school, but he definitely did not abandon his immersion in the intellectual world of Mālikism.

77 Andrea Brigaglia, "*Tafsīr* and the Intellectual History of Islam in West Africa: The Nigerian Case" in *Tafsīr and Intellectual History*, 379–415; 384.
78 Gumi, *Where I Stand*, 3.
79 Gumi, *Where I Stand*, 36.

Within politics, Gumi was a partisan of northern Nigeria, which he regarded as a cultural, religious, and political unit even after its administrative breakup.[80] Despite his participation in Saudi-backed global Muslim institutions, this perspective on the north often oriented Gumi's concerns to the local rather than the global level. Gumi paired his anti-Sufism with an anticolonialism, and discussed both concerns primarily as they figured in the Nigerian arena. In *Al-ʿAqīda,* Gumi described a stunted postcolonialism, where colonialism and Sufism were mutually reinforcing causes of Nigeria's troubles. He wrote,

> The enemies of Islam first used as a basis the writing of books to destroy the sunna, in the name of illumination and "sainthood" (*wilāya*), and smuggled them into the Islamic umma by means of the sectarian shaykhs who glorify them and give them absolute power, and replaced knowledge with ignorance, and reason with arbitrary personal opinions, and guidance with error, and the truth with distortions. Then, second, they built schools to teach the destructive culture of the West, and they began by teaching the children of pagan rejecters whose fathers used to walk naked in the land . . . and put them in sensitive governmental positions; and they began to control the Muslims whose minds were sleeping.[81]

These passages, although compatible with Salafism, also mark Gumi as one of the many African graduates of colonial schools who felt ambivalent about the colonial encounter even as his schooling continued to shape his textualism and rejection of local religious authority. Finally, in another reflection of his local orientation, Gumi embraced political stances – such as his statement on the eve of the 1983 election that it was more important for women to vote than to pray – that might have horrified some Salafis. In light of his continued *madhhab* allegiance, his open endorsement of politics over piety, and his lack of engagement with the Salafi canon, we can say that Gumi was not fully Salafi. Rather, he was a bridge between local anti-Sufism and global Salafism. The Izala organization, which he helped to found, also epitomizes this process.

Izala

In the late 1970s and 1980s, new Islamic tendencies flourished in northern Nigeria. One new movement was the mass anti-Sufi movement *Jamāʿat Izālat al-Bidʿa wa-Iqāmat al-Sunna* (The Society for Removing Heretical Innovation and Establishing the Sunna), which Jaʿfar Ādam and other future Salafi preachers joined in the 1980s. Izala was founded in 1978 in Jos under the leadership of Shaykh Ismail Idris (1937–2000),

[80] Allan Christelow, "Three Islamic Voices in Contemporary Nigeria" in *Islam and the Political Economy of Meaning*, edited by William Roff (London: Croon Helm, 1987), 226–53.

[81] Abubakar Gumi, Al-ʿAqīda al-Ṣaḥīḥa bi-Muwāfaqat al-Sharīʿa (Beirut: Dār al-ʿArabiyya, 1972), 78–9.

who graduated from the School of Arabic Studies in 1967 and served as an imam in the Nigerian army before creating Izala. Idris became a follower of Gumi, teaching his *Al-ʿAqīda* in Kaduna soon after its publication. Idris had also received education in Mālikī jurisprudence. As an army imam, Idris was drawn into theological debates with Sufis in towns he was stationed in, controversies that helped inspire the decision to found Izala.[82] Like Gumi, Idris seems to have had little exposure to the Salafi canon.

Gumi's heirs in Izala also sought to speak for dan Fodio. Izala took its name from dan Fodio's *Iḥyāʾ al-Sunna wa-Ikhmād al-Bidʿa* (Reviving the Sunna and Destroying Heresy). Izala references dan Fodio in diverse ways, and anchors its genealogy in local currents of reform.[83]

After its establishment in Jos, Izala established branches in other northern cities, including Kano. Izala's preachers encountered opposition from Sufis inside Kano's old city, but had greater success preaching in areas like Fagge, where Ādam partly grew up.[84] Izala's young preachers, like Ādam, taught children and adults how to read, recite, and interpret the Qurʾan, and offered lessons in *ḥadīth* and *fiqh* (jurisprudence).[85] This kind of generic education for adults and children is one method still used by Nigerian graduates of Medina.

In Kano, Izala spread by assembling a coalition of young preachers and adult businessmen who fought micro-political battles to create alternative religious spaces to the Sufi-dominated mosques. Kano's Emirate Council controlled the establishment of mosques, especially Friday mosques, of which there were only five in Kano by the early 1980s. Izala's activists established worship spaces in private homes and broadcast their sermons through loudspeakers. These tactics brought conflict with Sufis and the emir, who ultimately allowed Izala some freedom.[86] Izala's reinscription of urban space was paralleled by an inversion of older relationships between clerics and businessmen, a process that has occurred within other reformist movements elsewhere in Africa.[87] Rather than wealthy Sufi clerics "overshadowing" businessmen, businessmen began recruiting and supporting Izala's young preachers. In this pattern, "unlike the

[82] Ramzi Ben Amara, "Shaykh Ismaila Idris (1937–2000), the Founder of the Izala movement in Nigeria," *Annual Review on Islam in Africa* 11 (2012): 74–8.

[83] Abdoulaye Sounaye, "Les héritiers du cheikh: Izala et ses appropriations d'Usman Dan Fodio au Niger," *Cahiers d'Études Africaines* 206/207 (2012): 427–47.

[84] Ousmane Kane, *Muslim Modernity in Postcolonial Nigeria: A Study of the Society for the Removal of Innovation and Reinstatement of Tradition* (Boston: Brill, 2003), 90; Rijiyar Lemo, *Ayyāmī*, 8.

[85] Jaʿfar Maḥmūd Ādam, "Tarihin Rayuwata a Ilmi" (recorded lecture, no date).

[86] Kane, *Muslim Modernity*, 90.

[87] See Østebø, *Localising Salafism: Religious Change among Oromo Muslims in Bale, Ethiopia* (Leiden; Boston: Brill, 2012) on this tendency in Ethiopia; and Kobo, *Unveiling Modernity*, on Ghana and Burkina Faso.

Sufi Shaykh, the cleric is not supposed to have any extraordinary powers. So, spiritually, he is assumed to be the equal of the businessman."[88] Funding from Saudi Arabia and Gumi's personal connections to the Kingdom played a role in Izala's spread. But during the 1980s, many of the movement's preachers were trained within northern Nigeria, and much of its funding came from local businesspersons.

Ādam would eventually reassess his relationship with Izala, most of whose senior leaders continue to be locally educated. Izala did, however, provide an entry point for preachers like Ādam into the worldviews and networks that would ultimately connect him and his peers to global Salafism. The next chapter discusses the young preachers' trajectories in greater detail, but here it is relevant to note that it was through Izala that Ādam came into contact with books like *Kitāb al-Tawḥīd* and with the circles most likely to be the object of outreach from the Islamic University of Medina.

Changes in Saudi Arabian Outreach to Africa

Saudi Arabia's outreach to Nigeria gradually overcame its initial difficulties. Over time, Salafi proselytizers established a broader network of contacts in Africa. They communicated seriously with those partners about the lay of the land, rather than assuming, as they had in the early 1960s, that they could bring African Sufis to Medina and remold them in a straightforward and heavy-handed manner.

The new Salafi institutions also provided vehicles for intellectuals to describe, for a global audience, the conditions in African countries. In the June 1978 *Journal of the Muslim World League*, the Nigeria-based Indian Professor A. R. I. Doi, then director of the Centre for Islamic Legal Studies at Ahmadu Bello University, Zaria, contributed an article titled "Education in Nigeria: Teaching of Islamic Studies as an Academic Subject." Doi discussed the history of Islamic education during precolonial, colonial, and postcolonial times. Doi's article did not reflect a Salafi creed. However, Salafis would likely have appreciated the informational content of the article, as well as Doi's emphasis on eliminating "syncretic superstitions" and his skepticism concerning Qur'anic education methods that deemphasized the acquisition of Arabic fluency.[89]

Saudi Arabia also had success at recruiting students from southwestern Nigeria, who reinforced the Kingdom's network of partners once they returned home. Iysa Ade Bello (b. 1949) obtained an LL.B. in Islamic Law from the Islamic University in 1976; he later earned a Ph.D. from

[88] Kane, *Muslim Modernity*, 92.

[89] A. R. I. Doi, "Education in Nigeria: Teaching of Islamic Studies as an Academic Subject," *Journal of the Muslim World League* (June 1978): 33–8; 37.

the University of Toronto in 1986.[90] Bello's writings suggest someone who is not Salafi – his dissertation at Toronto, for example, focused on the intellectual and philosophical debates between al-Ghazali and Ibn Rushd, two figures sometimes excluded from the Salafi canon (especially al-Ghazali), just as the discipline of philosophy is itself considered heretical by Salafis. Yet Bello did help edit a 1973 Yoruba translation of the meanings of the Qurʾan, which was published by the Muslim World League, making him another local partner for Saudi Arabia of the type represented by Ahmadu Bello – a non-Salafi who found areas of overlapping interest with the Kingdom, including the project of making Islam's foundational texts more accessible to lay, literate Muslims.

Another influential southwestern graduate is Abdurrasheed Hadiyyatullah, who entered the University in the 1960s. He wrote an article for the *Journal of the Islamic University in Medina* in 1969 entitled "Facts about Nigeria,"[91] providing the Islamic University with yet another snapshot of Muslim life in Nigeria. Hadiyyatullah has remained a key partner for the Kingdom. In 1988, he founded the Sharia College of Nigeria in Iwo, Osun State. The college was renamed Sheikh Abdul-Azeez bin Abdullahi bin Baaz Sharia College in 1999 "because of [Ibn Bāz's] immense scholarly contributions to the upliftment of Islamic Institutions and most especially his financially and morally support for the College."[92] Hadiyyatullah remains close to the Islamic University, attending a conference there in May 2015 on the theme of "historical relations between the Kingdom of Saudi Arabia and Africa and ways of strengthening it [sic]." He spoke on the topic "Ways of strengthening the Afro-Saudi relations through the Islamic advocacy support to the African continent."[93]

In the north, it was not until the 1980s that the Islamic University began to have sustained success in recruiting Nigerian students who would respond positively to its curriculum and goals. This success was connected to the university's new and systematic global outreach through its *dawrāt* (tours). On these tours, university staff taught and tested potential students. Official figures show that the university conducted 296 *dawrāt* in eighteen countries between 1982 and 1997, involving 1,362 teachers and 29,725 students. Of all these countries, which ranged from Senegal to Britain to Sri Lanka, Nigeria had the highest participation, involving 245 teachers and 8,146 students.[94] Several major Salafi preachers in Nigeria were recruited through these study tours.

90 Iysa Ade Bello Curriculum Vitae, circa 2004.

91 ʿAbd al-Rashīd Hadiyyat Allāh, "Ḥaqā'iq ʿan Nayjīrīyā," *Majallat al-Jāmiʿa al-Islāmiyya bi-l-Madīna* 6 (December 1969): 126–34.

92 Sharia College of Nigeria website, www.shariahcollege.com; accessed September 2015.

93 Islamic University of Medina, "Islamic University Organizes a Seminar on the Historical Relations between Saudi Arabia and Africa," 3 May 2015. Available at: www.iu.edu.sa/en/News/Pages/2009111.aspx, accessed September 2015.

94 Al-Ghāmidī, *Al-Kitāb al-wathāʾiqī*, 230.

Nigeria became one of the largest sources of students for the Islamic University. Between the time of its first graduating class in 1965 and 2001, the latest date for which I found figures, 856 Nigerians graduated from the university, including 389 who obtained a B.A., nine who obtained an M.A., and two who obtained Ph.D.s. In the number of its nationals who graduated from the Islamic University during this period, Nigeria outranked most countries, save Yemen (1,634 graduates), Pakistan (1,560), Indonesia (1,238), India (952), and Eritrea (915).[95] The university's attention to Nigeria was a major factor in generating a strong Salafi movement there.

Conclusion

The establishment of the Islamic University of Medina marked a new phase in the institutionalization of Salafism. This institutionalization enhanced Salafis' abilities to project their creed into new regions of the Muslim world.

Africa emerged as a special zone for Salafi outreach. Salafis perceived the continent as a dynamic space, full of possibility and ripe for instruction as it emerged out of colonialism. Initial efforts at outreach to African Muslims sometimes faltered, including when the first Nigerian students at Medina found the environment there shocking. Yet African Salafis resident in Saudi Arabia helped to theorize and implement forms of Salafi outreach that took account of particularities of African countries' religious environments, including the strong presence of Sufi orders.

The Islamic University and the Kingdom's African Salafis also cultivated local partners in Africa who, although not always fully Salafi themselves, were receptive to the ideals of international Muslim organizations and ready to accept financial and moral assistance to pursue their own projects. Two of the Kingdom's foremost partners were northern Nigeria's ruler Ahmadu Bello and his religious advisor Abubakar Gumi. Bello's efforts to unify northern Muslims and convert non-Muslims to Islam won him admiration from Salafis in the Kingdom. Gumi emerged as a figure with Salafi leanings who was eager to denounce Sufism.

Outreach from Medina and the Muslim World League to Africa became more sophisticated through the 1980s. It incorporated mechanisms like the study tours that the university organized. The stage was set for African Muslim students to be recruited in ways that ensured they

[95] *Buḥūth Multaqā Khādim al-ḥaramayn al-Sharīfayn li-Khirrijī al-Jāmiʿāt al-Saʿūdīyya: Min Ifrīqiyā, al-Awwal: Al-muqām bi-Nayjīriyā, Kānū taḥta Ishrāf al-Jāmiʿa al-Islāmīyya bi-l-Madīna al-Munawwara, 9–11/10/1422 H, 25–27/12/2002 M* (Medina: al-Mamlaka al-ʿArabiyya al-Saʿūdiyya, Wizārat al-Taʿlīm al-ʿālī, al-Jāmiʿa al-Islāmiyya bi-l-Madīna al-Munawwara, ʿImādat al-Baḥth al-ʿIlmī, 2003), 1056–65, with figures for Nigeria on page 1064.

would know better what to expect at the university. This process helps to explain why the Nigerian students who attended the university in the 1980s and 1990s had different experiences than their predecessors in the 1960s, and why the later group returned to Nigeria with the intellectual resources – including a mastery of the Salafi canon – that helped them popularize not just anti-Sufism but a detailed understanding of the Salafi creed.

Tracing the movement from anti-Sufism to Salafism is about more than just splitting hairs over definitions of Salafism. At stake are key questions about the incorporation of diverse local movements into a unified Salafi identity; this process, which unfolded over decades, needs to be historicized and contextualized with reference to both generational change in recipient countries and institutional change in Saudi Arabia. In Nigeria, the transmission of the canon, and of stances like anti-*madhhab*ism, has transformed and widened the intellectual horizons of preachers who emerged from the Izala fold. The difference between Gumi and the Medina graduates is not just one of style. The difference concerns the role that each played in mediating transnational encounters. Gumi was a local partner to Saudi Arabia whose interests resonated with the Kingdom's when it came to the question of anti-Sufism; figures like Ādam, in contrast, had available to them a fully formed intellectual system that they sought not to lay over northwest Africa's textual universe but to install in place of it. This difference does not mean that the Medina graduates are "transnational" or "global" figures disconnected from local realities; indeed, the Salafi canon constitutes a powerful intellectual resource useful for localizing and recontextualizing Salafi discourses. This resource gives the Medina graduates tools that were unavailable to Gumi – the canon allows them to make a more expansive case that struggles in Nigeria are not just an effort to reassert the early Muslim community's alleged values but also a part of a global struggle occurring around the world at the present time.

3 Nigerians in Medina

How did Salafism emerge in northern Nigeria? What role did the Islamic University of Medina play in this process? How, and for whom, did the Salafi canon become a standard of reference in northern Nigeria?

The previous chapter discussed the Nigerian Shaykh Abubakar Gumi (1924–92) and the anti-Sufi movement he patronized, Izala. I noted that Gumi, despite his decades-long contact with Saudi Arabia, remained an anti-Sufi Mālikī who was more attuned to local political and religious conflicts than to the intellectual flows of global Salafism. Gumi and most of Izala's early leaders had limited engagement with the Salafi canon.

The wide spread of what might be called "full" Salafism in northern Nigeria – a kind of Salafism infused with references to the canon, and attuned not only to anti-Sufism but also to anti-*madhhab*ism – began with graduates of the Islamic University of Medina who returned home in the 1990s and 2000s. Figures like Shaykh Jaʿfar Maḥmūd Ādam started their careers as preachers in Izala and remained associated with Izala throughout their lives. At the Islamic University of Medina, however, Ādam and his circle had deep exposure to the Salafi canon. This exposure led them to embrace a new self-identification that emphasized global and transhistorical Salafi affiliations.

This chapter argues that the canon provided the central mechanism through which Ādam and his circle distinguished their Salafism from Izala's anti-Sufism, although in practice, dividing lines between the two groups remain blurry. The graduates of Medina learned this canon primarily at the Islamic University, which sought to define a Salafi creed and teach techniques for transmitting it. Defining the creed involved refuting a large catalogue of rivals – not just Sufis, but the Shīʿa, the Ashʿarī theological school, and others. The university's students also received teachings that rejected affiliation to any legal school. Students in Medina engaged a Salafi canon whose contents could be deployed to challenge not only Sufis but also the anti-Sufi reformists in Izala.

The graduates of Medina differentiated themselves from Izala in several ways. First, they considered canonical figures like Ibn Taymiyya, as well as the canonical authorities of contemporary Salafism – Shaykhs Muḥammad Nāṣir al-Dīn al-Albānī, ʿAbd al-ʿAzīz ibn Bāz, and Muḥammad ibn Ṣāliḥ al-ʿUthaymīn – to be their preeminent intellectual guides, rather than Gumi. Second, they adopted distinctively Salafi discursive styles, such as introducing their lectures and sermons with the Prophet Muḥammad's Sermon of Necessity (see Appendix 1), a text that al-Albānī had revived and spread widely among his Salafi audiences. These discursive styles included the graduates' efforts to put the canon at the center of their teaching, which I discuss in the next chapter. Third, the graduates of Medina referred to themselves not as members of Izala but as Ahl al-Sunna wa-l-Jamāʿa (The People of the Sunna and the Muslim Community, colloquially "Ahlussunnah")[1] – a synonym for "Sunni" and an assertion of continuity with those whom Salafis consider "pure" Muslims around the world and in past epochs.

For Ādam and his circle, the experience of studying the canon at the Islamic University intersected in powerful ways with the politics of generational change inside northern Nigeria's anti-Sufi milieu. Ādam returned home just one year after Gumi's death, at a time when Izala was negotiating both internal schisms and changes in leadership. With the incentives and the tools to establish themselves as religious authorities semi-independent of Izala, Ādam and his circle elaborated a full Salafi identity, one that attracted a wide audience.

Much scholarship depicts African graduates of Saudi Arabian universities as embittered figures who, denied access to government jobs or institutional positions of religious leadership, are working at the margins of society to overthrow tradition.[2] In northern Nigeria, however, many graduates are influential preachers. Some have served in prominent institutional positions, for example, as senior bureaucrats in state governments, faculty members at universities, or advisors to the Central Bank of Nigeria.

The Medina graduates' appeal stems from the combination of forces they embody. They work to project an image of themselves as deeply learned scholars and as energetic activists leading a movement that has accrued considerable momentum. This movement, they assert, is

[1] The notion of "jamāʿa" also conveys the idea of agreement about the meaning and importance of the sunna. For a Salafi explanation of what this entire phrase means to the Salafi movement, see Muḥammad ibn Ṣāliḥ al-ʿUthaymīn, *Sharḥ al-ʿAqīda al-Wāsiṭiyya li-Shaykh al-Islām Ibn Taymiyya* (ʿAyn Shams: Maktabat al-Hady al-Muḥammadī, 2011), 24–25.

[2] Various essays in René Otayek, ed., *Le radicalisme islamique au sud du Sahara: Daʿwa, arabisation et critique de l'Occident* (Paris: Karthala, 1993); and Galilou Abdoulaye, "The Graduates of Islamic Universities in Benin: A Modern Elite Seeking Social, Religious and Political Recognition" in *Islam in Africa*, eds. Thomas Bierschenk and Georg Stauth, 129–46 (Berlin: Lit Verlag, 2002).

purifying Islam in northern Nigeria and democratizing Islamic knowledge, thereby enabling youth, married women, poor people, and other marginalized groups to access Islam's foundational texts. Such promises are not new in the context of West Africa; Izala itself has been promising and offering an expanded access to Islamic knowledge for decades,[3] including through a wide network of schools.[4] What the Medina graduates add is their forceful assertion that by studying with them, Nigerian Muslims can participate in a translocal and transhistorical community of pure Muslims, one in which purity and learning, rather than genealogy or charisma, are the currency of authority. By offering up the canon as an intellectual resource and a platform for Muslim activism, moreover, they propose not just shortcuts to accessing foundational Islamic texts but an entire new textual universe governed by rules and methods that promise to disrupt other, more hierarchical and esoteric models of spiritual authority. The Medina graduates offer a way of approaching Islam that promises to give its adherents an almost mathematical certainty that they can derive correct belief and practice from certain core, easily understandable premises. At the same time, the canon allows them to center their preaching and instruction on an affirmative message of spreading a highly specific creed, rather than on the negative message of denouncing Sufism.

The Medina graduates in Nigeria also operate in a broader field where many youth-based Muslim movements are undergoing changes. For example, Izala is also strong across the border in Niger, in part because the border between Nigeria and Niger is political rather than linguistic. Yet in Niamey and elsewhere, new religious entrepreneurs (including Medina graduates) and their youthful followers have sometimes distanced themselves, to different degrees, from Izala. These youth break with Izala's harsh anti-Sufism and its spiritual austerity in favor of more affirmative, flexible messages.[5] In southwestern Nigeria, youth have also grown restless within older Muslim organizations. Efforts like the Yoruba-dominated Naṣrul-Lahi-L-Fātih (Naṣr Allāh al-Fātiḥ, meaning "The Help/Victory of God, The Victorious" and abbreviated NASFAT) represent both a bid to revitalize Islamic practice on a "non-sectarian and non-political" basis, and a response to the dynamic preaching of Pentecostal Christians. NASFAT has itself, however, been prone to schisms, reflecting the centrifugal tendency of much new Muslim activism in

[3] Ousmane Kane, *Muslim Modernity in Postcolonial Nigeria: A Study of the Society for the Removal of Innovation and Reinstatement of Tradition* (Leiden: Brill, 2003).

[4] Elisha Renne, "Educating Muslim Women and the Izala Movement in Zaria City, Nigeria," *Islamic Africa* 3:1 (2012): 55–86.

[5] Abdoulaye Sounaye, "Irwo Sunnance yan-no! 1: Youth Claiming, Contesting and Transforming Salafism," *Islamic Africa* 6:1–2 (July 2015): 82–108.

Africa and elsewhere.[6] Such tendencies can result in radicalization, as Part III of this study discusses, but can also generate new combinations of piety and aesthetics. In northern Nigeria, the Medina graduates closely study the experiences of both peer movements and rival groups in Nigeria and elsewhere. Their preference for a loose organizational structure over a formal associational one partly reflects their sense that formal associations are not only rigid but even spiritually dangerous if they obstruct a sense of Muslim unity.

Generational Changes and Schisms in Izala

Most of the graduates of Medina discussed in this section started their public careers as preachers in Izala in the 1980s. The society connected them with teachers, patrons, and audiences, as well as with one another. Looking back from the vantage of the 2000s, Ādam would posit continuity between the 1980s and his later career, presenting his trajectory as one of uninterrupted participation in "Ahlussunnah." But to understand the subtleties of Ādam's trajectory, it is necessary to summarize the history of Izala's schisms and show how these schisms reverberated in faraway Medina during the early 1990s.

As the previous chapter discussed, Izala was founded in 1978 by Shaykh Ismail Idris (1937–2000), a student of Abubakar Gumi. Although Idris led Izala's transformation into a mass movement, his confrontational personality and uncompromising anti-Sufism contributed to splits within Izala after Gumi's death.[7] Political questions also divided the society, even during Gumi's lifetime. In Kano, for example, "one patron tried to turn the preachers into an institutional channel for the negotiation of relations with the state," a move that sidelined and alienated some members.[8]

Theologically, the society became divided over the question of whether Sufis should be regarded as Muslims.[9] By the mid-1980s, even before they went to Medina, figures like Muḥammad Sani ʿUmar Rijiyar Lemo began to disagree with hardline anti-Sufis within Izala. Rijiyar Lemo writes, "I had some heated situations with some of the extremists (*mutaṭarrifīn*) in [Izala], for I leaned more toward reviving correct

6 Benjamin Soares, "An Islamic Social Movement in Contemporary West Africa: NASFAT of Nigeria" in *Movers and Shakers: Social Movements in Africa*, edited by Stephen Ellis and Ineke van Kessel, 178–96 (Leiden: Brill, 2009), 180.

7 Ramzi Ben Amara, "Shaykh Ismaila Idris (1937–2000), the Founder of the Izala Movement in Nigeria," *Annual Review of Islam in Africa* 11 (2012): 74–8.

8 Kane, *Muslim Modernity*, 217.

9 Muhammad Sani Umar, "Education and Islamic Trends in Northern Nigeria: 1970–1990s" in *Africa Today*, 48:2 (Summer 2001): 127–50; 136.

knowledge and spreading it than toward establishing preaching assemblies (*tajammuʿāt waʿẓiyya*)." Rijiyar Lemo also wrote a critique of Gumi's *Al-ʿAqīda*, which he sent to the Shaykh.[10] By 1989–90, when Ādam and Rijiyar Lemo left for Medina, anti-Sufi reformism in northern Nigeria was facing considerable strain.

These strains broke into an open schism during Ādam's time in Medina. In the early 1990s, Izala split into two factions. One group was attached to Idris and was based in his home city of Jos. Another group was headquartered in Kaduna, where Gumi had spent much of his adult life. Reasons for the split included the tensions that had grown within the movement during the 1980s as well as other factors: personality conflicts among senior leaders, disruption resulting from Gumi's death in 1992, and differences of opinion on international issues such as the Iraqi invasion of Kuwait and the ensuing Gulf War.[11] Most of the Nigerian students in Medina inclined toward the Kaduna side, which they believed exhibited more nuance in its treatment of Sufis and more openness in its leadership culture. The Kaduna branch also had more in common, intellectually, with the students in Medina. The senior leaders of the Jos branch, such as Shaykh Sani Yahaya Jingir (b. 1950), have been educated within Nigeria[12] and have not adopted the global Salafi discursive styles that have marked the graduates of Medina. Meanwhile, Medina graduates rose within the Kaduna branch.

There were leadership struggles even within the Kaduna branch. Rivals contended to replace Gumi as the leading preacher at the Sultan Bello Mosque in Kaduna, which Gumi had used as a base to build a local and, through radio, national audience.[13] Ādam reportedly lost out in his efforts to secure this position, not only when Gumi died but also later, when the position passed to Gumi's son Dr. Aḥmad Gumi (b. 1960).[14] A confluence of factors – growing intellectual and theological differences, but also struggles over power – influenced the decision of Ādam and other graduates to assert their own, semi-independent religious authority.

[10] Muḥammad al-Thānī ʿUmar Mūsā Rijiyar Lemo, *Ayyāmī maʿa Dāʿiyat al-Jīl wa-Mufassir al-Tanzīl* (Kano: Dar al-Ḥikma li-l-Kitāb al-Islāmī, 2011), 14.

[11] Ramzi Ben Amara, "The Izala Movement in Nigeria: Its Split, Relationship to Sufis and Perception of Sharīʿa Re-Implementation," Ph.D. dissertation, Bayreuth University, 2011.

[12] For his biography see Ben Amara, "Izala Movement," 186–7.

[13] Andrea Brigaglia, "The Radio Kaduna Tafsīr (1978–1992) and the Construction of Public Images of Muslim Scholars in the Nigerian Media," *Journal for Islamic Studies* 27 (2007): 173–210.

[14] "How I succeeded Dr. Gumi – Sheikh Alhassan Jos," *The Nigerian Voice*, 4 September 2010. Available at: www.thenigerianvoice.com/nvnews/33700/1/how-i-succeeded-dr-gumi-sheikh-alhassan-jos.html; accessed February 2015.

Paths to Medina[15]

We can gain a better understanding of the shift from Izala to "Ahlussunnah" by examining the biographies of five graduates of Medina who were based in Kano before and after their time in Saudi Arabia: Ādam, Rijiyar Lemo, Shaykh Abdulwahhab Abdullah (b. 1953), Dr. Bashīr ʿAliyu ʿUmar (b. 1961), and Dr. Abdullah Ṣāliḥ Pakistan (b. 1957). As discussed subsequently, the first four men no longer identified themselves primarily as members of Izala by the 2000s, while Pakistan remained a senior Izala leader in Kano (affiliated to the Kaduna branch). The movement's leadership includes women: Shaykha Halima Shitu, who is married to Abdullah, has gained renown for the religious lessons she offers to women in their home and for her work as a Hisbah commissioner under Kano Governor Ibrahim Shekarau (served 2003–11). She is a graduate of Umm al-Qura University in Mecca.

Ādam was the most prominent of the graduates of Medina. Since his assassination on 13 April 2007 by unknown gunmen, his fame and influence have continued to grow. He remains the most visible public face (often literally, on CD and DVD covers, and in the names of mosques and streets) of Salafism in Kano.

Graduates of Medina came from different social backgrounds. ʿUmar's grandfather and other male ancestors were Imams of Kano, and Rijiyar Lemo comes from a family of Kano scholars. Ādam had humbler origins. Some, like Rijiyar Lemo and ʿUmar, are Kano men. Others immigrated to Kano, like Ādam and Pakistan (both from Daura, in Katsina State) and Abdullah (from Sansanamango in the Republic of Togo).

The graduates' educational backgrounds differed, although all of them experienced and blended different educational tracks, formal and informal. Some, like Abdullah and Ādam, studied extensively inside the traditional system. Others initially had greater exposure to Western-style schools and universities. ʿUmar said that his "first contact with deep Islamic education" came only in his twenties. Through different means – Qurʾan schooling, attendance at Western-style schools, and study with Arabs in Kano – most of them achieved Arabic proficiency before leaving Nigeria. Although for brevity's sake I refer to this group as "graduates of

[15] This section is based on interviews with Dr. Bashir Aliyu ʿUmar (2 October 2011, Kano), Shaykh Abdulwahhab Abdallah (5 October 2011, Kano), Shaykh Muhammad Nazifi Inuwa (12 October 2011), Dr. Abdullahi Saleh Pakistan (22 October 2011, Kano); on several informal conservations with Shaykh Abdulwahhab Abdullah and Shaykh Nazifi Inuwa; and on field notes from visits to Kano in July–August 2010 and September 2011–January 2012. I have also benefited from Andrea Brigaglia's biographical sketch of Ādam: Brigaglia, "A Contribution to the History of the Wahhabi Daʿwa in West Africa: The Career and the Murder of Shaykh Jaʿfar Mahmoud Adam (Daura, ca. 1961/1962-Kano 2007)," *Islamic Africa* 3:1 (Spring 2012): 1–23.

Medina," it is worth bearing in mind that their learning represents the intertwining of multiple institutional and tutorial strands.

The paths these men took to Saudi Arabia varied, although the tightly networked nature of the group meant that some went at the suggestion of their friends. Some were recruited through the Islamic University's *dawrāt* (Arabic: "tours," singular *dawra*), educational programs that partly aimed to bring students to the University. As the previous chapter noted, Saudi Arabia began its *dawrāt* in northern Nigeria in 1981, and Nigeria became the site of the most intensive *dawra* program in the world.

The first members of "Ahlussunnah" to go to Saudi Arabia were Pakistan and Abdullah. In 1981, after participating in the *dawra*, they went respectively to Medina and Mecca. Pakistan, who held a secondary certificate from the Arabic Teachers' College in Gwale, a school where several members of this network studied, completed a B.A. in Qur'anic Studies at the Islamic University of Medina in 1985. From 1986 to 1991, he lived in Pakistan. He completed an M.A. at the Islamic University in Islamabad in 1989 and, from 1989 to 1991, supervised schools run by the Muslim World League. Abdullah attended primary and secondary school in Mecca before proceeding to Medina, where he obtained his B.A. in 1991.

'Umar enrolled in Electrical Engineering at Ahmadu Bello University in Zaria in 1978. He joined Nigeria's Muslim Students' Society at a time when the Iranian Revolution of 1979 was inspiring many of the society's members to more strident activism. After helping his peers destroy the alcohol at the university faculty club, 'Umar was expelled. Back in Kano, he worked as a water engineer but continued to study Islamic subjects and give religious lectures. He participated in the *dawra* in 1981 but declined a scholarship to Saudi Arabia, partly out of concern that abandoning his career might produce family conflict. After a period of soul-searching, he gave up his post to pursue the path of Islamic learning. When he made the pilgrimage to Saudi Arabia in 1986, Abdullah convinced him to apply to the Islamic University of Medina; he joined the Faculty of Ḥadīth in 1988. He obtained his B.A., M.A., and Ph.D. from Medina, completing the last of these in 2004.

Ādam took a different route to Medina. As a youth, he memorized the Qur'an as an itinerant student. He then studied with classically trained scholars in Kano, learning Mālikī legal manuals like the *Mukhtaṣar* (Compendium) of Khalīl, but also reading works like Shaykh Muḥammad ibn 'Abd al-Wahhāb's *Kitāb al-Tawḥīd* – one of the few texts in the Salafi canon taught widely in Nigeria at that time. He also studied with Shaykh Jazuli Nuhu, one of only two members of the first Nigerian cohort at Medina to remain and complete a degree at the Islamic University. Another key mentor to the future Medina graduates and their peers was Dr. Ahmad Bamba of the Bayero University Kano mosque, a ḥadīth specialist who continues to be a major figure in Kano's Salafi community. The early 1980s was a pivotal time for Ādam. He studied at an evening literacy program. At the Egyptian Cultural Center, an Egyptian Arabic instructor taught him the recitation of the Qur'an (*tajwīd*), an experience that Ādam would later say brought his Qur'anic learning to life.[16] Undoubtedly this training played a role in Ādam's victory in a 1987 Qur'an competition, another turning point in his life. After winning the Nigerian competition, Ādam placed fifth at the international competition in Saudi Arabia. This accomplishment solidified his status as a rising Izala preacher and paved the way for his scholarship to Medina. In 1987, Ādam obtained a secondary diploma at the Arabic Teachers' College of Gwale.[17] In 1989, he obtained a scholarship to Medina, where he joined the Qur'an College.

Rijiyar Lemo, who attended primary and secondary schools in Kano, completed a higher secondary certificate at the Arabic Teachers' College in 1989 and joined Ādam at the Islamic University the following year. Despite the diverse paths these men took to Medina, significant commonalities emerge, including exposure to traditional northern Nigerian Islamic educational curricula and, in almost all cases, some attendance at Nigerian secondary schools and/or universities.

Life and Study in Medina

The future Nigerian Salafi leaders were in Saudi Arabia during a period of political tension and change. Events in the Kingdom would have implications for the construction of global Salafi canonical authority. The period of the Nigerians' studies (roughly 1981–2005 for the whole group, with some members staying for just four years and others staying well over a decade) largely overlapped with the reign of one king, Fahd (1923–2005, ruled 1982–2005, with then-Crown Prince Abdullah serving as *de facto* ruler after Fahd's 1995 stroke).

Despite continuity on the throne, this period saw major upheavals, particularly the 1990–1 Gulf War, which brought American soldiers to Saudi soil and triggered widespread political-religious dissent in the Kingdom. In the face of this dissent – the outgrowth of decades-old Muslim Brotherhood influences in Saudi Arabia, including at the Islamic University – the Kingdom's Grand Mufti ʿAbd al-ʿAzīz ibn Bāz strove to defend the religious legitimacy of the King's policy choices. The political suppression of the Muslim Brotherhood-inspired dissent was accompanied by an assertion of senior scholars' religious authority as well as systematic

[16] Jaʿfar Maḥmūd Ādam, "Tarihin Rayuwata a Ilmi," undated recording.
[17] Rijiyar Lemo, *Ayyāmī*, 30–1.

efforts (led by thinkers at the Islamic University) to attack the theological integrity of the Muslim Brotherhood, especially its thinker Sayyid Quṭb (1906–66).[18]

Nigerian Salafis, after they returned home, did not typically comment on these events – but from their continued admiration of Ibn Bāz and their lack of references to any of the Muslim Brotherhood-inspired Salafis, it seems clear that they sided with the global canonical authorities and the Islamic University's "quietists" against the Saudi dissidents. Even though Nigerian Salafis would become politically outspoken at home, they would do so within a framework that continued to position figures like Ibn Bāz as the contemporary world's foremost scholars. Finally, it should be noted that the 1990s represented the apex of the career of Ibn Bāz (who was appointed Grand Mufti of Saudi Arabia in 1993). The deaths of al-Albānī, Ibn Bāz, and Ibn ʿUthaymīn in 1999–2001 occasioned new reflections among Salafis worldwide about the canonical status of these three shaykhs. In short, Nigerian Salafis studied in Medina at a time when the construction of contemporary canonical authority took on a new urgency.

In interviews, graduates of Medina characterized the religious landscape in the Kingdom both positively and negatively. Shaykh Nazifi Inuwa (b. 1970) mentioned that Saudi Arabian society was more closed to new ideas than either Sudan (where he also studied) or Nigeria, but he said that this atmosphere did not make his time in the Kingdom unpleasant.[19] Dr. Pakistan said that Saudi Arabia funds charity and social welfare much more lavishly than Nigeria does, but he added that Nigerian society is more pious. Another difference Pakistan mentioned is that in Saudi Arabia, the government pays and supervises preachers and imams. "Therefore," he said approvingly, "unrest seldom occurs there." In Nigeria, he continued, people (i.e., Sufis) say whatever they want. They live by what they can get from their supporters, which leads to *kadhib* (lying) and *dajl* (trickery) – a reference to Salafis' feeling that many Sufi shaykhs are charlatans who exploit their followers.[20]

Nigerian students were impressed with the care the Islamic University put into welcoming and hosting them,[21] but their relations with Arabs were not free of racial discrimination. ʿUmar mentioned several incidents of racism to me, including harassment by Saudi Arabian traffic police.

18 Stéphane Lacroix, *Awakening Islam: The Politics of Religious Dissent in Contemporary Saudi Arabia*, translated by George Holoch (Cambridge: Harvard University Press, 2011); Rabīʿ ibn Hādī al-Madkhalī, *Aḍwāʾ Islāmiyya ʿalā ʿAqīdat Sayyid Quṭb wa-Fikrihi* (Al-Madīna: Maktabat al-Ghurabāʾ al-Atharīyya, 1993).

19 Interview with Inuwa, 12 October 2011, Kano.

20 Interview with Pakistan, 22 October 2011, Kano.

21 'Al-Jāmiʿa al-Islāmiyya Taltaqī Kharījī al-Jāmiʿāt al-Saʿūdiyya fī Nayjīrīyā,' *Al-Jazirah*, 22 December 2001. Available at: www.al-jazirah.com/2001/20011222/fu1.htm; accessed February 2015.

Once, he related, he was with his son in the library of the Prophet's Mosque. His son sneezed. An attendant brought a tissue, but another attendant said he should not bring children to the mosque, citing a *ḥadīth*. When ʿUmar told him this *ḥadīth* was weak, the attendant said that an African could not challenge him on a *ḥadīth*. Some Saudis, ʿUmar said, think Africans have "no background knowledge of Islam." Saudi Arabia's growing sophistication in recruitment and outreach strategies, in other words, did not mean that Nigerian students felt completely comfortable in the Kingdom.

ʿUmar's rebuttal in the mosque was no accident: at the Islamic University, the Nigerian students delved into the study of *ḥadīth*. ʿUmar and Rijiyar Lemo studied in the Department of Ḥadīth Sciences (*Qism ʿUlūm al-Ḥadīth*), where they learned the Salafi canon and Salafi methods of *ḥadīth* criticism. Rijiyar Lemo's M.A. thesis was entitled 'Ḍawābiṭ al-Jarḥ wa-l-Taʿdīl ʿind al-Ḥāfiẓ al-Dhahabī min khilāl Kitābihi *Siyar al-Aʿlām al-Nubalā'*: Jamʿan wa-Dirāsatan' (Al-Dhahabī's Rules of Critique and Evaluation through His Book *The Biographies of the Noble Scholars*: A Collection and a Study).[22] The title shows Rijiyar Lemo's engagement with a canonical figure (a fourteenth-century Damascene *ḥadīth* collector and historian, and a student of Ibn Taymiyya). The title also reflects Rijiyar Lemo's immersion in methods honed and reimagined by prominent Salafi scholars such al-Albānī and the Saudi scholar Dr. Rabīʿ al-Madkhalī, a longtime teacher at the Islamic University who is known for his contemporary interpretation of *al-jarḥ wa-l-taʿdīl* (critique and evaluation, or disparagement and praise, which in Salafi hands is a method for deciding whether a scholar is qualified).[23] For their doctoral theses in the same Department, ʿUmar and Rijiyar Lemo examined classical *ḥadīth* scholarship. ʿUmar wrote on Aḥmad ibn Ḥanbal (and the resulting book was published in Saudi Arabia).[24] Rijiyar Lemo examined the study of *ḥadīth* in the early Muslim community in Mecca and Medina.[25] Nigerian Salafis would return home equipped with an advanced knowledge not just of the canon, but of its foundational principles, especially *ḥadīth* criticism, which also involved painstaking research on the early Muslim community.

[22] Muḥammad al-Thānī ʿUmar Mūsā, 'Ḍawābiṭ al-Jarḥ wa-l-Taʿdīl ʿind al-Ḥāfiẓ al-Dhahabī min khilāl Kitābihi *Siyar al-Aʿlām al-Nubalā'*: Jamʿan wa-Dirāsatan,' M.A. thesis, Islamic University of Medina, 1999.

[23] Roel Meijer, "Politicizing *al-jarh wa-l-taʿdil*: Rabi b. Hadi al-Madkhali and the Transnational Battle for Religious Authority," in *The Transmission and Dynamics of the Textual Sources of Islam: Essays in Honour of Harald Motzki*, eds. Nicolet Boekhoff-van der Voort, Kees Versteegh and Joas Wagemakers, 375–99 (Leiden: Brill, 2011).

[24] Bashīr ʿAlī ʿUmar, *Manhaj al-Imām Aḥmad fī Iʿlāl al-Ḥadīth* (Waqf al-Salām 2005).

[25] Muḥammad al-Thānī ʿUmar Mūsā, 'Al-Madrasa al-Ḥadīthiyya fī Makka wa-l-Madīna wa-Atharuhā fī al-Ḥadīth wa-ʿUlūmihi min Nash'atihā ḥattā Nihāyat al-Qarn al-Thānī al-Hijrī,' Ph.D. dissertation, Islamic University of Medina, 2005.

In addition to their classroom learning, the Nigerians studied extensively with scholars in mosques. ʿUmar said the atmosphere was lively in Medina during his undergraduate days: "Everything was new to me." He had classes from morning until the mid-afternoon prayer, then he would read at home. At evening prayer, he came to the mosque for lessons. During his first two years at Medina, a former Vice Chancellor of the University and an associate of Shaykh Ibn Bāz, Shaykh ʿAbd al-Muḥsin al-ʿAbbād (b. 1934), taught *Ṣaḥīḥ al-Bukhārī*, the most famous *ḥadīth* collection in the Muslim world.[26] This kind of study enhanced the young preachers' command of scripture and their ability to cite textual evidence in lectures and debates back home in Nigeria.

Paths Back to Nigeria

Salafi leaders maintained ties to Nigeria throughout their time in Medina, visiting Nigeria periodically and remaining abreast of developments there through correspondence. They returned permanently to Nigeria at different times – Abdullah in 1991, Ādam in 1993, and ʿUmar and Rijiyar Lemo, who obtained Ph.D.s in Medina, in 2004 and 2005, respectively.

Following his homecoming, Ādam returned to the teaching and lecturing circuits to which he had belonged before leaving for Medina. He also created new institutions. He became director of the ʿUthmān bin Affan group, a mosque and school complex named after the third caliph. The complex was established in the Gadon Kaya neighborhood of Kano's Old City by one of Ādam's local patrons. Shaykh Abdulwahhab Abdullah worked closely with him there.[27] Ādam's circle received some support from international Muslim charities such as al-Muntada al-Islāmī,[28] but local financial support strongly aided their rise to prominence. The mosque in Gadon Kaya has remained a central institution for the movement. Rijiyar Lemo and Abdullah still offer lessons there. ʿUmar began his preaching there after his return from Saudi Arabia, before Al-Furqān mosque, where he became imam, opened in 2007. Graduates of Medina have maintained connections to Saudi Arabia through pilgrimages and visits; in 2011, for example, ʿUmar was a royal guest on the hajj.

The Islamic University was often not the endpoint of Kano Salafis' educational trajectories. Ādam, after completing his B.A. in Medina, later entered (and subsequently left, amid some controversy) an M.A.

26 Interview with Umar, 2 October 2011, Kano.
27 Rijiyar Lemo, *Ayyāmī*, 46.
28 Andrea Brigaglia, "Jaʿfar Mahmood Adam, Mohammed Yusuf and al-Muntada Islamic Trust: Reflections on the Genesis of the Boko Haram Phenomenon in Nigeria," *Annual Review of Islam in Africa* 11 (2012): 35–44.

program in Islamic Studies at Bayero University Kano. He completed an M.A. at the Africa International University in Khartoum and enrolled in a Ph.D. program at Usman Danfodiyo University in Sokoto (where Dr. Pakistan obtained his Ph.D. in 2006). Paths that led to Medina often led back to Nigeria or to other destinations in Africa or the Arab world.

Advanced educational credentials placed the graduates of Medina in a tiny minority of Nigerians and helped them to reach diverse audiences. Despite their own relative youth within a scholarly gerontocracy, Ādam and other preachers earned a following among Kano youth. These youth saw them as credible scholars but also as down-to-earth speakers who address, without resorting to euphemism, issues such as marriage, sex, family, and politics. Although audiences at study circles have often been primarily male, the Medina graduates have reached women through radio, recordings, and co-educational lectures in mosques. Advanced educational credentials have earned the graduates some following among politicians, civil servants, and professionals. The relationships between graduates of Medina and these different groups show how Salafi preachers have partially tailored lectures to local audiences' concerns, a theme that is discussed more in the next three chapters.

Ādam's popularity and influence began to soar by the end of the 1990s. In 2000, as the Kano State government was moving to reimplement *sharīʿa*, he served on a ten-man review committee for the draft *sharīʿa* code, indicating his position as a representative of a major religious constituency.[29] By 1999, Ādam's followers began systematically recording his lectures, hundreds of which still circulate in northern Nigeria and online. By the mid-2000s, after Rijiyar Lemo and ʿUmar returned home, the Medina graduates and their local Salafi peers had representatives in some of the city's most prominent institutions, including Bayero University Kano (ʿUmar) and the Shekarau administration (Abdullah, ʿUmar). Over three decades, "Ahlussunnah" became a major force in the religious and political life of one of Nigeria's largest cities.

Ethnographic Snapshots of the Medina Graduates in Kano

Salafis around the world are often depicted as grim, conservative, and fanatical. To add humanity and complexity to this study's portrait of Kano's Salafis, it is important to note their frequent use of humor as well as other potentially surprising aspects of their demeanor. Ādam often began his lectures with personal anecdotes and made frequent

[29] Ibrahim Na'iya Sada, "The Making of the Zamfara and Kano State Sharia Penal Codes," in *Shari'a Implementation in Northern Nigeria, 1999–2006*, edited by Philip Ostien (Ibadan: Spectrum Books, 2007), 29.

use of self-deprecating humor. Audiences can often be heard laughing in the recordings. In person, Shaykh Abdulwahhab Abdullah regularly made jokes. At his house one evening, my research assistant Usman and I witnessed the shaykh discussing plans with a group of about twenty young followers to take up a collection for slaughtering animals at Eid. The shaykh at one point teased a young man whom he was sending out to buy phone recharge cards, calling him *shege* (Hausa: "bastard") in a kind of joking banter that would be out of character for most *ʿulamāʾ* in Kano. Other researchers have also noted the striking egalitarianism in Nigerian Salafi and anti-Sufi circles.[30]

Nigerian Salafis draw sharp theological boundaries in their lectures, and their followers have sometimes clashed violently with Sufis; yet in day-to-day life, many Salafis interact on polite and even friendly terms with Sufis. During the period of my research, I attended an evening prayer and social circle in Kano, whose members had met daily for years. One member was an outspoken Salafi who knew the major Salafi preachers of the city well, but he faithfully attended this evening prayer circle, whose habitual attendees included Sufis and other non-Salafis. He participated in group prayer, common meals, and lively discussions with his non-Salafi friends. In general, relations between Salafis and the Qadiriyya order seemed more respectful than those between Salafis and the Tijāniyya. For example, Abdullah emphasized his study with the Qadiri Sufi Shaykh Nāṣir Kabara (1912–96), yet asked me intently whether I was a Tijānī upon hearing that I had done prior research in Senegal.

As Salafis have moved into positions of intellectual, political, and religious authority, they have interacted with a wide range of other Muslims, influencing them but at the same time taking on the responsibilities of having a wider audience and constituency. Several Salafis, including graduates of Medina and Sudan's International University of Africa, teach at the Aminu Kano College of Islamic and Legal Studies, a well-regarded tertiary institution in Kano that trains future legal elites. These Salafis held positions as deans and heads of departments. In these capacities, they could shape the curriculum, but they also had to work closely with scholars and administrators from other theological backgrounds. The changes Nigerian Salafis have experienced as their social status rises recall Robert Launay's description of how one prominent Muslim leader in Côte d'Ivoire transitioned from outspoken anti-Sufism to accommodation with Sufism as he became a local elder and took on a range of social roles "that flagrantly contradicted his Wahhabi ideas."[31] Although the transitions are not so dramatic in Nigeria, some Nigerian Salafis

[30] Kane, *Muslim Modernity*.

[31] Robert Launay, *Beyond the Stream: Islam and Society in a West African Town* (Berkeley: University of California Press, 1992), 90.

have had to negotiate what it means to present themselves not just as Salafi leaders but as authorities for larger Muslim communities. At the same time, their institutional positions can afford them opportunities to present the fundamentals of Salafism as a kind of "generic Islam"[32] and to attempt to Salafize colleagues and students.

In line with this, some Salafi-controlled mosques are hubs for many kinds of activity, especially the pursuit of adult education by Muslims who are not necessarily "full" Salafis but who have an interest in and sympathy for Salafi styles of teaching scripture. Al-Furqān, where ʿUmar became imam, is a huge, gleaming mosque in the Government Reserve Area, a wealthy neighborhood in Kano. During prayer times, many expensive cars are parked out front, as well as some motorbikes. Out front, one vendor might be selling oranges, while another sells MP3s and DVDs of recordings of prominent Nigerian *ʿulamāʾ* – not just of Salafis like Ādam but also of prominent Sufis like Shaykh Isa Waziri (1925–2013), a prominent adviser to the late emir of Kano, Ado Bayero. The mosque has an active program of adult Arabic education, offering courses on *tajwīd* (recitation) and other subjects. Al-Furqān attracts pupils and worshippers who are not Salafi. The influence of the Medina graduates extends far beyond just those Nigerians who fully accept the Salafi theological vision.

The Medina graduates have obtained financial support from various sources. Global Islamic charities have been one key source: Al-Muntada al-Islāmī Trust was key to Ādam's establishment of his network of mosques and schools in Kano and later to the establishment of Al-Furqān Mosque. At the same time, the role of external funders should not overshadow the importance of local funders: Muhammad Indimi (or Ndimi), founder and chairman of the oil company Oriental Energy Resources, built the mosque in Maiduguri where Ādam delivered *tafsīr* during Ramadan; the Sabuwar Gandu mosque in Kano was built with the support of local businessmen, such as the Izala member Muhammad Ahmad. For book publishing, Salafis have turned to both Nigerian and Arab publishers, including institutions like Al-Muntada. The Islamic University and Saudi publishers also sometimes help graduates of Medina publish M.A. and doctoral theses. For the recording and dissemination of lectures, Salafis have relied primarily on existing networks of technicians, small shops, and peddlers in Kano and other cities.

Many Salafi preachers are not personally wealthy. They often live middle-class lifestyles, drawing personal incomes from multiple sources, especially teaching at schools and universities and/or serving in

[32] Benjamin Soares, *Islam and the Prayer Economy. History and Authority in a Malian Town* (Ann Arbor: University of Michigan Press, 2005), 224.

government posts. For example, during the period of my fieldwork, one of the younger graduates of Medina, Nazifi Inuwa, was operating his own private school, serving as the head of the Department of Qur'anic Studies at the state government-run tertiary institution The Aminu Kano College of Islamic and Legal Studies, offering lessons at mosques in Kano, and conducting two radio programs. Some Salafis have important connections elsewhere in Nigeria – the Kano-based preacher Shaykh Muhammad bin Uthman, for example, traveled regularly to preach in Port Harcourt during the period of my fieldwork – that may supplement their incomes. Salafis do not, however, have access to the same level of redistributive financial power that the most prominent Sufi shaykhs do, nor have any Salafi preachers emerged as major businessmen at the level of, for example, the Kano-based Tijani Shaykh Isyaku Rabiu or his son Abdulsamad Rabiu, Nigeria's fourth richest man as of 2015.[33]

Breaking with Izala

At the Islamic University, Ādam and Rijiyar Lemo underwent two intellectual shifts. First, deepening their disagreements with Izala hardliners, they adopted somewhat greater tolerance for Sufis. Second, they began preaching outside of the context of a formalized, hierarchical organization. The university and the canon have remained a potent reference point in Rijiyar Lemo's presentation of his circle's break with Izala: he invokes the canon as the standard of authority by which he measured Izala's claims to represent Salafism.

Networks formed by Izala continued to link the Nigerian students in Medina even as their studies opened new questions about Izala's theological integrity. Rijiyar Lemo relates that he, Ādam, and Dr. Ibrāhīm Jalo of Taraba State formed an extracurricular study circle dedicated to reading works by Ibn Taymiyya. "One doctrinal affiliation brought us together, and that was affiliation to [Izala], as *duʿāt* [preachers] in it. We were comrades before the university, and we became more connected at the university."[34] At the Islamic University, however, the young preachers cultivated the spirit of open debate that they felt Izala lacked. Ādam later said, "We would gather books and read, or we would open a chapter in a book. [Rijiyar Lemo] would read or I would read and we would comment on it to each other. Sometimes we would agree, sometimes we would differ, and so forth."[35] This atmosphere encouraged the

[33] *Forbes* profile of Abdulsamad Rabiu, 2015. Available at: www.forbes.com/profile/abdulsamad-rabiu/; accessed October 2015.
[34] Rijiyar Lemo, *Ayyāmī*, 23.
[35] Ādam, "Tarihin Rayuwata."

investigations that led the students in Medina to reevaluate their relationship to Izala and to foreground the Salafi canon.

During their time at the Islamic University, the circle around Ādam came to feel that they had textual evidence to support their stances against the Izala hardliners – a significant asset in a community that prizes textual evidence as the decisive criterion for settling disputes. Rijiyar Lemo wrote that study and debate in Medina took on a wider scope than discussions inside Izala circles at home. "When we met together at the campus of the Islamic University, we would re-examine many of the preaching issues (*al-qaḍāya al-daʿwiyya*) that [Izala] had adopted" such as "the issue of prayer behind the heretical innovator (*mubtadiʿ*), or the one whose status is hidden (*al-mastūr*), and the issue of eating something sacrificed by Sufis (*masʾalat akl dhabīḥat al-ṭuruqiyyīn*)."[36] On this issue, Rijiyar Lemo mentioned that reading the works of two canonical authorities, Shaykhs Ṣiddīq Ḥasan Khān al-Qannūjī and Muḥammad al-Shawkānī, "increased my conviction (*qanāʿati*) in my stance."[37]

Rijiyar Lemo's invocation of these figures has at least two salient contexts. First, he mentioned them while recalling a legal debate with Izala hardliners in the 1990s; canonical Salafis became intellectual authorities supporting his stances. Second, he mentioned these figures in a book attempting to define Ādam's legacy – and the identity of his successors in the "Ahlussunnah" network – after the shaykh's death. By invoking canonical Salafis, Rijiyar Lemo suggested that time in Medina expanded his and Ādam's command of the canon to a degree the Izala hardliners could not match. The mention of Khān and al-Shawkānī also highlights how the canon taught at the Islamic University was broader than just Wahhābī works.

In 1991, while Ādam and Rijiyar Lemo were at the Islamic University, Izala split into two camps. As noted earlier, one camp was based in Jos and the other in Kaduna. The sympathies of Ādam and Rijiyar Lemo lay with the latter, which they perceived as more moderate and less authoritarian. The Jos camp, Rijiyar Lemo wrote, went too far in "excommunicating without any thinking" (*takfīr bilā adna tafkīr*).[38] Significantly, in Kano, where Izala also split, the leader of those aligned with Kaduna was Abdullah Pakistan, an alumnus of Medina. Dr. Ibrāhīm Jalo, another close friend of Ādam's at the Islamic University, also affiliated himself with the Kaduna branch.[39] To the students in Medina, this branch seemed to offer a less authoritarian, more intellectual, and even more Salafi worldview.

[36] Rijiyar Lemo, *Ayyāmī*, 25.
[37] Rijiyar Lemo, *Ayyāmī*, 26.
[38] Rijiyar Lemo, *Ayyāmī*, 29–30.
[39] Ben Amara, "'Izala Movement,'" 194.

Despite their sympathies for Kaduna, many Nigerian students at Medina attempted to remain neutral. Rijiyar Lemo wrote, "When this split occurred, we decided to meet with all the students in the University belonging to [Izala], and take one stance characterized by neutrality (*al-ḥiyādiyya*) and justice (*al-ʿadāla*), and not support a side against the other side." They authored a "letter of advice" (*risāla naṣīḥa*) to the two sides and delegated Ādam to deliver it.[40] Rijiyar Lemo described this episode as a formative experience in Ādam's career as a preacher:

> There is no doubt that this stance that the students took then is what formed for the brother [Ādam], may Allah have mercy on him, an intellectual basis for launching his preaching after his return to Nigeria. It created for the Salafi *daʿwa* a special air, and gave it a distinguished dimension in Nigerian society. After some of the students had been fettered by the decisions [Izala] issued, they became free in their *daʿwa* and free in their approach, not compelled to follow a certain person who would impose his views on them.[41]

This new platform for *daʿwa* was the Salafi canon. In their debates with Izala, the graduates of Medina invoked their learning at Medina, their mastery of Salafi methodologies, and their respect for thinkers in the global Salafi canon.

Not all Nigerian Salafis had the same experience at the university. Some members of Izala remained within the fold. Still others promoted reform within Izala. Dr. Pakistan, who rose to leadership within the Kaduna-affiliated branch of Izala in Kano after 1991, told me that he moved the society's emphasis from *takfīr* (anathematization) to *taʿlīm* (education).[42]

It is important not to exaggerate the extent of the split between Ādam's circle and Izala. The graduates emphasized their break with Izala in some contexts while downplaying it in others. Rijiyar Lemo's biography of Ādam – the place where the graduates' rejection of Izala is most clearly and sharply articulated – was written in Arabic, not Hausa. Given the large number of Nigerian figures and places Rijiyar Lemo mentions in the book, Rijiyar Lemo may have envisioned Nigerian Arabophone scholars as his primary audience. The biography, in other words, was not necessarily aimed at a mass audience. Worth noting too is that Ādam, in his oral, Hausa-language intellectual autobiography *Tarihin Rayuwata a Ilmi* (The History of My Life in Knowledge), mentioned the Islamic University only briefly, and he included little discussion of the Salafi intellectual canon. Ādam often glossed over his circle's split with Izala, referring to his membership in Izala in the 1980s without rancor and, simultaneously, identifying Izala – even in the 1980s – as part of

40 Rijiyar Lemo, *Ayyāmī*, 32.
41 Rijiyar Lemo, *Ayyāmī*, 33.
42 Interview with Pakistan.

"Ahlussunnah."[43] These lectures were intended for mass audiences. In different contexts, the graduates of Medina have framed their relationship with Izala, and the significance of their time in Medina for that relationship, differently.

Within the broader anti-Sufi fold, there have been sharp differences of opinion about theology. The graduates of Medina have invoked the Salafi canon to defend their positions and distinguish themselves from Izala. Partly for this reason, the Medina graduates came to be perceived as a distinct and troublesome group by some Izala leaders.[44] Yet the Salafis around Ādam continued to work with Izala, especially with reformers like Pakistan. All of these leaders are interconnected through friendship, marriage, and kinship. In conflicts with hereditary Muslim rulers and other adversaries, Izala and the graduates of Medina have often presented a united front.

The subtle differences between the Medina graduates and Izala did, however, have consequences in terms of discursive styles and the content of preaching. For Ādam and his circle, shifting the emphasis from identifying themselves as members of Izala to describing themselves as representatives of Salafism was a way of universalizing their identity. One graduate of Medina, Shaykh Abdullahi Garangamawa, explained that from the perspective of the graduates, Izala is "only an organization," one with a specific history and context. Being part of "Ahlussunnah," on the other hand, is "an approach, dating from the time of the Messenger of God." This approach is distinguished by adherence to the Qurʾan and the Sunna. "Everyone you see inside [Izala] is Ahlussunnah, but it is not necessary for everyone who is Ahlussunnah to be inside [Izala]." Some Salafis preferred not to label themselves as Izala, Garangamawa added, "Because in the past, there was foolishness . . . and excommunications and some things that had no basis."[45] Referring to Salafism as an "approach" is itself one marker of a global Salafi identity.

In the 1990s, as Ādam and his circle began to present Salafism as a category that transcended the boundaries of Izala as an organization, their preaching became accessible to new constituencies, especially professionals and civil servants. Rijiyar Lemo wrote:

> There had been among them some who evaded the Sunna because of the harshness (*ghilẓa*) in social interaction, cruelty in expression, and excess in *takfīr* and driving people out (*tanfīr*) which characterized some individuals of the Society. Then when they saw a form of *daʿwa* unaligned with a sect, not fanatic toward a group, and at the same time one whose leaders were endowed with the

[43] In the latter lecture (delivered in Kano, 2006), for example, when discussing Sufi attempts to shut down a Salafi mosque in the mid-1980s, Adam says, "The number of Kano's Ahlussunnah at that time did not reach a tenth of Kano's Ahlussunnah now."

[44] Ben Amara, "The Izala Movement," 267.

[45] Interview with Garangamawa, Kano.

spirit of good treatment toward the one who is different, they appreciated the Sunna. [Ādam], may Allah have mercy on him, was a pioneer and a leader in this direction.[46]

The graduates of Medina placed a premium on the ability to demonstrate textual knowledge. In recruiting teachers for lessons at the mosque, Ādam emphasized scholarly credentials, for he "saw the majority of those who undertook *da'wa* and instruction as weak in knowledge and poor in understanding."[47] Graduates of Medina were attempting to enforce a new standard for intellectual accomplishment among reformist preachers and to shift the tone and focus of their preaching.

One of the greatest testimonies to the efficacy of the graduates' bid to pioneer a new style of preaching and education has been their success in influencing and even producing locally trained Salafis. For example, one prominent Nigerian Salafi is Shaykh Aminu Daurawa (b. 1969), whose televised lectures on Islamic history have earned him attention, along with his preaching and his service as commander general of the Kano State Hisbah (a law enforcement body with responsibility for public morality) starting in 2011. Daurawa's education occurred within Nigeria rather than at the Islamic University. Daurawa writes in his intellectual autobiography that he studied with numerous scholars in Nigeria. He emphasizes his relationship with Shaykh Abdulwahhab Abdullah, one of the Medina graduates. He adds, "There are some scholars who influenced me in my life, but by means of studying their books and listening to their cassettes." He lists Ibn 'Uthaymīn and al-Albānī as two major influences and also mentions canonical authorities such as Ibn Taymiyya. Of al-Albānī, Daurawa writes, "All his books that have appeared in the market, and the cassettes, I purchase them, because of their many benefits."[48] The Medina graduates, in other words, have helped bring domestically trained northern Nigerian Salafis into intensive contact with the global Salafi canon.

When considering the relationship between Izala and "Ahlussunnah," an interesting comparative case is the relationship between Al-Gam'iyya al-Shar'iyya and Anṣār al-Sunna al-Muḥammadiyya in Egypt. Richard Gauvain categories the latter as Salafi but notes that the former is not, even though they are widely perceived as Salafi. The former maintain an Ash'arī theological affiliation and work within the schools of law, and even (unlike Nigeria's Izala) show sympathy for Sufism. Yet there is institutional and social overlap between the two movements; preachers

46 Rijiyar Lemo, *Ayyāmī*, 33.
47 Rijiyar Lemo, *Ayyāmī*, 48.
48 Aminu Ibrahim Daurawa, "Tarihin Shaikh Aminu Ibrahim Daurawa," 2013. Available at: http://zakariahdg.blogspot.com/2013/12/tarihin-shaikh-aminu-ibrahim-daurawa.html; accessed October 2014.

within Anṣār al-Sunna al-Muḥammadiyya regularly speak in mosques affiliated with Al-Gamʿiyya al-Sharʿiyya.[49] In Egypt as in Nigeria, Salafis who adhere strictly to the Salafi canon nonetheless operate within a broader religious field of sympathetic allies.

Local Daʿwa in the Context of Universal History

In their own eyes, the Nigerian graduates returned from Medina as spokesmen for a global Salafi worldview, rather than a parochial Nigerian anti-Sufism with questionable textual bases. Religious action, for the graduates of Medina, centres on *daʿwa*, a category that is intended to be at once an embodiment of a universal Islamic mission and a locally situated practice.

The Arabic word *daʿwa* can be translated as the "call" to Islam. Those who practice *daʿwa* are *duʿāt* (singular *dāʿiya*). Rijiyar Lemo's memoir of Ādam bears the Arabic subtitle *Dāʿiyat al-Jīl wa-Mufassir al-Tanzīl* (The Preacher of the Generation and the Exegete of the Revelation). These epithets stress two core aspects of Salafi identity: an activist stance toward Islamic reform and a mastery of scripture. Salafi leaders enjoined followers in Kano to be activists too. In one 2006 lecture, Ādam told the crowd, "Understanding sunna does not mean 'registering' with some 'registration card' such that if you enter your name, that's it, you become a member.... The creed of *Ahl al-Sunna wa-l-Jamāʿa* does not mean ... *daʿwa* with the mouth alone without any work that makes it real on a daily basis."[50]

Daʿwa, in Salafi discourses worldwide, is not limited to converting non-Muslims to Islam; it includes calling other Muslims to become better Muslims. The *dāʿiya* is, for Salafi thinkers in Saudi Arabia and elsewhere, a universal category. An article published in the journal of the Muslim World League in 1990 outlined how the *dāʿiya* needed to possess certain qualities to succeed, including "following the example of the Messenger" (*iqtifāʾ āthār al-rasūl*). The article presented the *dāʿiya*'s struggle as basically unchanging:

> For if our pious predecessors were fought by ignorant classes (*ṭabaqāt jāhila*), failed leaderships (*riʾāsāt fāshila*), obscure tribes, and belligerent, combative peoples, we today are fought by classes who claim they are cultured. Indeed, we are fought by unbelieving governments who have jointly decided and jointly stated that they will fight Islam and unite to block its *daʿwa* and to judge its men.[51]

[49] Gauvain, *Salafi Ritual Purity: In the Presence of God* (New York: Routledge, 2013), 37–38.

[50] Jaʿfar Maḥmūd Ādam, untitled lecture, mid-2000s, Kano.

[51] Muḥammad Maḥmūd al-Sawwāb, "Shakhsiyyat al-Dāʿiya Hiya al-ʿĀmil al-Asāsī fī Najāḥihi," *Al-Rābiṭa*, 29:34 (May 1990), 21.

Nigerian Salafi leaders' conception of *da'wa* is similar. Just as Nigerian Salafis have viewed their historical circumstances as fundamentally similar to those of other Salafis, so too have they viewed their core mission as identical to that of other Salafi figures, past and present.

The Nigerian graduates of Medina have urged their followers to view themselves as part of a broader community of people who understand monotheism correctly. Nigerian Salafi leaders narrate local events in ways that attempt to transcend local chronologies and geographies. The community to which Nigerian Salafis link their local community's experiences includes the Qur'anic prophets before Muḥammad, but its historical center is the Prophet and his Companions. The community extends forward in time from the Prophet to any Muslim, in any place, considered to follow his Sunna. As Chapter 6 details, Salafi leaders have presented their struggles in Kano as part of an ongoing struggle wherein true Muslims, surrounded by hostile communities and/or faithless Muslims, are a permanent vanguard and a vulnerable minority.

African graduates of Saudi Arabian universities have noted that local contexts shape the challenges each *dā'iya* faces. In this way, they echo the theorizations of Salafi outreach that al-Jāmī proposed decades earlier (see Chapter 2). In 2001, at a conference the Saudi Arabian government held in Kano for African graduates of Saudi Islamic universities, a Malian scholar outlined five challenges for the African *dā'iya*: converting non-Muslims, purifying Islamic practices, fighting "Christianization" (*al-tanṣīr*) and Westernization, opposing Sufism, and confronting "waves of Shī'ism." In West Africa, the scholar continued, fighting polytheistic beliefs and opposing Sufism were the most salient challenges, due to the historical linkages between Sufism and the initial Islamization of the region.[52]

Strikingly, however, in keeping with their effort to project a universal Salafi identity, the graduates of Medina have identified a broad range of theological enemies, including sects with a minimal presence in Nigeria. Attacking sects perceived as heterodox has allowed Salafis to draw boundaries around their identity, emphasizing what it is at the same time that they emphasize what it is not. Salafis in Kano are known for opposing Sufism, especially the Tijaniyya order, which they charge with introducing heresies into Islam. Yet they also oppose the Shī'a, the Ahmadiyya, and "Qur'āniyyūn," meaning people who take the Qur'an as their sole scriptural authority, rejecting the Sunnah. All of these groups represent, for Salafis, present incarnations of longstanding threats to genuine

[52] Muḥammad al-Bashīr Dakūrī, "Al-Da'wa wa-al-Du'ā fī Ifrīqiyā: Al-Wāqi' wa-l-Taṭallu'āt," in *Buḥūth Multaqa Khādim al-Haramayn al-Sharīfayn li-Khirriji al-Jāmi'āt al-Sa'ūdiyya min Ifrīqiya, al-Awwal: al-Muqām bi-Nayjīriyā, Kanu taḥta Ishrāf al-Jāmi'a al-Islāmiyya bi-l-Madīna al-Munawwara* (Medina: al-Jāmi'a al-Islāmiyya bi-l-Madīna al-Munawwara, 2003), 539.

Muslims. In a lecture on the Qurʾāniyyūn, Ādam traced their founding back to doctrinal controversies in the early centuries of the Muslim community, citing the Shīʿa, the Muʿtazila, and the Kharijites as the forerunners of the Qurʾāniyyūn. These three sects, he said, "are groups that began refusing to apply the *aḥādīth* of the Messenger of Allah, may Allah bless him and grant him peace, except they did not say so openly. They followed some principles and methods that they invented . . . by means of which they brought these evil creeds and caused destruction with them."[53] Qurʾanism, Ādam said, met the same fate in all of its historical incarnations: "contempt in the world and the afterlife. Here in the world Allah humiliates them."[54] As often in his lectures, Ādam stressed the importance of avoiding any heresy: "We must distance ourselves from any heresy, for every heresy is an error, and a path toward fire. Therefore any form of worship that the Messenger of Allah, may Allah bless him and grant him peace, did not use to worship Allah, may He be glorified and exalted, and the Companions did not use to worship Allah, is not worship."[55] Viewing Nigeria through the lens of global Salafism has meant, for the graduates of Medina, reading the local religious landscape as a reinstantiation of primordial theological conflicts in Islam. This attitude treats not just Sufism but any sect perceived to deviate from Sunni orthodoxy as a dangerous rival.

Conclusion

Graduates of the Islamic University of Medina are prominent leaders in the "Ahlussunnah" network in Kano. They have made use of their learning at the university and of different aspects of the classical and contemporary Salafi canons to promote a global Salafi identity. The Medina graduates built a wide audience, including youth but also married women and certain social and political elites, partly through their ability to shift intellectual registers. As the next chapters show, the Medina graduates' popular messages have often emphasized scripture in an accessible way, while in other intellectual settings Salafi leaders demonstrated their mastery of Salafi methodologies of *ḥadīth* criticism and engaged a variety of Salafi thinkers. Mastery of Salafi methodologies and the Salafi canon proved particularly useful to the Medina graduates when they engaged in technical debates with rival Nigerian Salafis such as "hardliners" from the Izala movement or with the radical preacher Muḥammad Yūsuf (see Chapter 7). The graduates invoked their learning at Medina

[53] Jaʿfar Maḥmūd Ādam, *'Yan Alkuraniyyun: ('Yan Tatsine, Kala-Kato): Tarihin Kafuwarsu da Akidunsu* (Kano: Usman bin Affan Islamic Trust, 2005), 4.

[54] Ādam, *'Yan Alkuraniyyun*, 24–5.

[55] Ādam, *'Yan Alkuraniyyun*, 26.

and the authority of contemporary Salafi thinkers in such debates to discredit rivals and present them as intellectually deficient. These intellectual attacks on their rivals reinforced Salafi leaders' self-presentations as highly credentialed, sober representatives of Islamic *daʿwa*.

The Salafi *daʿwa* in Kano and throughout northern Nigeria departs in key ways from the anti-Sufi reformism that preceded it and still competes with it. Despite shared priorities between Izala and the Medina graduates, the Ahlussunnah network emphasizes a broader canon, identifies a wider range of theological enemies, and presents a larger identity that links local and global concerns outside the framework of a hierarchical organization. The Medina graduates have invoked the full Salafi canon to delegitimize the positions of their rivals in Izala. The graduates have at times downplayed their connections to Izala in favor of asserting an allegedly universal identity as Salafis. Yet the graduates have then reinscribed this universal identity in the local environment by connecting local struggles to broader histories and geographies. An ability to shift between local concerns and translocal identities has lain at the heart of these Salafis' rhetorical power.

Part II

The Canon in Action

4 Teaching the Canon

On the evening of Wednesday, August 16, 2006, Shaykh Jaʿfar Maḥmūd Ādam arrived late to the Saʿd Ibn Abī Waqqāṣ Mosque in Kano, Nigeria.[1] He apologized to the crowd. He was tired from travel but would still deliver his lecture as planned. He would overcome his fatigue, he explained, because his speaking style was calibrated to the mood of his audience:

> I'm one of the kind of people who, often, if I start to speak, those who are in front of me have an influence on what I should say, with the assistance of the Lord. I mean, those who are around me – if they are sleeping, there is a kind of speaking I will do. If, too, if they are disciplined, there is a kind of speaking I will do. If they are old, there is a kind of speaking I will do. Or if they are youth, the vanguard . . .

At this, the assembled young men erupted into cheers and laughter. The Shaykh laughed too. But then he turned serious, and introduced his subject. When he spoke a name, the room fell silent.

> Imam Aḥmad ibn Ḥanbal: one of the scholars of the Sunna who came earliest in history. He is given the nickname "Imam of *Ahl al-Sunna wa-l-Jamāʿa*." He is a man whose life the Lord Allah oriented toward working with *ḥadīth* reports of the Messenger of Allah, may Allah bless him and grant him peace. Writing them down, compiling them, teaching them to the Muslim community. He put them into practice during his lifetime. . . . Imam Aḥmad ibn Ḥanbal has a small abbreviated book that his son wrote himself from his mouth, in other words from the mouth of his father. In it he mentions some principles, or you might say poles, or pillars, on which the creed of Ahlussunnah is built.[2]

This excerpt of Ādam's lecture confronts the outsider with the question at the heart of this study: Why would scores of young Nigerian Muslims flock to a mosque on a Wednesday night to hear about an eighth-century *ḥadīth* compiler?

In the previous two chapters, I showed that exposure to the Salafi canon was a primary source of differences between Izala and the graduates of

[1] Saʿd Ibn Abī Waqqāṣ (d. ca. 674) was a Companion of the Prophet Muḥammad and an important military, political, and diplomatic leader in the early Muslim community.

[2] Jaʿar Ādam, untitled lecture, 16 August 2006, Kano.

Medina. Here I argue that teaching the canon represents the Medina graduates' fundamental mechanism for transmitting a Salafi identity in Nigeria. For audiences, the canon has a multifaceted appeal rooted in its ability to anchor their Salafi identity in a long and global scholarly tradition.

Aspects of Salafi thought and identity can be, and often are, transmitted without reference to the canon. To put it crudely, one can grow a long beard, wear short trousers, criticize Sufis' prayers and behaviors, and denounce the Shīʿa without having read Ibn Taymiyya. Moreover, as subsequent chapters explain further, Nigerian Salafis often shift discursive registers. For popular audiences, Salafis tend to emphasize Qurʾan and *ḥadīth* but downplay the broader canon.

Yet it is familiarity with the canon that equips aspiring Salafis with the intellectual tools most valuable for articulating their worldview. This familiarity also allows Salafis to defend canonical authors such as Ibn Taymiyya and Ibn ʿAbd al-Wahhāb, and thereby refute charges against themselves, especially the idea that they practice a kind of "Wahhābism" that, in the eyes of Salafis' critics, introduces a blameworthy innovation into Allah's religion. Teaching the canon allows Salafis to offer their pupils an affirmative identity and a scholarly path that allows for improvisation within a set of authorized discourses.

In contrast to highly technical discussions with theological rivals (including fellow Salafis and/or Salafi-jihadis), where they invoke the canon heavily, Salafis teach in what might be called a middle register. In the middle register, Salafis teach core works in the canon, especially *ḥadīth* collections and famous texts on creed such as Ibn ʿAbd al-Wahhāb's *Kitāb al-Tawḥīd*. The success of this method can be seen in the crowds that fill mosques when Salafi shaykhs lecture. Additionally, as noted in the previous chapter, there are now many Nigerian Salafis who were educated inside Nigeria, but who are nevertheless deeply familiar with the full range of canonical authority and look to figures like Shaykhs Muḥammad Nāṣir al-Dīn al-Albānī, ʿAbd al-ʿAzīz ibn Bāz, and Muḥammad ibn al-ʿUthaymīn as standards for defining creed and handling foundational texts. These canonical shaykhs frequently switched registers themselves, sometimes articulating the Salafi creed with reference to Qurʾan and *ḥadīth* alone.[3] Around the world, Salafi pedagogy is characterized by significant flexibility.

The Salafi educational model in Nigeria makes *ḥadīth* the queen of the Islamic sciences, rather than Mālikī jurisprudence, which is the centerpiece of the classical model in northwest Africa. Salafis teach *ḥadīth* through canonical collections such as the *Forty Hadith* collection of

[3] Muḥammad Ṣāliḥ al-ʿUthaymīn, *ʿAqīdat Ahl al-Sunna wa-l-Jamāʿa* (Al-Riyāḍ: Muʾassasat al-Shaykh Muḥammad Ṣāliḥ al-ʿUthaymīn al-Khayriyya, 2009).

Shaykh Yaḥyā ibn Sharaf al-Nawawī (1233–77). *Ḥadīth* collections have been Nigerian Salafis' most effective tool for popularizing the study of the Salafi canon as a whole.

Alongside their efforts to teach *ḥadīth*, Nigerian Salafis have worked to spread the best-known canonical authors, particularly Ibn Taymiyya and Ibn ʿAbd al-Wahhāb. Shaykh Jaʿfar Ādam, Dr. Muḥammad Sani ʿUmar Rijiyar Lemo, and others in their circle have translated, in book form and in oral lessons, key texts by these canonical authors. Lessons about canonical authors, like lessons about *ḥadīth*, offer students deeper insight into the textual basis of the Salafi worldview. Lessons about these authors also provide opportunities to discuss the moral and intellectual examples set by these authors and to apply such examples to contemporary circumstances and problems. By teaching the canon, Nigerian Salafis aim to bring it to life.

As the last chapter noted, Nigerian Salafis have built a complex infrastructure for spreading their doctrine and increasing their followership. This infrastructure includes a network of mosques, a strong presence in electronic media, and a circuit of speaking engagements facilitated through the mosque network. This infrastructure supports, and is strengthened by, the informal courses that Nigerian Salafis offer on *ḥadīth* collections and canonical texts. Kano-based Salafis travel across northern Nigeria delivering lectures and courses. Ādam offered courses in Kano and Bauchi, an annual Ramadan *tafsīr* (Qurʾanic exegesis) in Maiduguri, and twice-weekly lectures at a university in Katsina (together with Rijiyar Lemo).[4] Salafis based in other cities delivered their own courses, such as Shaykh Muḥammad Awwal 'Albānī' in Zaria (1960–2014) and Dr. Aḥmad Gumi in Kaduna. In these diverse settings, Salafis offered up scriptural and canonical knowledge to thousands of formal and informal students – and then multiplied their audience by disseminating their teachings through recordings and online.

Challenging the Classical Model of Islamic Education

Nigerian Salafis have elaborated a full-fledged educational model that both borrows from and competes with the classical model of Islamic education in northwest Africa. The latter model centers on the person-to-person transmission of texts from specialist teachers to students who have come to study a specific text with a specific person. Students typically begin their studies with the Qurʾan, memorizing part or all of it under the supervision of a teacher. Following the completion of the Qurʾan,

[4] Muḥammad al-Thānī ʿUmar Mūsā Rijiyar Lemo, *Ayyāmī maʿa Dāʿiyat al-Jīl wa-Mufassir al-Tanzīl* (Kano: Dar al-Ḥikma li-l-Kitāb al-Islāmī, 2011), 72.

students seek instruction in different branches of Islamic knowledge, with an emphasis on Mālikī jurisprudence. The classical model also includes the study of grammar, creed, Sufism, Arabic literature, exegesis, and other subjects. Because students learn from specialists, a full education often requires moving from teacher to teacher, and sometimes from place to place, over years or decades.

The classical model features a largely standardized curriculum, particularly for Mālikī jurisprudence. The curriculum consists primarily of North African and Andalusian Arab authors who lived during the first ten centuries of Islam.[5] As they advance through the classical curriculum, students read more and more complicated manuals of jurisprudence. Students first learn the essentials of creed and worship through texts like the *Mukhtaṣar al-Akhḍarī* (Al-Akhḍarī's Summary). The classical model does not treat such texts, in and of themselves, as sufficient for transmitting correct practice: students depend on teachers to explain the meaning of terms (through translation from classical Arabic into vernacular languages) and to answer detailed questions about practicalities (for example, how far to wash up the forearms when performing ablutions). The teacher's presence and commentary are essential to the effective transmission of knowledge.

Ḥadīth was part of this classical curriculum, but *ḥadīth* reports often appeared within other texts and only sometimes as their own branch of study. Tal Tamari comments, regarding her field research on the classical model in Mali, that "hadith, although frequently mentioned in descriptions of West African curricula, and reasonably well represented in West African libraries, seems not to have been studied as an independent subject by members of my sample, except for the two less traditionally educated, Wahhabi-leaning scholars."[6] This does not mean that classical scholars were unfamiliar with *ḥadīth*. Bruce Hall and Charles Stewart, who have traced a "core curriculum" in Sahelian Africa by cross-referencing the contents of private libraries with prominent citations in works by well-known precolonial scholars, identify *ḥadīth* as a subset of studies of the Prophet Muḥammad, one of six major areas in the core curriculum. West African scholars studied the *ḥadīth* collections of al-Bukhārī and Muslim. Classical scholars also studied small collections such as those in the "Forty Hadith" genre, including the collection of al-Nawawī,[7] which is a favorite for contemporary Salafis. Many of the

[5] Tal Tamari, "Islamic Higher Education in West Africa: Some Examples from Mali" in *Islam in Africa*, edited by Thomas Bierschenk and Georg Stauth (Münster: Lit Verlag, 2002), 91–128; M. Abdurrahman and Peter Canham, *The Ink of the Scholar: The Islamic Tradition of Education in Nigeria* (Lagos: Macmillan Nigeria, 1978).

[6] Tamari, "Islamic Higher Education," 109.

[7] Bruce Hall and Charles Stewart, "The Historic 'Core Curriculum' and the Book Market in Islamic West Africa," in *The Trans-Saharan Book Trade: Manuscript Culture, Arabic*

best-known scholars in precolonial Islamic Africa were masters of *ḥadīth*: for example, the Timbuktu-based Shaykh Aḥmad Bābā (1556–1627) described his father as "a specialist in *ḥadīth*, in jurisprudence, rhetoric, and logic."[8] Nevertheless, in the classical model, jurisprudence was the queen of the Islamic sciences.

The Salafi educational model parallels the classical model in its emphasis on studying texts under the personalized tutelage of a specialist. The Salafi model is more horizontal, however: students can begin with a variety of texts, rather than following a more or less set sequence as in the classical model. The Salafi model in Nigeria reflects the intertwining of two influences: first, the local environment (as discussed in Chapter 3, many Nigerian Salafis initially studied in classical settings in Nigeria); and second, the study circles (*ḥalaqāt*, singular *ḥalqa*) that many Nigerian Salafis attended in Saudi Arabia, for example at the Prophet's Mosque in Medina. Alongside their forays into establishing institutionalized schools, Salafis have adopted a tutorial style both because it is familiar to Nigerian audiences and because it reflects their own experiences at home and in Saudi Arabia.

Given this overlap, we can say that the Salafi educational model in Nigeria diverges from the classical model more in content than in pedagogy. The two models also share some material. Both, for example, favorably invoke the Andalusian scholar al-Qāḍī ʿIyāḍ ibn Mūsā (1083–1149). Yet differences loom large. The Salafi curriculum emphasizes creed and *ḥadīth*, rather than jurisprudence. The curriculum Nigerian Salafis offered resembles, in condensed form, the curriculum that shaykhs like Ibn Bāz offered in Saudi Arabia. One Saudi Arabian student who attended the *ḥalaqāt* of Ibn Bāz during the last two decades of the Shaykh's life studied major *ḥadīth* collections, works by Ibn Taymiyya and Ibn ʿAbd al-Wahhāb, and various works in exegesis, jurisprudence, and creed.[9]

There are deep, local historical antecedents to the Nigerian Salafi pedagogical model. In West Africa, reformists of different stripes, including Salafis, have challenged the classical model since the late colonial period. These reformist challenges have taken numerous forms. Strongly influenced by both colonial schools and institutions like Egypt's Al-Azhar University, reformists began to found their own schools in the 1940s. In both Anglophone and Francophone West Africa, these hybrid schools incorporated study of the Qurʾan, but also mathematics and physical

Literacy and Intellectual History in Muslim Africa, edited by Graziano Krätli and Ghislaine Lydon, 109–74 (Leiden: Brill, 2011).

8 Quoted in John Hunwick, "Timbuktu: A Refuge of Scholarly and Righteous Folk," *Sudanic Africa* 14 (2003): 13–20; 15.

9 "Al-Sīra al-Dhātiyya," website of Dr. Saʿīd ibn ʿAlī bin Wahf al-Qaḥṭānī, undated. Available at: www.binwahaf.com/portal/pages/view/22.html; accessed December 2014.

sciences. Above all, hybrid schools have promoted the study of the Arabic language with the goal that students will attain fluency more rapidly than in the classical model. Hybrid schools – whether the Franco-Arabe "medersas" of Mali, Senegal, and elsewhere, or the "Islamiyya" schools of northern Nigeria[10] – have competed with both classical Islamic schools and Western-style government schools.

In addition to promoting new forms of schooling, reformists repackaged the raw materials of classical curricula. In late colonial Northern Nigeria, Shaykh (later Professor) Haliru Binji, a colleague of Shaykh Abubakar Gumi and like Gumi a graduate of the School for Arabic Studies, abridged Mālikī texts and translated them into Hausa to facilitate direct access to Islamic law for the growing population of northern Nigerian elites literate in Hausa.[11] In late colonial Guinea, the reformist Kabiné Diané published works with titles like *Recueil des cinq piliers de l'Islam* (Compendium of the Five Pillars of Islam) that sought to present streamlined, easily accessible Islamic teachings.[12] Reformists in the late colonial and early independence period began translating Qur'anic verses and *aḥādīth* into European and vernacular languages, partly to meet the growing demand for religious knowledge among African graduates of colonial schools who had no mastery of Arabic.[13] Four decades before Ādam translated al-Nawawī's *Forty Ḥadīth* into Hausa, Gumi had already done so.

Postcolonial Salafis have built on this diverse reformist legacy while marrying it with the Salafi emphasis on direct, unmediated engagement with the Qur'an and *ḥadīth*. For Salafis, the way to popularize Islamic knowledge is not by streamlining the Mālikī curriculum but by promoting knowledge of *ḥadīth*. Salafis walk their students through an increasingly complicated series of *ḥadīth* collections and in the process discuss techniques for evaluating the reliability of the reports themselves. Key texts in the Salafi curriculum include, in addition to al-Nawawī's *Forty Ḥadīth*, the collections *Riyāḍ al-Ṣāliḥīn* (The Gardens of the Righteous), also by al-Nawawī, and *Bulūgh al-Marām min Adillat al-Aḥkām* (Attaining the Objective by the Evidences of Rulings) by Ibn Ḥajar al-ʿAsqalānī (1372–1449). Nigerian Salafis have taught these collections as well as the two most famous collections by al-Bukhārī and Muslim. For Salafis, jurisprudence comes close to being merely one kind of applied *ḥadīth* study – in

[10] Jonathan Reynolds, *The Time of Politics (Zamanin Siyasa): Islam and the Politics of Legitimacy in Northern Nigeria (1950–1966)* (San Francisco: International Scholars Publications, 1998).

[11] Haliru Binji, *Ibada da Hukunci a Addinin Musulunci*, Parts I and II (Zaria: Gaskiya Corporation, 1957 and 1960).

[12] Kabiné Diané, *Recueil des cinq piliers de l'Islam* (Imprimerie A. Diop, 1959).

[13] Vincent Monteil, "Un visionnaire musulman sénégalais (1946–1965)," *Archives de sociologie des religions* 19:19 (1965): 69–98.

the terminology of al-Albānī, Salafis rely not on the established schools, but on *fiqh al-ḥadīth* (the jurisprudence of *ḥadīth*).[14]

Ḥadīth collections have been incorporated into the Salafi canon in their own right and also through the numerous commentaries that have built up around them. For example, the eighteenth-century Yemeni scholar Ibn al-Amīr wrote an explanatory commentary on *Bulūgh al-Marām* entitled *Subul al-Salām* (The Ways of Peace), which in turn became the object of a commentary by al-Albānī. Saudi institutions have invested in disseminating (and thereby laying claim to) such collections. Or to take another example, the Muslim World League produced an edition of *Riyāḍ al-Ṣāliḥīn* with footnotes explaining difficult terms. The league did not articulate strategic or ideological goals surrounding the publication but seemed to indicate that simply disseminating *ḥadīth* would benefit Muslims: the League's Secretary General spoke of the collection's "small size and great benefit."[15] These collections are not exclusive to the Salafi canon – as we saw earlier, the classical Mālikī model of northwest Africa also incorporated al-Nawawī – but in Salafi hands, these collections serve the purpose of giving Salafi audiences access to the raw materials that Salafis use to react to life situations.

These collections derive *aḥādīth* from the six canonical Sunni *ḥadīth* collections but render them more accessible to the nonexpert than those voluminous and detail-rich works. For example, al-Nawawī's *Forty Ḥadīth* does not include the full chains of narrators (*asānīd*, singular *isnād*) for each *ḥadīth*, but rather the text of the report and the first narrator only. In oral and written lessons, Salafis can walk students through the process of sourcing and evaluating reports. Ādam's Hausa translation of *Forty Ḥadīth* repeatedly refers the reader to the six canonical collections, as well as to works in the Salafi canon, such as al-Albānī's *Silsilat al-Aḥādīth al-Ṣaḥīḥa*, which lists *ḥadīth* reports that al-Albani had personally verified according to his standards.[16] In other words, small collections offer the beginner an introduction to *ḥadīth* study while offering the advanced student insight into the larger world of Salafi *ḥadīth* scholarship. Even as Salafis use collections like *Forty Ḥadīth* in teaching, they have treated the *aḥādīth* in them with the same critical tools they have used for evaluating the reports in the larger collections of al-Bukhārī, Muslim, and others.

[14] Stéphane Lacroix, "Between Revolution and Apoliticism: Nasir al-Din al-Albani and His Impact on the Shaping of Contemporary Salafism" in *Global Salafism: Islam's New Religious Movement*, edited by Roel Meijer, 58–80 (New York: Columbia University Press, 2009), 65.

[15] ʿAbd Allāh ibn ʿAbd al-Muḥsin al-Turkī, "Introduction" in Yaḥyā ibn Sharaf al-Nawawī, *Riyāḍ al-Ṣāliḥīn* (Mecca: The Muslim World League, undated), 5.

[16] Yahya al-Nawawi, *Al-Arbaʿuna Hadithan*, translated and annotated by Sheikh Jaʿafar Mahmoud Adam, edited by Muhammad Rabiʿu Umar Rijiyar Lemo and Muhammad Sani Umar R/Lemo, second edition (Kano: Sheikh Jaʿafar Islamic Documentation Centre, 2011).

Teaching Qur᾽an and Ḥadīth

As Wilfred Cantwell Smith and William Graham have argued, scripture is more than just a written genre. Smith calls scripture "a human activity," pointing to the layers of interpretation and contestation that surround texts.[17] Among these layers is the oral dimension of scripture. Graham writes, "The spoken word of scripture has been overwhelmingly the most important medium through which religious persons and groups throughout history have known and interacted with scriptural texts."[18] This oral dimension of scripture comes to the foreground in education, or attempts to transmit scriptures to new audiences. Both the classical model of Islamic education in Northwest Africa and the Salafi pedagogical model emphasize oral engagement with scripture.

Graham's emphasis on orality raises questions that are useful for understanding how Nigerian Salafis teach scripture and how they teach the Salafi canon. As Graham comments,

> We need to know more about the ways in which memorization and recitation of scriptural texts are related to movements of revival and reform. In addition to any connection between the upsurge in reading, recitation, and memorization of scripture and the renewed stress on the authority and meaning of scripture, other factors also deserve attention. For example, the "internalizing" of important texts through memorization and recitation can serve as an effective educational or indoctrinational discipline. Nor should we overlook the importance of publicly bolstering piety and faith and increasing personal and group enthusiasm by providing for constant reading and reciting of a community's authoritative scripture in every aspect of its life, from ritual to instruction. A shared text – one that can be chanted in unison and constantly referred to as a proof text common to an entire community – is a powerful binding factor in any group, and especially in a minority group at odds with and bent on reforming or converting the larger society around it.[19]

All of these factors come into play for Salafis in northern Nigeria. Salafis have built large audiences through the seemingly simple practice of offering lessons in Qur᾽anic memorization.

Alongside the factors Graham mentions, there is the importance of scriptural translation to many movements of Islamic revival and reform. In East Africa, Swahili translations of the meanings of the Qur᾽an became theological battlegrounds, as figures like Shaykh Abdalla Saleh al-Farsy (1912–82) used their own translations to refute and undermine translations undertaken by sects like the Ahmadiyya.[20] Meanwhile, oral

[17] Wilfred Cantwell Smith, *What Is Scripture? A Comparative Approach* (Minneapolis: Fortress Press, 2005 [1993]), 18.

[18] William Graham, *Beyond the Written Word: Oral Aspects of Scripture in the History of Religion* (Cambridge: Cambridge University Press, 1987), 155.

[19] Graham, *Beyond the Written Word*, 161.

[20] Justo Lacunza-Balda, "Translations of the Quran into Swahili, and Contemporary Islamic Revival in East Africa," in *African Islam and Islam in Africa: Encounters between*

glosses can serve to demonstrate African scholars' Arabic proficiency and scriptural mastery. Recounting his intellectual career in one lecture, Ādam described how he began teaching a small group of adults in sessions where they read and recited ten verses of *Sūrat al-Baqara* (The Chapter of the Cow, the second and longest chapter of the Qur'an) each week. In 2011, I attended a lesson with a similar format at al-Furqān Mosque in Kano. The Salafi Shaykh Muḥammad Nazīfi Inuwa, a graduate of the Islamic University of Medina, guided a crowd of more than five hundred adult men and women in reciting ten verses of *Sūrat Nūḥ* (The Chapter of the Prophet Noah). Afterward, Inuwa gave a careful Hausa translation of the verses, devoting particular attention to vocabulary that would be obscure to his audience.

As Graham comments, there can be an "interpenetration of the written and the spoken word."[21] Although Ādam wrote relatively little during his lifetime, the Sheikh Ja'afar Islamic Documentation Centre in Kano has published posthumous written editions of lessons that Ādam delivered orally, such as his lessons on and translation of al-Nawawī's *Forty Ḥadīth*.[22] Lessons and texts provide a mutually reinforcing framework for Salafi authority.

The Anatomy of Salafi Ḥadīth Lessons in Northern Nigeria

The critical study of *ḥadīth* is central to Salafism, and Nigerian Salafis have invested considerable time in teaching *ḥadīth*. As Chapter 1 discussed, a distinguishing mark of Salafism is not just its emphasis on these reports but its willingness to reexamine core assumptions about the texts, as in al-Albānī's reevaluations of collections by al-Bukhārī and Muslim. For Salafis, the critical study of *ḥadīth* has had wide-ranging theological and political implications. In Medina, Nigerian Salafis immersed themselves in studying techniques like *takhrīj* – the "extraction" of reports used in other texts, an extraction undertaken to reevaluate the reports' quality – as well as *al-jarḥ wa-l-ta'dīl* (disparagement and praise), which can be used to assess the trustworthiness of *ḥadīth* transmitters, but also for assessing the religious qualifications of other scholars.[23]

Sufis and Islamists, edited by Eva Rosander and David Westerlund, 95–126 (Athens: Ohio University Press, 1997), 123.

21 Graham, *Beyond the Written Word*, 156.

22 Yahya al-Nawawi, *Al-Arba'una Hadithan*, translated and annotated by Sheikh Ja'afar Mahmoud Adam.

23 Roel Meijer, "Politicising *al-Jarḥ wa-l-Ta'dīl*: Rabī' b. Hādī al-Madkhalī and the Transnational Battle for Religious Authority," in *The Transmission and Dynamics of the Textual Sources of Islam: Essays in Honour of Harald Motzki*, edited by Nicolet Boekhoff-Van Der Voort, Kees Versteegh, and Joas Wagemakers, 375–99 (Leiden: Brill, 2011).

Nigerian Salafis teach *ḥadīth* collections in a relatively loose format involving weekly meetings in mosques, schools, or homes. Salafi teachers often sit at a desk piled with books while students sit on the floor. Teachers begin each lesson with the Prophet Muḥammad's *Khuṭbat al-Ḥāja* (The Sermon of Necessity, itself a *ḥadīth*), the same doxology the Medina graduates use for all their lectures. Teachers then proceed to a discussion built around word-for-word translations of the texts – a method also central to the classical model. These translations lead into extended commentaries. In sixty- or ninety-minute lessons, Salafi teachers might cover only a handful of *ḥadīth* reports. At the end of the lesson, the teacher typically takes questions from the audience. Students with burning questions can interrupt the lesson to ask them.

Many of the courses have been recorded and are available for purchase on CDs or as MP3 files or, increasingly, for free on Salafi-run websites and YouTube. In recent years, videos of lessons have spread online. This availability extends the lifetime and the audience of the lessons, allowing homebound women, taxi drivers, travelers, and others to follow along. For students who attend lessons in person, such courses expand opportunities to build a lifestyle suffused with Salafi pedagogy and worship. Weekly courses, Thursday night lectures on diverse topics, Friday communal prayers at Salafi mosques, and other opportunities allow for immersion in the Salafi community.

Nigerian Salafi teachers' commentaries have multiple facets, each of which represents particular aims. For one thing, Salafi shaykhs introduce the science of understanding and evaluating *ḥadīth* reports. They explain the meanings of technical terms and introduce principles for working with the reports. For example, commenting on a *ḥadīth* stating that two Muslims who fought each other to the death with swords would both enter hell (*al-nār*), Ādam explained that the *ḥadīth* covered any kind of weapon.[24] Such reports offer opportunities to discuss when to generalize and when not to. The lessons presume no Arabic proficiency on the part of the students, but Salafi scholars assume that many of their students have a basic ability to pronounce Arabic characters – an ability that many students might have derived from introductory studies within the classical system, including the memorization of the Qurʾan inside classical Qurʾan schools.

This technical knowledge holds a profound appeal as a tool for living a more virtuous and pure life, an aim that motivates many Muslims in movements of revival and reform.[25] For Salafis as for many other Muslims, *ḥadīth* reports provide keys for refining one's practice and

[24] Jaʿfar Maḥmūd Ādam, recording of third lesson on *Riyāḍ al-Ṣāliḥīn*, 13 March 1999. Available at: www.youtube.com/watch?v=AB2qE6oTAKU; accessed December 2014.

[25] Saba Mahmood, *Politics of Piety: The Islamic Revival and the Feminist Subject* (Princeton: Princeton University Press, 2005).

understanding of Islam, especially in an environment perceived as distracting and potentially sinful. Building from a *ḥadīth* that extolled the virtue of collective as opposed to individual daily prayer, Ādam told his students,

> Really, it's appropriate that if I know that at 8:00 one will conduct the prayer, at 7:45 one will call the prayer, then let's say at 7:30 I should come to the mosque. How many hours [are spent] at the office, and on my worldly affairs, an association, politics, a campaign for seeking office – and how many hours for glorifying Allah (*don girman Allah*)? If one holds a meeting for an electoral campaign, everyone knows the time it's happening but no one has set a time for getting up from it, and what about prayer? You'll only spend a quarter of an hour [on it]? . . . Come and spend thirty minutes in the mosque. You'll receive a major spiritual reward.[26]

Attending lessons on *ḥadīth* collections was not meant to check a spiritual box but to help progressively orient one's life toward purity.

Salafis familiarize their students with the most famous transmitters of *ḥadīth*, who included some of the Prophet Muḥammad's best-known Companions, such as his wife ʿĀʾisha.[27] For Salafis, studying the science of *ḥadīth* means immersing oneself in the values and modes of the Prophet's community, a form of knowledge key to the Salafi worldview. In one lecture, Ādam defined the criteria for being a Companion of the Prophet – interacting with him, having faith in his message, and dying in a state of fate. Ādam then underscored the preeminent status of the Companions in Sunni Islam, explaining that even though as individuals the Companions had sometimes erred, this "did not remove them from the status that Allah gave them" (*bai cire su daga matsayin da Allah ya ba su*). Ādam emphasized the importance of refraining from any insult against the Companions.[28] Working through these foundational ideas of Sunni Islam – and of Salafism – prepared audiences to handle more complex ideas, including the central Salafi contention that if a practice was unknown to the Companions, it was un-Islamic.

Familiarizing students with the science of *ḥadīth* prepares them to produce textual evidence to support Salafi positions in debates with opponents. Introducing a series of lessons on *Riyāḍ al-Ṣāliḥīn*, Ādam explained categories of *ḥadīth* such as *ṣaḥīḥ* (sound), *ḥasan* (good), and *ḍaʿīf* (weak). He added, "So both the sound *ḥadīth* and the good *ḥadīth*, one uses both of them for proof, in what concerns creed, in what concerns worship, in what concerns social relations. One does not use the weak *ḥadīth* for proof." (*To da hadisi sahihi da hadisi hasan dukkaninsu ana hujja da su, cikin abinda ya shafi akida, cikin abinda ya shafi ibada, cikin abinda ya shafi*

26 Ādam, recording of third lesson on *Riyāḍ al-Ṣāliḥīn*.
27 Ādam, recording of second lesson on *Riyāḍ al-Ṣāliḥīn*, 6 March 1999. Available at: www.youtube.com/watch?v=5GUiVbxB2LQ; accessed December 2014.
28 Ādam, recording of second lesson on *Riyāḍ al-Ṣāliḥīn*.

mu'amala. Hadisi da'ifi ba a hujja da shi).[29] Salafis' *ḥadīth* lessons are accessible to beginners. The shaykhs can count on their lessons having generic appeal in a broader social context that prizes the acquisition of Islamic knowledge.

Salafis situate *ḥadīth* collections historically. They recount the lives and aims of compilers, familiarizing audiences with al-Nawawī, al-Bukhārī, and others. Salafis describe the historical circumstances surrounding *ḥadīth* reports, introducing another avenue for teaching Muslim history. Narrating this history involves discussing other reports, and the resulting commentaries can facilitate a form of Qur'anic exegesis to the extent that *aḥādīth* can clarify the meanings of Qur'anic verses and vice versa. History lessons show how the Qur'an and the *ḥadīth* work together to undergird the Salafi worldview.

Commentaries on *ḥadīth* collections serve as gateways for Nigerian Salafis to introduce readers and students to the broader canon. In his discussion of *Riyāḍ al-Ṣāliḥīn*, Ādam cited texts such as Ibn al-Qayyim's *Ṭarīq al-Hijratayn wa-Bāb al-Sa'ādatayn* (The Path of the Two Migrations and the Door of the Two Happinesses) to expand on the meanings of individual reports.[30] Meanwhile, Salafi teachers introduce supplementary texts with cautions and framings, underscoring the sense that any piece of Islamic scholarship should be evaluated against the standard represented by the canon. For example, Shaykh Muḥammad Awwal 'Albānī' Zaria was one of the most famous Nigerian Salafi teachers of *ḥadīth*. In one introductory lesson on *Ṣaḥīḥ Muslim*, he noted that his lessons would incorporate various commentaries. He marked some of these commentaries as canonically legitimate, and others as useful but not entirely trustworthy. He introduced *Al-Mu'lim bi-Fawā'id Muslim* (The Informer of the Benefits of *Muslim*) by Shaykh Abū 'Abd Allāh al-Māzirī (1061–1141) with several qualifications. This commentary was useful for understanding issues in *Ṣaḥīḥ Muslim* related to jurisprudence, language, and history, he said,

> But as for what concerns creed, little of the book is reliable, for no other reason than that he has a sort of Ash'arī creed. Also, sometimes you see a confusion (*iḍṭirāb*) between Mu'tazilism and Jahmism [a Salafi term for proponents of a created Qur'an] . . . [One day] I may read something from his commentary in order to help us, because these mistakes don't mean that the book has become useless – it is a work by a human being.[31]

29 Ādam, recording of first lesson on *Riyāḍ al-Ṣāliḥīn*, Available at: www.youtube.com/watch?v=wcSvfvpnvBc; accessed December 2014.

30 Ādam, recording of first lesson on *Riyāḍ al-Ṣāliḥīn*, 27 February 1999.

31 Muḥammad Awwal 'Albānī' Zaria, recording of introduction to course of lessons on *Ṣaḥīḥ Muslim*, 10 October 2011. Available at: www.youtube.com/watch?v=2s28iXNk79c; accessed December 2014.

Salafis were especially concerned with safeguarding their students' understanding of creed. Noting uncertainties surrounding the creed of another commentator, al-Nawawī, Albānī Zaria told his students that he would be drawing not only on al-Nawawī's commentary on *Ṣaḥīḥ Muslim* but also on a contemporary Salafi commentary on al-Nawawī, *Al-Dalā'il al-Wafiyya fī Taḥqīq 'Aqīdat al-Imām al-Nawawī: A-Salafiyya am Khalafiyya?* (The Reliable Evidences in Investigating the Creed of Imam al-Nawawī – Is It Salafi or Latter-Day?) by Shaykh Mashhūr ibn Ḥasan Āl Salmān (b. 1960/1), a student of al-Albānī (the Albanian, not the Nigerian). Albānī Zaria went on to mention abridgements and commentaries he would use by al-Albānī himself, and by Ṣiddīq Ḥasan Khān, al-Madkhalī, and other members of the contemporary canon. The interaction among these texts highlights how Nigerian Salafi teachers might move from the basics of *ḥadīth* to the complexities of the contemporary canon, all within a single lesson.

Salafis often return to the question of how to operationalize *aḥādīth* in one's own life. In his introductory lesson on *Riyāḍ al-Ṣāliḥīn*, Ādam commented, "*Riyāḍ al-Ṣāliḥīn* is a book that contains *aḥādīth* of the Messenger of Allah, may Allah bless him and grant him peace, in chapters that teach social relations, in chapters that teach character in order to refine people's character from an evil state to a beautiful state."[32] Individual reports could lead into discussions of moral dilemmas: after reading the Prophet's statement, "There is no *hijra* (emigration) after the conquest [of Mecca]," Ādam proceeded to discuss how to determine whether a city counted as part of Islam's territory or not, which in turn determined whether it was necessary for Muslims to emigrate away from that place.[33] In this way, lessons on *ḥadīth* led to forays into politics, sometimes obliquely.

Even when Salafi shaykhs do not invoke the full canon in lessons, the canon's attitudes toward *ḥadīth* are implicitly present. Nigerian Salafis emphasize the idea that because *ḥadīth* reports are so important to defining creed and practice, they must be carefully evaluated. If one could not perform such evaluation oneself, turning to the canon was the appropriate solution. Commenting on Ādam's affinity for the works of al-Albānī, Rijiyar Lemo writes,

> He was always saying to me: "We are not able to trace *aḥādīth* to their likely places of origin (*miẓānihā*), and cite them [by verifying their chains of transmission], and judge between them, sound and weak. All that concerns us is that people known for their mastery in this field are working with them; like Shaykh Nāṣir al-Dīn al-Albānī, and we should hold fast to the results of their researches unless

[32] Ādam, recording of first lesson on *Riyāḍ al-Ṣāliḥīn*.
[33] Ādam, recording of second lesson on *Riyāḍ al-Ṣāliḥīn*.

the difference between it, and the proof and clear evidence (*al-ḥujja wa-l-burhān*), becomes plain to us."[34]

Ādam's students received an understanding of *ḥadīth* that had been filtered through the Medina graduates' extensive engagement not only with the foundational texts themselves but also with specifically Salafi treatments of these texts.

Teaching Ibn Taymiyya and Ibn ʿAbd Al-WahhāB

Of all the authors in the Salafi canon, Nigerian transmitters of the canon pay the most attention to Ibn Taymiyya and Ibn ʿAbd al-Wahhāb. This is not to say that figures like al-Albānī, Ibn Bāz, and Ibn ʿUthaymīn are unimportant to Nigerian Salafis – on the contrary, Nigerians frequently invoke these figures when attempting to discredit theological opponents and verify *aḥādīth* for use in their own writings. But in teaching, Nigerian Salafis are most concerned with ensuring that their students are familiar with more classical authors. As the beginning of this chapter noted, Ibn Taymiyya and Ibn ʿAbd al-Wahhāb featured heavily in the mosque lessons offered by Ibn Bāz himself.

In lessons, Ādam and Rijiyar Lemo stressed the global fame of Ibn Taymiyya and Ibn ʿAbd al-Wahhāb but also assumed little contextual knowledge on the part of their audiences. In 2008, Rijiyar Lemo taught Ibn Taymiyya's *Al-Tuḥfa al-ʿIrāqiyya fī al-Aʿmāl al-Qalbiyya* (The Iraqi Masterpiece on Actions of the Heart) in Katsina. His first lecture introduced Ibn Taymiyya's life and works. This was necessary, Rijiyar Lemo explained, because "there is no doubt, few know who Ibn Taymiyya is" (*babu shakka, kadan ne suka san wanene Ibn Taymiyya*).[35] Studying these shaykhs' writings, Nigerian Salafis suggested, was part of being an educated Muslim – and it gave students an intellectual advantage over many other Muslims.[36]

Ādam and other graduates of Medina did not initiate the teaching of works by Ibn Taymiyya and Ibn ʿAbd al-Wahhāb in northern Nigeria; Ādam himself studied *Kitāb al-Tawḥīd* in Kano before leaving for Medina. Yet the Medina graduates dedicated themselves with particular energy to the task of teaching these works. The earliest recording of Ādam in my possession captures a course of forty-five lectures he delivered on *Kitāb al-Tawḥīd* in 1997; he also taught Ibn ʿAbd al-Wahhāb's *Kashf*

[34] Rijiyar Lemo, *Ayyāmī*, 57.

[35] Muḥammad Sani ʿUmar Rijiyar Lemo, recording of first lesson on *al-Tuḥfa al-ʿIrāqiyya fī al-Aʿmāl al-Qalbiyya*, 13 May 2008.

[36] Jaʿfar Maḥmūd Ādam, recording of first lesson on *Kitāb al-Tawḥīd*, 6 September 1997; Muḥammad Sani ʿUmar Rijiyar Lemo, recording of first lesson on *Al-ʿUbūdiyya*, December 2005.

al-Shubuhāt (The Clearing of Doubts).[37] With these texts as with *ḥadīth* collections, Salafis read through and translated texts word by word, diving as necessary into commentary.

Nigerian Salafis explicitly situate these texts as Salafi discourses. Introducing his lecture series on Ibn Taymiyya's *Al-Waṣiyya al-Kubrā* (The Greatest Commandment), Rijiyar Lemo called it one of the "writings that Ibn Taymiyya left, which up to the present are enlightening the Muslim world. . . . He wrote all of them based on the Qurʾan and the Sunna of the Prophet, may Allah bless him and grant him peace, and according to the understanding of the pious predecessors."[38] Rijiyar Lemo situated Ibn Taymiyya as a particular kind of activist in relation to the Sunna, noting "the kind of effort and struggle that he endured in order to spread the Sunna of the Prophet, may Allah bless him and grant him peace, in his time – and the hatred, enmity, and unpopularity that he met with from those who sought to evade the light of the Sunna of the Prophet."[39] As the next chapter discusses, the ideal of the pious scholar spreading the Sunna in a world of enemies furnishes the core of Salafi politics.

Salafi teachers urged their students to follow along closely in the texts. They encouraged students to prize knowledge and undergo hardship in its pursuit. Opening a series of lessons on Ibn Taymiyya's *Al-ʿUbūdiyya*, Rijiyar Lemo told his students, "The inability to get the book in the market or the shortage [of copies] among the community (*karancinsa a hannun jamaʿa*) should not become a reason for not reading it." He urged them to copy the book by machine or even by hand, adding, "Don't you forget that when our scholarly forebears were studying, there was no photocopy machine. Not at all. If a scholar wanted a book, if he was able, he gave money for a copy of it, the entire book. . . . If you don't have money, take it and copy it [yourself]."

The theme of hardship in learning tracked closely with Salafi teachers' emphasis on the personal suffering that canonical scholars like Ibn Taymiyya had undergone in acquiring knowledge or defending the creed. Rijiyar Lemo added that such hardship had not ceased in recent times, connecting Ibn Taymiyya, and his own students in twenty-first-century Kano, to more contemporary canonical authorities:

Even in recent history, Muḥammad Nāṣir al-Dīn al-Albānī, at the very beginning of his search for knowledge, had no wealth (*a tarihi ma na kurkusa Muhammad Nasir al-Din al-Albani a farko-farkon nemansa da ilimi ba wani wadata ce da shi ba*). . . . He used to sit in al-Ẓāhiriyya Library studying. If he saw a book that

[37] Al-Imam Yahaya An-Nawawi, *Al-Arbaʿuna Hadithan*, translated by Sheikh Jaʿfar Mahmoud Ādam (Kano: Sheikh Jaʿafar Islamic Documentation Center, second edition, 2011), xii.

[38] Muḥammad Sani ʿUmar Rijiyar Lemo, recording of first lesson on *Al-Waṣiyya al-Kubrā*, 9 January 2007.

[39] Rijiyar Lemo, recording of first lesson on *Al-Waṣiyya al-Kubrā*.

interested him, he would sit and copy it. . . . Not a long time ago, but recently. So that's how scholars obtain knowledge – with difficulty (*da wahala*).[40]

The theme of suffering to obtain knowledge was not unique to Salafi circles – indeed, they shared this concern with the classical model of Islamic education – but the idea of suffering took on special resonance in the context of Salafis' self-perception as a vanguard surrounded by enemies (see Chapter 6). Another implicit message to students was that by working hard they could retrace the path worn by Ibn Taymiyya and al-Albānī: although the Salafi educational model emphasized group study with a highly credentialed teacher, it simultaneously valorized autodidactic study of the kind that al-Albānī had undertaken.

Nigerian Salafis taught works by Ibn Taymiyya and Ibn ʿAbd al-Wahhāb for several reasons. One was to help themselves and their students refute the charge that Salafism was a new and heterodox sect in the Nigerian context. In his introductory 1997 lecture on *Kitāb al-Tawḥīd*, Ādam stated that much scholarship on Ibn ʿAbd al-Wahhāb had "sought to bury the light of [his] *daʿwa*" and paint anyone who responded to that *daʿwa* as a "Wahhābī." This charge, Ādam noted, had been thrown at Izala. Detractors of Ibn ʿAbd al-Wahhāb and Ibn Taymiyya, Ādam went on, tended to accuse these shaykhs of insulting the Prophet Muḥammad. Ādam responded that one could challenge such accusers by asking them to bring proof from the shaykhs' own writings: "He will not be able to bring one word in his book that verifies this accusation" (*ba iya kawo kalma daya a cikin littafinsa wadda ke gaskata wannan tuhumi*).[41] Ādam added that the canonical shaykhs had even written tracts against insulting the Prophet, such as Ibn Taymiyya's *Al-Ṣārim al-Maslūl ʿalā Shātim al-Rasūl* (The Drawn Sword Against the Insulter of the Prophet).

A second reason for teaching the canon was the expansive opportunities it provided to discuss Qurʾanic verses and *aḥādīth*. Much of Ādam's course on *Kitāb al-Tawḥīd* was devoted to translating, analyzing, and contextualizing the reports Ibn ʿAbd al-Wahhāb had cited. In Rijiyar Lemo's lessons on Ibn Taymiyya, he frequently discussed scriptural passages, both those cited by Ibn Taymiyya and others that could be relevant to a larger discussion of Salafism.

We saw this process working the other way when Salafi shaykhs taught *ḥadīth* collections and alluded to the larger canon. In this manner, teaching foundational texts and teaching the canon are mutually reinforcing techniques. They give the impression that the Qurʾan, *aḥādīth*, and Salafi canonical texts form a seamless whole. This impression facilitates the claim that scholarship by Ibn Taymiyya and others was nothing more,

40 Rijiyar Lemo, recording of first lesson on *Al-ʿUbūdiyya*.

41 Jaʿfar Maḥmūd Ādam, recording of first lesson on *Kitāb al-Tawḥīd*, 6 September 1997.

and nothing less, than an attempt to explain, defend, and spread the Sunna.

Lessons on canonical works emphasized precision with regard to citation and stressed the need to produce compelling textual evidence. Lectures on one text inevitably led into discussions of numerous other texts, and not just scripture. Salafis went into great detail when discussing outside texts. Rijiyar Lemo's first lesson on Ibn Taymiyya's *Al-Waṣiyya al-Kubrā* delved into the text's background. This venture involved repeated citations from works by historians such as al-Dhahabī and Ibn Kathīr, both students of Ibn Taymiyya.[42] When citing works, Salafi shaykhs often provided exact titles and page numbers and offered detailed biographies of authors. These citations trained audiences to expect precision from their teachers – and to demand precision from their theological opponents, a theme discussed in Chapter 5. By implication, Salafis disparaged the real or hypothetical debate partner who stumbled in citations or made recourse to other forms of authority (experience, inherited practices, charisma). Detailed citations made Salafis' lessons on individual texts into occasions for immersing audiences in a wider textual universe and exploring interrelationships among authors, which reinforced the sense that individual works belonged to a larger, and coherent, canon.

Finally, canonical texts could have special relevance within intra-Muslim debates in contemporary northern Nigeria. Teaching canonical texts could help Salafis reinforce and disseminate anti-Sufi arguments, but with a greater degree of nuance and subtlety than was possible in shorter, more polemical genres and settings. *Al-Waṣiyya al-Kubrā* represented Ibn Taymiyya's counsel, or warning, to the followers of the Syrian-Iraqi Shaykh ʿAdī ibn Musāfir (d. 1162). A canonical edition of the text, published in Saudi Arabia in 1987, framed Ibn Taymiyya's epistle within the context of a perceived pattern where certain sects deviated from the creed of true Islam and pious scholars arose to correct them. The canonizers lauded Ibn Musāfir, but wrote:

> After his death, may Allah have mercy on him, an extravagant sect (*firqa ghāliya*) arose, which crossed the line in its glorification of Shaykh ʿAdī. It exceeded all bounds, contradicting the foundations of the Islamic creed, to which Shaykh ʿAdī himself had adhered. So it was necessary for the *ʿulamāʾ* of the Muslims, those possessing the correct creed (*dhawī al-ʿaqīda al-ṣaḥīḥa*), to correct the distortion and to bring the deniers of truth (*al-jāmiḥīn ʿan al-ḥaqq*) to the way of the straight path. This is what Shaykh al-Islām Ibn Taymiyya did, may Allah have mercy on him. He wrote a letter to the followers of ʿAdī ibn Musāfir, reminding them in it of what their predecessors (*salafihim*) among the shaykhs whom they imitated and to whose path (*ṭarīqa*) they belonged used to believe; explaining to them

42 Rijiyar Lemo, recording of first lesson on *al-Waṣiyya al-Kubrā*.

what they had to do to adhere to the Book and Sunna; and warning them of the causes of error.[43]

For these canonizers as for Rijiyar Lemo, the text represented a model of Salafi engagement with deviant Muslims, as well as an authoritative statement of the true creed. Reading *Al-Waṣiyya* offered an opportunity to discuss at length sensitive issues such as whether Muslims can see Allah in this lifetime.[44]

Often, these discussions proceeded without explicit reference to Sufis and their beliefs. Yet as Rijiyar Lemo noted at the beginning of the series, Ibn Musāfir was a contemporary of Shaykh ʿAbd al-Qādir al-Jīlānī, the namesake of the Qadiriyya Sufi order, which is popular in northern Nigeria. For Rijiyar Lemo, Ibn Musāfir and al-Jīlānī were admirable Muslim scholars whose images had been distorted by overzealous disciples. By praising such shaykhs, disassociating them from their followers' practices, and depicting their followers as being in need of correction and advice from Salafis, Rijiyar Lemo and his peers could make a complex argument about Salafi-Sufi relations, an argument that went beyond condemnation and positioned Salafis as firm but well-intentioned teachers.

In their discourses on Sufism, Nigerian Salafis have ranged from harshly critical to cautiously conciliatory. In lessons on canonical texts, Salafi teachers emphasized the theme of giving well-intentioned advice to straying Muslims rather than pronouncing *takfīr* against them (declaring them apostates). In the lesson on *Ṣaḥīḥ Muslim* mentioned earlier, where Albānī Zaria noted some "confusion" surrounding the creedal purity of al-Nawawī, he warned his students of the dangers of rash *takfīr*. He recalled an incident that had occurred in Medina in the 1990s when "some youth" attempted to burn al-Nawawī's commentary because they perceived impurities in it. He mentioned how shaykhs, including one of his teachers from the Islamic University of Medina, stopped the burning. He added:

It was an error: just because [al-Nawawī] had made a certain mistake in creed, that did not make him an infidel (*ba ya kafirta shi ba*). If he put himself in a state of error, or a certain disposition, just hope that Allah will pardon him, just hope that Allah will show mercy toward him. Often there have been our scholars in this country who have put themselves into this situation, such as Shehu Usman dan Fodio, such as Shehu Abdullahi Gwandu, such as Muhammad Bello, the Commander of the Faithful. If you read some of their books, for them too you will see Ashʿarism (*Ashʿariyyance*), you will see speculative theology (*ʿilm al-kalām*), you will see philosophy (*falsafa*). I myself, among the books that I edited

[43] Muḥammad ʿAbd Allāh al-Nimr and ʿUthmān Jumʿa al-Ḍamīriyya, "Muqaddimat al-Taḥqīq," in Ibn Taymiyya, *Al-Waṣiyya al-Kubrā*, edited by Muḥammad ʿAbd Allāh al-Nimr and ʿUthmān Jumʿa al-Ḍamīriyya (Al-Ṭā'if: Maktabat al-Ṣiddīq, 1987), 8.

[44] Rijiyar Lemo, recordings of twenty-first and twenty-second lessons on *al-Waṣiyya al-Kubrā*, 17 July 2007 and 24 July 2007.

by dan Fodio, there are books that dan Fodio wrote solely in order to defend speculative theology, in order to show that it is a proof (*hujja*) among proofs, a way (*hanya*) among the ways that one can know the correct understanding of monotheism (*ingantaccen tawhidi*). You see, it's a mistake, but that should not lead you to declare him an infidel. Rather you should say he was guilty of a blameworthy innovation (*balle ka bidi'antad da shi*). That's because you will see that he himself, in his later writings, he came to correct such things.[45]

In this pedagogical mode, Nigerian Salafis sought to police the boundaries of creed while at the same time discouraging *takfīr*. This emphasis fit with the Medina graduates' larger intellectual orientation and the shifts in attitude toward Sufism they experienced at the Islamic University, where their own encounter with the canon convinced them that *ta'līm* (education) was better than *takfīr*. As Nigerian Salafis suggested to their students back home, reading scripture could strengthen one's hand in theological debates. Reading canonical texts that came in the form of "advice" to straying Muslims provided a template for "correcting," rather than anathematizing, one's rivals. The canon offered a tool for defining the community but also for interacting with those outside it.

Written Engagement with the Canon

Nigerian Salafis have not just taught the canon but have also worked to make it available to the individual, Hausophone autodidact. Hausa translations of canonical works have spread with increasing rapidity over the past two decades. Ādam and his circle produced written translations of works by Ibn Taymiyya, as well as commentaries on the Shaykh's writings. Ādam personally translated *Al-Wāsiṭa bayn al-Ḥaqq wa-l-Khalq* (The Connection between the Creator and the Created).[46] Such translations are published in Hausar Boko (Latin script) rather than Hausar 'Ajami (a modified Arabic script). As such, the translations aim to reach the wide audience of readers literate in Hausar Boko, a constituency that has grown rapidly since the colonial period, thanks to colonial and postcolonial elite education.

Such translations and commentaries were collective projects that grew out of Nigerian Salafis' time together in Medina. In his translation to *Al-Wāsiṭa*, Ādam thanked Rijiyar Lemo and their companion Dr. Ibrāhīm Jalo for their help. As noted in Chapter 3, these men carefully studied Ibn Taymiyya's works during their time together as students at the Islamic University. Other influences from Saudi Arabia appear in such

45 'Albānī' Zaria, recording of introduction to course of lessons on *Ṣaḥīḥ Muslim*.
46 Ibn Taymiyya, *Al-Wāsiṭa bayn al-Ḥaqq wa-l-Khalq*, translated by Ja'far Maḥmūd Ādam (Kano: Al-Muntada al-Islāmī Trust, 1999).

translations: Ādam not only translated Ibn Taymiyya's text, he also translated an introduction to the text by the Syrian Shaykh Muḥammad Jamīl Zaynū (1925–2010), who taught at Dār al-Ḥadīth al-Khayriyya in Mecca. Translation projects reinforced Nigerian Salafis' intellectual and material connections to the Kingdom and to global Salafism.

Works by more contemporary canonical authorities have also begun to appear in written Hausa translation, sometimes with the support of Saudi Arabian institutions. Saudi Arabia's Ministry of Islamic Affairs, Endowments, Da'wa, and Guidance sponsored a Hausa translation of Ibn 'Uthaymīn's *'Aqīdat Ahl al-Sunna wa-l-Jamā'a* (The Creed of the People of the Prophet's Model and the Muslim Community).[47] The same ministry also sponsored a translation by Dr. Bashīr 'Aliyu 'Umar, of the book *Ḥiṣn al-Muslim min Adhkār al-Kitāb wa-l-Sunna* (The Muslim's Protection by Means of Quotations from the Book and the Sunna). This book's author, Shaykh Sa'īd ibn 'Alī ibn Wahf al-Qaḥṭānī (b. 1953), trained under Ibn Bāz and obtained his B.A., M.A., and doctorate at Imām Muhammad ibn Sa'ūd Islamic University.[48] The canon itself served as an aid in translating such works. 'Umar wrote:

> I depended heavily on books of *ḥadīth* commentary (*sharḥ*), like *Fatḥ al-Bārī* the commentary on *Ṣaḥīḥ al-Bukhārī*, and Imam al-Nawawī's commentary on *Ṣaḥīḥ Muslim* and others, as well as on books for explaining the Arabic words that appear in *aḥādīth*, such as Ibn al-Athīr's *Al-Nihāya*, and al-Qāḍī 'Iyāḍ's *Mashrik al-Anwār*, in order to determine the appropriate translation.[49]

'Umar added his own commentary in the margins of the translation.

The permeable boundary between translation and commentary highlights how northern Nigerian Salafis have sought not only to teach and disseminate the canon, but also to contribute to it. These contributions have come in Hausa as well as Arabic. Rijiyar Lemo has shown particular dedication to writing Arabic works, including his Arabic-language biography of Ādam. Rijiyar Lemo also wrote an Arabic commentary titled *Bughyat al-Mushtāq fī Sharḥ Risālat Shaykh al-Islām Ibn Taymiyya ilā Ahl al-'Irāq* (The Aim of the One Desirous to Comment on the Epistle of the Shaykh of Islam Ibn Taymiyya to the People of Iraq).[50] This work

47 Muḥammad Ṣāliḥ al-'Uthaymīn, *Akidar Ahlus-Sunna*, translated by Shu'aib Abubakar Umar (Riyadh: Ministry of Islamic Affairs, Endowments, Da'wa, and Guidance, 1999/2000).

48 'Al-Sīra al-Dhātiyya.'

49 Bashir Aliyu Umar, translator, *Garkuwar Musulmi Ta Addu'o'i Daga Alkur'ani Da Sunna* by Shaikh Sa'īd bin 'Alī bin Wahf al-Qaḥṭānī, edited by Muhammad Sani Umar and Abubakar Muhammad Sani (Riyad: Ministry of Islamic Affairs, Endowments, Da'wa, and Guidance; Kano: al-Dar al-Salafiyya, second printing, 2000), 14.

50 Muḥammad al-Thānī 'Umar Mūsā, *Bughyat al-Mushtāq fī Sharḥ Risāla Shaykh al-Islām Ibn Taymiyya ilā Ahl al-'Irāq* (Kano: Al-Imamul Bukhari Centre for Research and Translation, 2011).

references numerous canonical thinkers, including Ibn al-Amīr al-Ṣanʿānī, al-Shawkānī, al-Albānī, and ʿAbd al-Raḥmān al-Saʿdī (1889–1956). From Nigeria, Rijiyar Lemo has added to a key subset of the global Salafi canon: works analyzing and promoting the writings of Ibn Taymiyya.

The Medina graduates' references to contemporary, extra-local Salafi thinkers like al-Albānī or Ibn Bāz have often occurred within technical discussions on specific legal matters. Examples of this pattern come from Shaykh Abdulwahhab Abdullah's books *Ramadan a kan Koyarwar Alkur'ani da Sunnah bisa Fahimtar Magabata na Kwarai* (Hausa: Ramadan According to the Teaching of the Qur'an and the Sunna According to the Understanding of the Pious Predecessors) and *Fatawoyin Aikin Hajji da Umrah da Ziyara a kan Koyarwar Alkur'ani da Sunnah da Fahimtar Magabata na Kwarai* (Rulings on Hajj, ʿUmra [the lesser pilgrimage], and Ziyara [visiting] According to the Teaching of the Qur'an, the Sunna, and the Understanding of the Pious Predecessors).[51] In these books, Abdullah not only cited scripture to support his positions, he provided precise references within canonical *ḥadīth* collections such as those of al-Bukhārī and Muslim. He discussed the status of each report according to Salafi methodologies of *ḥadīth* criticism. Citations of al-Albānī as an arbiter of a *ḥadīth*'s strength or weakness were ubiquitous.

In written works as in their teaching, the Medina graduates move between registers, invoking the contemporary canon most heavily in more technical and specialized registers. In all of these registers, texts authored by Nigerian Salafis supplement their teaching of the canon and reinforce their image as religious authorities who mediate between local concerns and a global intellectual stage.

Conclusion

In a wider context of changes to Islamic education in northern Nigeria, Salafis have promoted study of their canon. Graduates of Medina have concentrated on teaching their students collections of *ḥadīth*. They situate these collections in a Salafi framework of knowledge, action, and identity. Salafis have also concentrated on teaching works by Ibn Taymiyya and Ibn ʿAbd al-Wahhāb, two of the best-known authors in the canon. For Salafi teachers, a close relationship exists between these two genres of texts: *ḥadīth* collections can introduce broader discussions of the canon, and canonical texts contain *ḥadīth* reports that require explication.

[51] Sheikh Abdulwahab bin Abdallah, *Ramadan a kan Koyarwar Alkur'ani da Sunnah bisa Fahimtar Magabata na Kwarai* (Kano: Kumurya Prints U/Uku, 2009); *Fatawoyin Aikin Hajji da Umrah da Ziyara a kan Koyarwar Alkur'ani da Sunnah da Fahimtar Magabata na Kwarai* (Kano: Supreme Council for Shariʿa in Nigeria; Garewa Printing Press, second edition, 2004).

Robert Hefner has written that there is "a dilemma . . . at the heart of Islamic education today":

> Is the purpose of Islamic education to teach fidelity to a fixed and finished canon? Or should religious education offer a high-minded but general religious ethics that looks outward on creation and encourages a plurality of methods for fathoming and engaging its wonder?[52]

Nigeria's Salafis would likely object to how Hefner frames this dilemma. For Salafis, teaching their canon does not solely represent a backward-looking allegiance to a set of texts. It also aims to transmit a body of knowledge that will allow students to practice, debate, and improvise with confidence. Salafis believe that extending one's mastery over scripture will not just enrich religious knowledge but refine one's life ethically, reorienting one's values from worldly affairs to those of the mosque. Studying works by Ibn Taymiyya or Ibn ʿAbd al-Wahhāb vividly connects the past to the present, and prepares Salafis' students to contest other Muslims' creeds and practices.

Ironically, Hefner's dilemma would also be questioned by proponents of the classical model of Islamic education in northwest Africa. For these Muslims, a canon was also a foundation rather than a stopping point. As Rudolph Ware has argued, "Traditional Islam never made change impossible or even undesirable, but it did seek to keep it from the unqualified. . . . Mastery has always been the precondition for improvisation."[53] For both the Salafis and their classical opponents, canons transmitted identities and ethical orientations; the canon defined the community. The difference lies in how each community conceives of the rules that govern claims to intellectual and spiritual authority.

Alongside their underlying similarities in aims, the two models share core pedagogical methods. Salafis, like classical teachers, provide word-for-word translations and commentaries on Arabic texts. In both settings, the transmission of texts takes on a personal and communal character – although, it should be added, Salafis' energetic distribution of recorded lessons extended the lifetime and scope of their teaching, making it possible for individuals to study or restudy texts on their own. Salafi pedagogy was also informed by the structure of study circles in mosques in Saudi Arabia, where teaching was highly personalized as well. Nevertheless, the resemblance of Nigerian Salafi pedagogy to classical pedagogy made Salafi instruction familiar and accessible to Nigerian students.

52 Robert Hefner, "Introduction: The Culture, Politics, and Future of Muslim Education" in *Schooling Islam: The Culture and Politics of Modern Muslim Education*, edited by Robert Hefner and Muhammad Qasim Zaman, 1–39 (Princeton: Princeton University Press), 35.

53 Rudolph Ware, *The Walking Qur'an: Islamic Education, Embodied Knowledge, and History in West Africa* (Chapel Hill: University of North Carolina Press, 2014), 70.

This process highlights what Terje Østebø has called the "localization" of Salafism. At the same time, Salafis also sought to inculcate in their students a sense of belonging to a wider Salafi community, global in scope and centuries old. This sense of identity would come strongly into play in Salafis' political discourses, the topic of the Chapter 6. First, however, it will be worthwhile to examine in greater detail how Salafis and Sufis debate, especially in electronic media, where each side has made important epistemological maneuvers and compromises.

5 The Canon in Religious Debates and Electronic Media

In November 2006, Shaykh Jaʿfar Ādam addressed supporters in Kano. In his lecture, "The Struggle between Falsehood and Truth," he treated a controversy surrounding a mosque in Kano's Sabuwar Gandu neighborhood. He explained that the Salafi community had built the mosque. But, he claimed, Kano's most powerful forces had blocked Salafis' choice of imam. These forces numbered three: the Tijaniyya Sufi order, for which Kano has been a stronghold since the early twentieth century; Emir Ado Bayero (1930–2014, reigned 1963–2014), the city's hereditary Muslim ruler and a member of the Tijaniyya; and politicians such as Governor Ibrahim Shekarau (b. 1955, served 2003–11), whom Ādam accused of catering to the Tijaniyya and the emir.

Against this perceived coalition, Ādam deployed one of the Salafi community's main assets: media engagement. In a recorded lecture, he marshaled proof-texts to make his case for the Salafi community's ownership of the mosque. He cited Qurʾanic verses and *ḥadīth* reports, but he also extended Salafism's ideal of textualism to include secular documents, such as news clips, legal documents, and letters. In Kano's diverse and charged media landscape, Ādam's lecture circulated in recorded form. The lecture contributed to tensions that culminated in violence between Salafis and the Tijaniyya, as well as a legal suit Salafis launched against the emir and the governor. The physical conflict ended with a literal standoff: Salafis retained control in Sabuwar Gandu, but the Tijaniyya built an imposing new mosque within sight of the Salafi enclave. In the media, however, the conflict continued: Salafis systematically promoted their narrative, seeking to define understandings of the controversy within Kano even after the question of mosque control was resolved. As Salafis mediatize conflict such as Sabuwar Gandu, meanwhile, Sufis and other critics of Salafism have begun turning to electronic media to denounce Salafism, question its canon, and assert the value of other canons.

In the twentieth and twenty-first centuries, the rise of electronic media has confronted religious communities with dramatic changes. Electronic media have thrust some believers into new spaces where the meaning of texts, the boundary between public and private, and the nature of religious authority are transformed.[1] Scholars of religion have highlighted how religious media can affect "local, everyday, embodied forms of religious practice and affinity,"[2] or modes of ethical "self-fashioning."[3] These interactions do not simply affect media producers and isolated consumers; media circulate within "institutions of sociability, empathy, and sharing."[4] Such circulation can have unpredictable consequences, as audiences reimagine content in ways that producers did not intend. In Pentecostal Christian circles in Ghana, Birgit Meyer writes, the rapid circulation of new media products places religious leaders in a partly reactive position. The changes stemming from new media production have been "criticized at times from within, as pastors and believers fear losing control."[5] What some producers see as a loss of control, however, others may see as opportunity. Hence there is an "an increasingly complicated negotiation" surrounding electronic media – negotiation "between the private and public spheres,"[6] or between producers and audiences – as well as fierce competition between rival producers and rival communities.

Many scriptural literalists and "fundamentalists" have adapted creatively to new media landscapes.[7] To understand these communities' approaches to media, we require an understanding of their styles of argumentation, as well as their conceptions of media itself. Salafis in northern Nigeria have cultivated an awareness of what makes audiences respond – what rhetorical maneuvers preemptively address concerns about the intellectual legitimacy of different positions, what maneuvers provoke outrage among opponents, and what kind of speech will energize and rally core supporters. Nigerian Salafis have reason to believe that media engagement will broaden their following, particularly in an environment where their opponents have greater institutional power. The dissemination of their broadcasts and recordings has helped draw youth, women, and others to the Salafi worldview. Yet engagement with electronic media has also encouraged nuance and compromise in how Nigerian Salafis

1 Hent de Vries, "In Media Res: Global Religion, Public Spheres, and the Task of Contemporary Comparative Religious Studies" in *Religion and Media*, edited by Hent de Vries and Samuel Weber, 3–42 (Stanford: Stanford University Press).

2 Jeremy Stolow, "Religion and/as Media," *Theory, Culture, and Society* 22.4 (August 2005): 119–45; 123.

3 Charles Hirschkind, *The Ethical Soundscape: Casette Sermons and Islamic Counterpublics* (New York: Columbia University Press, 2006), 22–3.

4 Dorothea Schulz, *Muslims and New Media in West Africa: Pathways to God* (Bloomington: Indiana University Press, 2012), 201.

5 Birgit Meyer, "Impossible Representations: Pentecostalism, Vision, and Video Technology in Ghana" in *Religion, Media, and the Public Sphere*, edited by Birgit Meyer and Annelies Moors, 290–312 (Bloomington: Indiana University Press, 2006), 308.

6 De Vries, "In Media Res," 17.

7 Stewart Hoover and Nadia Kaneva, "Fundamental Mediations: Religion, Meaning, and Identity in Global Context" in *Fundamentalisms and the Media*, edited by Stewart Hoover and Nadia Kaneva, 1–22 (London and New York: Continuum, 2009).

frame religious knowledge. Salafis work creatively and strategically with religious knowledge: they extend the status of proof-texts to media other than scripture, and they present messages in locally resonant idioms.

I make two, intertwined arguments in this chapter. First, I argue that Salafism's epistemological foundations facilitate certain approaches to electronic media. The Salafi rhetorical contention that knowledge is transparent, or that "Islam is easy to understand,"[8] helps Salafis to advance the ideal of electronic media as spaces where an intellectual meritocracy, based on the ability to deploy proof-texts, can flourish. This ideal reflects Salafis' confidence that they can identify singular, exclusive interpretations of proof-texts. In this meritocracy, they hope, audiences will judge arguments by the proof-texts that speakers produce to support their arguments. As Bernard Haykel writes, part of Salafism's appeal lies in its "claims to religious certainty," which the movement pairs with a "seemingly limitless ability to cite scripture to back these [claims] up."[9] In radio broadcasts and recorded lectures, Salafis see opportunities to lay out scriptural and canonical evidence that will win over undecided audiences. As they harness electronic media, Nigerian Salafis have both deployed and repackaged their canon. In Nigeria, the dissemination of Salafism – and the dissemination of the canon – has often occurred through the nexus of textual and electronic media.

Second, I argue that Salafis' media engagement is one factor in broader transformations that concern the social construction of knowledge both within the Salafi community and among Muslims who respond to the Salafi media challenge. As the Sabuwar Gandu episode shows, Salafis' media engagement frequently ends not in unmitigated triumph, but in compromise. Such compromise can extend to the domain of knowledge – Salafis work to present their arguments in locally resonant terms, and they grant some authority to secular media. Meanwhile, Salafis' opponents, especially the rising Sufi leaders and progressive Muslim intellectuals discussed at the end of this chapter, are also adapting to the new media environment. Engaging through radio, audiovisual recordings, and the Internet, they make a dual refutation of the Salafis: they reject the Salafi canon as a narrow conception of Islam, and they dismiss Salafis' aspirations to participate in intellectual meritocracy by portraying the Salafis as social climbers who cause division among Muslims for personal gain. At the same time, Salafis' opponents sometimes tacitly agree to make the presentation of proof-texts the fundamental currency of debate. This

8 Jonathan A. C. Brown, "Is Islam Easy to Understand or Not? Salafis, the Democratization of Interpretation, and the Need for the Ulema," *Journal of Islamic Studies* 26:2 (2015): 117–44.

9 Bernard Haykel, "On the Nature of Salafi Thought and Action" in *Global Salafism: Islam's New Religious Movement*, edited by Roel Meijer, 33–57 (New York: Columbia University Press, 2009), 36.

maneuver can sometimes appear to be a concession to the Salafis. Both sides make some compromises in media engagement.

In this chapter, I first analyze two media interventions by Salafi leaders in Kano: Ādam's earlier-mentioned lecture and a 2007 radio broadcast by his associate Dr. Muḥammad Sani ʿUmar Rijiyar Lemo. Each of these media engagements highlights Salafis' confidence in the persuasive power of proof-texts. Ādam's lecture demonstrates how Salafi leaders present proof-texts through mass media as a means of gaining followers and compensating for a relative lack of institutional power. The lecture also shows how Salafis grant the status of proof-texts to nonscriptural media – how they extend, into new spheres, the attitudes found in the canon. Rijiyar Lemo's broadcast highlights how Salafis seek to counter accusations that their ideas are foreign imports, and in this way to clear the ground for Salafi argumentation to proceed. This effort can blur the lines between the classical canon of northwest Africa and the Salafi canon: Nigerian Salafis present their ideas as fundamental not just to Salafism but to any orthodox understanding of Islam.

I then analyze two mediatized responses to Salafis. The first is from young Sufi graduates of Arab universities, who rival the Medina graduates in spoken Arabic fluency, university credentials, and savvy for building institutions. The second is from a famous progressive Muslim intellectual, Sanusi Lamido Sanusi, who used multiple media – newspapers, academic scholarship, and the Internet – to attack Ādam's credibility. These anti-Salafi responses help show how electronic media have become a key domain for contention over the meaning of Islamic knowledge, a struggle that pits canon against canon.

Muslim Electronic Media Engagement in Northern Nigeria

In Africa, "new generations of Muslim intellectuals, preachers, and activists have come of age in the era of liberalization."[10] These figures are working creatively with the rich array of media and civic associations that liberalization has helped to flourish.[11] Nigerian graduates of Medina operate within this liberalized environment, taking full advantage of electronic media to disseminate their messages. Through electronic media, Salafis have sought to counterbalance some of their opponents' greater political and institutional power. For decades, Salafis represented

[10] René Otayek and Benjamin Soares, "Introduction: Islam and Muslim Politics in Africa" in *Islam and Muslim Politics in Africa*, edited by Benjamin Soares and René Otayek, 1–24 (New York: Palgrave MacMillan, 2007), 13.

[11] On civic associations in northern Nigeria, see Tahir Gwarzo, "Activities of Islamic Civic Associations in the Northwest of Nigeria: With Particular Reference to Kano State," *Africa Spectrum* 38:3 (2003): 289–318.

a minority of Nigeria's estimated eighty-five million Muslims. But by 2006, when Ādam gave his lecture on Sabuwar Gandu, radio broadcasts and recorded lectures had made Salafi leaders household names in the north. To the extent that Nigerian Salafis have won some battles – for control of the Sabuwar Gandu mosque, for example – their victories have owed partly to media engagement. Such engagement has reinforced Salafis' activities in spaces like mosques and law courts and has constituted a powerful channel for the transmission of Salafis' literalist and exclusivist interpretations of texts. Invoking Brian Larkin's notion of media as "infrastructure" or "institutionalized networks that facilitate the flow of goods in a wider cultural as well as physical sense,"[12] we can say that media have become "infrastructure" for Nigerian Salafis, complementing their physical infrastructure of mosques and schools, as well as the intellectual infrastructure provided by the global Salafi canon.

The Medina graduates' media engagement built on a foundation laid by other Nigerian Muslim leaders. As Larkin has pointed out, northern Nigerian Muslim scholars – including Sufis – came to embrace electronic media over the course of the twentieth century. Scholars skeptical of new media, such as those who opposed broadcasts of Qur'anic recitation in the 1950s, lost out. By the century's end, Larkin writes, prominent Muslim scholars dismissed earlier resistance to electronic media as a product of ignorance. In these scholars' eyes, the new "position of knowledge and familiarity with technology is not just the result of Hausa people's becoming more Westernized and more familiar with Western technology but also, significantly, because of their better education *Islamically*."[13] By the time Ādam and Rijiyar Lemo returned from Medina in the 1990s and 2000s, radio, television, and cassette tapes were familiar parts of the religious and media landscape – their content could be controversial, but the fact of their use by Muslim scholars was not.

Salafis built on Izala leaders' forays into electronic media. Beginning in the 1960s, radio and print provided venues in which future Izala leaders cultivated media personae and debated questions of orthodoxy with Sufis.[14] Izala's spiritual patron Shaykh Abubakar Gumi (1924–92) began broadcasting Qur'anic exegeses in 1967.[15] Izala's formal leader Shaykh

[12] Brian Larkin, *Signal and Noise: Media, Infrastructure, and Urban Culture in Nigeria* (Durham, NC: Duke University Press, 2008), 4.

[13] Larkin, *Signal and Noise*, 9.

[14] Andrea Brigaglia, "The Radio Kaduna 'Tafsir' (1978–1992) and the Construction of Public Images of Muslim Scholars in the Nigerian Media," *Journal for Islamic Studies* 27 (2007): 173–210.

[15] Abubakar Gumi with Ismaila Tsiga, *Where I Stand* (Ibadan, Nigeria: Spectrum Books, 1992).

Ismail Idris (1937–2000) recorded lectures in the 1980s and after.[16] As part of their identification with the global Salafi sphere, Ādam and Rijiyar Lemo were also influenced by the electronic media engagement of Salafi scholars like Saudi Arabia's Shaykh ʿAbd al-ʿAzīz ibn Bāz, who delivered *fatāwā* (edicts) on the program *Nūr ʿalā al-Darb* (Light on the Path) on Saudi radio.[17]

New and independent vehicles for intra-Muslim debate were founded in the 1990s and early 2000s. These included the northern Nigerian Internet forum Gamji (founded 1994), the northern newspaper company Media Trust Nigeria Ltd. (founded 1998), and Kano's Freedom Radio (founded 2003). By the 1990s, platforms like the BBC's Hausa Service had stimulated Nigerian Muslims' interest in developments affecting Muslim communities elsewhere.[18]

In Kano, electronic media have permeated urban dwellers' quotidian religiosity, from religious programming on television and radio to mobile telephone ringtones featuring recitations of Qurʾanic verses. Kano has a teeming media landscape, attuned heavily but not exclusively to orality. Survey data showed in 2012 that 92.6 percent of Nigerians had a radio in their home.[19] Internet use is rapidly rising, especially because of the proliferation of smartphones: one data set indicates that for news consumption, the Internet is beginning to displace radio and television among Nigerians, although radio and television remain dominant.[20] Visual media content comes from Kano's Hausa-language film industry ("Kannywood") and Nigerian television stations. English- and Arabic-language satellite television (legally or illegally obtained) connects northern Nigerians to international news and sports media. The BBC, Deutsche Welle, Voice of America, and other international outlets have Hausa-language services that broadcast domestic and international news several times daily. Nigerian newspapers have a significant urban readership and a formidable online presence. All of these media interact with one another and create overlapping audiences.

[16] Muhammad Sani Umar, "Changing Islamic Identity in Nigeria from the 1960s to the 1980s: From Sufism to Anti-Sufism" in *Muslim Identity and Social Change in Sub-Saharan Africa*, edited by Louis Brenner, 154–78 (Bloomington: Indiana University Press, 1993).

[17] Collections of these edicts can be found at the Shaykh's memorial website: www.binbaz.org.sa/noor; accessed March 2015.

[18] Muhammad S. Umar, "Education and Islamic Trends in Northern Nigeria: 1970s–1990s," *Africa Today* 48: 2 (Summer 2001): 127–50.

[19] Broadcasting Board of Governors/Gallup, *Nigeria Media Use 2012* (2012). Available at: www.bbg.gov/wp-content/media/2012/08/gallup-nigeria-brief.pdf; accessed June 2013.

[20] Broadcasting Board of Governors/Gallup, *Contemporary Media Use in Nigeria* (2014). Available at: www.bbg.gov/wp-content/media/2014/05/Nigeria-research-brief.pdf; accessed March 2015.

Recorded music and religious lectures circulate widely, a trend that facilitates the dissemination of Salafi media. Abdoulaye Sounaye, in the (closely related) context of Niger, has referred to a "tripartite structure" of preachers, audiences, and the "Islamic discotheques" that sell recorded religious materials.[21] Similarly, in Kano, recordings of Salafi lectures circulate through a system of shops, mobile salespeople, displays in front of mosques, and informal sharing among friends. Rising rates of mobile telephone ownership – 87 percent of the population by 2014[22] – allow easy and rapid transmission of audio content. Significantly, mobile telephones can store recorded religious lectures as MP3 files, extending the portability of recordings.

The growing diversity of Kano's media parallels a growth in educational institutions in the city since Nigeria's oil boom in the 1970s. Many of the city's new schools are privately run Islamic schools, which proliferated after the 1980s, when the federal government of Nigeria scaled back its ambitions to provide universal primary education. Changes in schooling have created new classes of media consumers eager to receive a variety of content, including religious content, through oral, print, and virtual media. The penetration of electronic media affected religious discourses in Kano by the late 1990s. Islamic scholars, even from traditional backgrounds, evinced a growing interest in commenting on global affairs and debating topics like the "secularity of the Nigerian state, gender equality, human rights, democracy, and rights of ethnic and religious minorities."[23] Electronic media created opportunities for religious leaders to engage broader audiences in new ways, operating in the spaces where textual traditions and mass mobilization intersect.

Kano's Salafi leaders invest considerable time into oral performances captured through electronic media. The Salafi Shaykh Muhammad Nazifi Inuwa, for example, conducts *Al-Azkar* (Supplications), one of the most popular radio programs in the city in the early 2010s. *Al-Azkar* is a live Arabic-to-Hausa translation, every Friday morning, of the congregational sermon delivered in Mecca, followed by commentary in Hausa on the sermon's context. *Al-Azkar* and other performances highlight Salafi preachers' rhetorical abilities in Arabic and Hausa. This focus on orality and electronic media is a deliberate strategic choice: Inuwa explained in one *Al-Azkar* episode, broadcast 14 October 2011, that because few Kano residents read newspapers or attend lectures in mosques, it was important to propound "righteous speech" (*maganar adalci*) on the radio. Kano's Salafi leaders author texts in Arabic and Hausa, but they invest

[21] Abdoulaye Sounaye, "La «discothèque» islamique: CD et DVD au cœur de la réislamisation nigérienne," ethnographiques.org, Number 22 (May 2011). Available at: www.ethnographiques.org/2011/Sounaye; accessed November 2014.

[22] Broadcasting Board of Governors/Gallup, *Contemporary Media Use in Nigeria.*

[23] Umar, "Education and Islamic Trends," 131.

less energy in writing than in lectures and electronic media interventions. Salafis' investment in electronic media involves decisions about how to manage the relationships among different media.

Salafi preachers' awareness that their live performances will be recorded or broadcast affects the content of these performances. As Hirschkind argues in the case of Egypt, recording promotes greater attention to citations and accuracy: "As the life of the sermon has been extended through the use of tapes and its spatial and temporal frame expanded, the sermon is now more readily subjected to critical scrutiny on scholarly grounds."[24] When they emphasize proof-texts, Salafi preachers in Kano not only anticipate such scrutiny, they encourage it.

Hoping to outcompete rivals within a meritocracy, Salafis demand a larger niche within Kano's media landscape. This ambition parallels and enhances their efforts to expand their network of mosques and schools. In Kano as elsewhere, media represent and feed into a web of relationships: when Salafis circulate recorded lectures, appear on radio and television, and generate Web content, they broadcast their messages beyond the mosque or the study circle but also work to draw more Muslims to the physical sites where Salafism is discussed and transmitted.

Ādam's Lecture on Sabuwar Gandu

Ādam's lecture on the Sabuwar Gandu mosque controversy showcases Salafis' view of electronic media. For Salafis, electronic media are a space that enables an intellectual meritocracy based on the ability to deploy proof-texts. This section explores how the lecture treated other media and how it related to the Salafis' overall position with Kano's media landscape and institutional politics.

Before analyzing the lecture, it will be helpful to trace how the controversy unfolded from the perspective of Salafis in Kano. I draw on a written narrative by Muhammad Ahmad,[25] a Salafi, a member of Izala, and a prime mover in the mosque project. Ahmad's account merits attention not only as background to Ādam's lecture, but also as an extension of it. Ahmad's book shares its title with the lecture, and amplifies Ādam's effort to shape narratives about the controversy. The book reproduces numerous written media, such as official correspondence and newspaper reports, and thereby anthologizes the proof-texts Salafis produced to support their case. The book, like the lecture, depicts Salafis as a minority oppressed by opponents with greater institutional power. The book aims to set the record straight by collecting and deploying other media. This

[24] Hirschkind, *The Ethical Soundscape*, 147.

[25] Muhammad Ahmad, *Gwagwarmaya tsakanin Gaskiya da Karya akan Mallakar Masallacin Juma'a na Sheikh Ja'afar Mahmud Adam, Sabuwar Gandu – Kano* (Kano: Al-Kitab Printing Press Ltd., 2010).

strategy reflects Salafis' faith in the power of intellectual meritocracy, as well as the partial confidence Salafis extend to nonscriptural media as proof-texts.

Ahmad purchased a space for a Friday congregational mosque in Sabuwar Gandu in 1995. After years of paperwork and inspections by local and state government authorities, he secured approval to build the mosque from Kano's Emirate Council, a circle of advisers to the emir of Kano. The council oversees Friday mosques. In 2005, the Salafis proposed candidates for the mosque's leadership: Inuwa (the host of *Al-Azkar*, mentioned earlier) as imam, and Mallam Iliyasu Muhammad as deputy imam. The Imam of Kano, Shaykh Idris Kuliya Alkali (d. 2011), tested and approved the candidates. The emir gave permission for the mosque to open on 15 September 2006.

According to Ahmad, Salafis then encountered resistance from Sufi shaykhs, especially those of the Tijaniyya, as well as from the Emirate Council. Advisers urged the emir to revoke Inuwa's appointment as imam. Defying the emir and the Tijaniyya, Salafis opened the mosque on 29 September 2006 and clashed violently with Sufis.

Ahmad reports that Governor Ibrahim Shekarau sided with the emir and the Tijaniyya in attempting to deny Salafis control of the mosque. Shekarau, who won election in 2003 in large part because of promises to reinvigorate the implementation of *sharīʿa* in Kano, was widely popular among *ʿulamāʾ* in Kano, but was particularly close to the Palace, and his father had been a friend of the emir's. Over time, Shekarau lost the support of some Salafi leaders, including Ādam, who came to perceive the governor as part of an anti-Salafi coalition.

On 5 October, the emir appointed a scholar from the Tijaniyya, Dr. Yusuf Ali (b. 1949), as imam of the mosque. Ali earned his university degrees from Bayero University Kano and worked for more than three decades as a *sharīʿa* judge in Kano. Ali had already sparred with Salafis earlier in the decade, when his high-profile practice of *rukiyya* (Islamic exorcism) caused controversy in Kano.[26] Ali's appointment as imam of the Sabuwar Gandu mosque outraged Salafis.

After further violence, police closed the mosque. A court battle followed, and a compromise was struck: Inuwa and Ali withdrew, and Shaykh Abdullahi Ishaq Garangamawa (b. ca. 1956), a Salafi graduate of Medina, was appointed as imam. The mosque reopened on 21 December 2007. The Tijanis built their own mosque nearby, with Ali as imam. Although Ali has appeared on radio and television throughout his career,[27] he placed little emphasis on engaging the Sabuwar Gandu controversy in the media, perhaps hoping to avoid further violence.

[26] Susan O'Brien, "La charia contestée: démocratie, débat et diversité musulmane dans les «États charia» du Nigeria," *Politique Africaine* 2:106 (2007): 46–68.

[27] Yusuf Ali, "Tarihin Rayuwar Ustaz Dakta Yusuf Ali." Available at: www.ustazyusufali.faithweb.com/tarihinustaz004.html; accessed April 2014.

Ādam's lecture on Sabuwar Gandu came at the height of the controversy, in November 2006. The lecture's title, "The Struggle between Falsehood and Truth," referred to the recurring conflict he perceived between true Muslims and their enemies. The lecture included six major sections. First, he described historical moments where Muslims and pre-Islamic prophets preached reform in contexts of corruption and sin. He drew heavily on the Qur'an to weave these narratives. Second, he recounted struggles between Salafis and Sufis for control of mosques in Kano between the 1980s and the 2000s, analogizing these conflicts to the historical moments he invoked at the beginning. Third, he discussed the Sabuwar Gandu controversy. Fourth, he identified three "enemies" of Salafis – Kano's hereditary Muslim rulers, elected politicians, and Sufi shaykhs – and discussed their (alleged) reasons for opposing Salafis. Fifth, he explained why Salafis would not relinquish control of the Sabuwar Gandu mosque. Lastly, he suggested ways of resolving the mosque controversy and the broader conflict between Ahlussunnah and its opponents. During the lecture, Ādam referenced numerous media, including scripture. In doing so, he also articulated attitudes about the relationship between media and truth.[28]

Like Ahmad would later do, Ādam constructed the Salafi case by presenting proof-texts. When Ādam came in to his lecture to the Sabuwar Gandu mosque, he stressed that its builders had followed bureaucratic requirements outlined in well-regulated documents. The builders, he emphasized, also held documents proving ownership and attesting to Inuwa's approval as imam. After the Imam of Kano had tested Inuwa, Ādam narrated, "He wrote in Arabic, the language of Islam. He presented to His Highness the emir of Kano a letter – we have a copy of it in our hands."[29] During the lecture, an Izala leader (Dr. Pakistan) then flourished the document itself. This physical exhibition of proof-texts underscores the way the lecture as an event, even before its dissemination on recording, formed part of a chain of media products. The lecture presented, organized, and interpreted textual media.

In Ādam's view, proof-texts testified not only to Salafis' ownership of the mosque, but also to their opponents' lack of an Islamic legal basis for contesting Inuwa's appointment. "The mosque is ours. We have the power to appoint the imam. . . . We have confirmed that there is nowhere in *Bukhārī* or *Muslim* [two canonical *ḥadīth* collections] where it is said that if you have an imam who has not been approved, your imam is no good."[30] For Ādam, mosque ownership rested on documentation, rather than on the prerogative the Palace claimed to administer the mosque and

28 Ja'far Maḥmūd Ādam, "Gwagwarmaya tsakanin Gaskiya da Karya," recorded lecture, November 2006, Kano.
29 Ādam, "Gwagwarmaya."
30 Ibid.

its endowment on behalf of God and the wider community. Ādam's lecture, like Ahmad's book, compiled proof-texts into a larger proof-text, a media intervention that acted as a brief for the Salafi movement within the Sabuwar Gandu controversy. Ādam accorded decisive evidentiary value not only to scripture but also to secular legal documents. Fundamental attitudes embedded in the canon – namely, the feeling that the primary or even sole function of texts is, if they are found credible, to determine practice – appeared in the shaykh's treatment of even noncanonical documentary materials.

Ādam used media to attack his opponents' credibility. Part of Salafis' refusal to relinquish control of Sabuwar Gandu concerned alleged heresies uttered by Ali. In discussing these utterances, Ādam signaled to listeners that Salafis were carefully tracking and evaluating media, including media from abroad. He presented these efforts as a form of transparency that was available to all listeners, even Salafis' opponents. In other words, he invoked media to level the playing field. Referring to an Al Jazeera broadcast, he told listeners, "If you want, go on the Internet, open the file, and you will see." The availability of media promoted accountability. Recalling a meeting of Kano shaykhs who had denounced Ali, Ādam said, "We, we will not forget, even if you forget. . . . The videocassette exists."[31] Accountability reinforced meritocracy: the best arguments, the shaykh implied, would withstand scrutiny.

Also at stake were Ali's reported attitudes toward media and scripture. Again invoking an outside media product, Ādam denounced a letter Ali had sent to filmmakers. Under the Shekarau administration, Kano's film industry became a site of struggles over public morality, with some filmmakers facing censorship and imprisonment.[32] By associating Ali with filmmakers, Ādam linked his adversary with a community that some Kano Muslims considered a source of immoral media. At least three media came into play in this discussion: Ali's letter, fictional films, and *ḥadīth* reports. Ali, in Ādam's eyes, exhibited a blasphemous flexibility in his treatment of these media. Ādam narrated:

He wrote in a letter to filmmakers that they could continue making films, they could keep on with theatrical performances (*wasan kwaikwaiyo*) because . . . the prophets were all theatrical performers. He said if you want a proof (*hujja*), see the second *ḥadīth* in *Forty Hadith* about the Angel Gabriel [in which Gabriel appeared to the Prophet and asked him a series of questions about Islam] when he came in the form of "some villager" (*wani bakauye*). . . . He said it was all a theatrical performance. . . . On the basis of this he said all the prophets were

[31] Ādam, "Gwagwarmaya."

[32] Carmen McCain, "The Politics of Exposure: Contested Cosmopolitanisms, Revelation of Secrets, and Intermedial Reflexivity in Hausa Popular Expression," Ph.D. dissertation, University of Wisconsin–Madison, 2014.

theatrical performers. Is this a Muslim or an unbeliever (*arne*)? [Crowd: "*Arne*!"] So why would one appoint an unbeliever as imam?[33]

For Ādam, Ali's (alleged) metaphorical reading of the *ḥadīth* highlighted an epistemological conflict: for Ali, a *ḥadīth*'s outer form could mask hidden realities. For Ādam, this was a perversion of the idea of a proof-text, and hence a sacrilege. Any destabilization of clarity and transparency in textual media threatened Salafi scriptural methodologies as well as Salafi media strategies. The conflict between Ādam and Ali was not just about what media meant but also about the rules for approaching media.

Ādam went further than merely presenting proofs against his opponents: he systematically attacked forms of authority based on criteria other than textually based religious truth. To Salafis' possession and exhibition of clear proof-texts, Ādam contrasted what he depicted as the illegitimate, socially constructed authority of Sufi shaykhs, elected politicians, and hereditary Muslim rulers. Salafis, he argued, saw through these social constructs to grasp the alleged weakness of, for example, the Palace's claims that it possessed authority to regulate Friday mosques. In this case, Nigeria's secular constitution was Ādam's proof-text: "For we, we already know that in the political system of the country it is written nowhere . . . that you may not build a mosque unless the Palace agrees. That is written nowhere constitutionally in the political system of Nigeria." Ādam suggested that Salafis entered voluntarily into a social contract with hereditary Muslim rulers "out of an effort at politeness and obedience." But, he added, "Today if we stop coming [to ask their permission to open a mosque], we have not broken the law of the nation."[34] Because the Palace's authority lacked a documentary basis, Ādam suggested, Salafis' social contract with the Palace could be annulled. Authority was ultimately textual, even if the relevant text was not Islamic.

Yet Ādam compromised. He did not call for dismantling the aristocracy, removing elected politicians, and installing an Islamic state. Believing that Kano's political structures were rigged against Salafis, he nonetheless urged a limited and strategic intra-Muslim pluralism. Salafis, he suggested, would gain popularity if they were given space to propagate their message, especially in mosques and media. At the end of his lecture, Ādam proposed solutions to the Sabuwar Gandu conflict. Beyond ensuring that the mosque remain in Salafi hands, Ādam urged the emir to give Ahlussunah an equal share of the annual Ramadan *tafsīr* (Qurʾanic exegesis) conducted at the Palace:

33 Ādam, "Gwagwarmaya."
34 Ibid.

Why, why is there one person only who performs *tafsīr* at the Palace in Kano? We are not saying to take it and give it to us. Let it be split into three parts. The first ten [days] Tijaniyya. The middle ten Qadiriyya. The last ten? [Audience shouts: Sunna, Sunna, Sunna]! . . . If it is put on radio and television, everyone will see! We will differentiate between good thread and poor, between grains and pebbles, by Allah, by Allah, I guarantee if the Palace of Kano does this, it will do justice.[35]

Ādam further asked for airtime on Radio Kano, a government-run radio station, so that Salafis could explain their beliefs and match Sufis proof-text for proof-text. Between controlling mosques and accessing mass media, he suggested, Ahlussunnah's message would spread, let authorities and Sufis do what they might. This conviction reflected another side of the Salafi attitude toward evidence and the Salafi ideal of media spaces as intellectual meritocracies: if every side has the opportunity to present its proofs and evidence, truth can but triumph – as, in Ādam's eyes, it always had. A short-term investment in cultivating a media-based intellectual meritocracy, he reasoned, would yield long-term institutional power.

The lecture showcased Ādam's strategic approach to media. Extending Salafis' reliance on proof-texts to legal documents, news reports, videos, the Internet, and other media, he presented a legal case (both in terms of *sharīʿa* and the Nigerian legal system) that relied on textual and electronic media. As one of the many lectures that his followers recorded with the intention of distributing them, the Sabuwar Gandu intervention was a performance not only for a physical gathering of the Salafi community at a moment of crisis, but also a media product intended to circulate and generate responses from both supporters and opponents. In combination with Ahmad's book, these Salafi-generated media represent a powerful and enduring bid to dominate the narrative around Sabuwar Gandu; both the recorded lecture and the book remain in circulation. Both products also aimed to support Salafis' bid for greater control of media and mosques, the primary spaces in which they seek to win audiences to their side through carefully marshaled proof-texts.

Rijiyar Lemo's Radio Broadcast on *Mawlid*

The preceding analysis of Ādam's lecture highlighted how Salafis use different media as proof-texts. My treatment of Rijiyar Lemo's radio broadcast examines how Salafi leaders seek to present their ideas within locally resonant idioms, and in this way dispel accusations that could cloud Salafis' ideal of a media-based intellectual meritocracy. Terje Østebø has discussed the "'localisation" of Salafism in Ethiopia through

[35] Ibid.

"dialectic interactions between impetus and response, between agents and audiences."[36] For Nigerian Salafis, electronic media help make such dialectic interactions possible. For this reason, they make strategic choices in their media interventions about how to engage local intellectual traditions.

Rijiyar Lemo appeared on Freedom Radio on 31 March 2007 to discuss *mawlid*, or the celebration of the Prophet Muḥammad's birthday. Freedom, founded in 2003, is Kano's first privately owned radio station. In an interview, Kabiru Umaru Abdallahi, the station's director of Islamic programming, stated that Freedom's religious offerings were its most popular. From its inception, the station sought young preachers who offered dynamic content. In an example of how media engagements build on each other, Abdallahi explained that Freedom often invited preachers based on the reputations they had generated through lecturing in mosques and circulating recordings.[37] Salafis, including Ādam, have appeared frequently at Freedom.[38] Rijiyar Lemo's broadcast on *mawlid* fit the station's programming preferences and reflected Salafi media strategies.

In his broadcast, Rijiyar Lemo marshaled texts to depict *mawlid* as an un-Islamic innovation, and to counter accusations that opposition to *mawlid* was a foreign import. Rijiyar Lemo hoped, through the medium of the radio, to bypass rival scholars and reach mass audiences who might, on the basis of textual references he provided them, verify his assertions for themselves. As in Ādam's lecture, Salafis' confidence in media as an intellectual meritocracy informed the broadcast, as did the strategic interweaving of different media to present a textually driven argument.

The Sufi reaction to this broadcast was dramatic, and it caused Freedom to exercise greater caution in its Islamic programming. Sufis appeared on Freedom to rebut Rijiyar Lemo's broadcast. Sufis also took their objections to the street. In a protest on 2 April 2007, Sufis hurled stones and burned the station's transmitter.[39] Freedom subsequently discouraged guest preachers from discussing creedal controversies,[40] a stance that reflects the evolution of Freedom's place within Kano's media landscape.

Salafi networks have not shied away from the controversy, however. The recording of Rijiyar Lemo's broadcast still circulated in Kano as

[36] Terje Østebø, *Localising Salafism: Religious Change among Oromo Muslims in Bale, Ethiopia* (Leiden: Brill, 2012), xix.

[37] Interview with Kabiru Umar Abdullahi, 16 November 2011, Kano.

[38] Andrea Brigaglia and Fauziyya Fiji, "'We Ain't Coming to Take People Away': A Sufi Praise-Song and the Representation of Police Forces in Northern Nigeria," *Annual Review of Islam in Africa* 10 (2008–2009): 50–7; 57, note 8.

[39] "Nigeria: Suspected Islamic Militants Attack Private Radio Station in Kano," AFP, 2 April 2007.

[40] Interview with Kabiru Umar Abdullahi.

of 2011. I purchased it as part of a collection provocatively titled, "Heretics: Admirers of the Prophet or Admirers of Latter-Day Pagans?" The recording's inclusion in the collection, which features lectures by various Salafi preachers against Sufism, frames the broadcast and the issue of *mawlid* as part of a broader Salafi-Sufi conflict. The recording's almost casual title, "Freedom Program on *Mawlid*," combined with the notoriety the 2007 broadcast attracted, suggests that the collection's compilers presumed their intended audience would be familiar with the incident. Not only the move from radio to recording, but also the legacy of the 2007 arson, affects the meaning of the original message within the media landscape.

Rijiyar Lemo structured the broadcast around four questions. First, does celebrating the Prophet's birthday indicate love (Hausa: *soyyaya*) for him? Second, when did the practice of *mawlid* start and who started it? Third, who has objected to the practice? Finally, if celebrating *mawlid* can be shown as an innovation introduced into Islam, under what legal category does it fall – is it a "good innovation" (*bidʿa ḥasana*) or not? Rijiyar Lemo marshaled textual evidence to support his answers, ultimately suggesting that *mawlid* is a "reprehensible innovation" (*bidʿa makrūha*).[41] Rijiyar Lemo's strategic presentation of textual evidence expounded the core Salafi argument that contemporary practices must be vetted according to the record of the early Muslim community. In a sense, this argument does not depend on local context, and Salafis have advanced it in diverse settings.

In Kano, however, Salafi leaders are aware of accusations that they are importing a foreign creed ("Wahhābism," in their opponents' parlance) and a foreign *madhhab* or legal school (in this case, the Ḥanbalī *madhhab*, rather than the Mālikī *madhhab*). Against this background of suspicion, Rijiyar Lemo also invoked the Mālikī canon of northwest Africa to delegitimize *mawlid* through the words of regionally and locally respected figures. He attempted to anticipate and undermine opponents' counterarguments by depicting disagreement with early Muslim and Mālikī authorities as unthinkable. Intellectual merit, he seemed convinced, would sway undecided audiences to the Salafi point of view, while the localizing thrust of his remarks would neutralize opponents' dismissal of Salafism as a foreign import.

These techniques appeared in a portion of the broadcast dealing with the early Muslim community. After saying that the practice of celebrating *mawlid* was unknown among the first three generations of Muslims, Rijiyar Lemo ruled out the possibility of contravening their example:

> You see if we're going to do justice toward them, we will give them the status that Allah gave them. We will never agree that [*mawlid*] shows love of the Prophet,

[41] Muḥammad Sani ʿUmar Rijiyar Lemo, "Shirin Freedom akan Maulidi," recorded radio broadcast, Freedom Radio, March 2007, Kano.

may Allah bless him and grant him peace. Because if we said so, it would be as though we were ruling (Hausa: *hukuntawa*) that they do not love the Prophet, may Allah bless him and grant him peace, which no one has enough arrogance (Hausa: *karfin halayya*, literally "strength of character") to say. I don't think there's anyone who will say that.[42]

Such an argument might suffice, in Salafis' eyes, to settle the question of *mawlid*. But Rijiyar Lemo invoked Mālikī canonical authorities to frame the issue in locally resonant terms:

I think in this city there is no book in which one has faith that it communicates what is due to the Messenger of Allah (Hausa: *hakkin Manzon Allah*), may Allah bless him and grant him peace, or his rights (*hakokinsa*) . . . like the book *Al Shifā'* [Arabic: *Al Shifā' bī Ta'rīf Ḥuqūq al-Muṣṭafā*, 'Healing by Recognizing the Rights of the Chosen One,' a biography of the Prophet], *Al Shifā'* of Qadi 'Iyād [1083–1149, a Mālikī scholar from present-day Ceuta and southern Spain]. The book *Al-Shifā'*. This is a book that has long been read for many years in this country. We've read, we've read, we've read, we came back and read, we read. Yet, we've never seen where he shows us that it is among the signs of loving [the Prophet] to do this meeting [i.e., *mawlid*]. Moreover, this meeting existed in the time of Qadi 'Iyad. But he didn't know, he didn't mention it among the signs of loving the Messenger of Allah. . . . I do not think there is anyone who believes that Qadi 'Iyād did not give the Messenger of Allah his due. There is no one.

Rijiyar Lemo made a similar argument concerning Shaykh 'Uthmān dan Fodio. Rijiyar Lemo's strategy of localization involved presenting texts that anchored his evidence in local legal and historical traditions. After reviewing several Mālikī texts, Rijiyar Lemo commented, "So you see it's not now that one has started talking [about *mawlid*] and it's not 'people of the Ḥanbalī *maddhab*' or 'Wahhābīs' or something. No. [It's] from within Mālikism whose books we read. They talk about it."[43] This invocation of Mālikism is striking in light of many Salafis' rejection of adherence to formal legal schools. Rijiyar Lemo's use of Mālikī sources in his broadcast seemed strategic, rather than a reflection of any Mālikī allegiances on his part.

Yet the strategic deployment of Mālikism does not contradict Salafi epistemological beliefs about singular and exclusive interpretations of scripture. In one ruling, Shaykh Muḥammad Nāṣir al-Dīn al-Albānī said that he evaluated the ideas and practices within legal schools according to scriptural proof-texts, rather than rejecting all of the content of the legal schools wholesale:

There are found in each one of the schools things that accord with the Book [i.e., the Qur'an] and the Sunna. They are accepted because of their conformity to the Book and the Sunna, not because it is the school of one of the imams.

[42] Rijiyar Lemo, "Shirin Freedom."
[43] Ibid.

When something is found in one of these imams' schools that contradicts the Book and the Sunna, it is refuted and refused, even if one of the imams said it.[44]

Figures from the legal schools, moreover, can be reframed as members of the Salafi canon, or at least as compatible with what Salafis see as genuine Sunni Islam. Salafism thus offers its adherents some flexibility in how they frame their views. This flexibility facilitates efforts at localization. Rijiyar Lemo conceived of the broadcast as a space that removed barriers between himself and the audience. He invoked Mālikī authorities to challenge stereotypes about Salafis that circulate in arenas where he has less access.

Whether this invocation of Mālikism is effective or not is another question. For skeptical audiences and for opponents of Salafism, Rijiyar Lemo's references to Mālikī authorities could be viewed not just as flexible and pragmatic, but as a form of dissimulation – a maneuver by an effectively Ḥanbalī speaker to obscure his Ḥanbalism. Critics of Salafism could even charge that the broader rhetoric of Salafism and anti-*madhhab*ism is itself a form of dissimulation, a strategic move to pretend to be something other than Wahhābī-Ḥanbalīs, which many Muslims believe Salafis, at heart, to be.

In Salafi eyes, however, Rijiyar Lemo's use of Mālikī and other sources emphasized, like Ādam's lecture on Sabuwar Gandu, transparency and accountability within media. Naming more than a dozen texts, Rijiyar Lemo provided detailed citations, identifying works' titles, stating authors' life spans, and giving page numbers for quotations. The broadcast functioned as a legal brief that assembled texts in service of its argument and also as a bibliography that listeners might use as a basis for their own investigations and verifications. Rijiyar Lemo's confidence in the power of media to cultivate intellectual meritocracy shone through.

Rijiyar Lemo, framing his mission as spreading knowledge, encouraged audiences to verify what he said. This framing aimed to dispel the criticism that he sought to provoke controversy, and in this way he hoped to answer another recurring Kano stereotype of Salafis as troublemakers. Throughout the broadcast, Rijiyar Lemo and the Freedom Radio host, Kabiru Umar Abdallahi, acknowledged that conflict had previously taken place over *mawlid* and that the broadcast itself could cause conflict. Against the charge that he sought conflict, Rijiyar Lemo contrasted the idea of spreading knowledge.

One should understand that really, the one who forbids [*mawlid*] did not start this. And it's not crisis (Hausa: *rigima*) that he wants. He's distributing some

[44] Muḥammad Nāṣir al-Dīn al-Albānī, *Fatāwā al-ʿAllāma Nāṣir al-Dīn al-Albānī*, collected and prepared by Abū ʿAbd al-Raḥmān ʿĀdil ibn Saʿd (Beirut: Dār al-Kutub al-ʿIlmiyya, 2011), 10.

knowledge to you. This kind of discussion makes knowledge progress.... But if someone says, "You, you talk, you say what you agree with, but one side should be sanctioned." ... So you see knowledge will not progress.... Let's open our hearts (*mun bude kirjinmu*), let's stop and listen to each side, let's hear the kind of proofs (*dalilan*) that they give.[45]

Opponents might object that the sheer fact of appearing on the radio to denounce *mawlid* was an irresponsibly provocative move. Rijiyar Lemo sought to preempt this charge. Like Ādam, Rijiyar Lemo called for a circumscribed pluralism in which both sides would present evidence and listeners would judge. Clarity of evidence was, for Rijiyar Lemo, the decisive criterion in this arena of public debate. Utilizing the flexibility the Salafi tradition has permitted in styles of argumentation, Rijiyar Lemo deployed textual evidence to both defend and localize his position on *mawlid*, while at the same time advocating the Salafi ideal of intellectual meritocracy based on proof-texts.

Other Muslims' Media Responses, Part One: Sufis

Throughout the world, Salafis' theological beliefs and reformist stances have often brought them into debates and conflicts with other Muslims, including other Sunnis. Salafism's canonical figures have themselves been objects of polemics and disagreement. Al-Albānī's refusal to be bound by the four major Sunni legal schools attracted criticism from figures like Dr. Sa'īd Ramaḍān al-Būṭī (1929–2013), a world-famous Syrian scholar who defended the classical structures of Sunni Islam and denounced "Salafism" as an innovation.[46] Opponents accuse Salafis of distorting and misreading Sunni textual traditions, sowing conflict and leading the masses astray, and abusing and denigrating classical Muslim authorities.

In Nigeria, Salafis face strong opposition from other Muslims, especially Sufis. The attention I give to Salafism and the Medina graduates in this book should not obscure the continued influence of Sufism in Kano and across northern Nigeria. It can be tempting, given Salafis' self-image as a Muslim vanguard and their self-conscious and strategic valorization of the role of youth in Islam, to adopt a binary construction that opposes the image of an aging, backward-looking, localized Sufi community to a youthful, energetic, transnationally engaged Salafi one. Such a construction would misrepresent realities in Nigeria or elsewhere in Africa. In northern Nigeria generally and Kano particularly, Sufism has undergone recurring waves of transformation and rejuvenation, including during

[45] Rijiyar Lemo, "Shirin Freedom."

[46] See Sa'īd Ramaḍān al-Būṭī, *Al-Lā Madhhabiyya: Akhṭar Bid'a Tuhaddid al-Sharī'a al-Islāmiyya*, third edition (Damascus: Dār al-Fārābī, 2005 [1985]).

the twentieth and twenty-first centuries. Sufi orders there retain broad followings, including among youth.

Important scholarship has documented how leading northern Nigerian Sufi shaykhs of the twentieth century, from both the Qadiriyya and Tijaniyya orders, popularized Sufism among wider audiences than ever before.[47] This expansion of Sufism involved new efforts to cultivate transnational ties, including with the Middle East (Morocco and Egypt for the Tijaniyya, and Iraq for the Qadiriyya, whose founder lived in twelfth-century Baghdad).[48] Less well documented is the way in which these same leaders – including the Qadiri shaykh Nāṣir Kabara (1912–96), the Tijani shaykhs Tijjānī ʿUthmān (1916–70) and Abū Bakr ʿAtīq (1909–74), and the Tijani businessman Mallam Uba Ringim (1919–99) – strategically prepared their own heirs to be highly credentialed, transnationally connected leaders with Arabic fluency, hybrid educations, and complex local bases of genealogical, scholarly, and institutional authority. The generation of Kabara, ʿUthmān, ʿAtīq, and Ringim undertook this strategic preparation in order to enable their sons and grandsons to keep pace with rapid social change. One major benefit of this preparation has been its utility in meeting the Salafi challenge to Sufism.

Among the generation of Sufis who are roughly the same age as the leading Medina graduates, several figures merit attention. Nāṣir Kabara's successor or *khalīfa* is his son Qaribullah, but his son ʿAbd al-Jabbār (b. 1970) has been particularly outspoken as a defender of Sufism. In lectures, the younger Kabara has worked to outline the textual basis for Sufi practices such as *mawlid* (the celebration of the Prophet's birthday) and *dhikr* (remembrance of God, e.g., through chanting a litany).[49] Kabara has also been a critic of Salafis' appropriation of concepts such as Sunna. In one lecture, he accused "those who call themselves scholars" of having "caused chaos in Islam (*suka hargitse musulunci*)" by "drawing a line in [Islam]" between the saved and the damned. These fake scholars had proceeded, he charged, from "a lack of understanding what the Sunna is." Kabara argued instead for a more expansive notion of Sunna than the Salafi version, which consists only of prophetic *aḥādīth* and yields only one answer to any question posed about its contents.

[47] John Paden, *Religion and Political Culture in Kano* (Berkeley and Los Angeles: University of California Press, 1973); Auwalu Anwar, "Struggle for Influence and Identity: The Ulama in Kano, 1937–1987," M.A. thesis, University of Maiduguri, 1989; and Roman Loimeier, *Islamic Reform and Political Change in Northern Nigeria* (Evanston: Northwestern University Press, 1997).

[48] Roman Loimeier, "Playing with Affiliations: Muslims in Northern Nigeria in the 20th Century" in *Entreprises religieuses transnationales en Afrique de l'Ouest*, edited by Laurent Fouchard, André Mary, and René Otayek, 349–72 (Paris: Karthala, 2005).

[49] Abduljabbar Nasir Kabara, "Garkuwar Mauludi (1/14)," recorded 17 June 2006. Available at: www.youtube.com/watch?v=3zN0PC5y-iA; accessed October 2015; Abduljabbar Nasir Kabara, "Wajabcin Zikir (1/2)," uploaded to YouTube 1 June 2012. Available at: www.youtube.com/watch/v=B0gxKjoGE_Q; accessed October 2015.

In place of this narrow Sunna, Kabara evoked a phrase from *Al-Risāla* (The Epistle), a core Mālikī text, the author of which referred to "traditions (*sunan*, the plural of *sunna*) – what they confirm, what is supererogatory according to them, what is desired according to them, and the kind of good manners associated with them."[50] In an extended discussion of this phrase, Kabara elaborated a more flexible, culturally situated notion of the Sunna.[51] As Kabara's use of Mālikī sources shows, when Sufis criticize Salafis for being narrow-minded, Sufis are speaking not just as "mystics" but as representatives of the classical model of Islamic education in northwest Africa, which they believe remains unparalleled as a mechanism for forming a complete Muslim, morally, intellectually, and spiritually. For Sufis, Salafis betray the narrowness of their learning when they emphasize *ḥadīth* over other Islamic sciences and when they constantly refer to a relatively small pool of canonized scholars. Many of the scholars in the Salafi canon, it should be noted, have a much lower stature in Sufi eyes than they do among Salafis.

Kabara has challenged Salafis by displaying considerable familiarity with their canonical authorities. He repositions such authorities, either by knocking them off of their Salafi pedestals or by appropriating them to make his own points. In his lecture on the Sunna, Kabara showed some respect for al-Albānī's scholarship on *aḥādīth* but criticized Nigerians who talked about al-Albānī's "authentication" of reports. Pointing to a core tension in Salafism between scholars' claims to be capable of *ijtihād* and their reliance on intermediaries, he called Nigerian Salafis "poor folk waiting to receive alms (*talakawa da suke jiran a karbu musu sadakar*)" from al-Albānī; Kabara called himself a "student with little knowledge (*ni almajiri ne rashin sani*)," but refused to accept that "a white man is going to come from Albania and . . . say he's going to teach me how to evaluate *aḥādīth*." This image evoked social divisions in Nigerian society, positioning Salafis as the passive poor while positioning Kabara as a humble, but more agentive, seeker of truth. A scholar was just a scholar, Kabara suggested, and no upstart could overturn Nigeria's own strongly established scholarly traditions.

Kabara's description of Nigerian Salafis as *talakawa* echoed a more widespread Sufi criticism of Salafis, which is that Salafis deliberately spread discord because they seek fame. Embedded in this criticism is a set of attitudes about the social origins of Salafis – a Sufi perception that Salafis are social climbers who use religion to compensate for or disguise their undistinguished origins. During my fieldwork, some Sufi

[50] Ibn Abī Zayd al-Qayrawānī, *Matn al-Risāla* (Beirut: Al-Maktaba al-Thaqāfiyya, undated), 4.

[51] Abduljabbar Nasir Kabara, "Menene Sunnah? (Part One)," uploaded to YouTube 7 February 2014. Available at: www.youtube.com/watch?v=7VpllZrFFOo; accessed October 2015.

friends expressed bafflement that I was studying figures like Ādam, whom they regarded as essentially an upstart boy who had possessed no serious learning. Even more damningly, some Sufis saw Boko Haram as the predictable outgrowth of Salafis' confrontational stances toward Sufi and hereditary authority: the movement of upstart Salafis, they felt, was bound to turn violent at some point.

Elsewhere, Kabara has reappropriated reframed thinkers in the Salafi canon. In one Facebook post, Kabara used the words of Ibn Taymiyya in an effort not just to refute Salafis on one point (in this case, the idea that righteous Muslims might be able to work miracles, such as ʿAbd al-Qādir al-Jīlānī's legendary resurrection of a cooked chicken) but also to show that Salafis are ignorant of their own canon. Kabara cited a passage from Ibn Taymiyya that seemed to agree with the possibility of miracles worked by the righteous. Kabara concluded, "So our problem today is that the ignoramuses of Salafism (*jahilan Salafiyya*), those who see themselves as the ultimate scholars, have not even studied the books of their shaykhs."[52]

Both Qaribullah and ʿAbd al-Jabbār Kabara have played prominent roles in the institutional life of Kano. The *khalifa* sat on the *sharīʿa* implementation Review Committee in 2000 (along with other Sufis appointed, in part, to balance out the seats given to Salafis like Ādam).[53] Both brothers sit on the Governing Board of the Shaikh Nasir Kabara Research Centre, which was established in 2009 with a donation from the Kano state government and commissioned by Emir Ado Bayero in 2010.[54] Institutionalizing the memory of pivotal twentieth-century Sufis has been one strategy their successors have pursued to both consolidate their own authority and spread Sufism to new audiences.

Among the Tijanis, several styles of public engagement, including anti-Salafi engagement, obtain. Most of the prominent Tijanis in Kano belong to the Tijaniyya-Ibrāhīmiyya, named for the Senegalese shaykh Ibrāhīm Niasse (1900–75), who helped popularize the order throughout West Africa and beyond.[55] As noted earlier, twentieth-century leaders in this branch of the Tijaniyya, including Niasse himself, systematically sent their sons, grandsons, and the sons of their leading disciples to study in the Arab world, particularly at Egypt's al-Azhar University. This strategic

[52] Abduljabbar Kabara, Facebook posting, 29 August 2015. Available at: www.facebook.com/AbduljabbarKabara/posts/857797444273873; accessed October 2015.

[53] Ibrahim Na'iya Sada, "The Making of the Zamfara and Kano State Sharia Penal Codes" in *Sharia Implementation in Northern Nigeria: A Sourcebook, Volume 4*, edited by Philip Ostien, 22–32 (Ibadan: Spectrum Books, 2007), 29.

[54] Shaikh Nasir Kabara Research Centre, "Background," 17 August 2011. Available at: http://snkresearchcentre.blogspot.com/2011/08/background.html; accessed October 2015.

[55] Rüdiger Seesemann, *The Divine Flood: Ibrahim Niasse and the Roots of a Twentieth-Century Sufi Revival* (New York: Oxford University Press, 2011).

choice has resulted in a leadership class of the Tijaniyya in Kano that largely comprises graduates of al-Azhar and other Egyptian universities. These Tijanis have hybrid educations: their education at al-Azhar did not supplant immersion in the classical Islamic educational system of northwest Africa, but rather became a layer added to that training.[56]

The Tijani graduates of al-Azhar have been at the forefront of building new institutions for the Tijaniyya in Kano. These institutions include the Mai Masallaci ("The Mosque Owner's") Foundation, a center dedicated to research and documentation about Nigerian Sufism, which has an associated Islamic school. The "Islamiyya" schools that operate across Kano are hybrid, government-approved institutions that teach both Islamic sciences (such as jurisprudence) and a government-created curriculum. Studying at an Islamiyya school is meant to lead to government-recognized secondary school certificates and, ultimately, university admission. Various kinds of scholars and movements operate Islamiyya schools, but the Tijanis have become one strong participant in this field. A web of schools and other new institutions, many of them founded since the 1980s, allows the Tijaniyya to ensure that Salafis cannot claim a monopoly over Islamiyya schools, Qur'an recitation competitions, or other Islamic institutions in the city. Sufi-Salafi competition in the realm of institution building has meant that in several areas of Kano (including Gadon Kaya and, as discussed earlier, Sabuwar Gandu), one can find Sufi and Salafi mosques within a stone's throw of one another.

Tijani Muslims, like their Qadiri peers, voice fundamental criticisms of Salafis and their approach to Islamic knowledge. One Tijani scholar, Dr. Lawi 'Atīq (b. ca. 1962), is the son of Shaykh Abū Bakr 'Atīq, one of the most prominent Tijani leaders in Kano during the twentieth century. The younger 'Atīq is a major scholar and Tijani leader in his own right. He is a graduate of Al-Azhar, where he studied in the 1980s. Nevertheless, he had strong reservations about the claims to intellectual and religious authority made by some Nigerian graduates of Arab universities. In particular, 'Atīq was concerned by the way such graduates have presented their learning as all-encompassing, rather than deferring to the ethic of specialization that prevails in the classical northwest African model of Islamic education. Explaining the sources of what he called religious discord (*fitna*) in contemporary Nigeria, 'Atīq placed much of the responsibility on Arab-educated religious entrepreneurs:

You take someone who goes to Egypt. . . . When he gets an opportunity to go to Egypt, to obtain an academic scholarship, perhaps he was studying in a high

[56] This section is based on interviews with Shaykh Baba Uba Ibrahim, 1 December 2011 and 8 December 2011, Kano; Shaykh Kabiru Uba Ibrahim, 9 December 2011, Kano; and Shaykh Bashir Tijjani Uthman, 13 December 2011, Kano.

> school here in Kano. But in his house, he didn't study any book, he didn't study anything. Perhaps his father was a trader or a farmer. . . . He goes to Egypt or Saudi Arabia or Libya or any other place to study the principles of religion (*'ulūm al-dīn*). . . . And he returns to us in Nigeria, to Kano for example or to any place in Nigeria. And first of all, when he returns he has no background (*khalfiyya*) or foundation (*arḍiyya*) in knowledge or the principles of religion. When he goes there [to the Arab world] he goes and studies in a university, or any place of study, to obtain a degree on paper (*waraqat shahāda*). . . . When he returns to Nigeria, he is ninety-nine percent ignorant. In other words, he has one eye, he returns to the blind and wants to lead them. And therefore you find this *fitna*. . . . For example, how do you explain a person who went to Saudi Arabia, for example to study *ḥadīth*, or to Egypt to study the Arabic language, and he wants to return to Nigeria and call himself a scholar (*'ālim*) in the principles of religion, and a scholar in language, and a scholar in Sufism, and a scholar in everything – "General Enterprises"? . . . This is what has happened to Islam in Nigeria.[57]

'Atīq explained further that when specialists questioned such graduates on their knowledge in any particular branch of learning, the graduates were found deficient. He compared them to car mechanics who felt themselves qualified to be electricians as well. In contrast, 'Atīq said, the classical model developed mastery in particular specializations, and also fostered humility in terms of overall claims to intellectual and religious authority. University degrees threatened to displace a system that is considered, by 'Atīq and many other Nigerian scholars, a more rigorous form of credentialing and authorization.

As Sufis debate Salafis, both sides are affected, and the stakes are high. In some ways, current Sufi-Salafi debates reenact earlier polemics that raged between Abubakar Gumi on the one hand and Kabara, 'Uthmān, and 'Atīq on the other. The 1972 publication of Gumi's *Al-'Aqīda al-Ṣaḥīḥa bi-Muwāfaqat al-Sharī'a* (The Correct Creed Is in Accordance with the *Sharī'a*) triggered polemical responses from Kabara and various Tijani shaykhs.[58] Some of these twentieth-century shaykhs' sons feel that an ethic of politeness that characterized the earlier debate has now slipped away; Lawi 'Atīq remembered that Gumi had come to pay his respects when 'Atīq's father died. The younger 'Atīq felt that he lacked any equivalent personal connection or sense of mutual respect with Salafis today. Nevertheless, violence featured in debates even in the time of Gumi and the older Sufis: Gumi experienced threats and assassination attempts in the 1970s, and Sufis killed Izala supporters after the riots associated with the (non-Izala) preacher Maitatsine in the first

57 Interview with Dr. Lawi 'Atīq, 25 January 2012, Kano.

58 Roman Loimeier, *Islamic Reform and Political Change in Northern Nigeria* (Evanston: Northwestern University Press, 1997).

half of the 1980s.[59] Violence today has antecedents in the past. Today's Salafi-Sufi conflicts, moreover, take place amid a broad "sense of insecurity" for many northern Nigerian Muslims,[60] which may contribute to both sides' willingness to turn from violent words to violent acts. Kano in particular is one of the region's "hotspots" for interreligious violence, including violence between Muslim sects.[61] Given the importance of Sufism to many ordinary Nigerian Muslims, moreover, Sufi-Salafi conflicts can have upsetting and divisive ramifications at the level even of individual households, pitting fathers against sons or neighbors against neighbors.

Meanwhile, young Sufis today may, wittingly or unwittingly, make a profound compromise if they let Salafis set the epistemological terms of the debate. Even as Sufis seek to show that their own learning is broader and deeper than the education Salafis receive in Medina or the ideas contained in the Salafi canon, there is a strong sense that the final currency of debate is textual proofs and evidence. As scholars like ʿAbd al-Jabbār Kabara mount an aggressive, public defense of Sufism by offering textual proofs for Sufi practices and worldviews, they risk implicitly suggesting that the Salafis are right about how Islamic knowledge should work, even if Sufis disagree with their conclusions. Here, too, the past is present: in the 1970s and 1980s, intra-Sufi debates broke out in response to Gumi's anti-Sufi tract. Some Tijanis sought to present a "reformed" version of their order, stripped of a few controversial elements, and other Tijanis objected.[62] Today, as a new generation of Sufis responds to Salafi attacks, they face the same dilemma, especially if personalized authority and charisma are subordinated to concerns about who can produce the most authoritative text.

Other Muslims' Media Responses, Part Two: Progressive Intellectuals

Northern Nigerian intellectuals of a progressive bent have also criticized Salafis, echoing Sufis' criticisms but putting forward other rival canons and different arguments about the proper sources of religious authority. Such intellectuals do not necessarily speak for broad constituencies, but they frequently have major platforms at universities, nongovernmental

[59] Ousmane Kane, *Muslim Modernity in Postcolonial Nigeria: A Study of the Society for the Removal of Innovation and the Reinstatement of Tradition* (Leiden: Brill, 2003).

[60] Murray Last, "The Search for Security in Muslim Northern Nigeria," *Africa: The Journal of the International African Institute* 78:1 (2008): 41–63; 43.

[61] Murray Last, "Muslims and Christians in Nigeria: An Economy of Political Panic," *The Round Table: The Commonwealth Journal of International Affairs* 96:392 (2007): 605–16.

[62] Rüdiger Seesemann, "The Takfīr Debate: Sources for the Study of a Contemporary Dispute among African Sufis, Part One: The Nigerian Arena," *Sudanic Africa* 9 (1998): 39–70; and "Part Two: The Sudanese Arena," *Sudanic Africa* 10 (1999): 65–110.

organizations, or in government. One powerful critique, which personally targeted Ādam, came from Sanusi Lamido Sanusi (b. 1961), an immensely influential hereditary Muslim ruler and public intellectual whose diverse roles have included being emir of Kano (since 2014) and serving as governor of the Central Bank of Nigeria (2009–14, until he was suspended after publicly accusing then-President Goodluck Jonathan of corruption). During most of the 2000s, Sanusi worked as a banker and acted as a public intellectual, commenting frequently on issues relating to Islam, politics, and the implementation of *sharīʿa* in northern states. Sanusi's hybrid educational background, which includes an M.A. in Islamic Law from the International University of Africa in Sudan, enables him to debate Salafis in multiple spheres.

In 2005, Sanusi published a two-part response to Ādam on the question of defining religious, political, and ethnic identity in northern Nigeria, particularly with reference to the nature of *sharīʿa*. The conflict concerned two visions of Islam: Ādam's emphasis on Islam as a set of pan-historical truths interpreted through an exclusivist framework, versus Sanusi's idea of an internal Muslim pluralism that treats Islam and Muslim identities as constructs, while conceptualizing *sharīʿa* as a system for promoting socioeconomic justice. The immediate trigger for Sanusi's two essays was a remark by Ādam in the newspaper *Daily Trust* that people like Sanusi "don't know where they come from. They don't have the identity of the religion they belong to. They equally don't have the identity of the tribe they belong."[63] Sanusi's essays were published on the Internet forum Gamji, where they evoked numerous counter-responses as the debate shifted from print to online.

For Sanusi, the issue of having an identity, like the issue of defining *sharīʿa*, came down to questions of how to define Islam as a whole: "If Jaʿfar argues that I do not have an Islamic identity, all that it means to me is that my interpretation of what Islam is differs in fundamental respects from his." This difference of interpretation highlighted the question of intellectual authority in Islam. Tension between himself and Ādam, Sanusi wrote, arose because "those who are used to unquestioning subservience from the intellectually immature have to deal with independent thinkers, and suddenly find their claims to certain knowledge relativized and decentered."[64]

Sanusi attacked Ādam's personal and educational background, depicting the shaykh as a narrow-minded fundamentalist and a hypocrite and

[63] Sanusi Lamido Sanusi, "Identity, Political Ethics and Parochialism: Engagement with Jaʿfar Adam (1)," Gamji, 27 April 2005. Available at: www.gamji.com/sanusi/sanusi49.htm; accessed April 2013.

[64] Sanusi Lamido Sanusi, "Identity, Political Ethics and Parochialism: Engagement with Jaʿfar Adam (2)," 3 May 2005. Available at: www.gamji.com/sanusi/sanusi50.htm; accessed April 2013.

dismissing his Salafi activism as a desperate search for personal fulfillment. Drawing on the account of Ādam's early life found in Ousmane Kane's *Muslim Modernity in Postcolonial Nigeria*, Sanusi called Ādam

> an ambulant who grew up without stability or parental care; a charm maker who turned into a fanatical wahhabite; an alien and settler in his place of abode; a Nigerian who was educated on the charity of Saudi Arabia and whose mosque and school – his source of livelihood – are funded by Arabs; a strong advocate of anti-Americanism whose patron is doing good business with the Great Satan himself; in other words, a man whose life has been a series of dislocations, contradictions and alienation; an exile throughout his life, groping for *terra ferma* beneath his feet; an unknown quantity that rides on the back of religious fundamentalism to gain social relevancy. Such a person needs an anchor desperately because of his inherent insecurity and instability, and he finds it in paranoid and parochial identities. He needs an identity, because without one he is nothing. And if he has none, he must construct it.[65]

By attacking Ādam's background, Sanusi could dismiss the central component of Ādam's religious authority, namely the contention that the shaykh derived and applied universal religious truths with reference to canonical texts and thinkers. Sanusi used one of the Salafis' most revered canonical authorities, Ibn Taymiyya, to symbolize the gap he perceived between Salafis' allegedly narrow knowledge of classical religious thought and the complexities of contemporary political reality:

> The problem we have with some of our scholars is their presumption that every Muslim must rely on them for mediation not just in understanding religious texts, in which they may or may not have achieved a standard of competence, but also in matters beyond their competence, such as the question of negotiating the difficult terrain of politics and developing true concepts of citizenship in plural societies. There is nothing wrong with an Imam participating in political discourse, but he must understand that memorizing thirteenth century texts written by Ibn Taimiya will not make him an authority in contemporary political thought, nor provide him with immunity from ridicule, the just recompense for pretentious posturing.[66]

The critiques that Sufis and progressives make of Salafis align in this passage. Yet in addition to positioning his Salafi opponents as intellectually unsophisticated, Sanusi offered up a different canon, namely modern Western-style scholarship and philosophy. This alternative canon, Sanusi argued, destabilized the identities that Salafis desperately wished to see as fixed:

> I do not expect Jaʿfar to be familiar with philosophical works on this topic [of the social construction of identity]. For example I doubt if he has read the books of the contemporary African philosopher, Kwame Anthony Appiah, such as

[65] Sanusi, "Identity (1)"; the relevant pages in Kane are 108–10.
[66] Sanusi, "Identity (1)."

The Ethics of Identity or *In My Father's House: Africa in the Philosophy of Culture*. I doubt if he has even read Majid Fakhry's *Ethical Theories of Islam* or Sohail Hashmi's *Islamic Political Ethics: Civil Society, Pluralism and Conflict*. I do not expect that he has ever come across Segun Gbadegesin's brilliant article "Yoruba Philosophy: Individuality, Community and the Moral Order"; Anthony Kirk-Greene's "'Mutumin Kirki': The Concept of the Good Man in Hausa"; or Sa ʾad Abubakar's equally insightful analysis of the concept of *Pulaku* among the Fulani in his master-piece of Adamawa history, *The Lamibe of Fombina*.[67]

Much criticism of Salafis, then, has focused on attacking their learning – in other words, on saying that Salafis have insufficient understanding of important canons (be it the classical scholarly canon of northwest Africa, or more contemporary philosophical and academic canons). This criticism goes on to say that the Salafis' own canon is simplistic, that it includes a few texts by Ibn Taymiyya and a few *ḥadīth*. Sanusi blended media – academic scholarship, works of philosophy, and a reframed understanding of the value of the Salafi canon, all woven together in an Internet essay – to challenge not only Ādam's ideas but also his public, highly mediatized, construction of religious and political authority.

Conclusion

When assessing Nigerian Salafis' media strategies, two features stand out. First, Salafis apply their understanding of religious truth to seemingly secular media forms: just as Salafis deploy scriptural proof-texts to argue creedal and legal issues, so they invoke videos, websites, and government documents as proofs in intra-Muslim disputes over knowledge and rights. All of these media contribute to the ideal of intellectual meritocracy: Salafis encourage audiences to check references, whether by consulting classical texts or searching online. For Salafis, media is a kind of infrastructure that reinforces the physical infrastructure of mosques and schools. Salafis express confidence that if they obtain physical and virtual space to propagate their message, the preponderance of evidence they assemble cannot fail to convince listeners. Kano's Salafis view electronic media, in which they believe actors compete on a more even intellectual footing than in other spaces, as an especially favorable arena for the transmission of their ideas.

Second, Salafis invoke local textual traditions to counter portrayals of Salafism as a foreign import. Drawing on the flexibility that the Salafi tradition allows in argumentation, Salafis recognize the influence of locally resonant texts and traditions. Thus Rijiyar Lemo invoked Mālikī texts where he might have cited only *ḥadīth* and classical histories, or materials

[67] Sanusi, "Identity (1)."

from the Salafi canon. In their media strategies, Salafis show some willingness to compromise with prevailing social structures in Kano. This willingness is predicated, in part, on Salafis' confidence in media as an intellectual meritocracy. Thus Ādam called for greater radio airtime rather than an overthrow of the Palace or the governor. He believed that more airtime would, in the long run, allow Salafi messages to triumph.

As Salafis and their critics clash in the media, each side compromises: Salafis relativize and localize canonical authority, while Sufis give greater weight to textual evidence than they might otherwise do. At the same time, media battles expose the Salafi canon to risks and challenges: Salafis' opponents can propose rival canons, appropriate and reframe core Salafi thinkers, or depict the Salafi canon as the unsophisticated clutch of texts wielded by grasping social climbers. As Salafis seek to use electronic media to level the playing field and compensate for their opponents' greater institutional power, Salafis' critics can use media to reassert social hierarchies based on heredity and knowledge.

This chapter has examined one ideal embedded in the Salafi canon: the ideal of an intellectual meritocracy, where the argument with the strongest textual basis will, if given a fair hearing, carry the most weight. We have seen how an ideal provided by the canon can function even when the canon remains in the background – how, even, the ideal can function when expressed partly through the idiom of a different canon, such as the Mālikī heritage of northwest Africa. The next chapter turns to another ideal that is central to the canon: the ideal of Salafis as a vanguard of true Muslims. This latter ideal, the next chapter shows, structures Nigerian Salafis' interventions in local, national, and global politics.

6 The Canon in Politics

A famous *ḥadīth*, often cited by Salafis in Nigeria and elsewhere, relates that the Prophet Muḥammad said, "Islam began as a stranger and will return as a stranger as it began, so blessed are the strangers." Shaykh Ja'far Maḥmūd Ādam, building a lecture around this text, applied it to religious life in contemporary Nigeria:

> So in this place Muslims of the original kind have become strangers: strangers in their creed, for the creed is the unity of Allah, worshipping Him alone, amid people who worship idols. Then too, strangers in terms of attitude, traits, and their characters, because they live amid people that have evil characters. Strangers in terms of ethics because they live amid people who exist in blasphemy.[1]

The *ḥadīth*, and Ādam's commentary on it, imply that in the final days of the world, the community of true Muslims will be small. Heretics, hypocrites, and enemies will surround it. The *ḥadīth* could be understood as a call for the faithful to close ranks, yet Salafis worldwide have often seen it as a call to activism. In his lecture, Ādam recounted other versions of the report in which the Prophet's Companions asked him for clarifications about the identity of the strangers he mentioned. Alternate versions include definitions such as "those who pursue reform when people have become corrupt" and "those who reform what people have corrupted of my tradition (*sunnatī*)." These texts suggest that the role of the small community of true Muslims is to both embody purity and correct a fallen world.

As Chapter 4 discussed, Salafi preachers in northern Nigeria use multiple registers as they present Salafi ideals and teachings to their audiences. This pattern is not unusual among Salafis worldwide – Ibn Bāz and other Salafi canonical figures often used a stripped-down, scripture-based form of argumentation in their legal opinions (*fatāwā*) and other pronouncements intended for a broad audience.[2] Similarly, in their political commentary, Nigerian Salafi preachers tend to emphasize Qur'anic

[1] Ja'far Maḥmūd Ādam, recording of untitled lecture, Sokoto, 2004.

[2] 'Abd al-'Azīz ibn Bāz, *Al-Shaykh Ibn Bāz wa-Mawāqifuhu al-Thābita*, collected and edited by Aḥmad bin 'Abd Allāh al-Farīḥ (Kuwait: Maktabat al-Rushd, 2000).

verses and *ḥadīth* reports but downplay the broader set of canonical references. One reason for the Medina graduates' success in growing their followership in Kano from the 1990s to the present has been their ability to discuss politics in a highly accessible, scripture-heavy discursive style. Yet even as the canon seems to recede in political discourses, it structures the ideal of Salafis as a vanguard of pure Muslims. At times, Nigerian Salafis invoke canonical figures such as Ibn Taymiyya to reference an ideal and situate the present in relation to it.

Scholars of Salafism have described the movement as theologically unitary and politically diverse. Bernard Haykel sees theology as the core of Salafism,[3] while Quintan Wiktorowicz has created a political typology for Salafis, categorizing them as political quietists, nonviolent political dissidents, and jihadis.[4] In this chapter, I argue that there is a unified political ideal, stemming from Salafism's theological core, that underlies all Salafis' political behaviors. This ideal depicts Salafis as "strangers" to a world of deceit and corruption. In methodological terms, studying the political ideals expressed in the Salafi canon helps us to go beyond the narrow confines of studying intellectual genealogies. Being part of a canon allows Nigerian Salafis to draw on a huge repertoire of Salafi models, beyond just those they saw at the Islamic University.

Within the context of northern Nigerian politics, the Salafi community is fragmented. Some individual preachers maintain affiliations to different elected officials, whereas other preachers attempt to remain aloof from politicians (although not from commenting on major political developments perceived to affect Islam). Salafi leaders took different stances toward Kano's Governor Ibrahim Shekarau, who cultivated an image as an ardent champion of *sharīʿa* implementation. Abdulwahhab Abdullah served as a member of the Zakat Committee, the Sharīʿa Commission, and the Shura Committee under Shekarau. Ādam was a member of the Sharīʿa Review Committee during the first term of Governor Rabiu Musa Kwankwaso, who served from 1999–2003 and again from 2011–15; Ādam also held bureaucratic appointments under Shekarau, but he resigned in 2005, with open bitterness over Shekarau's alleged lack of commitment to Islamizing Kano. Ādam openly opposed Shekarau by 2007.[5] During his lifetime, Ādam seemed torn between pursuing an ideal of remaining aloof from elected politicians and pursuing the

3 Bernard Haykel, "On the Nature of Salafi Thought and Action" in *Global Salafism: Islam's New Religious Movement*, edited by Roel Meijer, 33–57 (New York: Columbia University Press, 2009).

4 Quintan Wiktorowicz, "Anatomy of the Salafi Movement," *Studies in Conflict & Terrorism* 29 (2006), 207–39.

5 Haruna Wakili, "Islam and the Political Arena in Nigeria: The Ulama and the 2007 Elections," Northwestern University Institute for the Study of Islamic Thought in Africa Working Paper 09–004, March 2009.

advantages of participating in politics; his decision to resign from Shekarau's government may have reflected not just distaste with the governor but also ambivalence about the merits of serving in government at all. Following Ādam's death, his associates have pursued different political paths, which strains the Salafi community's unity. In 2011, some Salafis endorsed Kwankwaso and served in his second administration despite the criticisms he received during his first term for being "weak" on *sharīʿa* implementation.[6] The most prominent Salafi in Kano politics since 2011 has been Shaykh Aminu Daurawa (b. 1969), Commander General of the Hisbah Board under Governor Kwankwaso and then, after the 2015 elections, under Kwankwaso's successor and former deputy, Abdullahi Ganduje. Daurawa has used this position to strengthen the Salafi movement and, when opportunities present themselves, to turn political crises into occasions for attacking Sufism. At such moments, Salafis tend to unite.

The Salafi Daʿwa versus Islamist Activism

Around the world, Salafis have had to negotiate relationships with other Muslim activist movements, particularly Islamists, who focus on capturing state power to Islamize society from the top down. In contrast to Salafism's well-defined theological creed, the theological core of Islamism, as represented by Egypt's Muslim Brotherhood and its offshoots and peers, consists primarily of "generic Sunni Islam," that is, a set of propositions about what Islam is that do not involve fine-grained distinctions on theological questions such as the nature of the attributes of Allah.[7] Islamism's "generic Islam" means that areas of strategic compromises are possible between Islamists and Salafis, but it also means that the two tendencies have different priorities. In Sudan, for example, Salafis have had ambivalent attitudes toward the Islamist government that came to power in 1989. Although Sudanese Salafis endorsed the Islamist project "in principle," they "remained highly critical of both the method and the content of Islamist political activism . . . [and] saw themselves (using the classical idiom of *nasiha*, or advice) in the role of reforming a regime not yet fully in line with the principles of what Salafis understood to be correct doctrine."[8] In Egypt, multiparty elections after the 2011 revolution brought Salafis' differences with Islamist actors to

6 Alex Thurston, "Muslim Politics and Shariʿa in Kano, Nigeria," *African Affairs* 114: 454 (January 2015): 28–51.

7 For more on "generic Islam," see Benjamin Soares, *The Prayer Economy: History and Authority in a Malian Town* (Ann Arbor: University of Michigan Press, 2005), 224.

8 Noah Salomon, "The Salafi Critique of Islamism: Doctrine, Difference and the Problem of Islamic Political Action in Contemporary Sudan" in *Global Salafism*, 143–68; 146. See also Einas Ahmed, "Militant Salafism in Sudan," *Islamic Africa* 6:1–2 (July 2015): 164–84.

the fore. The Salafi Al-Nūr Party ran its own candidate for president. In Saudi Arabia, state-affiliated Salafi authorities – including canonical figures like Ibn Bāz – negotiated their position vis-à-vis many younger Saudis' enthusiasm for Islamist thinkers like Sayyid Quṭb. Salafis often enter into political Islam with a sharp sense that what matters most is the purity of Muslims' creed. Moreover, some Salafis fear that belonging to formal associations such as the Brotherhood might create sectarianism within the Muslim community or lead to spiritually dangerous compromises with regimes.[9]

In northern Nigeria, Salafis have not had to compete and interact with organized Islamist movements to the same degree that their Arab peers have. The Muslim Brotherhood does not have any significant presence in Nigeria, and the most recognizably Islamist voices in an ideological sense – as opposed to the mass of Muslims broadly interested in living in a more pious society, and the elected politicians who are strategically and selectively Islamist – are limited to certain university intellectuals. Yet Nigerian Salafis, like their Sudanese counterparts, expressed concern about the doctrinal and methodological character of northern states' efforts to implement *sharīʿa* after 1999. Ādam questioned who would administer *sharīʿa*-affiliated bureaucracies before the law came into effect, and he and several other Salafis resigned from bureaucracies under Governor Ibrahim Shekarau in 2005, after they came to feel that Shekarau was too close to the Sufi orders and the emir of Kano.

Nigerian Salafis are certainly aware of the Brotherhood. When Nigerian Salafis talk about the Brotherhood, they note and sometimes praise the efforts that figures like the Brotherhood's founder Ḥasan al-Banna (1906–49) have made in Islamic activism. Yet they do not embrace the Brotherhood. In one lecture, Rijiyar Lemo categorized the Brotherhood as one of many "jihad associations" (*kungiyoyin jihadi*) that had emerged between the fall of the Ottoman Caliphate in 1924 and the present; such groups, he said, had largely failed, and he made little distinction between the Brotherhood and its violent offshoots. Rijiyar Lemo's voice in the lecture was that of a historian who sympathized with fellow Muslims' efforts to resist outside aggression in places like Palestine, Afghanistan, Iraq, and the Philippines: "All these places, Muslims everywhere in the world now agree that they are defensive jihad" (*Wadannan gurare duk, musulmi na koina a duniya yanzu ya yi ittifaki a cewa suna da jihad al-dafʿi*).[10] Yet Rijiyar Lemo pronounced an unequivocal verdict that many Islamist and jihadist groups, especially those coming out of the Egyptian radical milieu, fell into "some opinions and some creeds and also taking

9 Quintan Wiktorowicz, *The Management of Islamic Activism: Salafis, the Muslim Brotherhood, and State Power in Jordan* (Albany: State University of New York Press, 2001), 131–3.

10 Muḥammad Sani ʿUmar Rijiyar Lemo, "Kungiyoyin Jihadi (2)," Maiduguri, April 2009.

a certain approach that violated the approach of Ahlussunnah" (*wadansu tunanai-tunanai da wasu akidu da kuma daukan wani manhaji wanda ya saba wa manhajin Ahlussunnah*). He objected to the Brotherhood's simultaneous proclamation of Salafi and Sufi affiliations.[11] He also stressed that many Islamist and jihadist organizations had been founded or led by youth, and moreover youth who were not trained as *ʿulamāʾ* but rather as doctors and engineers.[12] Rijiyar Lemo carefully noted that al-Banna "was not a scholar."[13]

Rijiyar Lemo also argued pragmatically that many violent Islamist actions had failed to alter political realities. He pointed to Egyptian President Hosni Mubarak's continued relations with Israel even after the assassination of his predecessor Anwar al-Sadat in 1981 by jihadi activists. Naming the leaders of the assassination plot, Rijiyar Lemo asked, "What ʿAbd al-Salām Faraj did, what Yaḥyā Hashim did, what Khālid Islambouli did, did it change anything? It didn't change anything."[14] In contrast, Rijiyar Lemo pointed admiringly to the growth of Salafi activism in Egypt.

> Praise to Allah, Ahlussunnah have made efforts to become strong in Egypt, whereas in the past, you would say, "There is knowledge there, but there is a lack of Sunna." Since the time they appeared, Ahlussunnah have established activities for spreading knowledge, and teaching, and striving to enlighten people about the Sunna of the Prophet, may Allah bless him and grant him peace.[15]

With this reference to the growth of Salafism and the spread of orthodoxy, Rijiyar Lemo directed attention to the Salafi conviction that the greatest social project was not competition over political leadership, but the effort to reorient society's thinking, values, and practices.

The Brotherhood's minimal influence in Nigeria has had two consequences. First, there are no Salafi-Brotherhood hybrids of the type found in Saudi Arabia.[16] Second, Nigerian Salafis have not had as strong an incentive as their peers in, for example, Egypt after the 2011 revolution, to establish political parties or even gravitate toward one political party in particular; it should also be noted that Nigeria's Constitution (Part III, Section 222(e)) implies that parties with religious bases are forbidden. When Nigerian Salafis participate in politics, their primary competitors are not the Brotherhood but rather Sufis, hereditary rulers, progressive intellectuals, and Christians. The main arenas of competition have been

[11] Rijiyar Lemo, "Kungiyoyin Jihadi (2)."
[12] Muḥammad Sani ʿUmar Rijiyar Lemo, "Kungiyoyin Jihadi (1)," Maiduguri, April 2009.
[13] Rijiyar Lemo, "Kungiyoyin Jihadi (1)."
[14] Rijiyar Lemo, "Kungiyoyin Jihadi (2)."
[15] Ibid.
[16] Stéphane Lacroix, *Awakening Islam: The Politics of Religious Dissent in Contemporary Saudi Arabia*, translated by George Holoch (Cambridge: Harvard University Press, 2011).

not elections but preaching and the control of institutions, ranging from neighborhood mosques to state government bureaucracies. Salafis are not "the 'other' Islamists" or some kind of U.S.-style "Tea Party" pressuring the Muslim Brotherhood from the "right."[17] Indeed, a "left-right" spectrum has little meaning in the context of Muslim politics, where so-called fundamentalists often blend commitments to social welfare and women's education with a rejection of manmade laws and the notion of a pluralistic society. In contrast to Islamist politics, Salafi politics aims to actualize a specific theology in various domains of life and is often more concerned with purifying society than with state power.

The Salafi Vanguard and Metonymy

The ideal of a pure vanguard surrounded by enemies finds diverse expressions in Salafism and its canon. In politics, the classical canon offers two models: the quietist persecuted by authorities, but unwilling to surrender his beliefs; and the activist who works to purify the societies around him. These two models are two sides of the same coin, namely the idea of a pure vanguard of Muslims fighting to maintain the truth in a world full of backsliders and enemies.

For Salafis, Ibn Ḥanbal, Ibn Taymiyya, and Ibn ʿAbd al-Wahhāb exemplify both creedal purity and the courage necessary for its defense. The canon's coherence derives in part from the ways in which it views these diverse actualizations of the ideal as equally legitimate according to their different contexts. As noted in Chapter 1, the canon celebrates Ibn Ḥanbal's steadfast reluctance to participate in politics or to be intimidated by the ʿAbbāsid Caliphs' theological inquisition. It also lauds Ibn Taymiyya's intellectual battles against perceived heresies in the shadow of the Mongol assault on Muslim heartlands, as well as Ibn ʿAbd al-Wahhāb's confrontational approach to perceived heresy in his own time.

If the canon can authorize both quietism and confrontation, it becomes easier to understand the political attitudes of Nigerian graduates of the Islamic University of Medina. At the Islamic University, they came under the strong influence of "purist" and "quietist" Salafi scholars. Yet they returned to Nigeria and acted like "politicos," to use Wiktorowicz's term. Sometimes, they even praised jihadis, including al-Qāʿida (in a context in which figures like Osama bin Ladin had significant popularity). They criticized everything from elected Nigerian politicians to hereditary northern Nigerian Muslim rulers to the U.S.-led war in Iraq – even as they continued to invoke the canonical authority of Saudi quietists.

17 Shadi Hamid, *Temptations of Power: Islamists and Illiberal Democracy in a New Middle East* (New York: Oxford University Press, 2014), 13; 18.

The ideal of a pure vanguard provides a template that structures Salafis' political behaviors. This ideal is inherently political in that it represents an ambition for reorganizing society.[18] It positions the vanguard in relation to other social groups, including other Muslims, and suggests that the vanguard knows best how to safeguard the interests of Islam. In northern Nigeria, Salafi politics does not always distinguish between theological rivals and political enemies. As we saw in the previous chapter, Salafis have depicted these rivals and enemies as part of a unified coalition that operates against them.

The ideal of the vanguard underlies diverse, even contradictory forms of Salafi political expression, yet these forms share common features, especially a common attitude toward time. The Salafi political ideal reflects what Patrick Gaffney has labeled metonymy in religious discourses. In his study of preachers in 1970s Upper Egypt, Gaffney concluded that some preachers used metaphor to relate "revelation and the world," which these preachers saw as "two separate systems . . . which have structural parallels." Other preachers, in contrast, spoke within a discourse of metonymy, where "a logic of association dominates which does not specify an intervening interpretive phase or any distinct institution standing between the divine will and the human imperative."[19] Salafis preachers in northern Nigeria operate in the latter mode. They have characterized the present – be it their struggles to control mosques in Kano, or the United States' invasion of Iraq – as part of a larger, unchanging pattern, namely the battle of true monotheism against its internal and external enemies. For Nigerian Salafis, the early Muslim community's struggles against Arab pagans, or Ibn Taymiyya's suffering in fourteenth-century Egypt and Syria, are not metaphors for their own struggles; rather, all of these moments form part of a seamless whole.

Metonymy can make Salafi politics more encompassing than other, more familiar notions of Muslim activism. The framework of "Muslim politics," as developed by Dale Eickelman and James Piscatori,[20] and applied in an African context by Benjamin Soares and René Otayek, offers more possibilities for analysis of Salafism than does the limited category "Islamist." The latter authors' emphasis on the political implications of the question "what does it mean to be Muslim?" points to the ways in which the micro and the quotidian can intersect with larger political spheres. They write, "In many parts of the Muslim world, not just in

[18] Rémy Leveau, "Les mouvements islamiques," *Pouvoirs* 62 (September 1992): 45–58; see also the discussion of Islamism and reformism in Ousmane Kane, *Muslim Modernity in Postcolonial Nigeria: A Study of the Society for the Removal of Innovation and the Reinstatement of Tradition* (Leiden: Brill, 2003).

[19] Patrick Gaffney, *The Prophet's Pulpit: Islamic Preaching in Contemporary Egypt* (Berkeley: University of California Press, 1994), 52–3.

[20] Dale Eickelman and James Piscatori, *Muslim Politics* (Princeton: Princeton University Press, 1996).

Africa, Muslims are increasingly concerned with questions of religiosity, the correct practice of Islam, and ethical reform and improvement."[21] These concerns animate much Salafi discourse and activism in northern Nigeria.

These questions, for Salafis, are not confined to the micro-politics of daily decision making and ethical self-improvement. For Nigeria's Salafis, metonymy operates not just by positioning the present as a part of a seamless historical whole but also by depicting individuals' daily lives as parts of broader theological struggles. For example, Nigerian Salafis have delivered numerous lectures on marital problems. Widespread concern exists in Kano, among Salafis as well as other Muslims, over what is perceived to be a high incidence of divorce, as well as the perception that ordinary Muslims are experiencing increasing difficulty in making successful matches and avoiding marital conflict. This sense of crisis helps explain why one of Ādam's only lectures to be transcribed and published as a book – and one that remained widely available, in audio and text forms, years after his death – is titled *Matakan Mallakar Miji* (Steps for Controlling a Husband).

The text represents a form of Salafi quotidian politics, articulated in a register that deemphasizes the canon. Delivered as a lecture at ʿUthmān bin Affān Mosque in 1999 and published in 2000, the text uses Qurʾanic verses and *ḥadīth* reports to explain how women can achieve marital harmony. Ādam presented these suggestions as an Islamic (and Salafi) alternative to local practices, which included women's visits to people whom Ādam called *boka* (spiritual healer) or *malamin tsibbo* (charm maker). In his introduction, Ādam wrote that the Islamic alternative he offered had generated substantial popular interest:

> Then we said, if Islam forbids going to [spiritual healers and charm makers] . . . there are prayers that one can do, that do not clash with shariʿa. . . . This cassette spread, and I got no rest due to the amount of calls from different programs in the north of this country [asking] about these prayers for controlling a husband, and where could one find them?[22]

This work delegitimized certain local practices while offering an accessible version of Salafi practice as an alternative. Its quotidian politics offered as a solution to life's problems the idea that there is one unchanging model of piety that provides unchanging answers. Metonymy in this sphere is political in the sense that Salafis' answers to the questions of how to worship and live are frequently divisive. The resulting conflicts spill over into intra-Muslim debates and even electoral politics.

21 René Otayek and Benjamin Soares, "Introduction: Islam and Muslim Politics in Africa" in *Islam and Muslim Politics in Africa*, edited by Benjamin Soares and René Otayek, 1–24 (New York: Palgrave Macmillan, 2007), 17.

22 Jaʿfar Maḥmūd Ādam, *Matakan Mallakar Miji* (Kano, 2000), 12.

Islam and Politics in Fourth Republic Nigeria

As discussed in the last chapter, Ādam's earliest lecture courses, dating from the late 1990s, involved teaching canonical works. The Medina graduates' systematic discussions of Nigerian domestic politics and geopolitics date from the early 2000s, after Nigeria returned to civilian rule. Their increasing political outspokenness likely reflected the changing political environment. Under General Sani Abacha (1943–98, ruled 1993–8), Nigeria experienced one of the harshest periods of military rule in its history. Many critics and opponents of the regime were imprisoned and even executed. Even though Abacha was a Muslim northerner, prominent northern Muslim critics like General Shehu Yar'Adua (1943–97), who had served as second-in-command of a military government in the late 1970s, could suffer imprisonment and worse – Yar'Adua died in prison under mysterious circumstances. Fears of repression may have restrained political outspokenness on the part of newly returned graduates of Medina in the 1990s, especially given that Kano, their base, was Abacha's birthplace.

For these reasons, Nigerian Salafis' political outspokenness in the 2000s should be viewed partly in the context of partial democratization in Nigeria and Africa more broadly. Starting in that decade, many African single-party states and military rulers bowed to popular and external pressures to hold multiparty elections. Rulers also liberalized regulations governing media and associational life. (Or, like Abacha, their unwillingness to permit transitions to civilian rule may have contributed to their demise.)

As Otayek and Soares have pointed out, liberalization broke the monopolies of national, government-sponsored Muslim organizations in many African countries. Liberalization opened the doors to new associations, which "became vehicles for expressing Muslim religiosity and sociality." These new associations have drawn strength from their access to liberalized and new media. Many new Muslim leaders are at heart media stars,[23] like some of the Medina graduates.

Even as the state's tight control over public space has weakened in West Africa, however, the state and Muslim activism remain in dialogue. William Miles argues that the state and its performance bear directly on the trajectories of Muslim activist projects: "Islam is not an independent variable in West African politics. Its power depends on how well the post-colonial state manages to salvage its legitimacy in the wake of economic decline and urban insecurity."[24] Nigeria partly conforms, and partially diverges, from these regional trends.

[23] Otayek and Soares, "Introduction," 12.

[24] William F. S. Miles, "West Africa Transformed: The New Mosque-State Relationship" in *Political Islam in West Africa: State-Society Relations Transformed*, edited by William

In Nigeria, the religious arena was highly diverse and openly fragmented long before the end of military rule. Also, some of the best-known Muslim associations in the country were founded under military rule, such as Izala in 1978 and the Federation of Muslim Women's Associations in Nigeria in 1985.[25] Nigeria did not have a national Muslim association with the same monopolistic control as the Malian Association for the Unity and Progress of Islam or the Islamic Association of Niger. Yet several factors did combine to produce a more open and dynamic public arena during the 1990s – the period when graduates of Medina were beginning to attain prominence. One of these was the proliferation of new media platforms discussed in the last chapter and how these media connected northern Nigerians to developments elsewhere in the Muslim world. Nigerian Salafis have tapped into this global awareness with lectures that relate the local to the global, as will be seen later in the chapter.

Another factor was Nigeria's transition in 1999 to the Fourth Republic, which infused new energy into Nigerian politics. Although one party (the People's Democratic Party or PDP) dominated national politics until 2015, elections at the state level have sometimes proved highly competitive. State campaigns have provided occasions for experimental relationships between politicians and Muslim scholars. Meanwhile, violence has pervaded political expression and contestation. Although violence featured in Nigerian politics before 1999, under the Fourth Republic a host of actors have employed violence as they attempt to draw boundaries and articulate claims. As Carl LeVan points out, "Within months of the government's taking office [in 1999], ethnic riots shook the northern city of Kano, rebels in the Niger Delta took oil workers hostage, and communal clashes rocked the commercial capital of Lagos."[26] For many Muslims, violence contributes to an overall sense of physical and spiritual insecurity,[27] a climate that can empower new Muslim voices to address the anxiety even as those voices – like Ādam, who was ultimately assassinated – can themselves become targets of violence.

Simultaneously, debates recur over what it means to be Nigerian. Part of this questioning has centered on the role of religion in public life and national identity: although the 2006 census deliberately shied away from asking about religious and ethnic identity, 2006 survey data by Pew suggested that 76 percent of Nigerian Christians, and 91 percent

F. S. Miles, 183–93 (Boulder, CO; and London: Lynne Rienner Publishers, 2007), 193.

[25] Federation of Muslim Women's Associations in Nigeria, "About Us." Available at: www.fomwan.org/about_fomwan.php; accessed November 2014.

[26] A. Carl LeVan, *Dictators and Democracy in African Development: The Political Economy of Good Governance in Nigeria* (New York: Cambridge University Press, 2014), xiii.

[27] Murray Last, "The Search for Security in Muslim Northern Nigeria," *Africa* 78:1 (February 2008): 41–63.

of Nigerian Muslims, considered their religious identity more important than their national, ethnic, or African identities.[28] Fourth Republic politics have centered on elites' competition to control the country's wealth and resources, but elites' absorption in this competition has facilitated diverse forms of struggle at the margins. Overlapping struggles for control play out along different regional, religious, and ethnic cleavages. Indeed, competition for power and money at the center enabled the rise of figures who could build large constituencies – though not always large enough to attract Abuja's attention – as they mounted religio-political critiques from the sidelines.

New projects of defining and asserting Islamic identities occurred at the level of state government as well. Beginning in 1999, twelve northern states implemented "full *sharīʿa*" – penal codes enforcing the *Ḥudūd* punishments (corporal penalties identified in the Qurʾan) and criminalizing other offenses for the first time since independence. The implementation of *sharīʿa* generated new debates and tensions between Muslims and Christians but also among Muslims themselves. As governments established bureaucracies to administer *sharīʿa* and shape changing notions of public morality, Salafis joined in the fray as both participants in bureaucracies and critics of certain aspects of implementation. Ādam served on *sharīʿa*-related committees under both Governor Rabiu Kwankwaso and Governor Ibrahim Shekarau, but he and other Salafis publicly broke with Shekarau in 2005, resigning from committees in protest at Shekarau's alleged indifference to their suggestions.[29] In Kano and other northern states, the *sharīʿa* project intensified debates around Muslim identities and created new spaces in which Muslims contended for power.

Shaykh Jaʿfar Ādam's Geopolitics

As detailed in Chapter 3, Ādam built a substantial following in northern Nigeria, particularly after his return from Medina in 1993. His following resulted from his ability to speak on a wide range of topics, from marriage to creed. Politics was only one theme in his repertoire, but it was an important one. Ādam's political discourses achieved particular power from their ability to apply the same concerns at all levels, from the neighborhood level in Kano to the level of geopolitics. In lectures such as "Politics in Nigeria" and "The Struggle between Truth and Falsehood," Ādam used metonymy to articulate an integrated Salafi politics.

Ādam's political worldview placed the Salafi vanguard at the intersection of what he and other Salafi preachers saw as numerous tensions. The

[28] Robert Ruby and Timothy Samuel Shah, "Nigeria's Presidential Election: The Christian-Muslim Divide," Pew Forum on Religion and Public Life, 21 March 2007. Available at: www.pewforum.org/2007/03/21/nigerias-presidential-election-the-christian-muslim-divide; accessed November 2014.

[29] Thurston, "Muslim Politics."

Muslim community was growing but suffered from internal weaknesses. The Salafi *da'wa* was advancing in northern Nigeria, but the tyranny of a hostile non-Salafi majority threatened the Salafi minority. Ordinary Muslims recognized truth when they saw it, but predatory elites – religious and political – used their institutional power to deny Salafis platforms from which to present their evidence. Politics was fouled with corruption and hypocrisy, but Salafi scholars had to speak truth to power.

The Salafi ideal of the vanguard structured the northern Nigerian Salafi community's reaction to these tensions. As Ādam sought to purify and expand the Muslim community, he also sought to defend the Salafi vanguard from external enemies and the enmity of other Muslims and to avoid the debilitating effects of what he perceived as the inherent corruption and degradation of postcolonial Nigeria. Ādam positioned himself and his followers as practitioners of *da'wa* whose commitment to purification of self and society was total.

Like many other twentieth- and twenty-first-century Muslim activists around the world, Ādam felt that a lack of internal conviction weakened Muslims in the face of external challenges. In the lecture mentioned at the beginning of this chapter, where Ādam invoked the idea of Muslims as "strangers," he identified five qualities that had enabled the early Muslim community to win astonishing victories over more institutionally powerful enemies. These qualities were "adherence to principle" (*al-thabāt 'alā al-mabda'*), "attention to knowledge" (*al-ihtimām bi-l-'ilm*), "pride in religion" (*al-i'tizāz bi-l-dīn*), "the distinctive Islamic identity" (*al-huwiya al-islāmiyya al-mutamayyiza*), and "rightly guided leadership" (*al-qiyāda al-rāshida*).[30] Most contemporary Muslims, Ādam said, lacked these qualities.

Ādam then enumerated the external challenges the Muslim community faced. These challenges included crises in Palestine, Afghanistan, Kashmir, Chechnya, and elsewhere. In each case, Ādam mourned the spiritual and material losses Muslims had suffered as other groups and nations occupied their territory and killed them. Ādam vividly evoked this suffering in the case of Afghanistan:

> This is a problem that affects us, us Muslims. There is no one who can tell you the number of Muslims who have been killed in that place.... And there is no one who can tell you the amount of wealth that was lost at that time. There is no one who can tell you the number of women who became widows, or the number of children who became orphans as a result of the killing of their parents in the war in Afghanistan. There is no doubt that this is a problem that affects us, us Muslims.[31]

30 Ādam, untitled lecture (Sokoto, 2004).

31 Ja'far Maḥmūd Ādam, recording of lecture entitled "Siyasa a Nigeria," likely delivered in Kano, 13 July 2003.

With passages like this, Ādam cultivated and activated his audiences' emotional solidarity with Muslims elsewhere. This solidarity owed partly to the connections forged between northern Nigeria and the broader Muslim world through electronic media.

Ādam not only motivated but also informed his audiences. In recounting the conflict in Afghanistan he gave the audience a framework for understanding the conflict there, listing five historical stages: the Soviet invasion, the Afghan mujahideen's resistance, the formation of the government of Muḥammad Najibullah, the fall of Najibullah's government and the rise of the Taliban, and the American invasion after 9/11. Ādam discussed the motives of the various players. By incorporating detailed informational content into his political lectures, Ādam reinforced his argument that geopolitics affected all Muslims, and hence represented a subject worthy of study and discussion, as he sought to embody by displaying his own historical knowledge.[32] He depicted ways to understand contemporary developments like the war in Afghanistan as the result of geopolitical machinations, even as he described how they fulfilled the Prophet Muḥammad's foretelling of a time when the Muslim community would be vast but weak.

For Ādam, adopting a hard-nosed view about geopolitics entailed asking probing questions about why non-Muslim powers seemed so ruthless about pursuing their interests while Muslim countries suffered constant setbacks and predations. Here one can detect faint echoes of the revivalist and modernist contributions to contemporary Salafism, but one can also see how Salafism has made purification its solution to weakness, rather than modernization. In assessing the causes of Muslims' alleged weakness, Ādam leveled particular blame at political leaders in the Muslim world. He exempted no one, even Saudi Arabia's monarchs, from this critique. For many leaders, Ādam continued, Islam had been reduced to a kind of cultural baggage that they felt free to discard at will, as Tunisia's Habib Bourguiba did when he infamously broke the Ramadan fast in 1964. Such leaders, Ādam said, perennially failed to stand up for Muslims' rights in the face of outside aggression. Ādam condemned not only individual leaders, but also multilateral organizations like the Arab League and the Organization of Islamic Cooperation, which in his eyes had failed to protect Islam. In other words, Salafis were lonely figures in a turbulent world.

Ādam's Domestic Muslim Politics

Ādam saw the same problems – a lack of Muslim leadership and a corresponding failure to defend Islam – at work in northern Nigeria. He felt

[32] Ādam "Siyasa a Nigeria."

that Muslims were marginalized at the national level, with only "ceremonial ministers" in President Obasanjo's cabinet. State governors, he said, tended to place their own selfish interests before those of the community.[33]

The selfishness of politicians distorted the balance of intra-Muslim debates in the north. Ādam depicted civilian multiparty democracy as a ruthless process of grubbing for votes. This process would inevitably disadvantage the Salafi minority by bringing elected politicians into alignment with the more numerous adherents of Sufi orders:

> What do you need to win victory over your opponent, or your opponent to win victory over you? One vote. Everything over one vote is extra [Hausa: *nafila*, a religious term for supererogatory prayers and acts], but the obligatory duty [Hausa: *farilla*, another religious term] is one vote. If he has fifty-one votes, but you have fifty votes, he beats you.... You're looking for one! So the clever one among politicians is the one who doesn't want to lose even one vote, much less to lose millions of votes. So, since the way they think is that we are a minority, that most of us are strangers, that's it. He tries a little if he wants, but then he gives much to those with much. This is the kind of thinking that most governments do, looking at who has the most. That's why they support this war the Sufi orders have against us.[34]

Ādam also criticized hereditary Muslim rulers. Such rulers, he argued, were a shadow of their precolonial predecessors, who had possessed political leadership, religious authority, and popular support. He explained that of these three qualities, "the colonialist took away the first, that is political leadership (*shugabancin siyasa*), then [hereditary Muslim rulers] themselves threw away the second, which is what? Authority over people in religion (*shugabancin mutane a addini*). Then as for the third, there remains their esteem among the people (*kimarsu da mutane cikin gari*)." Yet this esteem, he added, was steadily declining as inherited authority produced rulers weak in religious knowledge and lacking in popular legitimacy.[35]

Finally, Ādam criticized the scholarly class of northern Nigeria, most of whose members, he said, fell into two categories: scholars with religious learning who lacked any understanding of modernity, and scholars with modern learning whose religious understanding was deficient. This multifaceted lack of leadership, Ādam explained, had nurtured weakness within Nigeria's Muslim community: weakness vis-à-vis non-Muslims, internal divisions along ethnic and communal lines, and an orientation toward worldly life rather than religious purity.[36]

33 Ibid.

34 Jaʿfar Maḥmūd Ādam, "Gwagwarmaya Tsakanin Karya da Gaskiya," Kano, 15 November 2006.

35 Ādam "Siyasa a Nigeria."

36 Ibid.

As Ādam shifted focus between a global, national, and local perspective, he resembled what Gaffney observed in one Egyptian preacher, namely a variable definition of "us" versus "them." Gaffney writes,

> At times it is "us" as servants of God against "them" as servants of Satan. Then it can become "us" as Muslims against "them" as non-Muslims. This can be reduced to "us" as true Muslims and "them" as corrupt or false Muslims. . . . He then can speak of "us" as against the government and against the people and the nation. He also elaborates his position as "us" against "them" as local civil authorities, functionaries, Sufi fraternities, and generally those with power, property, and education.[37]

Understanding these shifts in "us" versus "them" helps explain why Ādam both called for the expansion of the Muslim community and fought battles within the community to define it. He urged hereditary Muslim rulers to intensify their efforts to convert non-Muslim Hausa, yet he also challenged the right of those rulers to give permission for opening new mosques.

In his lectures from the 2000s, he drew on three decades of observing Salafi activism in the north – both as a participant, and as an observer from the vantage of Medina. He often spoke of Salafism's trajectory with excitement. Block by block, he said, Ahlussunnah had deepened its presence and expanded its numbers, even ten-fold, in cities like Kano.[38] Ādam's emphasis on street-level struggle bespoke his underlying confidence that ordinary Muslims, when provided with strong leadership and clear information, would make the right choices. He often expressed misgivings about what would happen if the wrong elites controlled systems – whether as leaders of Muslim countries around the world, or even within northern Nigerian states' *sharīʿa* bureaucracies – but he and other Salafis placed confidence in ordinary Muslims. Northern Nigerian Salafis openly and positively valued the roles that youth, women, and other subordinate groups could play in advancing the Salafi cause.

This emphasis on ordinary people's ability correlates with another Salafi political theme, namely the centrality of scholars to justice and purity. In many of his lectures, Ādam lamented what he saw as a shortage of scholars "who strive to speak truth to those in power, who try to give moral instruction to people on the basis of truth and keeping trust and feeling the fear of Allah and, too, knowing what is appropriate."[39] It is here that the ideal of the pure Muslim vanguard stands out most clearly: Ādam envisioned a class of scholars who could educate and purify

37 Gaffney, *Prophet's Pulpit*, 246.
38 Ādam "Gwagwarmaya."
39 Ādam "Siyasa a Nigeria."

society while giving political leaders the advice they required to govern with moral integrity. This ideal of the vanguard implicitly, and sometimes explicitly, reflected the influence of the Salafi canon.

The Canon in Politics

The Salafi canon has played two primary roles in structuring Salafis' political discourses in northern Nigeria. At times, the canon is barely mentioned, but it implicitly structures the ideal of the pure vanguard. At other times, Salafis explicitly invoke canonical figures' authority to anchor their interventions in contemporary Muslim politics in Nigeria.

Ādam often spoke on politics without systematically referencing the canon. But the ideal of the pure vanguard remained strongly present, particularly in the way he spoke about education and the role of scholars. In one lecture, he described most contemporary Muslim leaders as stooges of former colonial powers. Critically, for Ādam, their subversion had been accomplished through education. Such leaders, he explained, had been inculcated into serving the interests of Europe and America, reflecting their educational subversion "by means of an indirect method" (*ʿan ṭarīq ghayr mubāshir*). Their education left them ignorant of Islam and distorted their understanding of the totalizing role Islam should have in society:

> They have long sought to train our leaders into making a separation with regard to religion: "Religion is different, and life, too, is different. Religion is for those scholars in the mosque when they're giving the Friday sermon or the *tafsīr* (Qurʾanic exegesis) during the [Ramadan] fast."[40]

Ādam felt that a perverted education had divorced these leaders not just from the correct path represented by Salafism, but from any canonical tradition associated with Islam:

> A man does his first degree, he does his second degree, he even does his third degree, on many different aspects of life, many different aspects of progressive knowledge, yet at the same time he has never read *Akhḍarī*, or *Forty Ḥadīth*, or *Al-Uṣūl al-Thalātha*.[41]

The three books Adam mentioned here represent different canonical traditions. The first is *Mukhtasar al-Akhḍarī fī al-ʿIbadāt ʿalā Madhhab al-Imām Mālik* (*Al-Akhḍarī's Summary of Worship According to the School of Imam Mālik*), the introductory book of jurisprudence in the classical Mālikī curriculum taught throughout northwest Africa. The second

[40] Ibid.
[41] Ibid.

is al-Nawawī's *Al-Arbaʿūna Ḥadīth* (The Forty Hadith) an introductory collection of *ḥadīth* studied throughout the Sunni Muslim world (and taught by Salafis, as discussed in Chapter 4). And the last book is *Al-Uṣūl al-Thalātha* (The Three Principles) by Ibn ʿAbd al-Wahhāb, an introductory text on creed and part of the Salafi canon. By listing these books, Ādam implied that it would be better for Muslim leaders to be connected to any canon than to no canon at all. He offered up the Salafi canon as one possibility.

Another way the structuring ideas of the Salafi canon appear, even when the canon is not systematically invoked, is when Nigerian Salafis depict historical cycles. In the eyes of Nigerian Salafis, like most other Muslims, overall time is linear: it moves from creation through moments of revelation, through the Prophet Muḥammad's career as seal of the prophets, and toward the Day of Judgment. Yet for Salafis, embedded within this linear movement are cycles and patterns: again and again, Salafis feel, the vanguard of pure Muslims has faced off against hypocrites and enemies. Nigerian Salafis look to canonical figures, especially Ibn Taymiyya, as examples of this cycle at work, and they use metonymy to relate their struggles to his. It is no accident that many Salafi mosques and centers are named for Ibn Taymiyya, a reference that emphasizes not just the Shaykh al-Islam's scholarly authority but also his struggle against supposedly wayward Muslims in the time of the Mongols.

For the Nigerian Salafis, history is not only a template in which they are embedded, but a process that they can study and use. Rijiyar Lemo, comparing the Mongol invasion of Ibn Taymiyya's time to the Iraq War, elucidated his view of history in one lecture:

> As Allah says, "Such days we cause to follow by turns among men" [Q 3:140]. History is only a cycle of periods, a cycle of time. As they say, history is "*aḥdāth*" (events) and "*asbāb*" (causes) that combine. Things that are done and the reasons for their occurrence combine to produce history. Therefore what happened yesterday – if the reason for its occurrence yesterday reoccurs – will happen again. That is history.... We study history so that we may draw some lessons [from it].[42]

History, for Rijiyar Lemo, provides a framework for making sense of the present in religious terms, and a template for religious action: the creation of a ritually and theologically pure Muslim community that will rebuke heretics and point Muslims toward the sole path to salvation.

If at times the canon remains in the background, then at other times Nigerian Salafis foreground canonical authority, particularly in contexts where they have the space and incentive to develop more technically sophisticated arguments. For example, Ādam's companion and fellow

[42] Muḥammad Sani ʿUmar Rijiyar Lemo, recorded lecture, "Musulunci a Jiya da Yau," September 2008.

Medina graduate Shaykh Abdulwahhab Abdullah published *Hisbah: Its Aim, Its Principles, and Its Importance*. The book put forth a Salafi perspective on the Hisbah, an official body for regulating public morality. The book was published in 2008, at the height of controversies surrounding the Hisbah in Kano. Abdullah was well positioned to comment on these controversies, having served on multiple committees associated with *sharīʿa* implementation in Kano and Zamfara.

Hisbah forces were formed in several northern Nigerian states in the 2000s following the passage of *sharīʿa* codes. Hisbah groups have been objects of controversy both within northern states and between states and the federal government. At the state level, struggles to control the Hisbah have occurred, for example when independent Hisbah vigilante forces initially outpaced the Kano State government's efforts to create a Hisbah force in the early 2000s. Meanwhile, the federal government has sometimes challenged state governments' authority to operate Hisbah forces; Nigeria operates a National Police Force, and there are no state police forces, which means that under some interpretations of the constitution, a state-level Hisbah force usurps national policing authority. In 2006, the federal government detained Kano's Hisbah Chairman Yahaya Faruk Chedi for several months.

Hisbah: Its Aim, Its Principles, and Its Importance argued that Hisbah was an obligatory aspect of Muslim governance. The book defined and historicized Hisbah as an institution, discussing Hisbah under the Prophet Muḥammad and the four Rightly Guided Caliphs. The book then elaborated the different functions of Hisbah bodies, as well as the roles that different political and social actors (politicians, law enforcement, judges, journalists, and others) could play in constituting Hisbah bodies in contemporary Nigeria. In addition to its explicit invocation of canonical authority, discussed later, the book implicitly reflected the canon's ideals by reflecting what Ādam, Abdullah, and others saw as Salafi scholars' duty to counsel rulers. After offering scriptural texts on the necessity of ruling according to the revelation and the Sunna, Abdullah wrote,

> Here we give counsel (*nasiha*) to Muslim political leaders and hereditary rulers and major scholars: that they know that this position that Allah has given them is a trust, about which they will be asked on the Day of Judgment. Therefore let them make their utmost effort to discharge this responsibility in order to protect themselves on the Last Day. Moreover, it is obligatory that they make their utmost effort to ensure that Allah's religion and Islamic *sharīʿa* are over everything else.[43]

By offering this "counsel," the book's publication itself represented an effort to actualize the ideal of a pure vanguard, led by scholars, working

[43] Abdulwahhab Abdullah, *Hisbah: Manufarta da Ka'idodinta da Muhammancinta* (Kano: Majlis Ahlis Sunnah Wal-Jama'ah, 2008), 13.

to move society in the right direction. Just as Salafis counseled Sufis on religious matters, they would counsel politicians on issues of public morality.

Abdullah's *Hisbah* explicitly invoked Salafi canonical authority in three ways. First, the Shaykh repeatedly cited works from the canon, especially texts like Ibn Taymiyya's *Al-Ḥisba* (Hisbah) and *Al-Amr bi-l-Ma ʿrūf wa-l-Nahy ʿan al-Munkar* (Commanding the Right and Forbidding the Wrong, a concept central to Hisbah around the world). Abdullah drew on twentieth-century thinkers within the canon as well, for example, Ibn Bāz. These canonical citations reinforced Abdullah's use of Qurʾanic verses and *aḥādīth*, adding layers of specifically Salafi interpretation to his argument.

Second, Abdullah included references to twentieth-century Salafi shaykhs such as Aḥmad Shākir and al-Albānī, who had verified *ḥadīth* reports. Abdullah worked not just from *ḥadīth* collections considered canonical by the wider Sunni Muslim world, but from specifically Salafi iterations of those collections, in particular Shākir's edition of Aḥmad ibn Ḥanbal's *Al-Musnad*. Abdullah's methodology was a Salafi one: not just including scripture, but testing it against Salafi ideals of what constituted a strong or weak *ḥadīth*.

Finally, Abdullah pointed to examples of Salafi canonical authors acting in ways that actualized the ideal of Salafi scholars counseling rulers. He wrote, "Ibn Taymiyya wrote many letters to different rulers, in order to give them counsel."[44] In this context Abdullah also mentioned Shaykh ʿUthmān dan Fodio, but in a way that fit him into a Salafi pattern of counseling rulers: the Shehu "struggled to apply Allah's *sharīʿa* and restore to the Muslim religion its esteem and respect in this region of West Africa."[45] Abdullah also pointed to Ibn Bāz:

> In our time there are major scholars who have stood firmly (*tsaya tsayin-daka*) in giving rulers counsel. Among them there is this major scholar of Saudi Arabia, Shaykh ʿAbd al-ʿAziz bin ʿAbd Allah bin Baz, may Allah have mercy on him. When he was president of the Islamic University of Medina, he wrote a letter to the King of the country of Mecca, Faisal bin ʿAbd al-ʿAziz.[46]

Abdullah translated into Hausa an excerpt from the letter, wherein Ibn Bāz called for fuller application of *sharīʿa*. Abdullah went on to quote other writings by Ibn Bāz and Ibn ʿUthaymīn. References to Salafi canonical authority infused the content of the text, shaped its bibliographic universe and its treatment of scripture, and reinforced a meta-narrative

[44] Abdullah, *Hisbah*, 213.
[45] Ibid., 213.
[46] Ibid., 216.

depicting the text as part of a tradition where Muslim scholars give advice to rulers.

What was the content of Abdullah's counsel to the Muslim leaders of Nigeria? His longest chapter concerned the contributions that different forces in contemporary Nigerian society can make to the work of Hisbah. Abdullah placed these duties and contributions into a Salafi framework, referencing Salafi authority and making clear that politics is merely one venue in which Muslims are obligated to seek moral purity:

Here we want to explain what we understand about the explanation that the Shaykh of Islam [Ibn Taymiyya] has made, that every leader has a kind of contribution that he can make in the work of Hisbah, according to the power that Allah has given him, even if the community that he rules are not all Muslims. It is important for one seeking leadership, or a leader, to understand that this leadership is a form of worship (*ibada*), meaning seeking to come close to Allah. Therefore the leader should hold firm to his religion and his creed (*akidarsa*), and not make this leadership a path for seeking worldly gain (*abin duniya*) or the path of living easy and seeking fame. Doing so would bring him disappointment in this life and the afterlife.[47]

Abdullah devoted special attention to the role of politicians and state governors in Hisbah, outlining nineteen specific duties for politicians and eighteen for governors.

At times, Abdullah vividly connected these duties to contemporary social issues in northern Nigeria, relating the field of elite policymaking back to the concerns of Salafis' quotidian politics. For example, he wrote that governors should

take a firm stance against the hawking of goods that young girls do in markets and abandoned buildings where they are taught fornication. Sometimes even married women enter this type of corruption. It is obligatory to prevent them from doing this in order to protect the community from disobeying Allah and contracting modern diseases.[48]

Abdullah went on to recount an incident from 2008:

We heard an ugly report on Freedom Radio station . . . saying: four men had raped a twelve-year-old girl. This happened because of the hawking and begging that she was doing. And a major surprise was that among those who raped this girl were those religiously forbidden from having intercourse with her (*muharramanta*), namely her grandfather's younger brother and her mother's younger brother. And all of them bragged about doing it. Here we call on the recently elected government to carry out Allah's judgment on these people. And we call on the

[47] Abdullah, *Hisbah*, 129.
[48] Abdullah, *Hisbah*, 147.

media to stop spreading this kind of ugly news, because doing so violates the *sharīʿa* of Islam. [He cites Qur'an 24:19 as justification.][49]

A number of elements came together in these passages. Abdullah strove to connect contemporary circumstances to core elements of creed and law, making Ibn Taymiyya the bridge between past and present. He positioned himself as the scholar giving counsel to rulers, not simply to establish justice on earth but also to safeguard the community's long-term spiritual prospects.

For Abdullah, as for Ādam, Salafi politics involves being the voice that calls society to account. In this effort, Salafis make no distinction between their efforts in twenty-first-century Kano, the polemics of Ibn Taymiyya in fourteenth-century Damascus, and the deeds of the early Muslim community. Metonymy makes all these situations part of an integrated whole. The canon provides a template for understanding this totality and acting within it – a template also applicable to other Muslim political actors.

Conclusion

This chapter has argued that Salafi political thought is structured by the ideal of a vanguard of true Muslims, who fight for truth and moral reform even when outnumbered by heretics, backsliders, and enemies. This ideal derives from the Salafi canon. Salafis look to the political behaviors of figures like Aḥmad ibn Ḥanbal, Ibn Taymiyya, Ibn ʿAbd al-Wahhāb, and Ibn Bāz as diverse, contextually appropriate expressions of this ideal. Part of this ideal involves the notion of the scholar as a speaker of truth, someone who gives advice to those in power rather than someone who seeks to wield power directly. This image of the scholar emphasizes the importance of the canon: while Salafis seek to emulate the political behaviors of the Prophet and his Companions, they do not always seek to perform the full range of political actions undertaken by the early Muslim community.

In northern Nigeria, Salafis have positioned themselves as advocates of alleged Muslim interests but also as critics of various Muslim leaders on both the global and the national stages. Although educated in Medina and elsewhere in a "quietist" tradition, Nigerian Salafis behave like "politicos," tying discourses rooted in the canon to outspokenness on political issues. The canon implicitly and explicitly structures these discourses.

Being politically outspoken has had consequences that graduates of Medina did not intend. As Salafis have developed a new style of

[49] Abdullah, *Hisbah*, 147, note 147.

scripture-focused preaching, in which the canon sometimes recedes into the background, they have elaborated a template that others, less well-versed in the canon, can pick up and use in highly charged political preaching. Chapter 7 explores how Boko Haram, a movement that emerged in the Salafi milieu, picked up on certain strains within the canon to justify a rejection of Nigeria's political system, even as mainstream Salafis sought to work within that system. Ultimately, Boko Haram left much of the canon behind in favor of a jihadist platform.

Part III

Boko Haram and the Canon

7 Boko Haram from Salafism to Jihadism

The most infamous outgrowth of Nigerian Salafism is the violent movement *Ahl al-Sunna li-l-Daʿwa wa-l-Jihād* (Salafis for Proselytisation and Jihad), better known by its Hausa nickname Boko Haram (Western Education Is Forbidden by Islam).[1] In March 2015, Boko Haram reinforced its infamy by swearing allegiance to *Al-Dawla al-Islāmiyya fī al-ʿIrāq wa-l-Shām* (the Islamic State in Iraq and Syria, ISIS), a jihadi army and proto-state that blossomed amid the ashes of post-Saddam Hussein Iraq and war-torn Syria.[2] Given its local roots and global affiliations, what is the relationship between Salafism and jihadism for Boko Haram? What light does this case shed on the trajectory of so-called Salafi-jihadism worldwide?

Boko Haram's founder Muḥammad Yūsuf (1970–2009) was a Salafi rooted in the broader landscape of northern Nigerian Salafism. In his

[1] For discussions of Boko Haram's Arabic and Hausa names, see Paul Newman, "The Etymology of Hausa boko," Mega-Chad Research Network, 2013. Available at: www.megatchad.net/publications/Newman-2013-Etymology-of-Hausa-boko.pdf; accessed October 2014; and Alexander Thurston, "Boko Haram: What's in a Name?" Sahel Blog, 7 January 2013. Available at: http://sahelblog.wordpress.com/2013/01/07/boko-haram-whats-in-a-name/; accessed October 2014. For analyses of Boko Haram's history and messages, see Anonymous, "The Popular Discourses of Salafi Radicalism and Salafi Counter-Radicalism in Nigeria: A Case Study of Boko Haram," *Journal of Religion in Africa* 42:2 (2012): 118–44; Andrew Walker, "What Is Boko Haram?" United States Institute of Peace, June 2012. Available at: www.usip.org/sites/default/files/SR308.pdf; accessed September 2014; Aḥmad Murtaḍa, "Jamāʿat 'Boko Haram': Nash'atuhā wa-Mabādi'uhā wa-Aʿmāluhā fī Nayjīriyā," *Qirā'āt Ifrīqiyya*, 13 November 2012. Available at: www.qiraatafrican.com/view/?q=893 and in translation at: http://download.salafimanhaj.com/pdf/SalafiManhaj_BokoHaram.pdf; accessed October 2014; Kyari Mohammed, "The Message and Methods of Boko Haram" in *Boko Haram: Islamism, Politics, Security and the State in Nigeria*, edited by Marc-Antoine Pérouse de Montclos, 9–32 (Leiden: African Studies Centre, 2014); and Andrea Brigaglia, "Jaʿfar Mahmood Adam, Mohammed Yusuf and al-Muntada Islamic Trust: Reflections on the Genesis of the Boko Haram Phenomenon in Nigeria," *Annual Review of Islam in Africa* 11 (2012): 35–44.

[2] For overviews of ISIS, see Cole Bunzel, "From Paper State to Caliphate: The Ideology of the Islamic State," Brookings Institution, March 2015; Vice News (documentary), "The Islamic State," 26 December 2014; and Charles Lister, "Profiling the Islamic State," Brookings Institution, December 2014.

June 2009 "Open Letter to the Federal Government of Nigeria"[3] – one of the last lectures Yūsuf delivered before Boko Haram launched an ill-fated but consequential uprising the following month – his rhetorical debt to Jaʿfar Ādam was clear. Yūsuf was not a graduate of the Islamic University of Medina, but he rose to prominence as a member of the Salafi networks around the Medina graduates and he had been a protégé of Ādam. By 2009, Yūsuf's break with Ādam was complete: they had denounced each other publicly, and Ādam had been assassinated – perhaps by Yūsuf's followers – in 2007. But Yūsuf continued to draw on styles the Medina graduates had honed. In his June 2009 lecture, he began with the Sermon of Necessity and then, like Ādam had done in many of his lectures, launched into a methodical but free-flowing polemic against the political authorities. Unlike Ādam, however, Yūsuf exhorted his audience not just to criticize and correct the authorities, but to confront them.

Drawing on Yūsuf's manifesto and Boko Haram's propaganda videos, this chapter argues that Boko Harm first narrowed and then later deemphasized the Salafi canon. Boko Haram frequently invoked the Salafi canon during its phase of open preaching from 2002 to 2009. Yūsuf sought canonical legitimation for his most famous stances, his rejection of Western-style schools and his denunciation of secular government, as well as for his underlying framework of religious exclusivism. As he invoked the canon, however, he foregrounded particular, minority strains that are often invoked in global jihadi thought. These intellectual choices placed him partly outside the framework of the canon as the Medina graduates understood it. Since approximately 2010, Boko Haram has imitated the self-presentation of global jihadi actors, and the canon has played a less important role in its rhetoric. By 2014, as Boko Haram was declaring a "state among the states of Islam" (*dawla min duwal al-Islām*) in the northeastern Nigerian town of Gwoza,[4] the Salafi symbolism remained, but the group's intellectual references had shifted. Under Yūsuf's lieutenant and successor Abubakar Shekau (b. ca. 1968–75), Boko Haram has unleashed violence that has claimed thousands of lives, primarily in northeastern Nigeria. In propaganda, Shekau moved away from Salafi discursive markers like the Sermon of Necessity. References to the Salafi canon became rare. In place of disseminating the Salafi creed, Shekau emphasized an ideology that justified aggressive jihad. Over time, Boko Haram has become more jihadi than Salafi. What has remained constant is Boko Haram's antipathy toward the Nigerian state and other forces in Nigeria's political and religious life.

[3] Muḥammad Yūsuf, "Open Letter to the Government of Nigeria," 11 June 2009. Available at: www.youtube.com/watch?v=f89PvcpWSRg; accessed October 2014.
[4] "Video: Boko Haram Declares a New Caliphate in North Eastern Nigeria," Sahara TV, 24 August 2014. Available at: www.youtube.com/watch?v=Rl4IgD-nKg; accessed October 2014.

The question of whether Boko Haram's rank-and-file fighters are theologically Salafi is difficult to answer on the basis of available evidence,[5] but the leadership's ideological and theological message has at the very least contributed to and sought to rationalize a sustained willingness on the part of ordinary fighters to kill fellow Muslims in great numbers.[6] Does this make Boko Haram a "Salafi-jihadi" movement? As with other movements, this hybrid term can obscure more than it reveals.[7] The immersion of some jihadis in the canon makes it coherent to talk about "Salafi-jihadism" in some instances. For both ISIS and Boko Haram, Salafi discourses have remained a powerful tool, but one that sometimes seems opportunistic as they bid to claim theological legitimacy for their violence and to woo regional and global Muslim audiences with the promise of participating in a form of purity.

In both the Middle East and Nigeria, the jihadi worldview has begun to look distinct from Salafism. Some Salafi-jihadis have been constructing a selective version of the Salafi canon. This version downplays canonical scholars' skepticism about rebelling against Muslim authorities. As this trend has progressed, some jihadis have come to rely on their own distinctive canon, dipping into the broader Salafi canon rarely. The jihadi canon is notable for three features. First, it frames Ibn Taymiyya as a voice of violent Muslim exclusivism,[8] rather than as the foremost spokesman for a particular set of beliefs about creed, law, and the nature of God. Second, it expands the role of the Egyptian *ḥadīth* scholar Aḥmad Shākir while diminishing that of al-Albānī. Third, it foregrounds nineteenth-century Wahhābīs who argued for stark religious exclusivism, even if that meant anathematizing and fighting other Muslims.[9] What might be called "post-Salafi" jihadi movements exemplify how in the contemporary period, religious communities' canons are prone to fragmentation.

[5] For the best efforts to date to identify Boko Haram's social base, see Adam Higazi, "Les origines et la transformation de l'insurrection de Boko Haram dans le nord du Nigeria," *Politique Africaine* 130:2 (2013): 137–64; and Adam Higazi, "Mobilisation into and against Boko Haram in North-East Nigeria" in *Collective Mobilisations in Africa*, edited by Kadya Tall, Marie-Emmanuelle Pommerolle, and Michel Cahen, 305–58 (Leiden: Brill, 2015).

[6] Alexander Thurston, "'The Disease Is Unbelief': Boko Haram's Religious and Political Worldview," Brookings Institution Project on U.S.-Muslim World Relations, November 2015. For estimations of Boko Haram's casualties, see the Council on Foreign Relations' "Nigeria Security Tracker" (www.cfr.org/nigeria/nigeria-security-tracker/p29483) and Johns Hopkins University School of Advanced International Studies' "Nigeria Social Violence Project" (www.connectsaisafrica.org/research/african-studies-publications/social-violence-nigeria).

[7] Thomas Hegghammer, "Jihadi-Salafis or Revolutionaries? On Religion and Politics in the Study of Militant Islamism," in *Global Salafism: Islam's New Religious Movement*, edited by Roel Meijer, 244–66 (New York: Columbia University Press, 2009), 254.

[8] Daniel Lav, *Radical Islam and the Revival of Medieval Theology* (Cambridge: Cambridge University Press, 2012).

[9] Bunzel, "From Paper State to Caliphate."

The case of Boko Haram has lessons to offer for the broader inquiry into the relationship between religion and violence. The role of religious studies in this area has typically involved theorizing the role of religious doctrines in violence and extremism and/or applying these theories through case studies of violent groups.[10] However, the discipline can also help connect doctrines to the broader religious landscapes in which violent groups emerge. Although path-breaking studies of jihadi ideologues have appeared in recent years,[11] it remains difficult to understand the impact of these figures without a fuller sense of the context in which they operate. Detailed studies of how an entire religious field reacts to political crisis are rare.[12] As Stéphane Lacroix notes for the case of Islamic activism (violent and nonviolent) in Saudi Arabia, much literature "focuses on individualities ('charismatic preachers'... [and] 'dissident ulama'...) – as if contention was merely driven by individual motives – rather than on the structures and resources necessary for collective action."[13] In northern Nigeria, it is impossible to understand Boko Haram without a sense of the figures and forces from which Boko Haram borrowed, rhetorically and in terms of audiences. One lesson of the case of Boko Haram is the importance of incorporating attention to nonviolent Muslim authorities into analyses of jihadist movements. In other words, Boko Haram cannot be understood without understanding the Medina graduates.

An Arc of Instability?

I view Boko Haram primarily as an outgrowth of local religious and political struggles in northern Nigeria, but it is necessary to mention the wider context of jihadism in Africa. Some analysts have been overeager to fit Boko Haram into supposedly wider trends, be it an alleged "arc of

[10] Mark Juergensmeyer, *Terror in the Mind of God: The Global Rise of Religious Violence* (Berkeley: University of California Press, revised edition, 2003); Hans Kippenberg, *Violence as Worship: Religious Wars in the Age of Globalization*, trans. Brian McNeil (Palo Alto: Stanford University Press, 2011); and R. Scott Appleby, *The Ambivalence of the Sacred: Religion, Violence, and Reconciliation* (Lanham, MD: Rowman and Littlefield, 2000).

[11] Joas Wagemakers, *A Quietist Jihadi: The Ideology and Influence of Abu Muhammad al-Maqdisi* (Cambridge: Cambridge University Press, 2012); and Brynjar Lia, *Architect of Global Jihad: The Life of Al Qaeda Strategist Abu Mus'ab Al-Suri* (New York: Columbia University Press, 2008).

[12] For an important exception, see Thomas Pierret, *Religion and State in Syria: The Sunni Ulama from Coup to Revolution* (Cambridge: Cambridge University Press, 2013).

[13] Stéphane Lacroix, "Understanding Stability and Dissent in the Kingdom: The Double-Edged Role of the jama'at in Saudi Politics" in *Saudi Arabia in Transition: Insights on Social, Political, Economic and Religious Change*, eds. Bernard Haykel, Thomas Hegghamer, and Stéphane Lacroix, 167–80 (Cambridge: Cambridge University Press, 2015), 167–8.

instability" in Africa,[14] or the supposition that from an early point, Boko Haram was a puppet of al-Qāʿida.[15] Without lumping a set of discrete, locally and regionally grounded conflicts into one catch-all category, or believing that there must be an Arab mastermind behind any African jihadism, one can acknowledge some interaction, discursive and perhaps operational, between different jihadi groups.

There have been persistent, although in my view inconclusive, reports that the early Boko Haram trained with al-Qāʿida's northwest African affiliate, al-Qāʿida in the Islamic Maghreb (AQIM), or with its East African affiliate al-Shabāb. The antecedents of AQIM emerged in the context of Algeria's 1992–2002 conflict, positioning themselves as explicitly "Salafi-jihadi" challengers to both the Algerian state and other Muslim activist parties and armed groups. AQIM's predecessor organizations, however, found themselves marginalized in Algeria because of their brutality against civilians and fellow activists; starting in 2003, the future AQIM effected a turn to the Sahara and the Sahel, weaving a web of criminality and later playing a role in the jihadi coalition that controlled much of northern Mali in 2012–13. AQIM has fragmented into various groups.

Al-Shabāb, for its part, was a youth militia that initially formed part of the Islamic Courts Union, a coalition of clerics and businessmen that came to control much of southern and central Somalia around 2004–6; after a U.S.-backed Ethiopian occupation of Somalia toppled the Courts Union, al-Shabāb emerged as the most effective militia in southern and central Somalia, eventually controlling substantial territory after the Ethiopian withdrawal in early 2009. Al-Shabāb lost ground to the African Union Mission in Somalia, especially after 2012, but has retained the ability to conduct dramatic attacks in Somalia and neighboring Kenya, such as the killing of numerous civilians at Nairobi's Westgate Mall in 2013 and at Garissa University College in 2015.

Both AQIM and al-Shabāb invoke Salafism in their discourses and seek to pair it with jihadism. The complex histories of these groups,

[14] "'Arc of Instability' across Africa, If Left Unchecked, Could Turn Continent into Launch Pad for Larger-Scale Terrorist Attacks, Security Council Told," United Nations, 13 May 2013. Available at: www.un.org/press/en/2013/sc11004.doc.htm; accessed October 2015.

[15] The early Boko Haram had some correspondence with al-Qāʿida central and possibly received some funding from it, but interconnections do not appear to have been strong. See International Crisis Group, "Curbing Violence in Nigeria (II): The Boko Haram Insurgency," 3 April 2014, 23. Available at: www.crisisgroup.org/~/media/Files/africa/west-africa/nigeria/216-curbing-violence-in-nigeria-ii-the-boko-haram-insurgency.pdf; accessed March 2016; and Letter from Abubakar Shekau to al-Qaʿida, circa 2010, transcribed and published by the U.S. Office of the Director of National Intelligence (ODNI). Available at: www.dni.gov/files/documents/ubl2016/arabic/Arabic%20Praise%20be%20to%20God%20the%20Lord%20of%20all%20worlds.pdf; accessed April 2016.

however, underscore the need to view different African jihadi groups in their own particular contexts, rather than to uncritically view all three organizations as manifestations of one guiding hand or one undifferentiated phenomenon. Boko Haram has undoubtedly derived parts of its style from both AQIM and al-Shabāb, but Boko Haram's own domestic evolution merits special attention. Moreover, as seen with Boko Haram's eventual affiliation to the Islamic State, the group has a particular Salafi genealogy that ultimately proved more amenable to the Islamic State's brand than to al-Qāʿida's, suggesting that there are real limits to any influence al-Qāʿida may have had over the early Boko Haram. With this in mind, let us turn to the domestic context of Boko Haram.

A Brief History of Boko Haram

Most sources have settled on 2002 as the date of Boko Haram's founding. All accounts agree that its geographic headquarters was Maiduguri, the capital of Borno State in Nigeria's far northeast. Some accounts trace the movement's genesis to students at the University of Maiduguri who encountered Yūsuf in the 1990s.[16] In any case, the movement was part of a broader Salafi network in northern Nigeria. Maiduguri had its own Medina graduates, as well as a formidable Izala presence. Ādam regularly visited Maiduguri, including to give an annual Ramadan *tafsīr* (exegesis of the Qurʾan) at the mosque of a businessman named Muhammad Indimi. One Maiduguri-based commentator describes this period:

> [Ādam] also conducted Ramadan Tafseer (Qurʾan commentary) at the famous Indimi Islamic mosque on Damboa road in Maiduguri for 13 years [approximately 1994–2006]. The famous Indimi Mosque was always full to the brim as early as 2:00pm i.e. two hours prior the commencement of the Tafseer. People close [sic] their place of business from far and near to attend his preaching which is full of wisdom. I vividly recall how we rush [sic] from the University of Maiduguri to be part of the wisdom. His Tafseer was aired in many television and radio stations in the country.[17]

Although still a Sufi stronghold, Maiduguri was becoming a significant node in the Salafi network.

Yūsuf, evidencing a "will to power,"[18] sought to distinguish himself with a particularly strident political message that rejected Western-style education and secular government, a message undergirded by sharp

[16] Isa Gusau, "Boko Haram: How It All Began," *Sunday Trust*, 17 June 2011. Available at: http://sundaytrust.com.ng/index.php/the-arts/35-people-in-the-news/people-in-the-news/5869-boko-haram-how-it-all-began; accessed May 2014; and Shehu Sani, "Boko Haram: History, Ideas, Revolt," originally published in *Vanguard*, various issues, 2011.

[17] Ali Alhaji Ibrahim, "Sheikh Ja'afar Adam: Three Years On," Gamji forum, 2010. Available at: www.gamji.com/article9000/NEWS9076.htm; accessed October 2014.

[18] Anonymous, "Popular Discourses," 119.

distinctions between who did and did not count as a "true" Muslim. Why were people attracted to Yūsuf's preaching? Most analyses of Boko Haram cite poverty or religious radicalization as explanations for the movement's origins, but we require what Abdul Raufu Mustapha has called a "multi-dimensional evidence-based approach"; Mustapha foregrounds doctrine, poverty, politics, agency, and geography as variables in generating Boko Haram.[19] One might add history as another factor: Murray Last has shown how Boko Haram's style of dissent reflects longstanding patterns where fringe groups withdraw from the mainstream Muslim community in northern Nigeria.[20] A full consideration of Boko Haram's rise is beyond the scope of this book, but here I emphasize two factors that relate to contestation over the Salafi canon in northern Nigeria: the "fragmentation of sacred authority," and the relationship of Salafism to politics.

In a crowded religious marketplace, some preachers try to seize popular attention with strident rhetoric. Ousmane Kane identifies a "fragmentation of sacred authority" in northern Nigeria, which featured powerful challenges to Sufi orders and hereditary Muslim rulers.[21] The 1970s through the 1990s, the period when Boko Haram's leaders were growing up, saw a proliferation of Muslim movements in northern Nigeria, many of them politically outspoken. For example, there was the small but disruptive movement of "Muslim Brothers" led by Ibrahim al-Zakzaky (b. 1953), who draws inspiration from the Iranian Revolution of 1979. Nigerian Muslim activists sometimes had overlapping and shifting allegiances to domestic and external actors. The Nigerian scholar Aḥmad Murtaḍa situates Yūsuf in this context, arguing that Yūsuf was one of those "Shīʿites" who, after the "Muslim Brothers" fragmented in the mid-1990s, gravitated toward Izala. Within Maiduguri, Murtaḍa continues, further schisms occurred within Izala, leaving Yūsuf in control of one mosque.[22] Whether this depiction is accurate, the better documented break between Ādam and Yūsuf also marks Yūsuf as a product of religious fragmentation.

The fragmentation of sacred authority has intersected tragically with contentious electoral politics. Across Nigeria during the 1990s and after,

19 Abdul Raufu Mustapha, "Understanding Boko Haram," in *Sects & Social Disorder: Muslim Identities & Conflict in Northern Nigeria*, edited by Abdul Raufu Mustapha, 147–198 (London: James Currey, 2014), 166.

20 Murray Last, "From Dissent to Dissidence: The Genesis and Development of Reformist Islamic Groups in Northern Nigeria" in *Sects & Social Disorder: Muslim Identities & Conflict in Northern Nigeria*, edited by Abdul Raufu Mustapha, 18–53 (London: James Currey, 2014); and Abiodun Alao, "Islamic Radicalisation and Violence in Nigeria: Country Report," undated working paper. Available at: www.securityanddevelopment.org/pdf/ESRC%20Nigeria%20Overview.pdf; accessed August 2015.

21 Ousmane Kane, *Muslim Modernity in Postcolonial Nigeria: A Study of the Society for the Removal of Innovation and Reinstatement of Tradition* (Leiden: Brill, 2003).

22 Aḥmad Murtaḍa, "Jamāʿat 'Boko Haram.'"

vigilante groups "emerged . . . and operated with widespread popular support."[23] Vigilantes draw popularity from government failures but often enjoy some government support. Since the Fourth Republic began in 1999, many politicians have patronized vigilantes and thugs to win elections and maintain power.[24] After winning office, such politicians often discard – or attempt to discard – their violent supporters.

One factor in Boko Haram's rise was the group's political utility for Ali Modu Sheriff, who was elected governor of Borno State in 2003. Borno's first Fourth Republic governor, Mala Kachalla (1941–2007), fell out with Sheriff, his "former financier." Kachalla decamped to another party, while Sheriff retained control of the ruling All Nigeria People's Party (ANPP).[25] Sheriff allegedly enlisted Boko Haram's support to help win the 2003 election,[26] and Yūsuf may have been willing to work with the "pro-*sharīʿa*" Sheriff. As the wave of "sharīʿanization" rolled across northern Nigeria after 1999, Kachalla was seen as one of the few northern governors reluctant to implement *sharīʿa*; he waited until March 2003 to sign the Sharia Penal Code Law of 2001.[27] Youthful proponents of *sharīʿa* expressed impatience through violence.[28] For his part, Yūsuf saw the entire system as flawed. He sat on Kachalla's Sharia Implementation Committee, but later stated,

> The task they gave us was to investigate the judges that were in Borno, whether they were suitable for carrying out *sharīʿa* or not suitable for carrying out *sharīʿa*, and also what they were ruling at that time. We went around and we saw. Because of that, I began saying it was not *sharīʿa* that they were doing, according to what I know.[29]

Under Sheriff, the politics of *sharīʿa* shifted. Salafis won more appointments to state bureaucracies.[30] In 2005, the Borno State government

[23] Daniel Jordan Smith, "The Bakassi Boys: Vigilantism, Violence, and Political Imagination in Nigeria," *Cultural Anthropology* 19:3 (August 2004): 429–55; 429.

[24] Human Rights Watch "Criminal Politics: Violence, 'Godfathers,' and Corruption in Nigeria," October 2007, p. 1. Available at: www.hrw.org/sites/default/files/reports/nigeria1007webwcover_0.pdf; accessed March 2014.

[25] Leaked cable from U.S. Embassy Abuja, "Nigeria: Snapshot of Northern Gubernatorial Elections," 17 April 2003. Available at: www.wikileaks.org/plusd/cables/03ABUJA717_a.html; accessed October 2014.

[26] Marc-Antoine Pérouse de Montclos, "Boko Haram and Politics: From Insurgency to Terrorism" in *Boko Haram: Islamism, Politics, Security and the State in Nigeria*, edited by Marc-Antoine Pérouse de Montclos, 135–57 (Leiden: African Studies Centre, 2014).

[27] "The Centre for Islamic Legal Studies' Draft Harmonised Sharia Penal Code Annotated," in *Sharia Implementation in Northern Nigeria, 1999–2006: A Sourcebook*, edited by Philip Ostien (Ibadan: Spectrum Books, 2007), 34.

[28] Barnaby Philips, "Eclipse Triggers Nigeria Riot," BBC News, 10 January 2001. Available at: http://news.bbc.co.uk/2/hi/africa/1110791.stm; accessed September 2014.

[29] Debate between Shaykh Isa Ali Pantami and Muḥammad Yusuf, undated. Available at: www.youtube.com/watch?v=PFhYWeLWEyk; accessed October 2014.

[30] Alkali et al., "Overview," 30.

created a Ministry of Religious Affairs and Special Education,[31] and Sheriff appointed as its Commissioner a man named Buji Foi, a Boko Haram member. Foi, along with Yūsuf, was executed by security forces during the uprising of 2009,[32] and the extent of Boko Haram's early interactions with northeastern politicians remains unclear.

Circa 2003, Yūsuf was still a rising star within Ādam's network. Yet trouble arose. On the last day of 2003, an estimated two hundred fighters attacked targets in and around the village of Kannama, Yobe State.[33] These fighters came from a group that had made camp "about 30 kilometres south of Kannama where they were known for touring villages and preaching Islam." A local farmer told the BBC that the group "said they wanted to establish a new system of Sharia law, different from the one practised now."[34] The group reportedly included more than two thousand people who migrated to rural Yobe because they were "dissatisfied with the governments of Borno and Yobe."[35] After conflict with villagers and local authorities, the group attacked police stations in Kannama and Geidam,[36] assaulted Damaturu and Maiduguri, and was driven back by the military.[37]

The Kannama group was an offshoot of Yūsuf's emergent Boko Haram, although it remains unclear what its precise relationship to Yūsuf was. Yūsuf later told an interviewer, "These youths studied the Koran with me and with others. Afterwards they wanted to leave the town, which they thought impure, and head for the bush, believing that Muslims who do not share their ideology are infidels."[38] Whether he organized this violence or not, the clashes had dangerous implications for Yūsuf, who fled to Saudi Arabia.

31 Alkali et al., "Overview," 26.

32 "Nigeria: Prosecute Killings by Security Forces," Human Rights Watch, 26 November 2009. Available at: www.hrw.org/news/2009/11/26/nigeria-prosecute-killings-security-forces; accessed April 2014.

33 "Nigeria: 10,000 Displaced by Muslim Uprising in Northeast," IRIN News, 6 January 2004. Available at: www.irinnews.org/report/47921/nigeria-10-000-displaced-by-muslim-uprising-in-northeast; accessed October 2014.

34 Anna Borzello, "Tracking Down Nigeria's 'Taleban' Sect," BBC News, 14 January 2004. Available at: http://news.bbc.co.uk/2/hi/africa/3393963.stm; accessed October 2014.

35 Njadvara Musa, "Borno, Yobe Move to Check Militant Moslem Group," *The Guardian*, 6 January 2004. Available at: http://news.biafranigeriaworld.com/archive/2004/jan/06/111.html; accessed March 2014.

36 "Nigeria: Muslim Fundamentalist Uprising Raises Fears of Terrorism," IRIN News, 25 January 2004. Available at: http://www.irinnews.org/report/48247/; accessed October 2014.

37 "Muslim Cult Raises Fears of Terrorism in Nigeria," AFP, 16 January 2004. Available at: www.taipeitimes.com/News/world/archives/2004/01/16/2003091614; accessed October 2014.

38 Emmanuel Goujon and Aminu Abubakar, "Nigeria's 'Taliban' Plot Comeback from Hide-Outs," AFP, 11 January 2006. Available at: http://mg.co.za/article/2006-01-11-nigerias-taliban-plot-comeback-from-hideouts; accessed March 2014.

Sheriff's administration helped Yūsuf rehabilitate himself. Deputy Governor Adamu Dibal arranged for Yūsuf's return to Nigeria.[39] Dibal was not a member of Boko Haram, but he was reportedly part of the broader Salafi community in Maiduguri.[40] Between approximately 2005 and 2009, Yūsuf and his followers were able to operate openly in Maiduguri and elsewhere in the northeast.[41] After his return to Maiduguri, Yūsuf repaired ties with his followers who had fought in the Kannama uprising, and some of them would later fight in the 2009 uprising.[42]

Sheriff won reelection in 2007, but his relations with Yūsuf soured, setting the stage for Boko Haram's uprising. Authorities arrested Yūsuf and other Boko Haram members at several points in 2007–8.[43] Tensions between Yūsuf and Borno State authorities escalated, largely due to confrontations between Boko Haram and "Operation Flush." This law enforcement unit, run by the state government, had responsibility for eliminating road bandits. Yūsuf and his followers perceived it as Sheriff's tool for targeting them. In June 2009, Operation Flush stopped Boko Haram members who were returning from a funeral; in the ensuing confrontation, police killed and wounded as many as seventeen sect members. Yūsuf and his lieutenants called for retaliation.

On July 26, Boko Haram attacked police stations in Bauchi and Maiduguri. In response, security forces raided Boko Haram's strongholds.[44] Over the next four days, Boko Haram clashed with security forces in Bauchi, Kano, Gombe, Yobe, and Borno, and sect members were arrested in Adamawa.[45] On July 29, authorities stormed Boko Haram's main mosque in Maiduguri. By July 30, police had captured and killed Yūsuf.[46] Borno politicians disassociated themselves from the movement.

[39] Human Rights Watch, "Spiraling Violence: Boko Haram Attacks and Security Force Abuses in Nigeria," October 2012, 31. Available at: www.hrw.org/sites/default/files/reports/nigeria1012webwcover_0.pdf.

[40] Leaked cable from U.S. Embassy Abuja, "Politics of Nigeria's Northern Borno State," 3 November 2009. Available at: www.wikileaks.org/plusd/cables/09ABUJA2013_a.html; accessed April 2014.

[41] Murtaḍa, "Jamā'at 'Boko Haram.'"

[42] "Nigeria Clashes Rage as Death Toll Tops 300," AFP, 30 July 2009. Available at: http://www.dawn.com/news/851295/nigeria-clashes-rage-as-death-toll-tops-300; accessed March 2014.

[43] Taye Obateru, Kingsley Omonobi, Lawani Mikairu, and Daniel Idonor, "Boko Haram Leader Yusuf Killed," *Vanguard*, 30 July 2009. Available at: http://www.vanguardngr.com/2009/07/boko-haram-leader-yusuf-killed/; accessed May 2014.

[44] Ardo Hazzad, "Nigeria Forces Kill 32 after Attack on Police Station," *Reuters*, 26 July 2009. Available at: www.reuters.com/article/2009/07/26/us-nigeria-riots-idUSTRE56P0MA20090726; accessed April 2014.

[45] Patience Ogbodo, Abdul Salam Muhammad, and Umar Yusuf, "Bauchi Mayhem Spreads to Kano, Yola," *Vanguard*, 28 July 2009. Available at: www.vanguardngr.com/2009/07/bauchi-mayhem-spreads-to-kano-yola/; accessed April 2014.

[46] "Nigeria's Boko Haram Chief 'Killed,'" *Al Jazeera*, 31 July 2009. Available at: www.aljazeera.com/news/africa/2009/07/2009730174233896352.html; accessed April 2014.

Dibal acknowledged Yūsuf as a "brilliant" preacher who "had this kind of monopoly in convincing the youth about the Holy Koran and Islam," but also expressed confidence that without Yūsuf as "kingpin . . . it will be difficult for them to regroup."[47] His prediction would soon prove incorrect.

On 7 September 2010, Boko Haram broke into a prison in Bauchi, freeing 721 prisoners, including more than one hundred suspected sect members.[48] Along with a wave of assassinations in Borno State in summer and fall 2010, the attack marked the end of Boko Haram's quiet regrouping following their July 2009 uprising, and the beginning of a new and more violent phase of its existence. Under the formal leadership of Shekau, who had preached alongside Yūsuf and now claimed his mantle, Boko Haram plunged northeastern Nigeria into chronic violence, and periodically struck outside the northeast. Nigerian authorities mounted a brutal response, rounding up and sometimes executing suspected sect members, deploying soldiers to the northeast, and placing Borno, Yobe, and Adamawa under a State of Emergency from May 2013 to November 2014.

Yet violence continued. Boko Haram adopted various tactics: drive-by shootings on motorbikes, sabotage against mobile phone towers, arson at schools, kidnappings, and raids on military facilities. The sect has enjoyed little popular support, but they have evoked fear and respect. When Boko Haram attacked Kano during my fieldwork in January 2012, friends who were eyewitnesses to the violence told me they were shocked to see teenagers shooting semiautomatic weapons, but they also noted that shortly before Boko Haram struck, its fighters distributed leaflets warning civilians to evacuate targeted zones. Such tactics have sometimes made the movement appear more organized and lethal than the Nigerian security forces, earning it a grudging respect.

The group's targets have included the Nigerian state, Nigerian Muslims, and Nigerian Christians. The violence has exacerbated broader Muslim-Christian tensions. Some Muslims see Boko Haram as "a product of the scheming of the Christians, which aimed at tarnishing the image of Islam," and some Christians see Boko Haram as a war on Christianity sponsored by northern Muslim elites.[49]

47 Nick Tattersall, "Interview – Nigerian Sect Planned Bomb Attack during Ramadan," Reuters, 4 August 2009. Available at: http://in.mobile.reuters.com/article/worldNews/idINIndia-41523920090804; accessed April 2014.

48 "721 Inmates Freed in Nigeria's Prison Break," *Xinhua*, 8 September 2010. Available at: http://news.xinhuanet.com/english2010/world/2010–09/08/c_13485236.htm; accessed April 2014.

49 Hakeem Onapajo and Abubakar Usman, "Fuelling the Flames: Boko Haram and Deteriorating Christian-Muslim Relations in Nigeria," *Journal of Muslim Minority Affairs* 35:1 (2015): 106–22; 113.

Many observers believe that in its post-2010 incarnation, Boko Haram is composed of scattered factions.[50] It is true that the label "Boko Haram" has sometimes been applied to any and all criminal activity and inter-religious violence in northern Nigeria since 2010. At the same time, however, some of Boko Haram's actions, especially its failed state-building project in northeastern Nigeria in 2014–15, likely reflected a significant degree of internal unity. For the sake of analytical clarity, I treat Boko Haram as a relatively coherent organization, while recognizing that there is still much about the sect that remains unknown.

When Boko Haram reemerged in the fall of 2010, Nigerian politics had shifted. President Umaru Yar'Adua, a Muslim northerner, became incapacitated from illness in 2009 and died in May 2010. Vice President Goodluck Jonathan, hailing from the Niger Delta, assumed office. The unexpected power shift back to the south dismayed many northern elites and introduced lingering uncertainties about the capabilities, legitimacy, and intentions of the new president.

Some analyses reductively portray Boko Haram as a symptom of north-south rivalries or of Jonathan's accidental ascension. More darkly, conspiracy theories charge that frustrated northern elites manufactured Boko Haram to undermine Jonathan and return the presidency to the north. These analyses ignore Boko Haram's genesis and violence under Presidents Obasanjo and Yar'Adua. Nevertheless, national and subnational political contexts did affect Boko Haram's trajectory. Rather than depicting Boko Haram as a consequence of political turmoil, it will be fruitful to examine interactions between the movement and the surrounding environment.

Politics and violence collided with particular intensity in Borno. During the 2010–11 campaign season, as Sheriff neared the end of his second and final term, unidentified gunmen murdered at least four important

[50] For a detailed but partly speculative treatment of factionalization within Boko Haram, see International Crisis Group, "Curbing Violence in Nigeria II: The Boko Haram Insurgency," 3 April 2014. Available at: www.crisisgroup.org/~/media/Files/africa/west-africa/nigeria/216-curbing-violence-in-nigeria-ii-the-boko-haram-insurgency.pdf; accessed October 2014. This chapter deliberately does not analyze the splinter group Anṣār al-Muslimīn fī Bilād al-Sūdān (Defenders of Muslims in the Lands of the Blacks, or Defenders of Muslims in Black Africa), a group nicknamed "Ansaru" by Western analysts. Although Anṣār al-Muslimīn seemed to commit several attacks in Nigeria in 2012–13, the group's coherence, beliefs, and leadership structure remain too murky to permit a well-grounded analysis of it. For one effort at an analysis, see Jacob Zenn, "Cooperation or Competition: Boko Haram and Ansaru after the Mali Intervention," *CTC Sentinel* 6:3 (March 2013): 1–8. Zenn relies too confidently and selectively, however, on Nigerian government sources and Nigerian press reports. See also a translation of the group's founding charter at: https://azelin.files.wordpress.com/2013/04/jamc481_at-ane1b9a3c481r-al-muslimc4abn-fi-bilc481d-al-sc5abdc481n-e2809cthe-charter-of-jamc481_at-ane1b9a3c481r-al-muslimc4abn-fi-bilc481d-al-sc5abdc481ne2809d.pdf; accessed March 2015.

ANPP politicians in Borno, all of them close to Sheriff.[51] Suspicion for these incidents fell on Boko Haram. Ultimately, the ANPP's Kashim Shettima won the 2011 gubernatorial election, but Borno's elite entered the 2011–15 political cycle shaken. Sheriff spent the succeeding years in de facto exile from Borno.

In northern cities, rioting followed the announcement of Jonathan's victory in the presidential elections of 2011. More than eight hundred people died. Rioters targeted perceived supporters of Jonathan and the ruling People's Democracy Party (PDP), as well as Christians and settlers from southern Nigeria.[52] The official results showed Jonathan winning with 59.6 percent of the national vote, and meeting a legal threshold required by the Nigerian constitution wherein the winning presidential candidate must obtain at least 25 percent of the vote in at least two-thirds of Nigeria's states. Three-time opposition candidate and former military ruler General Muhammadu Buhari won 32.3 percent of the official national vote, and swept the northern states.[53] Some of Jonathan's worst state-level performances occurred in the northeast. The only states in which he won less than 20 percent of the vote were Kano, in the northwest, and Borno, Yobe, and Bauchi, all in the northeast.[54]

After the elections, Boko Haram conducted some of its most notorious attacks. On 16 June 2011, a suicide bomber detonated a car bomb at the National Police Force headquarters in Abuja. Little more than two months later, another suicide bomber struck the United Nations headquarters in the capital. Dramatic attacks continued in 2012, including coordinated bombings in Kano on 20 January that became one of Boko Haram's deadliest single attacks, claiming more than 180 lives. Boko Haram has continued to stage high-profile attacks, including two bombings in Abuja in April and June 2014. In July 2014, Shekau claimed responsibility for a June explosion at a Lagos fuel depot, which

[51] Ardo Hazzad, "Northern Nigerian Political Leader Killed by Suspected Islamic Militants," *Bloomberg*, 7 October 2010. Available at: www.bloomberg.com/news/2010–10–07/northern-nigerian-political-leader-killed-by-suspected-islamic-militants.html; accessed March 2014; Chidi Okoye, "Gunmen Assassinate Governor Sheriff's Brother, Cousin, and Four Others," *Daily Times*, 28 January 2011. Available at: www.dailytimes.com.ng/article/gunmen-assassinate-governor-sheriffs-brother-cousin-and-four-others; accessed March 2014; and "Gunmen Kill Alhaji Modu Gana Makanike, Borno ANPP Chieftain," *Nigeria News*, 28 March 2011. Available at: http://news2.onlinenigeria.com/news/top-stories/87441-gunmen-kill-alhaji-modu-gana-makanike-borno-anpp-chieftain.html; accessed March 2014.

[52] "Nigeria: Post-Election Violence Killed 800," Human Rights Watch, 16 May 2011. Available at: www.hrw.org/news/2011/05/16/nigeria-post-election-violence-killed-800; accessed September 2014.

[53] "Nigeria Election: Riots over Goodluck Jonathan Win," BBC News, 19 April 2011. Available at: www.bbc.co.uk/news/world-africa-13107867; accessed September 2014.

[54] Nigeria Elections Coalition, "Nigeria Presidential Elections – 2011 (FINAL)." Available at: http://nigeriaelections.org/presidential.php; accessed September 2014.

authorities had previously explained as an accident.[55] Boko Haram has not disrupted Nigeria's national economy, but its forays outside the northeast have caused panic.

Alongside urban terrorism, Boko Haram has attacked rural communities throughout northeastern Nigeria. The deployment of the military's Joint Task Force-Restore Order (JTF-RO, later renamed the Seventh Division), working with civilian vigilantes, partly succeeded in pushing Boko Haram out of Maiduguri in 2013, but in the countryside of Borno, and to a lesser extent Yobe and Adamawa, Boko Haram has targeted villages. Much of Boko Haram's rural violence has been predatory. Some has come in response to perceived provocations – after the emergence of so-called Civilian JTF units in northeastern Nigeria, Boko Haram began attacking villages where it believed members of that government-backed local militia were present. Boko Haram has also targeted schools, including its infamous kidnapping of 276 girls and young women from Government Girls' Secondary School in the northeastern town of Chibok in April 2014.

The response of the Nigerian security forces has exacerbated the group's hostility toward outsiders. Abuses by the security forces have received extended scrutiny from human rights organizations. Human Rights Watch, in an October 2012 report titled "Spiraling Violence," recounted evidence that the Joint Task Force had tortured, murdered, and unlawfully detained suspected Boko Haram members in the northeast.[56] Amnesty International warned that Nigeria was "trapped in the cycle of violence."[57] This pattern of abuses weakened civilians' trust in the government. The pattern also fit into Boko Haram's narrative of grievances. The group has framed many of its major actions since 2009 as reprisals against the Nigerian government. For example, Shekau justified the April 2014 Chibok schoolgirls kidnapping as a response to the Nigerian government's detention of women affiliated with the sect.[58]

In summer 2014, Boko Haram started capturing and holding towns and villages in the northeast. This shift responded to the movement's

[55] Tim Cocks and Isaac Abrak, "Boko Haram Leader Claims Blast in Nigeria's Lagos," Reuters, 13 July 2014. Available at: http://uk.reuters.com/article/2014/07/13/uk-nigeria-violence-idUKKBN0FI0IG20140713; accessed October 2014.

[56] Human Rights Watch, "Spiraling Violence: Boko Haram Attacks and Security Force Abuses in Nigeria," October 2012. Available at: www.hrw.org/sites/default/files/reports/nigeria1012webwcover_0.pdf; accessed September 2014.

[57] Amnesty International, "Nigeria: Trapped in the Cycle of Violence," November 2012. Available at: www.amnesty.org/en/library/asset/AFR44/043/2012/en/04ab8b67–8969–4c86-bdea-0f82059dff28/afr440432012en.pdf; accessed September 2014.

[58] Elizabeth Pearson and Jacob Zenn, "How Nigerian Police Also Detained Women and Children as Weapon of War," *The Guardian*, 6 May 2014. Available at: www.theguardian.com/world/2014/may/06/how-nigerian-police-also-detained-women-and-children-as-weapon-of-war; accessed November 2014.

increasingly untenable position in Maiduguri and its war with the C-JTF; the shift also reflected Boko Haram's continual willingness to experiment with new strategies and tactics. In August, Shekau declared the establishment of an "Islamic state" in the town of Gwoza. The territorial expansion peaked in January 2015, when Nigeria's neighbors, particularly Chad and Niger, began to fight Boko Haram inside Nigerian territory. As Boko Haram's violence came to overshadow Nigeria's 2015 presidential election campaign, the presidential election was postponed from 14 February to 28 March. Security forces undertook a campaign – backed by foreign mercenaries and loosely coordinated with Nigeria's neighbors – to dislodge Boko Haram. On 27 March, Nigerian forces recaptured Gwoza, symbolically and physically crushing Boko Haram's proto-state. This turn of events did not save Jonathan from electoral defeat, however – in a rematch of 2011, Muhammadu Buhari swept to victory, winning twenty-one of thirty-six states and taking nearly 54 percent of the popular vote.

Buhari's victory was hailed by many as a crucial step in defeating Boko Haram. With the austere former military ruler and longtime anti-corruption advocate at Nigeria's helm, many Nigerians and foreigners alike believed that the effort to crush the sect would be disciplined and strengthened. In the months after taking office on 29 May 2015, Buhari made significant gestures, moving the military's headquarters to Maiduguri, conducting state visits to Niger, Chad, and Cameroon, and appointing two officers from Borno State as Chief of Army Staff and National Security Advisor. Boko Haram, however, launched a wave of bombings in northeastern cities and massacres in northeastern villages, particularly during Ramadan (June/July) 2015. In the wider region, meanwhile, the sect evinced new reach with bombings in Chad's capital N'Djamena and consistent attacks in southeastern Niger and northern Cameroon. The local and regional insecurity threatened to embarrass and undermine Buhari's new administration, but the president's emphasis on regional cooperation and reform of the armed forces may curtail Boko Haram's ability to operate, resupply itself, and find new recruits.

Other theaters of jihadi activity on the African continent offer the disturbing lesson that jihadis' most notorious attacks can follow, rather than precede, their territorial losses: Somalia's al-Shabāb, for example, conducted its September 2013 attack at Nairobi's Westgate Mall, and its April 2015 shooting at Kenya's Garissa University College, long after African Union troops and Kenyan forces had retaken most of the group's territory. The problem of Boko Haram may trouble Nigeria for some time to come, even if its "Islamic state" has evaporated. In this context, it is vital to understand the movement's worldview, which necessitates examining its relationship to Salafism and the Salafi canon.

Muḥammad Yūsuf and the Canon

The Salafi canon deeply informed Yūsuf's discourses and symbolic postures, but Yūsuf's adoption of the canon was partial: he downplayed canonical voices who had warned against conducting violent rebellions against Muslim authorities, and he emphasized figures who had taken exceptionally narrow positions when defining the boundaries of what it means to be Muslim.

Yūsuf wrote a manifesto in 2009 titled *Hādhihi ʿAqīdatunā wa-Manhaj Daʿwatinā* (This Is Our Creed and the Method of Our Preaching).[59] He wrote the book in response to Salafi critics, namely, the Medina graduates, who denounced Boko Haram as unorthodox.[60] The book acted in multiple ways to assert a Salafi identity. It opened with the Sermon of Necessity. Much of the book contains straightforwardly Salafi ideas, as when Yūsuf wrote, "We call on the Muslim community to correct the creed of monotheism (*tawḥīd*) and follow the approach (*manhaj*) of the *salaf* in expressing Islam (*taʿbīr al-Islām*)." Like other Salafis, Yūsuf depicted his movement as a vanguard, invoking the famous *ḥadīth* "Islam began as a stranger and will return as a stranger as it began."[61] The book rehearsed standard Salafi arguments against perceived heresies, including the Shīʿa and the Tijaniyya, but its distinctive aspects are its denunciations of Western education and Western-style political institutions. Yūsuf rooted these condemnations in a highly exclusivist conception of Salafism.

In *Hādhihi ʿAqīdatunā*, Yūsuf cited numerous authorities from the Salafi canon. The 166-page tract invoked Ibn Taymiyya more than a dozen times, for example using the Shaykh al-Islam's *Majmūʿ al-Fatāwā* (Collection of Edicts) to denounce any system of government not anchored in the Qurʾan and Sunna. Yūsuf referred to other classical authorities, such as Ibn Ḥanbal and Ibn Taymiyya's students Ibn al-Qayyim and Ibn Kathīr. Yūsuf mentioned non-Wahhābī figures associated with the Salafi canon, such as Muḥammad al-Shawkānī and Rashīd Riḍā. These references show that Yūsuf was familiar with the broad canon.

Yūsuf drew on various Salafi sources to defend his views on education. Two sources deserve special mention. One was *Al-Madāris al-ʿĀlamiyya al-Ajnabiyya al-Istiʿmāriyya: Tārīkhuhā wa-Makhāṭiruhā* (Global, Foreign and Colonialist Schools: Their History and Dangers) by the Saudi

59 Boko Haram may have other statements of creed as well. A compatriot using the pseudonym ʿAlāʾ al-Dīn al-Barnāwī wrote a book called *Jāʾa al-Ḥaqq* (The Truth Has Come), but I have not located a copy. See Murtaḍa, "Jamāʿat 'Boko Haram.'"

60 Mohammed, "Message and Methods."

61 Abū Yūsuf Muḥammad ibn Yūsuf, *Hādhihi ʿAqīdatunā wa-Manhaj Daʿwatinā* (Maiduguri: Maktabat al-Ghurabāʾ likely 2009), 8.

Arabian Shaykh Bakr Abū Zayd (1944–2008).[62] Abū Zayd was a senior member of the Saudi religious establishment who had studied with Shaykhs Ibn Bāz and Muḥammad al-Amīn al-Shinqīṭī. *Al-Madāris al-ʿĀlamiyya* was not Abū Zayd's only work on the politics of Islam's encounter with the West: another title was *Al-Niẓām al-ʿĀlamī al-Jadīd wa-l-ʿAwlama: Al-Takattulāt al-Iqlīmiyya wa-Āthāruhā* (The New World Order and Globalisation: Regional Blocs and Their Influences).[63] In Abū Zayd, Yūsuf believed he had found a canonical authority who would legitimate his rejection of Western-style schools.

Another source for Yūsuf was Aḥmad Shākir, the Egyptian judge and *ḥadīth* scholar. Yūsuf cited Shākir's works *Ḥukm al-Jāhiliyya* (The Rule of Pre-Islamic Ignorance) and *Al-ʿIlmāniyya* (Secularism) in building his case against secular government. Shākir's works have informed the thought of other contemporary jihadist leaders.[64] Shākir's presence in *Hādhihi ʿAqīdatunā* partly supplanted that of al-Albānī, whose antipathy to jihad against Muslim rulers would have offered Yūsuf little in terms of canonical support for his politics. Like other Nigerian Salafis, Yūsuf cited al-Albānī as an authority on grading *ḥadīth*, and he cited Ibn ʿUthaymīn when the latter seemed to support his views about the impermissibility of Muslims studying in Western schools.[65] Yet Yūsuf remained strategically silent about those two shaykhs' many statements against aggressive jihad and *takfīr*. By marginalizing al-Albānī and reducing his role to that of mere *ḥadīth* evaluator, rather than *ḥadīth* interpreter, jihadis demarcate a more limited version of the broader Salafi canon. In this limited canon, a strain of rejectionist Salafism is particularly relevant.

Activating the Canon Against the State: Al-ʿUtaybī, Al-Maqdisī, and Yūsuf

Yūsuf picked up a strand of thought within Salafism that mobilizes the canon to delegitimize the state and advocate violence against it. This strand of thought connects Yūsuf to the Palestinian-Jordanian Salafi-jihadi theorist Abū Muhammad al-Maqdisī (b. 1959), and through al-Maqdisī to the Saudi Arabian rebel Juhaymān al-ʿUtaybī (ca. 1935–80), who led a two-week takeover of the Grand Mosque of Mecca in 1979.

62 For an analysis of Yūsuf's use of Abū Zayd, see Anonymous, "Popular Discourses."

63 Ṣuhayb Muḥammad Khayr Yūsuf, "Wafāt al-Shaykh Bakr Abū Zayd 'Ibn Qayyim al-ʿAṣr,'" Alukah, 7 February 2008. Available at: www.alukah.net/culture/10963/1882/; accessed April 2014.

64 For example, see Aḥmad al-ʿAshūsh, "Ilā al-ʿIlmāniyyīn al-Ashrār wa-Tābiʿīhim min al-Muslimīn al-Aghrār" (Mu'assasat al-Bayān al-Islāmī, 2012), 3. Available at: http://azelin.files.wordpress.com/2012/12/shaykh-ae1b8a5mad-ashc5absh-22to-the-wicked-secularists-and-their-followers-among-the-deceived-muslims22.pdf; accessed October 2014.

65 Yūsuf, *Hādhihi ʿAqīdatunā*, 90.

All three of these thinkers drew on highly exclusivist strains within nineteenth-century Wahhābī thought. This minority strain also contributed to the intellectual genealogy of ISIS.

Al-ʿUtaybī was the leader of a group called *Al-Jamāʿa al-Salafiyya al-Muḥtasiba* (The Salafi Society for Hisbah, i.e., commanding right and forbidding wrong). Comprising students at the Islamic University of Medina and other Salafis, the Society emerged in the 1960s. In its early stages, it enjoyed some official support from Saudi scholars like Ibn Bāz. The Society absorbed al-Albānī's teachings about operationalizing *ḥadīth*, and sought to correct other Saudi Muslims' worship and behavior. Over time, the group's minority interpretation of Islam brought condemnation from senior scholars. Al-ʿUtaybī led a faction that went underground and came to believe that one of its members was the Mahdi, a figure in the Islamic tradition who is expected to lead Muslims in the final battle against Satanic forces. The society's takeover of the Grand Mosque was meant to inaugurate the Mahdi's career.[66]

The society's ideas influenced al-Maqdisī, who may have encountered al-ʿUtaybī's followers during his informal studies in Saudi Arabia in the 1980s. In works such as *Al-Kawāshif al-Jaliyya fī Kufr al-Dawla al-Saʿūdiyya* (The Clear Demonstrations of the Infidelity of the Saudi State, 1989) and *Millat Ibrāhīm wa-Daʿwat al-Anbiyāʾ wa-l-Mursalīn* (The Community of Abraham and the Call of the Prophets and the Messengers, 1984), al-Maqdisī drew inspiration from portions of the Salafi canon, particularly nineteenth-century Wahhābī authorities who advocated a highly exclusive notion of Muslim identity.[67] Al-Maqdisī added Salafi legitimacy to ideas popularized by the non-Salafi Egyptian thinker Sayyid Quṭb (1906–66), who had argued that Arab rulers were non-Muslims and had called for their violent overthrow. Al-Maqdisī's ability to frame jihadism within Salafi idioms made him influential among Saudi Arabian jihadis, who were eager for fully Salafi justifications for violence.[68]

In *Hādhihi ʿAqīdatunā*, Yūsuf borrowed heavily from al-Maqdisī, although Yūsuf did not cite him. Al-Maqdisī also wrote a work entitled simply *Hādhihi ʿAqīdatunā*, which he did not intend to be an innovative statement of Salafi creed but rather a clarification of his positions in line with creeds written by Ibn Taymiyya and others; he composed the text "after it reached me that people were attributing to us, and making us out to have said, what we did not ever say, especially in the areas of unbelief and faith."[69] However, Yūsuf and al-Maqdisī both emphasized the

66 Thomas Hegghamer and Stéphane Lacroix, *The Meccan Rebellion: The Story of Juhayman al-ʿUtaybi Revisited* (London: Amal Press, 2010).
67 Wagemakers, *A Quietist Jihadi*.
68 Wagemakers, *A Quietist Jihadi*, 131.
69 Abū Muḥammad al-Maqdisī, *Hādhihi ʿAqīdatunā* (1997). Available at: www.tawhed.ws/r1?i=2&x=jzoyrjz8; accessed October 2014.

notion of *al-walā' wa-l-barā'* – literally "loyalty and disavowal" – which means exclusive loyalty toward the Muslim community and disavowal of non-Muslims and non-Islamic systems.

Yūsuf and al-Maqdisī drew on the same Wahhābī figures to anchor their discussion of *al-walā' wa-l-barā'* in Salafi canonical authority. In *Hādhihi 'Aqīdatunā*, Yūsuf refers to nineteenth-century Wahhābīs such as Shaykh Ḥamad ibn 'Atīq (d. 1883/4), who developed strongly exclusivist notions of *al-walā' wa-l-barā'* during political turmoil in present-day Saudi Arabia, including when a Saudi ruler called upon Ottoman help to defeat his rebellious brother. Al-Maqdisī also turned to Ibn 'Atīq, as had al-'Utaybī before him.[70] As Joas Wagemakers writes, "Whereas Ibn Taymiyya and others wrote about *al-walā' wa-al-barā'* as a tool to remain pure in one's faith, Wahhabi authors – particularly Ibn 'Atiq – turned the correct *walā'* and *barā'* into conditions for being Muslim."[71]

Yūsuf calls *al-walā' wa-l-barā'* "one of the pillars of *tawḥīd* and creed (*rukn min arkān al-tawḥīd wa-l-'aqīda*)."[72] He quotes Ibn 'Atīq's *Sabīl al-Najāt wa-l-Fakāk* (The Path of Salvation and Release): "Truly in the Book of Allah Most High there is no ruling (*ḥukm*) for which there is more and clearer evidence than this ruling – meaning *al-walā' wa-l-barā'* – other than the obligation of *tawḥīd* (*wujūb al-tawḥīd*) and the forbidding of what contradicts it (*taḥrīm ḍiddahu*)."[73] Like al-Maqdisī, Yūsuf drew on the collection of Wahhābī writings entitled *Al-Durar al-Saniyya fī al-Ajwiba al-Najdiyya* (The Glittering Jewels of the Najdi Responses). Al-Maqdisī encountered the collection in Saudi Arabia and it became a tool that "provided him with the fully Salafi arguments, concepts (such as *al-walā' wa-al-barā'*) and ideas that he wanted but, unlike the writings of al-Albani and Ibn Baz, these applied *takfīr* more easily."[74] The collection fulfilled a similar function for Yūsuf.

Yūsuf drew on this collection and other writings of Ibn 'Atīq to advance the related notion of *iẓhār al-dīn*, or manifesting religion. Yūsuf argued that in a non-Muslim land, it is not enough for Muslims to fulfill the ritual requirements of the religion; they must also actively oppose unbelief. Al-Maqdisī invoked this notion in his book *Millat Ibrāhīm*. He and Yūsuf sometimes cited the same passages from works like *Al-Durar al-Saniyya*.[75] The notion of Abraham's community as an example of exclusivist monotheistic commitment also connected al-Maqdisī to

70 Hegghamer and Lacroix, *The Meccan Rebellion.*
71 Wagemakers, *A Quietist Jihadi*, 152; see also David Commins, *The Wahhabi Mission and Saudi Arabia* (London and New York: I.B. Tauris, 2006), 61–6.
72 Yūsuf, *Hādhihi 'Aqīdatunā*, 159.
73 Yūsuf, *Hādhihi 'Aqīdatunā*, 162.
74 Wagemakers, *A Quietist Jihadi*, 36.
75 Compare Yūsuf, *Hādhihi 'Aqīdatunā*, 164 and Abū Muḥammad al-Maqdisī, *Millat Ibrāhīm wa-Da'wat al-Anbiyā' wa-l-Mursalīn* (1984), chapter 1. Available at: www.tawhed.ws/r1?i=1394&x=iti4u3zp; accessed October 2014.

al-ʿUtaybī.[76] These continuities point not only to Yūsuf's genealogical connections to al-Maqdisī and al-ʿUtabyī, but also to the ways in which Salafis advocating violence have approached the canon in similar ways.

Al-walāʾ wa-l-barāʾ represents an under-appreciated dimension of Yūsuf's thought. Most analyses of Boko Haram have emphasized the movement's opposition to Western-style education and secular government employment for Muslims, but underpinning these ideas – and other aspects of the group's thought and behavior – is an exclusivist conception of Muslim identity. This exclusivism had profound implications for how Yūsuf and the early Boko Haram viewed not just specific systems – education and government – but for how they viewed all of Nigerian society, and the relationship of Islam to it.

Hādhihi ʿAqīdatunā was meant to represent Yūsuf's thought within intra-Salafi debates, and to strengthen his followers' ability to represent the movement. Just as Ādam and Rijiyar Lemo taught canonical texts to their followers to help them refute Sufi allegations of heterodoxy, Yūsuf intended his manifesto as a weapon his followers could use against fellow Nigerian Salafis who criticized Boko Haram. Yūsuf taught the book orally to his followers, translating it phrase by phrase into Hausa and expanding on the book's ideas in extended Hausa commentaries that tied his ideas to street politics. In one recorded session, Yūsuf discussed *al-walāʾ wa-l-barāʾ*, drawing on his book. Yūsuf made the concept a unifying principle for rejecting political and religious practices that in his eyes contravened Islam. He insisted that individual believers had to embody *al-walāʾ wa-l-barāʾ* to be Muslim:

> What will make you a soldier of Allah first and foremost, you make a complete disavowal of every form of unbelief: the Constitution, the legislature . . . worshipping tombs, idols, whatever. You come to reject it in your speech and your body and your heart. Moreover, Allah and His Messenger and the believers, you love them in your speech and your body and your heart.[77]

Yūsuf viewed theological opposition to other Muslim sects and his movement's opposition to a non-Muslim society as an authentically Salafi position. Appropriating part of the canon, he distilled its messages into a strident political discourse. In so doing, he benefited from the Medina graduates' years of preaching on both the canon and politics – even as they opposed his rise. Unlike them, however, he did not extend Salafi textualism to non-Islamic textual sources: rather than invoking Nigeria's Constitution as a document with evidentiary value as Ādam had when

[76] Hegghammer and Lacroix, *The Meccan Rebellion*.

[77] Audio recording of Muḥammad Yusuf's commentary on *Hādhihi ʿAqīdatunā*, undated. Available at: www.youtube.com/watch?v=JWfWa2rfsKw&index=2&list=UUdXgmSgdkq3HIwFnZcYuweA; accessed October 2014.

discussing Sabuwar Gandu, Yūsuf identified the Constitution as a symbol of unbelief.

Exclusivist notions of Muslim identity came into play strongly in the lead-up to Boko Haram's confrontation with the authorities in 2009, reflecting how hard Yūsuf worked to activate ideas he derived from the canon. Operation Flush became the embodiment of Boko Haram's perception that it was living in an anti-Muslim society. As Yūsuf stated in his infamous June 2009 speech in which he denounced Operation Flush and vowed revenge,

> The Government of Nigeria has not been constructed so that it may do justice. It has not been constructed to promote Islam. It has not been constructed to protect Islam. It has not been constructed to protect Muslims. It has been constructed to fight Islam and kill Muslims. This is its work that it is carrying out even now in Plateau State, as is well known.[78]

With this reference to Plateau State, where Muslim-Christian clashes have raged since the early 2000s, and with other references to inter-religious clashes dating back to the 1980s, Yūsuf placed the perceived struggle of his community into a pattern that depicted the Nigerian state as a perennial anti-Muslim aggressor. If Muslims' loyalties had to be exclusive, Yūsuf made clear where they should lie.

In another lecture around this time, Yūsuf's fellow Boko Haram leader Muḥammad (Mamman) Nūr built an exclusivist discourse around the Qur'anic verses 39:54–55, which read, "Turn to your Lord (in repentance) and bow to His (Will), before the Penalty comes on you: after that you shall not be helped. And follow the best of what has been revealed to you from your Lord, before the Penalty comes on you – of a sudden while you do not feel it!"[79] In Nūr's hands, these verses became a call to practice exclusive loyalty to the Muslim community – and defend it – in times of crisis.

> Don't think that because you, in other words, if one harasses you with Flush, one harasses you with difficulties, if one harasses you with the high cost of food.... Don't think that if you go to the Afterlife, you'll receive it if you have not exhibited disavowal and rebellion against this government.[80]

When Boko Haram rose up in July 2009, its leaders framed the violence as an effort to actualize this exclusivist sense of a Muslim vanguard beset by hostile authorities and surrounded by hypocrites and enemies. The notion of *al-walāʾ wa-l-barāʾ*, rooted in a revolutionary branch of the Salafi canon, helped Boko Haram's leaders justify the uprising.

78 Yūsuf, "Open Letter."

79 Adapted from Abdullah Yusuf Ali, *The Holy Qur'an: Text, Translation, and Commentary*, Fourth Edition (Elmhurst, New York: Tahrike Tarsile Qur'an, 2004).

80 Video of Muḥammad Nur and Muḥammad Yūsuf, likely 2009. Available at: www.youtube.com/watch?v=cUot3BrT0FE; accessed October 2014.

In subsequent phases, the feeling of being an aggrieved constituency and a pure vanguard would continue to characterize Boko Haram's discourses, but connections to Salafi thought would weaken.

These trends connect Boko Haram to other jihadist movements. In the Middle East, al-Maqdisī's heirs and former pupils have gone in a direction that looks more like stripped-down jihadism than Salafism. During the 1990s, a gulf emerged between al-Maqdisī, who saw *da'wa* as a necessary precursor to jihad, and his pupil Abū Muṣ'ab al-Zarqāwī (1966–2006), who was ready to fight.[81] Al-Zarqāwī led a jihadi outfit in Iraq that became an affiliate of al-Qā'ida in 2004 – and was, ultimately, the forerunner of ISIS. Similarly, Yūsuf's heirs have abandoned Boko Haram's early scholarly trappings. The split between al-Maqdisī and al-Zarqāwī previewed, in certain ways, stylistic differences between Yūsuf and Shekau as leaders of Boko Haram.

Abubakar Shekau's Post-Salafi Discourses

Groups who adhere at one time to the Salafi creed can move away from it, including in the context of jihad. As Wagemakers writes, "The role of ideology in radicalisation can be part of a reciprocal relation between ideas and their political and socio-economic surroundings, a cross-fertilisation of text and context."[82] In the cases of Boko Haram and ISIS, their transformation has involved a shift away from the Salafi canon and toward a stripped-down, propagandistic style of jihadism.

References to the canon help index these changes. For example, in 2014, a laptop belonging to ISIS was recovered in Syria. The laptop contained videos, recordings, and texts by leaders of al-Qā'ida and affiliated groups, as well as by jihadi ideologues. Most of the names on the laptop belonged to figures who rose to infamy in the 1990s or 2000s. Some names belonged to older thinkers, such as Shākir and al-'Utaybī.[83] Conspicuously absent from the computer's files were major Salafi canonical figures such as al-Albānī, or even Ibn Taymiyya. The canon contained within the laptop is more jihadi than Salafi.

In his post-2009 messages, Boko Haram's new leader Abubakar Shekau has shifted away from standard Salafi canonical statements of creed and toward frames that seek to legitimate the sect's violence as an authentic jihad. His messages have focused on the political motivations behind Boko Haram's violence. The primary audiences of these

81 Wagemakers, *A Quietist Jihadi*, 215–17.

82 Wagemakers, *A Quietist Jihadi*, 248.

83 Harald Doornbos and Jenan Moussa, "Found: The Islamic State's Terror Laptop of Doom," *Foreign Policy*, 28 August 2014. Available at: www.foreignpolicy.com/articles/2014/08/28/found_the_islamic_state_terror_laptop_of_doom_bubonic_plague_weapons_of_mass_destruction_exclusive#_; accessed August 2014.

messages, released to Nigerian and international media as videos, seem to be the Nigerian state, as well as the media itself. Shekau sometimes directly addressed President Jonathan. There is little sense left that Boko Haram is seeking to educate other Muslims about creed; in his longest statement on the subject since 2010, an eighteen-minute video entitled "This Is Our Creed," Shekau outlined the basic Salafi understanding of *tawḥīd* but quickly moved into justifications for *takfīr* and violence.[84] Perhaps, in its own enclaves, the movement offers more rigorous instruction in Salafism to its followers, but in communications to the outside world, Shekau stresses politics over creed. In this sense, the primary goal of many Salafis around the world – education – no longer animates Boko Haram.

The politicization of the movement has pushed the canon into the background. As Chapter 6 discussed, strident Salafi political rhetoric has sometimes drawn only loosely on the canon, instead focusing on mounting political attacks and anchoring them in references to foundational texts. Boko Haram builds on this stripped-down Salafi political preaching, but it has abandoned some of the signature features of even these stripped-down Salafi discourses.

The following example illustrates this point. On 14 March 2014, Boko Haram attacked Giwa Barracks, a notorious detention site in Maiduguri operated by the Nigerian military. The attack freed hundreds of detainees.[85] The Nigerian military and vigilantes from the Civilian Joint Task Force fought back, perpetrating one of the worst episodes of human rights abuses in the conflict as they rounded up and murdered hundreds of detainees.[86] As the government drew condemnation for its harsh response, Boko Haram scored propaganda victories, first by striking openly at a symbol of Nigerian military power in the northeast, and second by releasing two videos, one that showed battle footage and another featuring a lengthy boast from Shekau.

In his video, Shekau claimed responsibility for the attack. His opening differed markedly from the Sermon of Necessity, which encapsulates the Salafi preoccupation with purifying creed and eliminating heresy. Like Yūsuf, Shekau had used the Sermon in his pre-uprising teachings, but in later years he reserved the Sermon for highly formal discourses, such

84 Abubakar Shekau, "Wannan Ne Akidarmu," likely 2015. Available at: www.liveleak.com/view?i=d4b_1421362369; accessed October 2015.

85 Hamza Idris, Yahaya Ibrahim, Ibrahim Sawab, and Ronald Mutum, "Boko Haram Attacks Barracks in Borno, Suffers Casualty," *Weekly Trust*, 15 March 2014. Available at: www.weeklytrust.com.ng/index.php/top-stories/15987-boko-haram-attacks-barracks-in-borno-suffers-casualty; accessed May 2014.

86 "Nigeria: War Crimes and Crimes Against Humanity as Violence Escalates in North-East," Amnesty International, 31 March 2014. Available at: www.amnesty.org/en/news/nigeria-war-crimes-and-crimes-against-humanity-violence-escalates-north-east-2014-03-31; accessed May 2014.

as his pledge of allegiance to ISIS. In the Giwa Barracks video, however, Shekau began:

In the name of Allah, the Beneficent, the Merciful, praise to Allah who made jihad a form of worship and made it for His servants one of the greatest forms of worship. And he purchased it by one of the two blessed outcomes: either victory or martyrdom.[87]

In contrast to the Qur'anic verses in the Sermon of Necessity, which emphasize pious fear of God, Shekau cited Qur'anic verses that stress the theme of fighting:

Verily Allah has purchased from the believers their persons and their goods; for theirs (in return) is the Garden. They fight in the way of Allah. They kill and are killed: a promise binding on Him in truth, in the Torah, the Gospel, and the Qur'an. And who is more faithful to his covenant than Allah? So rejoice in the bargain that you have concluded. That is the great victory. (9:111)

The ninth chapter of the Qur'an is a favorite source of quotations for jihadis around the world.

Boko Haram's core denunciations of Western institutions have remained present in Shekau's videos. In response to Jonathan's statement that Boko Haram was a "cancer," Shekau released a "Message to Jonathan" in which he replied, "We are not a 'cancer.' We are not a disease. . . . The disease is unbelief. . . . Everyone knows the Constitution is unbelief."[88] Yet Shekau now presents these ideas almost solely with reference to Qur'anic verses, rather than through a broader set of references to canonical authorities. For example, Shekau justified his assertion that "among the infidels are the democrats [i.e., participants in a democratic system]" (*wa min al-kuffār al-dīmuqrāṭiyyīn*) with a reference to 2:191: "And kill them wherever you overtake them and expel them from wherever they have expelled you, and *fitna* (chaos) is worse than killing."[89] In contrast to Yūsuf's willingness to give long expositions of his ideas, Shekau asserts but does not explain. In this way, Boko Haram's major ideas become slogans rather than part of a sustained intellectual argument. Shekau exhorts fellow Muslims to repent and presents life in a democratic context as incompatible with Islam, but Boko Haram under Shekau appears to be making little effort to win new recruits through sophisticated intellectual arguments. The notion of *al-walā' wa-l-barā'*

87 "Abubakar Shekau Claims Responsibility on Barracks Attack," TRAC Nigeria, 26 March 2014. Available at: www.youtube.com/watch?v=Pba8uvuf9Is; accessed May 2014.

88 Abubakar Shekau, "Message to Jonathan," 11 January 2012. Available at: www.youtube.com/watch?v=umkj50SUzck; accessed October 2014.

89 Abubakar Shekau, "Message to the World on Baga," January 2015. Available at: http://jihadology.net/2015/01/21/new-video-message-from-boko-%E1%B8%A5arams-jamaat-ahl-al-sunnah-li-dawah-wa-l-jihad-imam-abu-bakr-shekau-message-to-the-world-on-baga/; accessed March 2015.

still structures these discourses, but is no longer systematically and explicitly invoked, except through the Qur'anic verses from which the doctrine derives – a signal to fellow jihadis, perhaps, but not a detailed exposition with reference to the Salafi canon.

References to the canon sometimes appear in Shekau's propaganda. In his declaration of an Islamic state in Gwoza in August 2014, Shekau cited Ibn Taymiyya and Ibn al-Qayyim in his discussion of why the Nigerian state was a *ṭāghūt* (a tyrannical, infidel regime in open rebellion against Allah).[90] But such citations have become rare.

Even as Boko Haram has shifted to guerrilla attacks, terrorist violence, and territorial conquest, it has retained a sense that it is a true Muslim vanguard under constant threat from outsiders. Yet in Shekau's messages, there is little systematic effort to Salafize discourses. Indeed, there is a kind of "generic Islam," and Shekau (like other Salafis in Nigeria, including non-jihadis) has strategically invoked the legacy of ʿUthmān dan Fodio, omitting mention of dan Fodio's Sufi affiliations and presenting him as a symbol of pure, precolonial Islamic rule.[91]

Notably, ISIS has preserved more markers of Salafi discourse than Boko Haram. In his July 2014 sermon announcing his "caliphate," ISIS leader Abubakar al-Baghdādī opened with the Sermon of Necessity. Boko Haram used the sermon only in its announcement of its affiliation to ISIS,[92] although its pledge followed, verbatim, a formula used by other ISIS affiliates in swearing allegiance.[93] Canonical references were mostly absent from both of these important discourses, however: al-Baghdādī relied solely on Qur'anic verses and *ḥadīth* reports, and the pledge included a lone reference to Ibn Taymiyya, but otherwise no scholars were mentioned.

Like Yūsuf and Shekau, al-Baghdādī fit the narrative of his state into a litany of grievances, citing violence against Muslims from Africa to Burma as examples of the need to restore Muslims' "dignity, might, rights, and leadership."[94] Yet even as ISIS attempted to extend its sway over large portions of Iraq and Syria in 2013–15, jihadi theorists,

90 "Video: Boko Haram Declares a New Caliphate in North Eastern Nigeria," Sahara TV, 24 August 2014. Available at: www.youtube.com/watch?v=Rl4IgD–nKg; accessed October 2014.

91 Abubakar Shekau, "A Message to the Leaders of the Disbelievers," February 2015. Available at: http://jihadology.net/2015/02/17/al-urwah-al-wuthqa-foundation-presents-a-new-video-message-from-jamaat-ahl-al-sunnah-li-l-dawah-wa-l-jihads-boko-%E1%B8%A5aram-abu-bakr-shekau-a-message-to-the-leader/; accessed March 2015.

92 Abubakar Shekau, "Bayʿat Jamāʿat Ahl al-Sunna li-l-Daʿwa wa-l-Jihad li-Khalīfat al-Muslimīn Abī Bakr al-Baghdādī," 7 March 2015. Available at: http://jihadology.net/2015/03/07/al-urwah-al-wuthqa-foundation-presents-a-new-audio-message-from-jamaat-ahl-al-sunnah-li-l-dawah-wa-l-jihads-boko-%E1%B8%A5aram-abu-bakr-shekau-bayah-jama/; accessed March 2015.

93 Bunzel, "From Paper State to Caliphate," 42, footnote 229.

94 Abū Bakr al-Baghdādī, "Khuṭba," 5 July 2014. Available at: www.youtube.com/watch?v=P9o5KERTFIQ; accessed January 2015.

including al-Maqdisī, were denouncing ISIS's project and attacking the movement's religious credentials. The ideas of al-Maqdisī have influenced groups like Boko Haram and ISIS, but even within the Salafi-jihadi community, fierce debate rages.

One outcome of this debate may be to push groups like Boko Haram and ISIS even further from the original Salafi canon. ISIS has sometimes explicitly narrowed the canon, as it did when it compared itself to the original Wahhābī movement and suggested that al-Maqdisī was on the wrong side of history, just as, for ISIS, the Yemeni scholar Ibn al-Amīr (1688–1768) had been wrong in opposing the Wahhābī *da'wa*.[95] The corpus used by ISIS and Boko Haram takes hardline Wahhābī voices, frames their messages of religious exclusivism in a global Salafi language and excludes other voices in the broader Salafi canon.

As with al-'Utaybī and his assertion that the Mahdi had come, fraying relations with the broader Salafi community can lead fringe groups into wild millenarian visions that are barely anchored in any canon. ISIS's magazine *Dābiq*, named after the northern Syrian town where an apocalyptic battle will supposedly occur, is a case in point: many issues of the magazine contain no references to contemporary Salafi canonical authorities.[96] Rather, *Dābiq* claims the legacy of the Prophet's Companions, appropriates the memory of Usāma bin Lādin, and invokes Ibn Taymiyya and a few hardline representatives of the Wahhābī tradition (sometimes cited through texts like *Al-Durar al-Saniyya*, a favorite of al-Maqdisī and Yūsuf). Otherwise, the magazine concentrates on Qur'anic verses and *ḥadīth* reports. *Dābiq* uses the broad language of Salafism – in one passage, as an aside, an author equates "the 'aqīdah of the Islamic State" with "the 'aqīdah of Ahlus-Sunnah"[97] – but does not draw on the full Salafi canon. *Dābiq* privileges a political discourse whose main subjects are current events and whose main targets are rival jihadi groups and Western political actors. Similarly, Shekau's messaging is primarily oriented toward contemporary politics and features an even more stripped-down version of the Salafi canon.

Conclusion

Boko Haram initially relied on a selective version of the Salafi canon and on Salafi concepts such as *al-walā' wa-l-barā'*, but over time the canon and the markers of Salafi discourse receded in Boko Haram's public

95 Bunzel, "From Paper State to Caliphate," 11.
96 See the collected issues at: www.clarionproject.org/news/islamic-state-isis-isil-propaganda-magazine-dabiq; accessed March 2015.
97 *Dābiq* Issue 7 (English, January/February 2015), 33. Available at: http://media.clarionproject.org/files/islamic-state/islamic-state-dabiq-magazine-issue-7-from-hypocrisy-to-apostasy.pdf; accessed March 2015.

messaging. What is left is a movement more jihadi than Salafi, a sect that has retained a sense of exclusivism and grievance, but whose connection to Salafi theology is weakening.

Some possibility of dialogue with elements of the sect may remain – especially if the Nigerian state, credible mediators, and authoritative voices within Boko Haram can discuss issues such as prisoner releases, accountability for the killers of Yūsuf, and amnesty for some fighters. Yet President Buhari's current stance toward the group focuses more on eradicating it militarily than on finding issues that might be negotiated and discussed. The narrowed jihadi canon, meanwhile, gives Boko Haram a set of intellectual tools for interpreting all events through the lens of exclusivism. The solution to the crisis cannot be purely military, but its political aspect must be sophisticated enough to overcome the group's profound animosity toward outsiders.

Boko Haram's trajectory has comparative implications for the study of other jihadi groups. Although some violent movements with Salafi roots have retained them even after turning to violence – such as the Saudi Arabian jihadi groups influenced by al-Maqdisī – other groups abandon efforts to teach, and their discourses come to center on political demands. As the next chapter discusses, such trajectories have expanded openings for nonviolent Salafis to denounce jihadis, including by invoking canonical authority to deny jihadis theological and intellectual legitimacy. The struggles between Salafis and Salafi-jihadis, however, raise the question of whether the Salafi canon can retain its coherence amid the jihadi challenge.

8 Reclaiming the Canon

Salafism has never been a completely unified movement. The canon, this study's central framework for understanding Salafism, constitutes an evolving and contested terrain; the canon is a template for unity, but cannot guarantee it. The Salafi community as a whole negotiates, over time, who is admitted into and excluded from the canon, and who has the authority to determine the rules for inclusion and exclusion.

When scholars analyse intra-Salafi divisions, the Salafi community has famously been categorized into "purists," "politicos," and "jihadis." Yet it is easy to overstate the degree of internal division within the Salafi fold. It is possible to discern a mainstream within the Salafi community, namely the so-called "purists" or "quietists," although this label is misleading. As Jacob Olidort writes, Salafis whose "political actions are quiet, but [whose] political voice is loud" likely represent a majority of the movement worldwide.[1] The political behaviors of "quietists" move and shift along a continuum of political action, ranging from a steadfast refusal to engage politics to an active participation in party politics and political dissent. The boundary between "quietists" and "politicos" can be permeable and even meaningless. We have seen an example of this in Shaykh Jaʿfar Maḥmūd Ādam, an intellectual devotee of "quietist" Salafi scholars but also an outspoken political commentator and activist himself.

Perhaps it is simpler to talk not of three types of Salafism but of two: mainstream Salafis who are not involved in promoting aggressive jihad or working to carry it out, and Salafi-jihadis who are. At the same time, even the lines between jihadis and nonjihadis are blurred when it comes to the question of canons; as the previous chapter showed, Salafi-jihadis like Boko Haram and ISIS work hard to present their discourses as the latest and most authentic instance of continuity with the canon as they define it.

[1] Jacob Olidort, "The Politics of 'Quietist' Salafism," Brookings Institution (February 2015), 4. Available at: www.brookings.edu/~/media/research/files/papers/2015/02/salafism-quietist-politics-olidort/brookings-analysis-paper_jacob-olidort-inside_final_web.pdf; accessed March 2015.

In the face of jihadi violence and propaganda, mainstream Salafis are struggling to impose standards for who is and who is not a Salafi. Jihadis powerfully threaten mainstream Salafis, both intellectually and physically. Jihadi violence and propaganda now dominate outsiders' impressions of Salafism. For mainstream Salafis, this development can lead potential audiences astray; it also attracts hostile scrutiny from their own governments and from the West. As rhetorical contests to define Salafism intensify, mainstream Salafis can even become targets of jihadi violence themselves. In Yemen, gunmen suspected of ties to al-Qāʿida assassinated the Salafi Shaykh ʿAlī Bāwazīr in February 2014. Bāwazīr had reportedly asked local al-Qāʿida fighters to leave his district, and had criticized the group's killings of government security personnel. Bāwazīr's death alarmed Yemeni Salafis, who feared "the movement of assassinations from military leaders to shaykhs and leaders of the Salafi movement."[2]

In many countries, the jihadi challenge has further complicated mainstream Salafis' already fraught relations with the state. In Yemen, the local manifestation of the global "War on Terror" has contributed to the mainstream Salafi movement's "normalisation within Yemeni politics": after 2001, Salafis became important allies for the Yemeni President ʿAlī ʿAbd Allāh Ṣāliḥ (b. 1942, served 1990–2012). This alliance meant that influential Salafis escaped state repression as they, "willingly or not," helped the regime bolster its legitimacy against jihadi and Shīʿī challengers.[3] In postrevolutionary Egypt, the Muslim Brotherhood's short-lived presidency gave way to a countercoup and repression of Brotherhood activists, but Salafis – who had theological and strategic differences with the Brotherhood – took a different route. In 2015, as Egypt headed for its first legislative elections since the countercoup, the Salafi Al-Nūr ("Light") Party[4] pursued accommodation with the new military regime. The party presented itself as a partner for the regime in fighting terrorism – an approach "likely connected to the party's larger strategy of maintaining its voter base and its physical security in an effort to propagate its Salafi teachings."[5] In their relationships with states, mainstream Salafis face

[2] "Ightiyāl al-Shaykh ʿAlī Bāwazīr bi Ḥaḍramawt Yuthīr Makhāwif Salafiyyī al-Yaman," *Huna ʿAdan*, 25 February 2014. Available at: http://hunaaden.com/news/10985/; accessed May 2014.

[3] Laurent Bonnefoy, *Salafism in Yemen: Transnationalism and Religious Identity* (New York: Columbia University Press, 2011), 249.

[4] The party was founded in 2011 in the wake of the revolution by al-Daʿwa al-Salafiyya, an organization dating to the 1970s. Stéphane Lacroix, "Sheikhs and Politicians: Inside the New Egyptian Salafism," Brookings Institution, June 2012. Available at: www.brookings.edu/~/media/research/files/papers/2012/6/07-egyptian-salafism-lacroix/stephane-lacroix-policy-briefing-english.pdf; accessed March 2015.

[5] Jacob Olidort, "The al-Nour Party: A Salafi Partner in the Fight Against Terrorism?" Washington Institute for Near East Policy, 13 March 2015. Available at: www.washingtoninstitute.org/policy-analysis/view/the-al-nour-party-a-salafi-partner-in-the-fight-against-terrorism; accessed March 2015.

complicated incentives; they are pressured to balance self-preservation and credibility, and they risk losing their political and rhetorical autonomy from repressive regimes.

In northern Nigeria, mainstream Salafis have encountered their own difficulties. Mainstream Salafis represent a formidable form of theological opposition to Boko Haram. Because of their knowledge of the canon, mainstream Salafis can depict Boko Haram not just as un-Islamic but also as un-Salafi. Ādam and his companions denounced Muḥammad Yūsuf during his lifetime, and Ādam's successors have continued to denigrate Boko Haram even as mainstream Salafis have become targets of the sect. From the beginning, Boko Haram's violence targeted other Salafis, as evidenced by Boko Haram's destruction of an Izala mosque in 2009 – one of Boko Haram's first acts during its uprising. Ādam's assassination in 2007 was likely the work of Boko Haram. Boko Haram has assassinated several other Salafi preachers in the years since 2009. In February 2014, Abubakar Shekau claimed responsibility for the murder of Shaykh Awwal 'Albānī' Zaria (1960–2014), another prominent Salafi critic of the sect.[6] As I have argued elsewhere, mainstream Salafis have found themselves caught between the violence of Boko Haram and the Nigerian state's suspicions of most Salafis. Mainstream Salafis have been arrested and accused of having links to Boko Haram.[7] At the level of Nigeria's state governments, however, some mainstream Salafis have remained attractive partners for ambitious politicians.

Whereas my earlier work examined mainstream Nigerian Salafis' rhetoric regarding Boko Haram and the state, this chapter specifically examines how mainstream Salafis have worked to defend and reclaim their canon in the face of the challenge represented by Boko Haram. Placing the Nigerian experience into a global context, I note that the canon has suffered two major blows since the 1990s – the deaths of unifying canonical figures, and the rise of jihadi movements adept at borrowing Salafi rhetoric and styles. I argue, however, that the Salafi canon has remained a broadly unifying platform for the global Salafi community, especially because it is still backed by important physical institutions and is increasingly supported through virtual architectures. Nigerian Salafis have had partial success in refuting Boko Haram and institutionalizing their own access to media, government, and society. Their gains reflect a wider success on the part of mainstream Salafis around the world.

6 Salisu Bala, "Salafi Targets for 'Boko Haram': The Murder of Shaykh Muhammad Auwal Adam 'Albani' Zaria (d. 2014)," *Annual Review of Islam in Africa* 12:1 (2013/2014): 31–8.

7 Alex Thurston, "Nigeria's Mainstream Salafis between Boko Haram and the State," *Islamic Africa* 6:1–2 (July 2015): 109–34.

Global Transformations in Salafi Authority

Generational change has brought about a major transition in Salafi authority in the twenty-first century. This study has repeatedly stressed the prominent position in the Salafi canon of three contemporary figures: ʿAbd al-ʿAzīz ibn Bāz, Muḥammad ibn Ṣāliḥ al-ʿUthaymīn, and Muḥammad Nāṣir al-Dīn al-Albānī. All three shaykhs died between 1999 and 2001. None of them left a successor with the same personal, intellectual, and institutional charisma.

The institutions associated with Salafism cannot, on their own, compensate for the absence of scholars whose authority rested on their personal stature within the canon. Indeed, institutionalization was sometimes more a reflection of the authority such scholars had already accrued, rather than the cause of that authority. When Ibn Bāz reached the pinnacle of the Saudi Arabian religious establishment, serving as Grand Mufti from 1993 until his death in 1999, the timing was no accident: the position of Grand Mufti was resurrected after a long interregnum to meet the tests of legitimacy that Saudi Arabia's political and religious elite faced during the Gulf War, which saw American troops stationed in the country that contained the Muslim world's two holiest shrines.[8] This development called for special efforts to defend the monarchy and its religious allies as new movements challenged their orthodoxy, including in the form of a politically outspoken Salafi challenge from Muslim Brotherhood-inspired activists and in the form of the Salafi-inspired al-Qāʿida. That Ibn Bāz was selected for the role of Grand Mufti served as recognition of his distinguished career as a respected scholar and unifying religious figure. This recognition was especially notable in light of Ibn Bāz's social origins, for he was not a descendant of Ibn ʿAbd al-Wahhāb (i.e., not a member of Āl al-Shaykh). After Ibn Bāz's death, the position of Grand Mufti was retained, but it passed to a member of Āl al-Shaykh, ʿAbd al-ʿAzīz ibn ʿAbd Allāh (b. 1943). The new Grand Mufti is widely seen as having less personal charisma and influence than his predecessor. The institution cannot entirely compensate for the loss of Ibn Bāz.

Succession to Al-Albānī has been even more diffuse, even though he had many senior students and followers. Inside Saudi Arabia, there is Dr. Rabīʿ al-Madkhalī (b. 1931), whose quietist Salafism has been a major force at the Islamic University of Medina and throughout Salafi circles around the world. Outside Saudi Arabia, al-Albānī's prominent students and followers include the Palestinian-Jordanian Shaykh ʿAlī ibn Ḥasan al-Ḥalabī (b. 1960) and the Egyptian Shaykh Abū Isḥāq al-Ḥuwaynī

[8] Nabil Mouline, *The Clerics of Islam: Religious Authority and Political Power in Saudi Arabia*, translated by Ethan Rundell (New Haven: Yale University Press, 2014).

(b. 1956).[9] Nevertheless, despite various individuals' claims to have been al-Albānī's favorite student or his entrusted intellectual successor, tremendous contestation has arisen over the shaykh's legacy. Vitriolic exchanges occur offline and online about who has or has not distorted his work.

A generation born in the 1930s and educated in Saudi Arabia's universities was critical in disseminating Salafism and entrenching the canonical authority of the trio of al-Albānī, Ibn Bāz, and Ibn ʿUthaymīn. Some of the shaykhs from the 1930s generation have survived well into the twenty-first century. These scholars were prolific writers themselves and contributed significantly to the written canon. Perhaps the most prominent, both intellectually and institutionally, is Dr. Ṣāliḥ ibn Fawzān al-Fawzān (b. 1933), who serves on Saudi Arabia's Committee of Senior Scholars. Al-Madkhalī, although influential, has not been invited to join the committee. Others of this generation died in the 1990s or 2000s, leaving behind them a fragmented succession of their own. Shaykh Muqbil al-Wādiʿī (1933–2001) played a unifying role in Yemen after his return there in the 1980s, teaching from his school in Dammāj. Al-Wādiʿī left behind major students such as Yaḥyā al-Ḥajūrī, yet here too polemics rage concerning succession. Different members of the 1930s generation attack one another and attack purported successors of their peers. Among other struggles, al-Madkhalī and al-Ḥajūrī, and their supporters, have engaged in an extended polemic.[10]

Increasingly, a generation born in the 1950s and 1960s supplies the leadership of Salafi organizations and communities around the world. This generation still often claims direct intellectual links to the generation of al-Albānī, but they differ stylistically from the older generations. In particular, they are often fully fluent in the strategic use of electronic media. The older shaykhs did not shun television, radio, or recording, but neither did they market themselves as media stars. In this sense, Nigeria is no exception to broader trends in the Salafi world, and Nigerian Salafis' adeptness at using electronic media conforms to a wider pattern.

The large number of Salafi shaykhs of the 1950s and 1960s generation, combined with the ability of many preachers and scholars to build individual followings, contributes to a fragmentation in Salafi circles. It is here that the canon's role is being put to the test. As an ever-larger number of Salafi scholars appear on the scene, fewer and fewer of whom personally met or studied with figures like Ibn Bāz or al-Albānī, it remains to be seen how coherent the written canon will remain. At the same time,

[9] See Olidort, "The Politics of 'Quietist' Salafism"; Richard Gauvain, *Salafi Ritual Purity: In the Presence of God* (New York: Routledge, 2012).

[10] See Yaḥyā al-Ḥajūrī, "Al-Naṣḥ al-Rafīʿ li-l-Wālid al-ʿAllāma al-Shaykh Rabīʿ," al-Ḥajūrī's official website, 2 April 2013. Available at: www.sh-yahia.net/show_art_58.html; accessed October 2015.

many Salafis are keen to preserve the intellectual unity of their approach. One arena in which mainstream Salafis are putting up a spirited defense of the canon is the Internet.

Intra-Salafi Competition Online

Given the dramatic violence jihadis commit and the intense attention their media interventions attract, it is easy to overestimate the proportion of jihadis within the broader community of Salafis worldwide. Yet as Olidort writes, "If most Salafists globally were involved in forming political parties or in direct violent activity, the world would look very different."[11] This is true of the Internet as well, where mainstream Salafis are mounting a serious challenge to the notoriety and prominence of jihadi websites.

The Internet has created yet another layer of canonization. There are historical parallels here that offer grounds for comparison concerning the relationship between media infrastructure and texts. In the twentieth century, the accelerated spread of print publishing in the Arab world and the creation of institutions like the Islamic University of Medina ensured that the editions of canonical works that reached Arabic-reading audiences would be framed by specific commentaries and corrections. In the twenty-first century, the scanning and posting of printed works on the Web has further disseminated certain editions of canonical texts. Thousands of classical texts are available in PDF format online, often in editions created by Salafis and posted on Salafi websites. The student of Islam searching the web for works by Ibn Taymiyya will likely encounter the medieval shaykh through Salafi eyes.

On balance, the Internet has served a more unifying than fragmenting role vis-à-vis the legacy of al-Albānī, Ibn Bāz, and Ibn ʿUthaymīn. After their deaths, students and admirers of each shaykh established what I call a "legacy website" for their scholar – a place that gathers together the scholar's biography, writings, and audio recordings.[12] As the anonymous "volunteers" who founded al-Albānī's legacy website wrote, "This site aims to spread the knowledge and legacy (*turāth*) of the eminent scholar of *ḥadīth* Muḥammad Nāṣir al-Dīn al-Albānī – may Allah have mercy on him – by offering his books, his tapes, and his articles through the best of modern media that are convenient for general users."[13] These websites also seek to resolve any controversies that might arise concerning a scholar's stance on a particular theological or legal issue. For example, the authors of al-Albānī's legacy website have addressed the issue of whether

[11] Olidort, "The Politics of 'Quietist' Salafism," 4, footnote 1.

[12] See www.Alalbany.net, founded 2004; www.binbaz.org.sa, undated; and www.ibnothaimeen.com/index.shtml, founded 2004.

[13] "Man Naḥnu" at Al-Albānī's legacy website, undated. Available at: www.alalbany.net/%D9%85%D9%86-%D9%86%D8%AD%D9%86; accessed March 2015.

al-Albānī tried to require Muslims to use the Sermon of Necessity. Al-Albānī invoked that short text frequently in his writings as an opening doxology, but – the anonymous volunteers assert – he did not attempt to make it compulsory.[14] This effort to collect and clarify a scholar's contributions reinforces other forms of canonization occurring in print and in offline institutions.

The legacy websites entrench canonization in another way as well, namely, by providing a focal point for other Salafis online. One example is a prominent branch of Sudan's Anṣār al-Sunna al-Muḥammadiyya movement, itself an outgrowth of the Egyptian Salafi community. The movement's website lists links to legacy pages for Ibn Bāz, Ibn ʿUthaymīn, and al-Albānī under a column titled "useful sites."[15] The three legacy sites are the only webpages that appear in this column.

The three major Salafi shaykhs are not the only figures with personal websites. Virtually every major contemporary Salafi scholar, living or deceased, now has a personal site. Salafis have made increasing use of Facebook, Twitter, and YouTube, allowing them to interact directly with followers. Salafi movements also have websites, often well stocked with legal opinions (*fatāwā*), articles, audio recordings, and news.

The websites of mainstream Salafis have a major competitor in the form of the teeming jihadi Internet landscape. Jihadis constitute a challenge for mainstream Salafis not only because of the potential allure of jihadis' ideas and their specific efforts to refute non-jihadi Salafism, but also because jihadis often host the most prominent online editions of central works in the Salafi canon. One particularly noteworthy jihadi site is *Minbar al-Tawḥīd wa-l-Jihād* (The Pulpit of Monotheism and Jihad, www.tawhed.ws, founded circa 2002 and sometimes shut down for extended periods), operated by the Palestinian-Jordanian thinker Abū Muḥammad al-Maqdisī and his followers. The website's front page typically foregrounds recent polemics by jihadi thinkers and leaders, but the website's vast library includes extensive collections of texts by classical thinkers such as Ibn Taymiyya alongside more recent writings. The danger for mainstream Salafis is that the Salafi-jihadi websites portray a particular version of the Salafi canon, one that fully co-opts the core of the canon and brands it as not only Salafi but also Salafi-jihadi.

Mainstream Salafis have responded to the online jihadi challenge by establishing websites that seek to play a similarly comprehensive role as libraries of the Salafi canon. One example is *Al-Maktaba al-Shāmila* ("The Complete Library," www.shamela.ws), launched in 2005 by Saudi

[14] "Hal Yaqūl al-Shaykh al-Albānī Raḥimahu Allāh bi-Farīḍat Khuṭbat al-Ḥāja?" at Al-Albānī's legacy website, undated. Available at: www.alalbany.net/5746; accessed March 2015.

[15] Anṣār al-Sunna al-Muḥammadiyya bi-al-Sūdān, homepage, available at: http://ansar-alsuna.net/; accessed September 2014.

Arabia's Cooperative Office for Preaching, Guidance, and Enlightening Communities (*Al-Maktab al-Taʿāwunī li-l-Daʿwa wa-l-Irshād wa-Tawʿiyat al-Jāliyāt*). The office is a division of Saudi Arabia's Ministry of Islamic Affairs.[16] As of 2015, in online searches for various Arabic editions of works in the Salafi canon, the two websites often came up as the top two results – suggesting that jihadis and other Salafis are in fierce competition to determine who will gain the upper hand in defining and hosting the canon online. Mainstream Salafis' efforts to oppose jihadism online parallel the efforts by Saudi Arabian institutions, including the Islamic University of Medina, to oppose "extremism" through conferences and publications – even as Saudi Arabia still permits some Saudi clerics to call for jihad in Syria and elsewhere.[17]

The competition between *Minbar al-Tawḥīd wa-l-Jihād* and *Al-Maktaba al-Shāmila* is unspoken; other online, intra-Salafi rivalries are more blatant. Al-Madkhalī has his own official Arabic-language website (www.rabee.net), but his supporters operate TheMadkhalis.com, while his opponents operate Madkhalis.com, both of them English-language sites. At stake is al-Madkhalī's refutation of the Egyptian Muslim Brotherhood intellectual Sayyid Quṭb, who has inspired many jihadis around the world. In publications in the 1980s and 1990s, al-Madkhalī denounced Quṭb on theological grounds. Al-Madkhalī suggested that Quṭb held beliefs that contradicted core Salafi principles, such as the principle that all of the Prophet's Companions were exemplary Muslims. Online, the pro-Madkhalī group stresses the scholar's ties to Ibn Bāz, Ibn ʿUthaymīn, and al-Albānī, thereby attempting to place al-Madkhalī under the umbrella of these shaykhs' authority. One entry at the pro-Madkhalī website is titled "Imaam al-Albani to Shaykh Rabee: Everything with Which You Refuted Qutb for Is Correct and True and May Allaah Reward You for Fulfilling the Obligation of Exposing His Ignorance and Deviance."[18] The anti-Madkhalī website, meanwhile, claims the legacy of the same canonical shaykhs in an effort to refute al-Madkhalī and defend Quṭb; one entry quotes at length from an interview with al-Albānī to suggest that al-Albānī saw value in some of Quṭb's work, and

16 "ʿAn al-Maktaba al-Shāmila," undated, www.shamela.ws. Available at: http://shamela.ws/index.php/page/about-shamela; accessed March 2015. "Nabdha ʿan al-Maktab," al-Maktab al-Taʿāwunī li-l-Daʿwa wa-l-Irshād wa-Tawʿiyat al-Jāliyāt, 2012. Available at: www.altaawoni.org/index.php?op=pages&id=1; accessed March 2015.

17 On the Islamic University's role, see The Kingdom of Saudi Arabia, "Initiatives and Actions to Combat Terrorism," April 2015. Available at: https://saudiembassy.net/files/PDF/Reports/Counterterrorism.pdf; accessed October 2015.

18 "Imaam al-Albani to Shaykh Rabee: Everything with which You Refuted Qutb for Is Correct and True and May Allaah Reward You for Fulfilling the Obligation of Exposing His Ignorance and Deviance," TheMadkhalis.com, 7 January 2010. Available at: www.themadkhalis.com/md/articles/iosjk-imaam-al-albani-to-shaykh-rabee-everything-with-which-you-refuted-qutb-for-is-correct-and-true.cfm; accessed March 2015.

to further imply that al-Madkhalī had gone too far in his criticisms of Quṭb.[19] These efforts to claim canonical authority to determine Quṭb's status within the canon reflect a broader struggle over whether jihadism will be accepted as part of Salafism.

The fate of the canon online will have major repercussions for the Salafi community worldwide. Although face-to-face transmission – the teaching of the canon in mosques and schools – remains the primary mechanism for spreading Salafism in places like Nigeria, several developments make Internet *da'wa* indispensable to the movement. First, there is the Internet's ability to cultivate a sense of global solidarity – a particularly important facet of Salafi identity, and one that many Salafis are keen to reinforce by presenting a unified Salafi movement online. Second, the Internet is essential for reaching the growing population of Muslim autodidacts whose primary vehicle for learning is the Web, rather than a personal teacher or a physical library. Third, the Internet provides platforms to Salafi shaykhs who might otherwise be silenced when political repression and turmoil damage the physical infrastructures of Salafism. Thomas Pierret offers the example of Shaykh ʿAdnān al-ʿArʿūr (b. 1948), a Saudi Arabia-based Syrian preacher who inspired Syrian protesters after 2011 through his interventions on satellite television and the Internet. Pierret writes, "The new media . . . allowed for the involvement of actors who over recent decades had been excluded from the Syrian religious debate by the combined efforts of the state and the religious elite: the Salafis."[20] Finally, the Internet offers a vehicle for mainstream Salafis to achieve their ultimate hope: offering up Salafism not just as one Islamic interpretation among many, but as the commonsense, default, generic form of Sunni Islam. The Internet is an appealing arena for Salafis who believe that they need only present compelling textual evidence in order to win new audiences. If the new convert or the questioning young person, searching online, learns how to conduct the basic ritual obligations of Islam from Salafi websites, the Salafi community will have taken an important step toward winning these seekers over to its overall understanding of the faith.

The following sections examine these global trends in the northern Nigerian context. The same concerns that mainstream Salafis have elsewhere in the world – repulsing the jihadi challenge, building institutional influence, self-policing the movement, and strengthening their presence online – operate in northern Nigeria. In all of these domains, the Salafi canon is a central tool for mainstream Salafis.

[19] "In Defense of a Shaheed," Madkhalis.com, 17 June 2013. Available at: http://madkhalis.com/2013/06/in-defense-of-a-shaheed; accessed March 2015.

[20] Thomas Pierret, *Religion and State in Syria: The Sunni Ulama from Coup to Revolution* (Cambridge: Cambridge University Press, 2013), 236.

The Nigerian Arena: Competing Audiences

Around 2008, Muḥammad Yūsuf agreed to a debate with Dr. ʿĪsā ʿAlī Pantami, a British-educated ally of the Salafi graduates of Medina. Yūsuf agreed not only to discuss the legitimacy of his core teachings on issues such as Western-style education and secular government employment, but also to allow the debate to be recorded on video.

The video provides a visual display of the contest between Boko Haram and other Nigerian Salafis over canonical authority. The table in front of the two debaters was piled with books. In one exchange, Yūsuf invoked Saudi Arabia's Permanent Committee for Scholarly Research Projects and Issuing Rulings (*Al-Lajna al-Dāʾima li-l-Buḥūth al-ʿIlmiyya wa-l-Iftāʾ*), while Pantami referenced Ibn ʿUthaymīn. Yūsuf and Pantami, holding up books and disagreeing about the content of the canon, instantiated a global struggle over textual authority, not just between Salafis and other Muslims but among Salafis themselves.[21] Beyond the physical battlefield, where Boko Haram fights Nigerian soldiers and civilian vigilantes, fateful intellectual contests are occurring in Nigeria, paralleling struggles elsewhere. These rivalries have consequences for the trajectory of Salafism worldwide.

Nigerian graduates of the Islamic University of Medina, such as Shaykh Jaʿfar Ādam and Dr. Muḥammad Sani ʿUmar Rijiyar Lemo, devoted considerable efforts to refuting Boko Haram during Yūsuf's lifetime. As an anonymous expert has outlined, the graduates of Medina put forward both "intellectual" and "moral" counterarguments as they worked to discredit Yūsuf.[22] The expert points out that the graduates of Medina felt that their learning made them superior to Yūsuf. The graduates thought that Yūsuf was seeking a shortcut to prominence with his strident and divisive rhetoric. They attacked his learning and painted him as a tool of Christian and external interests hostile to Muslims.

Yūsuf responded in a recording titled "Warware Shubuhar Malamai" (Resolving Scholars' Doubts; a likely reference to Ibn ʿAbd al-Wahhāb's *Kashf al-Shubuhāt*, "Removing the Doubts"). Yūsuf described his encounters with Ādam, Ādam's companion Shaykh Abdulwahhab Abdullah, and other mainstream Salafis. In Maiduguri, Medina, and elsewhere, they repeatedly debated the meaning and veracity of various *ḥadīth* reports, as well as the merits of ideological positions taken by various Salafi authors. Here as in his text *Hādhihi ʿAqīdatunā wa-Manhaj Daʿwatinā* (This Is Our Creed and the Method of Our Preaching), Yūsuf

21 "Muqabala Mallam Isa Ali Bauchi da Mallam Muhammad Yusuf Maiduguri akan Karatun Boko Haram," circa 2008. Part 1 available at: www.youtube.com/watch?v=h-nhmj3faHc; accessed March 2015.

22 Anonymous, "The Popular Discourses of Salafi Radicalism and Salafi Counter-Radicalism in Nigeria: A Case Study of Boko Haram," *Journal of Religion in Africa* 42:2 (2012): 118–44.

argued that his ideas derived from canonical texts like *Al-ʿIlmāniyya* (Secularism) by the Egyptian Shaykh Aḥmad Shākir (1892–1958). Seeking to claim both global backing and local continuity, Yūsuf also claimed that his stances had the backing of a respected elder shaykh in Maiduguri, Shaykh Abba Aji (1942–2009), who had allegedly told him, "You have proof (*kana da hujja*)."[23] This lecture highlighted how the canon was not only a tool that Yūsuf used in his own teaching, but a form of common ground with his opponents. Despite the ferocity of the intra-Salafi debate, Yūsuf was willing to acknowledge this common ground and to debate on shared terms.

The canon, however, was a major tool the graduates of Medina used to discredit Yūsuf. In a famous anti-Yūsuf lecture, Ādam said,

> He thinks that major scholars in whom the scholarly world trusts, such as Shaykh Bin Bāz, Shaykh Nāṣir al-Dīn al-Albānī, Shaykh Ṣāliḥ ibn ʿUthaymīn, and other major scholars, either in Saudi Arabia or Egypt or other places, he thinks that all of them are ignorant. What they have studied is not learning. His own is learning.[24]

With this kind of denunciation, Ādam positioned Yūsuf as a reckless entrepreneur operating outside the boundaries of accepted Salafi knowledge. Simultaneously, Ādam positioned himself as the local interpreter of and spokesman for global Salafi authority – through references that invoked not only the Salafi canon, but also Ādam's elite access to it as a graduate of a Saudi university.

The Medina graduates recognized that they were competing with Yūsuf for an audience. In the lecture on jihad that he delivered in Maiduguri just a few months before Boko Haram's 2009 uprising, Rijiyar Lemo acknowledged the risk that jihadis would seduce Muslim audiences, including his own. This risk arose in part because of jihadis' use of the Salafi canon. Explaining the rise of jihadi movements since the 1970s, Rijiyar Lemo told his audience,

> I want you to know the background to what you are seeing now . . . Where is its origin? And who are those who are leading this affair? Because often, you'll hear talk of Ibn Taymiyya, Muḥammad ibn ʿAbd al-Wahhāb, so-and-so, so-and-so, so-and-so, Ibn ʿUthaymīn, but you won't know who *they* are, behind the scenes (*min warāʾ al-kawālīs*).[25]

By 2009, Rijijyar Lemo and other graduates of Medina were keenly aware of the competition Salafism faced from jihadi movements, and were

[23] Muḥammad Yūsuf, "Warware Shubuhar Malamai," audio recording circa 2008. Available at: www.youtube.com/watch?v=dWfv28iSEZQ; accessed March 2015.

[24] Jaʿfar Maḥmūd Ādam, "Me Ya Sa Suke Cewa Boko Haram Ne?" undated audio recording. Available at: www.youtube.com/watch?v=kkNDO0e2Jf8; accessed November 2012.

[25] Rijiyar Lemo, "Kungiyoyin Jihadi (2)."

nervous about historical precedents for intra-Salafi and intra-Muslim violence in 1990s Algeria and elsewhere. The Medina graduates seemed to anticipate Boko Haram's 2009 uprising, as evidenced by Rijiyar Lemo's carefully constructed remarks in Maiduguri on the eve of the violence. The Izala movement reportedly warned authorities about a looming rebellion in the northeast.[26] Mainstream Salafis invoked the canon to discredit their opponents and stress the need for broad-based, long-term Salafi *da'wa* as opposed to jihadi violence. These efforts to discredit Boko Haram continued after Boko Haram's turn to jihad in 2009, including in the context of mainstream Salafis' continued efforts to teach the canon, discussed subsequently.

Unifying the Salafi Movement in Nigeria

At various points in northern Nigeria's history, the region's Muslim constituencies have sought to put aside their differences in the face of an external challenge. In the 1980s, as Roman Loimeier has written, Izala and the Sufi orders made public displays of unity amid an upsurge in Christian political activity. Izala's spiritual patron Shaykh Abubakar Gumi reconciled with Sufi leaders like Shaykh Nāṣir Kabara of the Qadiriyya, even though they had engaged in harsh polemics little more than a decade before.[27]

Nigeria's mainstream Salafis have undertaken a similar effort to project a united Salafi front against Boko Haram. Most dramatically, in December 2011, the "Jos" and "Kaduna" factions of Izala – so named for the cities in which they were based – publicly reconciled after a twenty-year split. Izala affirmed the Jos leader, Shaykh Sani Yahaya Jingir, as its national leader, but also elevated young preachers like the politically outspoken Shaykh Muhammad Kabiru Gombe, who became National Secretary.[28] The incentives for intra-Salafi unity go well beyond the imperative of answering Boko Haram, and relations between Izala and other Salafis have often involved cooperation as well as rivalry. This reconciliation within Izala comes amid intensifying cooperation between Izala and other Salafis, including the graduates of Medina. But Boko Haram is undoubtedly a factor.

Two manifestations of this pan-Salafi unity are preaching sessions organized by Izala: the "Wa'azin Kasa" (National Preaching) and *tafsīr*

26 See U.S. Embassy Abuja's draft of the 2009 country report on terrorism for Nigeria, leaked through Wikileaks. 09ABUJA2254, "Nigeria: 2009 Country Reports on Terrorism," 11 December 2009. Available at: https://cablegatesearch.wikileaks.org/cable.php?id=09ABUJA2254; accessed March 2015.

27 Roman Loimeier, *Islamic Reform and Political Change in Northern Nigeria* (Evanston: Northwestern University Press, 1997).

28 Isa Sa'idu, "Izala Factions Unite," *Daily Trust*, 22 December 2011.

(Qur'anic exegesis) during Ramadan. The graduates of Medina and other like-minded Salafis have maintained discursive and stylistic differences from Izala, but they are often willing to speak under Izala's banner. Izala listed Rijiyar Lemo as one of its Ramadan exegetes for 2013,[29] and Abdulwahhab Abdullah was one of Izala's preachers in Togo (his native country) during the same year.[30] These frameworks allow Izala and the broader Salafi movement to project religious authority throughout Nigeria and West Africa.

Izala's reach extends to Boko Haram's heartland in northeastern Nigeria. Izala can give a platform to prominent northeastern shaykhs and can even conduct preaching in violence-stricken areas. In 2013, Izala held a session of its *wa'azin kasa* in the northern state of Jigawa. More than thirty preachers spoke, including Shaykh ʿAlī Muṣṭafā of Borno and Shaykh Muḥammad Kabiru Gombe of Gombe,[31] two states Boko Haram has repeatedly attacked. Muṣṭafā, a graduate of Medina, is one of the Salafis who along with Ādam intervened with Muḥammad Yūsuf in an attempt to dissuade him from opposing Western-style education.[32] During Ramadan 2013, preachers under Izala's banner performed *tafsīr* throughout Nigeria, including in many parts of the northeast, such as Yobe and Adamawa,[33] which were at that time under the federal government's state of emergency.

For Izala and other mainstream Salafis, these institutionalized preaching structures offer the possibility of controlling and supervising preaching – in other words, of working to prevent the rise of freelancing, hardline Salafis like Muḥammad Yūsuf. In 2014, before its Ramadan *tafsīr*, Izala

[29] Ibrahim Baba Suleman, "Jadawalin Sunayen Malaman da Jama'atu Izalatul Bida'ah wa Ikamatis Sunnah (JIBWIS) ta Kasa Ta Tura Gudanar da Tafsirin al-Qur'an na Shekarar 1434(H) 2013 a Jahohi," Izala, 2 July 2013. Available at: www.facebook.com/jamil.sanni/posts/521376997915366; accessed March 2015.

[30] "Jadawalin Sunayen Malaman da Jama'atil Izalatil Bid'ah wa Ikamatis Sunnah (JIBWIS) ta Kasa Ta Tura Gudanar da Tafsirin al-Qur'an na Shekarar 1434H – Kasashen Afirika ta Yamma," Izala, 2 July 2013. Available at: www.jibwisnigeria.org/jadawalin-sunayen-malaman-da-jamaatil-izalatil-bidah-wa-ikamatis-sunnahjibwis-ta-kasa-ta-tura-gudanar-da-tafsirin-al-quran-na-shekarar-1434h-kasashen-afirika-ta-yamma/; accessed March 2015.

[31] "Wa'azin Kasa! Maitagari/Jigawa 9/10/11/2013," Izala, 9 November 2013. Available at: http://jibwisnigeria.org/waazin-kasa-maigatarijigawa-910112013/; accessed October 2014.

[32] Muhammad Nur Alkali, Abubakar Kawu Monguno, and Ballama Shettima Mustafa, "Overview of Islamic Actors in Northeastern Nigeria," Nigeria Research Network Working Paper Number 2 (January 2012), 33, note 46. Available at: www3.qeh.ox.ac.uk/pdf/nrn/WP2Alkali.pdf; accessed October 2014.

[33] "Jadawalin Sunayen Malaman da Jama'atu Izalatul Bid'ah wa Ikamatis Sunnah (JIBWIS) ta Kasa ta Tura Gudanar da Tafsirin al-Qur'an na Shekarar 1434 (H) 2013 a Jahohi," Izala website, 2 July 2013. Available at: www.jibwisnigerian.org/2013/07/02/jadawalin-sunayen-malaman-da-jamaatu-izalatul-bidah-wa-ikamatis-sunnah-jibwis-ta-kasa-ta-tura-gudanar-da-tafsirin-al-quran-na-shekarar-1434h-2013-a-jahohi/; accessed October 2014.

held a two-day training for preachers in Nigeria's capital Abuja. Headlined by Izala's National Chairman Shaykh Abdullahi Bala Lau and the Kano Izala leader Dr. Abdullahi Saleh Pakistan (a graduate of Medina), the event sought to instill a discipline of apolitical preaching.[34] Nigerian state governments have sometimes sought to regulate preaching, as Borno State did in 2009 following Boko Haram's uprising there,[35] but Izala's effort to self-police the Salafi community in Nigeria may have wider success.

The Medina graduates benefit by operating at least partly under Izala's banner: they increase their access to Izala's resources and audiences, and they can work to bring Izala even more in line with global Salafism. Moreover, they can position themselves for even more prominent leadership positions in the organization when the next generational shift occurs. Graduates of Medina like Rijiyar Lemo and Nazifi Inuwa are two decades younger than Izala's Jingir and may be competitors for taking the reins of the organization.

Continuing to Teach the Canon

Amid violence and tensions with the state, Salafis have continued to teach their canon. This effort to transmit the canon can now be seen in a double context. In Chapter 4, I emphasized how by teaching canonical texts, Nigerian Salafi shaykhs equipped their students with the intellectual tools necessary to articulate a Salafi identity and rebut other Muslims' criticisms of Salafism and of figures like Ibn Taymiyya. With the rise of Boko Haram, this first goal has been joined by a second: by teaching the canon, mainstream Nigerian Salafis now also equip their students with the tools to refute Boko Haram and challenge Boko Haram's readings of Ibn Taymiyya and others. For example, in a lesson on Ibn Taymiyya's *Al-ʿAqīda al-Wāsiṭiyya*, Dr. Aḥmad Gumi stressed the text's foundational position as a statement of Salafi creed, particularly about the attributes of Allah.[36]

Such lessons also reinforced the primacy of textual evidence as the currency of Salafi debates. In another session, Gumi stressed that in discussing Allah's attributes, there were

> only two ways to know the attributes of Allah: either the Qurʾan or the Sunna of the Messenger of Allah, may Allah bless him and grant him peace . . . there is no analogy or independent interpretation (*babu qiyasi ko ijtihadi*) . . . [One cay say]

[34] Adam Umar, "JIBWIS Organises Seminar for Clerics on Ramadan," *Daily Trust*, 9 June 2014. Available at: www.dailytrust.com.ng/city-news/26042-jibwis-organises-seminar-for-clerics-on-ramadan; accessed March 2015.

[35] "Nigeria State Vets Muslim Clerics," BBC News, 25 August 2009. Available at: http://news.bbc.co.uk/2/hi/africa/8221154.stm; accessed March 2015.

[36] Aḥmad Gumi, "Al Aqidatul Wasidiyyah," 27 May 2012. Available at: www.youtube.com/watch?v=kNPbLP7-1q0; accessed October 2014.

"Allah said and the Messenger said (*qāl Allāh wa qāla rasūluhu*)," but there is no independent interpretation.[37]

Salafi have been champions of *ijtihād*, of course, but here Gumi reminded audiences that from a Salafi perspective, *ijtihād* has limits. Gumi was not only teaching his students the basics of Salafi textual engagement, but also warning them against religious entrepreneurs who constructed broad political programs without sufficient textual evidence – one of the main criticisms mainstream Salafis directed against Boko Haram. Gumi made this argument more explicitly in a 2013 *tafsīr* session:

What is *haram*, what is forbidden, must be written in black and white. If it's not written in black and white, then don't call it *haram*. . . . I'm talking about what Muslims now are doing, some Muslims, or some semi-educated Muslims. When they see a perfect system, perfected by non-Muslims, they label it as non-Islamic.[38]

Gumi sought to inculcate in his audience a pervasive skepticism about other preachers' intellectual legitimacy, particularly when it came to questions of determining what Islam does or does not authorize.

Salafis' deepening engagement with electronic media has reinforced their ability to continue teaching the canon amid Boko Haram's violence. In 2013, Izala launched a satellite television station called Sunnah TV. The station, which also has a YouTube channel and Twitter account, regularly features prominent Salafis such as Abdullah and Rijijyar Lemo, who discuss the canonical *ḥadīth* collections and other texts.[39] Notably, the station has provided a platform for Salafis from northeastern Nigeria even as they face violence from Boko Haram in their home region. On Sunnah TV, 'Alī Muṣṭafā has offered televised lessons in Salafi creed and jurisprudence. In a series of lectures for the program "*fiqh al-ʿaqīda*" (the jurisprudence of creed), he has drawn on Ibn ʿUthaymīn's *Al-Qawāʿid al-Muthlā* (The Exemplary Rules).[40] Such lessons represent efforts by mainstream Salafis to emphasize the importance of figures such as Ibn ʿUthaymīn – and, through him, to elevate creed over politics. Teaching the full Salafi canon also prevents the kind of narrowing of the canon that I described in the last chapter: if Salafi-jihadis are constructing a canon that compartmentalizes Ibn Bāz and Ibn ʿUthaymīn and reduces al-Albānī to an authenticator of *ḥadīth* rather than a spokesman for Salafism, then mainstream Salafis are pushing back by teaching a canon that still foregrounds these major scholars.

37 Aḥmad Gumi, "Al Aqidatul Wasidiyyah," 19 April 2012. Available at: www.youtube.com/watch?v=lIAXkaFyGIk; accessed March 2015.
38 Aḥmad Gumi, "Ramadan Tafseer," 17 July 2013. Available at: www.youtube.com/watch?v=W_SQuq6eI-Q; accessed May 2014.
39 See Sunnah TV Nigeria channel, Youtube. Available at: https://www.youtube.com/user/MySunnahTV; accessed October 2014.
40 ʿAlī Muṣṭafā, "Fiqhul Aqida 1," Sunnah TV, 2 October 2013. Available at: https://www.youtube.com/watch?v=LEBgeaTNj_4; accessed October 2014.

Such efforts to control the image and transmission of the canon are intimately tied to media projects. In a move that mirrors global trends within the Salafi community, Nigerian Salafis have increasingly cultivated an online infrastructure. As Chapter 5 discussed, the Medina graduates have invested considerable energies into developing their media presence. During Ādam's lifetime, radio and recordings were the major media for the movement. These media are now increasingly complemented by websites. The online infrastructure of Nigeria's mainstream Salafis includes Izala's website (www.jibwisnigeria.org) but also platforms more specifically oriented to highlighting the broader Nigerian Salafi community and its most prominent spokesmen. "Dandalin Sunnah" (www.dandalinsunnah.com) contains videos and audio of prominent Nigerian Salafis such as Dr. Ahmad Gumi and Shaykh Aminu Daurawa. Many Nigerian shaykhs have their own Facebook pages, for example, Rijiyar Lemo and Aminu Daurawa,[41] or Twitter accounts, for example, Abdullahi Bala Lau.[42]

Online infrastructure helps to spread the canon and assert the canon's relevance to ordinary Muslims. For example, one graduate of Medina, Dr. Ibrahim Jalo Jalingo, wrote a blog post for a Salafi-leaning website in which he defended the orthodoxy of Qur'an recitation competitions, a type of event popular among northern Nigerian Muslims of various theological stripes. Jalo responded to charges that because Salafis oppose celebrating the Prophet's birthday (*mawlid*), they should also oppose Qur'an recitation competitions. He invoked the authority of Ibn Taymiyya and the Ḥanbalī jurist Ibn Qudāma to defend the orthodoxy of these competitions, providing quotations from Arabic texts and translating them into Hausa.[43] Such websites provide platforms for original content, such as Jalo's post, as well as platforms for amplifying other media products, such as *tafsīr* recordings by Ādam and Rijiyar Lemo. The Internet has been a major force in the wider effort to canonize Ādam in northern Nigeria.

Institutionalizing Influence

Alongside their continued efforts to teach the canon, Salafis have continued to build their institutional power. Salafi leaders have continued

41 Facebook page of Muḥammad Sani 'Umar Rijiyar Lemo. Available at: www.facebook.com/pages/Dr-Muhd-Sani-Umar-Rlemo/355392177936441; accessed March 2015; Facebook page of Aminu Daurawa. Available at: www.facebook.com/amdaurawa; accessed October 2015.

42 Twitter account of Abdullahi Bala Lau. Available at: https://twitter.com/lau_bala; accessed March 2015.

43 Ibrahim Jalo Jalingo, "Musabakar Haddar al-Qurani ko Hadithi ko Wani Nau'in Ilmi a Mahangar Musulunci," Nibra's Blog, 26 January 2015. Available at: https://nibrasonline.wordpress.com/2015/01/26/musabakar-haddar-alqurani-ko-hadithi-ko-wani-nauin-ilmi-a-mahangar-musuluncidr-ibrahim-jalo-jalingo/; accessed March 2015.

to attain high posts with some state governments. Perhaps the highest-ranking Salafi official in the 2011–15 political cycle was the preacher Shaykh Aminu Daurawa, who was appointed Commander General of Kano State's Hisbah Board in 2011. Daurawa was not a graduate of Medina, but he was a member of Ādam's circle, and conforms discursively to the styles of the Medina graduates and the global Salafi movement.

As the Hisbah's Commander General, Daurawa has been responsible for helping to regulate public morality in Kano. He served first under Governor Rabiu Kwankwaso, who presented himself as a leftist social reformer in the mold of the Northern Nigerian progressive politician Aminu Kano (1920–83). Kwankwaso's progressivism and Daurawa's Salafism have produced interesting combinations in the Hisbah's work: one initiative has been mass marriages of widows and divorcees, a project that fulfills both the progressive desire to care for the socially and economically vulnerable and the Salafi desire (and the broader desire of many conservative northern Nigerian Muslims) to ensure that unmarried adults are returned to a condition where they pose no perceived threat to the community's sexual morality. The ability of Salafi leaders like Daurawa to work with different kinds of politicians in northern Nigeria suggests that the Salafi community can negotiate a role in electoral and bureaucratic politics. Notably, Daurawa was reappointed in 2015 under Kwankwaso's successor, Abdullahi Ganduje.

In Chapter 6, I highlighted Salafis' efforts to deploy the canon in politics and emphasize *daʿwa* over electoral politics. At the same time, it is important to point out how Salafis wield institutional power when they have it. One incident illustrates dramatically how Salafis can leverage their growing institutional influence to attack Sufism and reshape the religious field in Nigeria. In May 2015, a Tijani preacher named Abdul Nyass allegedly told an audience in Kano that Shaykh Ibrāhīm Niasse was greater than the Prophet. Abdul Nyass belongs to a subgroup within the Tijaniyya known as *ʾyan hakika*, or "people of [esoteric] reality." Whether this alleged statement was made, controversy – and violence – quickly spread through Kano. Even after authorities arrested Nyass and some of his followers, crowds burned Nyass' house and the court where he and the other detainees were set to appear. As pressure on authorities mounted, the Upper *Sharīʿa* Court in Kano sentenced Nyass and eight followers to death on June 25. Four days later, Kano's recently inaugurated new governor, Kwankwaso's former deputy Abdullahi Ganduje, announced his support for the verdict.[44] At the time of writing, it is unclear whether

[44] Ismail Mudashir, "Kano Backs Sentencing of 9 to Death over Blasphemy," *Daily Trust*, 30 June 2015. Available at: www.dailytrust.com.ng/daily/index.php/news-menu/news/58628-kano-backs-sentencing-of-9-to-death-over-blasphemy; accessed October 2015.

Kano's government will carry out the sentence; Ganduje may prefer to let the accused languish in prison until the controversy fades.

Amid the controversy, Salafi preachers took the opportunity to go on the offensive not just against Abdul Nyass, but against the Sufi orders more broadly. Preachers such as Dr. Ahmad Ibrahim of the Bayero University Kano Old Campus Mosque denounced Nyass and Sufism in recorded lectures. Senior Tijani shaykhs, such as Dahiru Bauchi and Isyaku Rabiu, disassociated themselves and the Tijaniyya from Nyass,[45] but such defensive maneuvers did not stop the Salafi offensive.

Some of the most formidable anti-Sufi statements came from Daurawa. Blurring his roles as Salafi preacher and government official, Daurawa made repeated statements during the controversy. In one Facebook post written days after the alleged blasphemy occurred, Daurawa said:

> What these Tijanis, these "people of the [spiritual flood, a reference to Ibrahim Niasse's core teachings]," these "people of esoteric reality" are doing in terms of insulting God's Messenger, it exceeds the unbelief of the Jews and Christians. It exceeds the unbelief of Pharaoh, Qarūn and Hāmān [two supporters of Pharaoh mentioned in Qur'anic verses such as 40:24] and of Abū Jahl [a Meccan opponent of the Prophet] and every unbeliever walking on the surface of the planet. . . . This is the reality of the Sufi order. There is a need to get rid of all the Sufi orders, since the Prophet, may Allah bless him and grant him peace, is being insulted inside them (*wannan shine hakikanin Darika. A kwai bukatar ayi watsi da dukkan dariku tunda ana zagin Annabi saw a ciki*).[46]

Even if he sought to speak in a strictly preaching capacity, rather than as the representative of the Kano state government, Daurawa's statement carried an implied threat that his institutional power – the specific mandate of the Hisbah to enforce ideals of Islamic public morality in the state – could be wielded against Sufis.

The incident with Abdul Nyass highlights the benefits Salafis can derive from participating in government, which give them new resources and platforms as they seek to Salafize Nigerian Muslims. At the same time, Salafis, with their emphasis on creedal purity, face particular risks by being in power. As the Egyptian example I mentioned at the beginning of this chapter shows, Salafis make trade-offs when they participate in electoral politics and governance. Pragmatism and participation can have political benefits but can also open the door to even greater intra-Salafi fragmentation over questions of politics and purity. As Nigeria's Salafis derive some of the benefits of holding senior bureaucratic appointments,

45 Abdulkadir Mukhtar and Haruna Yaya, "Dahiru Bauchi, Rabi'u, Dissociate Tijjaniyya from Blasphemous Preaching," *Daily Trust*, 21 May 2015. Available at: http://dailytrust.com.ng/daily/index.php/news-menu/news/55240-dahiru-bauchi-rabi-u-dissociate-tijjaniyya-from-blasphemous-preaching; accessed October 2015.

46 Aminu Daurawa, Facebook posting, 20 May 2015. Available at: www.facebook.com/amdaurawa/posts/845309232222932; accessed October 2015.

they also expose themselves to potential critiques that they have compromised the core Salafi mission of *da'wa*.

Other Nigerian Salafis do not hold formal government positions but intervene in political debates as prominent commentators. Reprising his father's role as a voice on electoral matters, Dr. Ahmad Gumi frequently made headlines during the 2014–15 presidential campaign, especially with his open letter to four-time presidential contender and former military ruler Muhammadu Buhari. In the letter, posted on Gumi's Facebook page and widely disseminated in the Nigerian press, Gumi discouraged Buhari from running, arguing that the general was too old and that Buhari's single-minded focus on fighting corruption left him vulnerable to exploitation by more sophisticated political allies. Gumi did not make explicitly Salafi arguments but did make generically Islamic ones. He framed his letter as a form of religious advice and warned Buhari that his candidacy, given some Nigerian Christians' fears of Buhari's allegedly Islamist agenda, would further divide Nigeria along religious lines.[47] Gumi's advice did not prevent Buhari from contesting – or winning – but the attention given to his letter reflected the media presence Gumi had built.

Mainstream Salafis have also continued to build influence within northern Nigerian higher education. As of 2016, Salafi-leaning faculty could be found at major institutions such as Bayero University Kano and Katsina Islamic University (also known as Al-Qalam University). Salafis' influence at such institutions should not be overstated, but their presence in faculties of Islamic Studies and other university departments allows them to build relationships with Western-educated and Nigerian-educated faculty members. Salafis sometimes share important goals with other faculty, such as systematically directing students to translate the corpus of *ḥadīth* into Hausa.

Conclusion

Through their media, preaching, and governmental platforms, mainstream Salafis wield considerable influence over thousands of followers in Nigeria and West Africa – even as Boko Haram seeks to establish psychological and territorial control in northeastern Nigeria, and to define Salafi Islam for Nigerian Muslims. Mainstream Nigerian Salafis have worked to defend their claim to the canon against the threat, not just physical but also intellectual, represented by Boko Haram. Reclaiming the canon involves unifying the Salafi movement, extending its influence

[47] See the full text of the letter, published 21 November 2014, at: www.premiumtimesng.com/news/headlines/169844-dont-contest-2015-election-prominent-islamic-cleric-sheikh-gumi-tells-buhari.html; accessed March 2015.

in media, politics, and education, and continuing to teach the canon. When Nigeria's mainstream Salafis teach works by figures such as Ibn ʿUthaymīn, they are foregrounding the quietist or mainstream strand of the contemporary canon, and thereby implicitly or explicitly challenging the selective, politicized, and exclusivist version of the canon that Boko Haram championed. When these mainstream Salafis teach texts by Ibn Taymiyya, they are seeking to shape how Nigerian audiences understand Boko Haram's favorite author. The mainstream preachers, in other words, hope to ensure that Ibn Taymiyya remains a pillar of Salafism rather than a pillar of jihadism.

I have argued in this chapter that struggles over the canon in northern Nigeria parallel struggles between mainstream Salafis and Salafi-jihadis elsewhere in the world. These struggles exist in physical space, as many mainstream Salafis strive to project religious and political influence amid suspicion from the state and violence by Salafi-jihadis. These struggles also play out online. Salafi-jihadis have used the Internet to great effect, a development that threatens mainstream Salafis' ability to define the canon and reach the growing population of Muslim autodidacts. Mainstream Salafis have responded by building an online infrastructure that, on the whole, plays a unifying role for the movement, including by reinforcing the canonization of contemporary shaykhs like Ibn Bāz, Ibn ʿUthaymīn, and al-Albānī. In this way, mainstream Nigerian Salafis' efforts to invoke and popularize this triumvirate, and their own deepening online engagement, contributes to a wider, global project of self-definition and self-policing by mainstream Salafis.

Conclusion

Africa is often reductively described as the recipient of outside influences, whether Western, Chinese, or Arab. This trend is particularly acute with regard to Islam, where "African Islam" is frequently caricatured as "syncretist" – and therefore open to powerful challenges from allegedly more "orthodox" Arab Muslims.

In the tense geopolitical atmosphere of the early twenty-first century and the "War on Terror," stereotypes of purist Arabs and syncretist Africans have been incorporated into narratives about the threat of global jihad. A lack of governance supposedly compounds this threat in Africa. Policy makers, analysts, and journalists frequently analogize the presumed experience of Afghanistan under the Taliban to other so-called ungoverned spaces or weak states, including in West Africa. Metaphors casting Africa passively – as a breeding ground of extremism, for example – often accompany such analogies. A commentator in the *Wall Street Journal* wrote in 2012,

> Oil money has funded extremist madrassas, or religious schools, to propagate a stripped-down, one-size-fits all ideology precisely suited for pollination across impoverished regions such as Somalia, Yemen, Nigeria, the Pakistani-Afghan border and the like. With money and threats, this international extremist franchise has targeted peaceful Muslim lands where the faith had blended with local customs or become more cosmopolitan through contact with other cultures. Places, in other words, where Islam had lost its aggression and exclusivity.[1]

West African "syncretists," in the language of this and other authors, become passive targets for Arab "extremists" who "pollinate" or "target" African communities. Commentators sometimes point to Nigeria, due to its population size and oil resources, as the "biggest prize" for Arab

[1] Melik Kaylan, "Radical Islamists Wage Muslim Civil War in Africa," *Wall Street Journal*, 13 July 2012. Available at: http://online.wsj.com/article/SB10001424052702303740704577523080072700486.html; accessed August 2013.

"extremists" interested in Africa.[2] Such depictions accord little agency or imagination to African Muslims.

This constellation of stereotypes focuses suspicious attention on African Muslims who travel to Arab countries for religious study. American think tanks routinely depict such Africans as conduits for the influence of Saudi Arabia, depicted as a shadowy country that bears responsibility for disseminating theological perspectives that led to the attacks of 11 September 2001. Saudi Arabia's religious outreach to Africa, for some analysts, threatens to radicalize the entire continent. At a Pew Forum titled "Religious Fault Lines in West Africa" in 2005, one speaker asserted that the factors involved in creating Muslim-Christian violence in northern Nigeria included "the stream of young radical preachers who return from higher studies in Saudi Arabia or Egypt and contest the allegedly impure Islam of their parents."[3] In contrast to such views, I have sought throughout this study to give a more complicated picture of what happens when "young preachers" travel to places like Saudi Arabia. Moreover, I challenge the idea that study in Saudi Arabia is inherently radicalizing.

The Salafi movement is one of the most important strands of Islamic thought and activism in Nigeria, Africa's most populous country. Salafis have achieved prominence as preachers but also as high-ranking officials in state governments and as faculty members in respected Nigerian universities. The attention so often paid to questions of radicalization in Africa can obscure the far-reaching changes that Salafi activists are producing in politics, education, and media. Put differently, the attention paid to figures like Boko Haram's Muḥammad Yūsuf and Abubakar Shekau (neither of whom graduated from a Saudi Arabian university) has prevented a more systematic discussion of mainstream Nigerian Salafis and how they are affecting the country's religious landscape.

By examining Salafism in Nigeria, this work has shown that twentieth-century texts are fundamental to wide-ranging and consequential debates over what it means to be Muslim. In contrast to the often-repeated equation of contemporary Salafism with "seventh-century Islam," I have argued that Salafism encompasses a canon that extends over all of Islamic history, as well as over multiple continents.

In northern Nigeria, the canon serves as a primary mechanism for transmitting Salafism. The major preachers discussed in this study –

[2] Richard Dowden, "Today Mali, Tomorrow Nigeria for Al Qaeda," *African Arguments*, 16 January 2013. Available at: http://africanarguments.org/2013/01/16/today-mali-tomorrow-nigeria-for-al-qaeda-%E2%80%93-by-richard-dowden/; accessed August 2013.

[3] Pew Forum, "Religious Fault Lines in West Africa," 15 March 2005. Transcript of remarks. Available at: www.pewforum.org/Politics-and-Elections/Religious-Fault-Lines-in-West-Africa.aspx; accessed August 2013.

Shaykh Jaʿfar Maḥmūd Ādam, Dr. Muḥammad Sani ʿUmar Rijiyar Lemo, Shaykh Abdulwahhab Abdullah, and others – studied the Salafi canon at the Islamic University of Medina between the 1980s and the 2000s. When they returned home, they taught the canon to a wide audience of students, equipping their followers with intellectual resources designed to rebut other Muslims' arguments against Salafism. The canon supplied powerful ideals – the notion of Salafis as a vanguard of true Muslims, and the ideal of media as an arena where an intellectual meritocracy operates – that structured Nigerian Salafis' interventions in politics. Around the world, as Salafis debate other Muslims, they rely heavily on the canon – not just on its contents, but also on its methodologies and attitudes toward texts and how texts should be used.

The canon is an object of struggles within the Salafi community, especially between mainstream Salafis and the Salafi fringe that embraces violence. If Salafism represents a narrowing of the broader world of Sunni Muslim scholarship, Salafi-jihadism further narrows the Salafi canon, preserving only those elements that can legitimate a highly exclusivist, activist politics based on violent rejection of the secular state and any Muslims who disagree with aggressive jihad. Mainstream Salafis – those uninvolved in violence and unwilling to anathematize Muslim rulers – have invoked the canon in an effort to delegitimize jihadis. Mainstream Salafis argue that jihadis are ignorant of foundational scholarship and that jihadis are unable to produce compelling textual evidence for their ideological stances. Even as Boko Haram has brought violence to much of northern Nigeria, including violence against prominent Nigerian Salafis, the mainstream Salafi movement there has continued to teach the canon and build its institutional influence in government, universities and schools, and the media. In an era in which Muslims are constantly asked to denounce the behavior of terrorists, contemporary Salafis employ the canon rather than Western-style human rights discourses to stand against violent groups in their midst.

This study of Nigeria has larger implications for understanding relations between religion and politics around the world. In early 2015, a debate raged about whether ISIS was "Islamic" or not. The debate was sparked by an article in *The Atlantic* titled "What ISIS Really Wants." The author relied heavily on the scholar of Salafism Bernard Haykel, who argued that ISIS was "smack in the middle of the medieval tradition and [was] bringing it wholesale into the present day."[4] Rebuttals of the article and of Haykel's quoted words surged forth, yet the debate missed what is, to me, the most important point. Ultimately, I disagree

[4] Graeme Wood, "What ISIS Really Wants," *The Atlantic*, March 2015. Available at: www.theatlantic.com/features/archive/2015/02/what-isis-really-wants/384980/; accessed March 2015.

with Haykel about the mechanism through which ISIS and the broader Salafi world interprets "the medieval tradition" – itself a construct whose coherence I would challenge. Salafis do not have an autonomous relationship with the Qur'an and the corpus of *ḥadīth*, or with medieval theologians like Ibn Taymiyya. Just like other Muslims today, Salafis read these texts through filters, namely the accumulated (and constantly reinterpreted) layers of meaning, interpretation, and politics that are embodied in distinct canons. The Salafi movement is of relatively recent origin, as demonstrated by the fact that some of its most prominent canonical authorities are twentieth-century scholars.

Even when a Salafi today picks up a text like *Ṣaḥīḥ al-Bukhārī*, the most famous classical collection of *ḥadīth*, he or she is likely to feel the conscious or unconscious influence of twentieth-century Salafi scholars' admonitions on how to decide which reports are actionable and which are not. Even when a Salafi today drenches himself or herself in a vocabulary that is directly borrowed from Ibn Taymiyya and other medieval scholars – describing himself or herself with terms like *ahl al-sunna wa-l-jamāʿa* (the people of the Prophet's model and the Muslim community) or *al-firqa al-nājiyya* (the saved sect) – he or she employs understandings of these terms that have been filtered through various intermediaries. After all, most contemporary Salafis do not read Ibn Taymiyya in manuscript form; they read him in editions that have moved through many human hands and minds that edited the texts, extracted and evaluated the *ḥadīth* reports contained within them, wrote introductions and footnotes, published them, and put them online. The question is not whether ISIS represents the "medieval tradition" but rather what tradition has been constructed, who constructed it, and how this construction has interacted with contemporary politics.

Acknowledging the power of contemporary lenses of interpretation should heighten, rather than diminish, our attention to the religious aspects of contemporary religious movements. That scholars should have to defend the religious nature of movements like Salafism or Salafi-jihadism may seem strange, but analysts often discuss Salafism (especially in Africa) solely as a product of Saudi Arabian material support, or as an escape for youth who allegedly might just as easily have turned to hip hop, drugs, or the dream of immigration to the West. As Ruth Marshall writes,

> Whether religion is understood in terms of a troublesome identity politics or in terms of local attempts to interpret global forces, it is considered as a medium for a message that is about something else, something nonreligious; the religious sphere is not interrogated *as such* for its political significance.[5]

5 Ruth Marshall, *Political Spiritualities: The Pentecostal Revolution in Nigeria* (Chicago: University of Chicago Press, 2009), 2.

Refocusing attention on texts is one way to explain the worldviews that differentiate religious activism from other forms of politics, and religious ideas from other kinds of ideas. Given the reductive stereotypes of Africa as a place where influences only arrive, but are not reshaped and retransmitted, it is particularly important to examine how religious texts are used, translated, and produced in countries like Nigeria.

The formation and dissemination of the Salafi canon exemplifies broader processes at work in contemporary religious communities today. Many practitioners are reimagining their traditions and developing new conceptions of religious authority. They neither jettison scripture nor rely solely on it but rather construct interpretive frameworks that provide, in their eyes, both authenticity and license for structured improvisation. My method for studying these frameworks of authority responds to calls to study Islam as a "discursive tradition,"[6] but also moves beyond that notion of Islam. What the idea of a discursive tradition has lacked is a sufficient discussion of religious authority – of the mechanisms by which authority is created and sustained, and the mechanisms by which religious authorities mediate between text and context, or what authorities ordinary practitioners look to as they negotiate those mediations.

The notion of canonization has helped me to understand how communities authorize certain kinds of texts and certain approaches to texts. Put differently, canonization has helped me to understand why Nigerian Muslims might care about figures like Shaykh Muḥammad Nāṣir al-Dīn al-Albānī and, more broadly, what processes created a situation in which Nigerian Muslims would have the possibility of caring about these men and their ideas. Authority, I have suggested, involves not just relationships of power but also relationships of imagination: through techniques like metonymy, contemporary Nigerian Salafis have crafted narratives that relate their audiences' predicaments to situations that earlier Muslims faced.

We can close by looking at ongoing processes of canonization within the Salafi community of northern Nigeria. Jaʿfar Ādam was assassinated in 2007, and already structures of canonization have grown up around him. After his death, his close associates reportedly discouraged mourners from wearing pins with the shaykh's image, fearing that such practices too closely resembled Sufi veneration of saints.[7] Yet Ādam's associates have assiduously worked to disseminate his writings and recorded lectures, including by founding new institutions like the Sheikh Jaʿafar Islamic Documentation Centre in Kano. Nigeria's Salafi community operates an increasing number of websites, many of which contain the biographies

[6] Talal Asad, "The Idea of an Anthropology of Islam," Georgetown University Center for Contemporary Arab Studies Occasional Papers Series, 1986.
[7] Field notes.

and audio recordings of Ādam and his peers. Fittingly for a figure who dedicated his career to disseminating the broader Salafi canon in Nigeria, in death Ādam has himself become an object of canonization, illustrating a trend that is reshaping personal and textual authority across the Muslim world today.

Appendix 1
The Sermon of Necessity (Khuṭbat al-Ḥāja)

The Sermon of Necessity, a text revived and reworked by Shaykh Muḥammad Nāṣir al-Dīn al-Albāni in the 1950s, is now widely used as a doxology by Salafi preachers and scholars. The version of the text reconstructed by al-Albāni is as follows:

All praise to Allah: We praise Him, we seek His aid, and we ask His pardon (*naḥmaduhu wa-nasta'īnuhu wa-nastaghfiruhu*). We seek refuge in Allah from the evils of our selves (*min shurūr anfusinā*) and from the sins of our deeds (*sayyi'āt a'mālinā*). He whom Allah guides, there is no one who can mislead him; and he who has strayed has no guide. I bear witness that there is no god but Allah, He alone with no partner to Him, and I bear witness that Muḥammad is His servant and His Messenger.

"O you who believe, fear Allah as He should be feared and do not die except as Muslims." (Qur'an 3:102)

"O you people, fear your Lord Who created you from one soul, and created from it its mate, and dispersed from both of them many men and women. And fear Allah, through whom ye demand your mutual (rights), and (reverence) the wombs (that bore you): for Allah ever watches over you." (Qur'an 4:1)

"O you who believe, fear Allah and speak correct words, that He may reform your actions for you and pardons your sins for you. Whosoever obeys Allah and His Messenger has won a great victory." (Qur'an 33:70–71)[1]

Furthermore: the truest speech is the Book of Allah and the best guidance is the guidance of Muḥammad (*inna aṣdaq al-ḥadīth kitāb Allāh wa-aḥsan al-hady hady Muḥammad*), may Allah bless him and grant him peace. And the worst of all things are innovations (*wa-sharr al-umūr muḥdathātuhā*), and every innovation is a heretical innovation (*bid'a*), and every heretical innovation is an error (*ḍalāla*), and every error is in hellfire.[2]

[1] Muḥammad Nāṣir al-Dīn al-Albānī, *Khuṭbat al-Ḥāja allatī Kāna Rasūl Allāh – Ṣallā Allāh 'alayhi wa-Sallam – Yu'allimuhā Aṣḥābahu* (Al-Riyāḍ: Maktabat al-Ma'ārif li-l-Nashr wa-l-Tawzī', 2000), 3. Qur'anic translation adapted from Abdullah Yusuf Ali, *The Holy Qur'an: Text, Translation, and Commentary*, fourth edition (Elmhurst, NY: Tahrike Tarsile Qur'an, 2004).

[2] This report, added by most Salafis who use the Sermon of Necessity, appears in the doxology to Muḥammad Nāṣir al-Dīn al-Albānī, *Silsilat al-Aḥādīth al-Ḍa'īfa wa-l-Mawḍū'a wa-Atharuhā al-Sayyi' fī al-Umma*, 40.

Glossary of Persons

Figures Incorporated into the Salafi Canon

Āl al-Shaykh, Muḥammad ibn Ibrāhīm (1893–1969) – Saudi Arabian scholar who served as Grand Mufti and as the first president of the Islamic University of Medina.

Al-ʿAbbād, ʿAbd al-Muḥsin (b. 1934) – Longtime teacher and administrator at the Islamic University of Medina.

Al-Albāni, Muḥammad Nāṣir al-Dīn (1914–1999) – Albanian-born, Damascus-raised evaluator of *ḥadīth.*

Al-Ālūsī, Nuʿman Khayr al-Dīn (1836–1899) – Iraqi scholar who wrote a defense of Ibn Taymiyya and corresponded with Ṣiddīq Ḥasan Khān.

Al-Bīṭār, Muḥammad Bahjat (1894–1976) – Syrian scholar invited by Saudi Arabia's King ʿAbd al-ʿAzīz to direct the Educational Institute (*al-Maʿhad al-ʿIlmī*) in Mecca.

Al-Fiqqī, Muḥammad Ḥāmid (1892–1959) – Founder of Egypt's Anṣār al-Sunna al-Muḥammadiyya, an early Salafi organization.

Abū al-Samaḥ, ʿAbd al-Ẓāhir (1881–1952) – Egyptian scholar invited by Saudi Arabia's King ʿAbd al-ʿAzīz to become imam of the Grand Mosque in Mecca.

Ibn ʿAbd al-Wahhāb, Muḥammad (1703–1792) – Anti-Sufi reformer who established a religiopolitical alliance with Muḥammad ibn Saʿūd (d. 1765) in present-day Saudi Arabia.

Ibn Bāz, ʿAbd al-ʿAzīz (1910–1999) – Saudi Arabian scholar who served as president of the Islamic University of Medina from 1970 to 1975 and as Grand Mufti of Saudi Arabia from 1993 to 1999.

Ibn Ḥajar al-ʿAsqalānī (1372–1449) – Egyptian scholar of *ḥadīth* and jurisprudential thinker within the Shāfiʿī school of Sunni Islam.

Ibn Ḥanbal, Aḥmad (780–855) – Eponym of the Ḥanbalī school – a theologian and jurist whose defense of the idea of the uncreated Qurʾan brought him persecution during the early ʿAbbāsid Caliphate.

Ibn Kathīr, Ismāʿīl (ca. 1300–1373) – Key student of Ibn Taymiyya, whose Qurʾanic exegesis and historical writing are well respected by contemporary Salafis.

Ibn al-Qayyim, Muḥammad (1292–1350) – Key student of Ibn Taymiyya, whose writings on law and creed remain important for contemporary Salafis.

Ibn Taymiyya, Aḥmad (1263–1328) – Damascene theologian and Ḥanbalī scholar whose literalist creeds, legal thought, and political writings are foundational for Salafism but remain deeply controversial, including among Salafis.

Al-Ifrīqī, ʿAbd al-Raḥmān (1908–1957) – Mali-born scholar who authored an influential anti-Tijaniyya polemic and taught in Saudi Arabia.

Al-Jāmī, Muḥammad Amān (1931–1996) – Ethiopia-born scholar who taught at the Islamic University of Medina and chaired the faculty of *ḥadīth*. A "quietist" Salafi tendency at the university and in Saudi Arabia bears his name.

Khān, Muḥammad Ṣiddīq Ḥasan (1832–1890) – Indian scholar and publisher who became a leader of the *ahl-e ḥadīth* movement, in part because he was inspired by al-Shawkānī.

Al-Madkhalī, Rabīʿ ibn Hādī (b. 1931) – Longtime instructor at the Islamic University of Medina, an opponent of Sayyid Quṭb, and a key thinker in the "quietist" movement also associated with Muḥammad Amān Al-Jāmī.

Al-Nawawī, Yaḥyā ibn Sharaf (1233–1277) – Syrian scholar of *ḥadīth* and jurisprudential thinker within the Shāfiʿī school of Sunni Islam.

Riḍā, Muḥammad Rashīd (1865–1935) – Syrian revivalist thinker who became an intellectual defender of the third Saudi state during the last decades of his life. Some of his students and junior contemporaries founded Egypt's Anṣār al-Sunna al-Muḥammadiyya.

Al-Ṣanʿānī, Muḥammad ibn Ismāʿīl al-Amīr (1688–1769) – Yemeni scholar of *ḥadīth*.

Shākir, Aḥmad (1892–1958) – Egyptian judge, *ḥadīth* scholar, and opponent of secularism.

Al-Shawkānī, Muḥammad ibn ʿAlī (1760–1834) – Yemeni jurist and scholar who claimed the right to absolute *ijtihād*.

Al-Shinqīṭī, Muḥammad al-Amīn (1907–1973) – Mauritania-born scholar who authored an influential exegesis of the Qurʾan, taught at the Islamic University of Medina, and served on Saudi Arabia's Committee of Senior Scholars.

Al-ʿUthaymīn, Muḥammad ibn Ṣāliḥ (1925–2001) – Saudi Arabian scholar and member of the Committee of Senior Scholars.

Al-Wādiʿī, Muqbil ibn Hādī (1933–2001) – Major Yemeni scholar, often identified as "quietist" but involved early in his life with Juhaymān al-ʿUtaybī.

Nigerian Salafis and Proto-Salafis

Abdullah, Abdulwahhab (b. 1953) – A graduate of Medina (B.A., 1991) and a close companion of Ja'far Ādam.

Ādam, Ja'far Maḥmūd (1961/2–2007) – A graduate of Medina (B.A., 1993) who became the most prominent Salafi preacher of his generation after he returned home.

"Albānī," Muḥammad Awwal (1960–2014) – A prominent *ḥadīth* scholar based in Zaria, who was assassinated by Boko Haram after criticizing the sect.

Daurawa, Aminu Ibrahim (b. 1969) – A Nigerian-trained Salafi, close to the Medina graduates, who became Commander General of Kano State's Hisbah Board in 2011 and was reappointed in 2015.

Gumi, Abubakar (1924–1992) – Northern Nigerian judge, scholar, and anti-Sufi polemicist, whose followers founded *Jamā'at Izālat al-Bid'a wa-Iqāmat al-Sunna* (The Society for the Removal of Heretical Innovation and the Establishment of the Prophetic Model, known as Izala) in 1978.

Gumi, Aḥmad (b. 1960) – Prominent son of Abubakar Gumi, who divides his time between Saudi Arabia and Nigeria and delivers in influential Ramadan *tafsīr* at Sultan Bello Mosque in Kaduna.

Idrīs, Ismā'īl (1936/7–2000) – Student of Abubakar Gumi and the founder and longtime leader of Izala.

Jingir, Muḥammad al-Thānī Yaḥyā (b. 1950) – A senior leader of Izala's "Jos" branch who became Izala's national leader after the Jos and Kaduna branches reconciled in 2011.

Pakistan, 'Abd Allāh Ṣāliḥ (b. 1957) – A graduate of Medina (B.A., 1985) and a major Izala leader in Kano.

Rijiyar Lemo, Muḥammad al-Thānī 'Umar (b. 1970) – A graduate of Medina (Ph.D., 2005) and a close companion of Ja'far Ādam.

'Umar, Bashīr 'Alī (b. 1961) – A graduate of Medina (Ph.D., 2004) who became imam of al-Furqān Mosque in Kano, a faculty member at the Department of Islamic Studies at Bayero University Kano, an advisor to Sanusi Lamido Sanusi during the latter's governorship of the Central Bank of Nigeria, and an internationally-recognized expert on Islamic finance.

Salafi-Jihadis

Al-Baghdādī, Abū Bakr (b. 1971) – Iraqi national and official leader of the Islamic State, also known as the Islamic State in Iraq and Syria (ISIS). In July 2014, he declared himself the Caliph Ibrahim.

Al-Maqdisī, Abū Muḥammad (b. 1959) – Palestinian-Jordanian theorist of Salafi-jihadism, and an inspiration to both Boko Haram and the Islamic State, although he has rejected the latter.

Shekau, Abū Bakr (b. ca. 1968–1975) – Nigerian-trained preacher and close associate of Muḥammad Yūsuf; he became Boko Haram's official leader after Yūsuf's death.

Al-ʿUtaybī, Juhaymān (ca. 1935–1980) – Saudi Arabian dissident who led a faction of *Al-Jamāʿa al-Salafiyya al-Muḥtasiba* (The Salafi Society for Hisbah, i.e., commanding right and forbidding wrong) to take over the Grand Mosque of Mecca in 1979.

Yūsuf, Muḥammad (1970–2009) – Nigerian-educated founder of Boko Haram; a one-time pupil of Jaʿfar Ādam.

Al-Zarqāwī, Abū Muṣʿab (1966–2006) – Jordanian militant and estranged student of al-Maqdisī who founded Al-Qāʿida in Iraq, a predecessor of the Islamic State.

Important Nigerian Non-Salafis

ʿAtīq, Abū Bakr (1909–1974) – Major Tijani scholar and leader in Kano.

ʿAtīq, Lawi (b. 1962) – A graduate of Al-Azhar and son of Abū Bakr ʿAtīq.

Buhari, Muhammadu (b. 1942) – Military ruler of Nigeria from 1983–1985, four-time opposition presidential candidate during the Fourth Republic, and civilian president since his election victory in 2015.

Jonathan, Goodluck (b. 1957) – President of Nigeria, 2010–2015. Originally took office on the death of his predecessor Umaru Yarʿ Adua, reelected for a full term in 2011, and defeated in the 2015 election.

Kabara, ʿAbd al-Jabbār (b. 1970) – Outspokenly anti-Salafi son of Nāṣir Kabara and younger brother of his father's *khalifa*, Qaribullah.

Kabara, Nāṣir (1912–1996) – Important scholar and leader of the Qadiriyya Sufi order in Kano.

Marwa, Muḥammad (d. 1980) – Eponymous founder of the Maitatsine ("He Who Curses") movement, a Qurʾan-only, antitechnology sect that rioted in northern Nigerian cities between 1980 and 1985.

Obasanjo, Olusegun (b. 1937) – Military ruler 1976–79 and then elected as Nigeria's first civilian president under the Fourth Republic, serving 1999–2007.

Rabiu, Isyaku (b. 1928) – Major Sufi shaykh and businessman in Kano.

Ringim, Uba (1919–1999) – Major Tijani businessman in Kano.

Sanusi, Sanusi Lamido (b. 1961) – Banker and public intellectual who served as governor of the Central Bank of Nigeria from 2009 to 2014 and became emir of Kano in 2014.

ʿUthmān, Bashīr Tijjānī (b. 1956) – Son of Tijjānī ʿUthmān, graduate of Al-Azhar University and proprietor of a large Islamiyya school in Kano.

ʿUthmān, Tijjānī (1916–1970) – Major Tijani Sufi scholar in Kano.

Yarʿ Adua, Umaru (1951–2010) – Nigeria's second civilian president under the Fourth Republic, serving 2007–2010.

Al-Zakzaky, Ibrahim (b. 1953) – Leader of the "Muslim Brothers," a politically confrontational Nigerian Shīʿī organization.

Glossary of Arabic Terms

Aḥādīth – plural of *ḥadīth*.

Ahl al-ḥadīth – "the people of *ḥadīth*," or those dedicated to deriving all belief and practice directly from Islam's foundational texts. In the Indian subcontinent, the *ahl-e ḥadīth* movement was a major contributor to the formation of Salafism.

Ahl al-sunna wa-l-jamāʿa – "the people of the Prophet's model and the community," a rough synonym for "Sunni" but also a phrase Salafis use to suggest that they are the only pure Muslims.

ʿĀlim – a Muslim scholar, plural *ʿulamāʾ*.

Anṣār al-Sunna al-Muḥammadiyya – "defenders of the Prophet's model," a Salafi movement founded in Egypt in 1926, with influential branches in Sudan and Chad.

ʿAqīda – "creed," a word Salafis use to describe what they consider the correct theological beliefs in Islam.

Ashʿariyya – an early school of Islamic theology that allowed metaphorical interpretation of God's attributes.

Bidʿa – "innovation," usually understood by Salafis to mean the introduction of a heretical belief or practice into the allegedly pure Islam of the pious predecessors.

Daʿwa – "calling" people to God, whether by enjoining non-Muslims to convert or by asking Muslims to "purify" their faith and practices. The one who performs *daʿwa* is a *dāʿiya*.

Fatwā – a scholar's legal opinion, usually issued in response to a question from a Muslim seeker or student.

Fitna – "disorder," especially political and military disorder that undermines Islam.

Ḥadīth – a report of something the Prophet Muḥammad said or did.

Ḥalqa – an extracurricular religious study circle that meets at a mosque.

Ḥanbalism – the school of Sunni jurisprudence widespread in Saudi Arabia; also a theological and political movement that champions ideas such as the uncreated nature of the Qurʾan and the need to literally interpret God's attributes as they are described in the Qurʾan.

Ijtihād – independent effort to derive a legal ruling; Salafis hold that this effort should be made outside the context of the established schools of jurisprudence, and using only Islam's foundational texts. The one who performs *ijtihād* is a *mujtahid*.

ʿIlm al-kalām – the discipline of speculative theology, a discipline and a set of schools rejected by Salafis.

Al-Jarḥ wa-l-taʿdīl – "critique and evaluation," or "disparagement and praise," which in Salafi hands is a method for deciding whether or not a scholar is qualified.

Madhhab – "school," referring to one of the four major Sunni schools of jurisprudence. Salafis reject adherence to these schools.

Mālikism – the school of Sunni jurisprudence widespread in northwest Africa, including Nigeria.

Manhaj – "approach," a term Salafis use to stress that their community is not a formal organization, but a way – in their eyes, the only proper way – of understanding Islam.

Mawlid – celebration of the Prophet's birthday.

Muʿtazila – a rationalist school of early Islamic theology.

Al-Salaf al-ṣāliḥ – "the pious predecessors," or the first three generations of Muslims, considered by Salafis to be the normative model of the Muslim community.

Sharīʿa – Islamic law.

Takfīr – declaring a Muslim an unbeliever.

Takhrīj – "extraction" of the *ḥadīth* reports used in a text, done in order to grade and authenticate the reports.

Tafsīr – exegesis of the Qurʾan.

Takyīf – "probing modality," i.e., asking how it is, for example, that God might have a throne.

Tamthīl – likening God's attributes to human characteristics, i.e., anthropomorphism.

Taqlīd – "emulation," or operating within the confines of a jurisprudential school. Often used pejoratively by Salafis.

Tawḥīd – the divine unity of God, and the scholastic discipline dedicated to study of the same.

Al-Walāʾ wa-l-barāʾ – "loyalty and disavowal," a phrase that for Salafi-jihadis connotes exclusive loyalty to those considered true Muslims and uncompromising rejection of all other persons and systems.

Bibliography

Al-ʿAbbād, ʿAbd al-Muḥsin. *Kutub wa-Rasāʾil ʿAbd al-Muḥsin ibn Ḥamad al-ʿAbbād al-Badr*. Al-Riyāḍ: Dār al-Tawḥīd li-l-Nashr, 2006.

Al-ʿAbbūdī, Muḥammad. "Dhikrayātī fī Ifrīqīyā." *Journal of the Islamic University of Medina* 1 (1966).

"Fī Ifrīqīyā al-Khaḍrā." *Journal of the Islamic University of Medina* 2 (1967).

ʿAbd al-Raḥmān, Maḥmūd ʿAbbās Aḥmad. *Al-Azhar wa-Afrīqiyā: Dirāsa Wathāʾiqīyya*. Al Haram, Giza: Al-Dār al-ʿĀlamiyya li-l-Nashr wa-l-Tawzīʿ, 2004.

Abdallah, Abdulwahhab. *Fatawoyin Aikin Hajji da Umrah da Ziyara a kan Koyarwar Alkurʾani da Sunnah da Fahimtar Magabata na Kwarai*. Second edition. Kano: Supreme Council for Shariʿa in Nigeria, 2004.

Hisbah: Manufarta da Ka'idodinta da Muhammancinta. Kano: Majlis Ahlis Sunnah Wal-Jama'ah, 2008.

Ramadan a kan Koyarwar Alkurʾani da Sunnah bisa Fahimtar Magabata na Kwarai. Kano: Kumurya Prints U/Uku, 2009.

Abdoulaye, Galilou. "The Graduates of Islamic Universities in Benin: A Modern Elite Seeking Social, Religious and Political Recognition." In *Islam in Africa*, edited by Thomas Bierschenk and Georg Stauth, 129–46. Munster: Lit Verlag, 2003.

Abdurrahman, M., and Peter Canham, *The Ink of the Scholar: The Islamic Tradition of Education in Nigeria*. Yaba, Lagos: Macmillan Nigeria, 1978.

Abou Zahab, Mariam. "Salafism in Pakistan: The Ahl-e Hadith Movement." In *Global Salafism*, edited by Roel Meijer, 126–42. New York: Columbia University Press, 2009.

Abubakar, Aliyu. *Al-Thaqāfa al-ʿArabiyya fī Nayjīriyā min 1804 ilā 1960 ʿĀm al-Istiqlāl*. Beirut: no publisher, 1972.

Ādam, Jaʿfar Maḥmūd. *Matakan Mallakar Miji*. Kano: Usman bin Affan Islamic Trust, 2000.

'Yan Alkuraniyyun: ('Yan Tatsine, Kala-Kato): Tarihin Kafuwarsu da Akidunsu. Kano: Usman bin Affan Islamic Trust, 2005.

Adesoji, Abimbola. "Between Maitatsine and Boko Haram: Islamic Fundamentalism and the Response of the Nigerian State." *Africa Today* 57:4 (2011): 98–119.

Ahmad, Muhammad. *Gwagwarmaya tsakanin Gaskiya da Karya akan Mallakar Masallacin Jumaʿa na Sheikh Jaʿafar Mahmud Adam, Sabuwar Gandu – Kano*. Kano: Al-Kitab Printing Press, 2010.

Ahmed, Chanfi. *West African ʿulamāʾ and Salafism in Mecca and Medina: Jawāb al-Ifrīqī – The Response of the African*. Leiden: Brill, 2015.

Ahmed, Einas. "Militant Salafism in Sudan." *Islamic Africa* 6:1–2 (July 2015): 164–84.

Āl Bassām, ʿAbd Allāh ibn ʿAbd al-Raḥmān ibn Ṣāliḥ. *ʿUlamāʾ Najd khilāl Thamāniyat Qurūn*. Second edition. Al-Riyāḍ: Dār al-ʿĀṣima li-l-Nashr wa-l-Tawzīʿ, 1998.

Āl Salmān, Mashhūr ibn Ḥasan. *Kutub Ḥadhdhara minhā al-ʿUlamāʾ*. Al-Riyāḍ: Dār al-Ṣamīʿī, 1995.

Alao, Abiodun. "Islamic Radicalisation and Violence in Nigeria: Country Report." Undated working paper.

Alavi, Seema. "Siddiq Hasan Khan (1832–1890) and the Creation of a Muslim Cosmopolitanism in the 19th Century." *Journal of the Economic and Social History of the Orient* 54 (2011): 1–38.

Al-Albānī, Muḥammad Nāṣir al-Dīn. *Ḍaʿīf al-Adab al-Mufrad li-l-Imām al-Bukhārī*. Al-Jubayl, Saudi Arabia: Dār al-Ṣiddīq, 1994.

Al-Dhabb al-Aḥmad ʿan Musnad al-Imām Aḥmad. Al-Jubayl, Saudi Arabia: Dār al-Ṣiddīq, 1999.

Fatāwā al-ʿAllāma Nāṣir al-Dīn al-Albānī. Collected and prepared by Abū ʿAbd al-Raḥmān ʿĀdil ibn Saʿd. Beirut: Dār al-Kutub al-ʿIlmiyya, 2011.

Fihris Makhṭūṭāt Dār al-Kutub al-Zāhiriyya: Al-Muntakhab min Makhṭūṭāt al-Ḥadīth. Damascus: Majmaʿ al-Lugha al-ʿArabiyya bi-Dimashq, 1970.

Khuṭbat al-Ḥāja allatī Kāna Rasūl Allāh – Ṣalla Allāh ʿalayhi wa-Sallam – Yuʿallimuhā Aṣḥābahu. Al-Riyāḍ: Maktabat al-Maʿārif li-l-Nashr wa-l-Tawzīʿ, 2000.

Silsilat al-Aḥādīth al-Ḍaʿīfa wa-l-Mawḍūʿa wa-Atharuhā al-Sayyiʾ fī al-Umma. Al-Riyāḍ: Maktabat al-Maʿārif, 1992.

Ali, Abdullah Yusuf, trans. *The Holy Qurʾan: Text, Translation, and Commentary*. Fourth edition. Elmhurst, NY: Tahrike Tarsile Qurʾan, 2004.

Aliyu, A. Y. et al. *Hajj Research Project Nigeria*. Volumes 1–4. Zaria: Ahmadu Bello University, 1983.

Alkali, Muhammad Nur, Abubakar Kawu Monguno, and Ballama Shettima Mustafa. "Overview of Islamic Actors in Northeastern Nigeria." Nigeria Research Network Working Paper Number 2 (January 2012).

Aluko, T. K. O. "An Evaluation of the Effects of the National Economic Empowerment and Development Strategy (Needs) on Poverty Reduction in Nigeria." In *Nigeria's Democratic Experience in the Fourth Republic Since 1999: Policies and Politics*, edited by A. Sat Obiyan and Kunle Amuwo, 360–79. Lanham, MD: University Press of America, 2013.

Al-Ālūsī, Nuʿman Khayr al-Dīn. *Al-Āyāt al-Bayyināt fī ʿAdam Samāʿ al-Amwāt ʿind al-Ḥanafiyya al-Sādāt*, edited by Muḥammad Nāṣir al-Dīn al-Albānī. Al-Riyāḍ: Maktabat al-Maʿārif li-l-Nashr wa-l-Tawzīʿ, 2005.

Jalāʾ al-ʿAynayn fī Muḥākamat al-Aḥmadayn. Cairo: Maṭbaʿat al-Madanī, 1980.

Amnesty International. "Nigeria: Trapped in the Cycle of Violence." November 2012.

"Nigeria: War Crimes and Crimes Against Humanity as Violence Escalates in North-East." 31 March 2014.

Anderson, Benedict. *Imagined Communities: Reflections on the Origin and Spread of Nationalism*. Revised Edition. London and New York: Verso, 1991.

Atharī, Muḥammad ibn Riyāḍ al-Aḥmad al-Salafī. *Riyāḍ al-Janna fī al-Ḥathth ʿalā al-Tamassuk bi-l-Sunna*. Beirut: Dār al-Kutub al-ʿIlmīyya, 2001.

Annual Reports of Northern Nigeria.

Anonymous. "The Popular Discourses of Salafi Radicalism and Salafi Counter-Radicalism in Nigeria: A Case Study of Boko Haram." *Journal of Religion in Africa* 42:2 (2012): 118–44.

Anwar, Auwalu. "Struggle for Influence and Identity: The Ulama in Kano, 1937–1987." MA Thesis, University of Maiduguri, 1989.

Appleby, R. Scott. *The Ambivalence of the Sacred: Religion, Violence, and Reconciliation.* Lanham, MD: Rowman and Littlefield, 2000.

Asad, Talal. "The Idea of an Anthropology of Islam." Georgetown University Center for Contemporary Arab Studies Occasional Papers Series, 1986.

Al-ʿAshūsh, Aḥmad. "Ilā al-ʿIlmāniyyīn al-Ashrār wa-Tābiʿīhim min al-Muslimīn al-Aghrār." Muʾassasat al-Bayān al-Islāmī, 2012.

Babou, Cheikh Anta. *Fighting the Greater Jihad: Amadu Bamba and the Founding of the Muridiyya of Senegal*, 1853–1913. Athens: Ohio University Press, 2007.

Bala, Salisu. "Salafi Targets for 'Boko Haram': The Murder of Shaykh Muhammad Auwal Adam 'Albani' Zaria (d. 2014)." *Annual Review of Islam in Africa* 12:1 (2013/2014): 31–8.

Barkindo, Bawuro. "Growing Islamism in Kano City since 1970: Causes, Form and Implications." In *Muslim Identity and Social Change in Sub-Saharan Africa*, edited by Louis Brenner, 91–105. Bloomington, IN: University of Indiana Press, 1993.

Bayart, Jean-Francois. "Le politique par le bas en Afrique noire: Questions de méthode." *Politique Africaine* 1 (1981): 53–82.

Bello, Ahmadu. *My Life.* Cambridge: Cambridge University Press, 1962.

Bello, Muḥammad. *Infāq al-Maysūr fī Tārīkh Bilād al-Takrūr.* Cairo: Egyptian Ministry of Endowments, 1964.

Ben Amara, Ramzi. "The Izala Movement in Nigeria: Its Split, Relationship to Sufis and Perception of Sharīʿa Re-Implementation." Ph.D. dissertation, University of Bayreuth, 2011.

"Shaykh Ismaila Idris (1937–2000), the Founder of the Izala movement in Nigeria." *Annual Review on Islam in Africa* 11 (2012): 74–8.

Bobboyi, Hamid. "Scholars and Scholarship in the Relations between the Maghrib and the Central Bilad al-Sudan during the Pre-Colonial Period." In *Reclaiming the Human Sciences and Humanities Through African Perspectives*, Volume 1, edited by Helen Lauer and Kofi Anyidoho, 746–760. Accra: Sub-Saharan Publishers, 2012.

Brenner, Louis. *Controlling Knowledge: Religion, Power, and Schooling in a West African Muslim Society.* Bloomington: Indiana University Press, 2001.

The Shehus of Kukawa: A History of the al-Kanemi Dynasty of Bornu. Oxford: Clarendon Press, 1973.

Brigaglia, Andrea. "A Contribution to the History of the Wahhabi Daʿwa in West Africa: The Career and the Murder of Shaykh Jaʿfar Mahmoud Adam (Daura, ca. 1961/1962-Kano 2007)." *Islamic Africa* 3:1 (Spring 2012): 1–23.

"Jaʿfar Mahmood Adam, Mohammed Yusuf and al-Muntada Islamic Trust: Reflections on the Genesis of the Boko Haram Phenomenon in Nigeria." *Annual Review of Islam in Africa* 11 (2012): 35–44.

"The Radio Kaduna Tafsīr (1978–1992) and the Construction of Public Images of Muslim Scholars in the Nigerian Media." *Journal for Islamic Studies* 27 (2007): 173–210.

"Tafsīr and the Intellectual History of Islam in West Africa: The Nigerian Case." In *Tafsīr and Intellectual History: Exploring the Boundaries of a Tradition*, edited by Andreas Görke and Johanna Pink, 379–415. Oxford: Oxford University Press, 2014.

and Fauziyya Fiji. "'We Ain't Coming to Take People Away': A Sufi Praise-Song and the Representation of Police Forces in Northern Nigeria." *Annual Review of Islam in Africa* 10 (2008–2009): 50–7.

Broadcasting Board of Governors/Gallup. *Nigeria Media Use 2012* (2012).

Broadcasting Board of Governors/Gallup. *Contemporary Media Use in Nigeria* (2014).

Brown, Jonathan A. C. *The Canonization of al-Bukhārī and Muslim: The Formation and Function of the Sunnī Ḥadīth Canon.* Leiden: Brill, 2007.

"From Quietism to Parliamentary Giant: Salafism in Egypt and the Nour Party of Alexandria." Unpublished paper.

"Is Islam Easy to Understand or Not?: Salafis, the Democratization of Interpretation, and the Need for the Ulema." *Journal of Islamic Studies* 26:2 (2015): 117–44.

Misquoting Muhammad: The Challenge and Choices of Interpreting the Prophet's Legacy. London: Oneworld, 2014.

"Salafis and Sufis in Egypt." Carnegie Endowment for International Peace, December 2011.

Bonnefoy, Laurent. *Salafism in Yemen: Transnationalism and Religious Identity.* New York: Columbia University Press, 2011.

Bunzel, Cole. "From Paper State to Caliphate: The Ideology of the Islamic State." Brookings Institution, March 2015.

Al-Būṭī, Saʿīd Ramaḍān. *Al-Lā Madhhabiyya: Akhṭar Bidʿa Tuhaddid al-Sharīʿa al-Islāmiyya.* Third Edition. Damascus: Dār al-Fārābī, 2005.

The Carter Center and the National Democratic Institute for International Affairs. *Observing the 1998–99 Nigerian Elections: Final Report.* Atlanta: The Carter Center, Summer 1999.

Central Intelligence Agency. "Nigeria." *World Factbook*, May 2012.

Chamberlin, John Weir. "The Development of Islamic Education in Kano City, Nigeria, with Emphasis on Legal Education in the 19th and 20th Centuries." Ph.D. dissertation, Columbia University, 1975.

Christelow, Allan. "Three Islamic Voices in Contemporary Nigeria." In *Islam and the Political Economy of Meaning*, edited by William R. Roff, 226–53. Berkeley: University of California Press, 1987.

Commins, David. "From Wahhabi to Salafi." In *Saudi Arabia in Transition: Insights on Social, Political, Economic and Religious Change*, edited by Bernard Haykel, Thomas Hegghammer, and Stéphane Lacroix, 151–66. Cambridge: Cambridge University Press, 2015.

Islamic Reform: Politics and Social Change in Late Ottoman Syria. Oxford: Oxford University Press, 1990.

The Wahhabi Mission and Saudi Arabia. London: I.B. Tauris, 2006.

Cook, Michael. *Commanding Right and Forbidding Wrong in Islamic Thought.* Cambridge: Cambridge University Press, 2001.

"On the Origins of Wahhabism." *Journal of the Royal Asiatic Society*, Third Series, 2:2 (July 1992): 191–202.

Csordas, Thomas. "Introduction: Modalities of Transnational Transcendence." In *Transnational Transcendence: Essays on Religion and Globalization*, edited by Thomas Csordas, 1–30. Berkeley: University of California Press, 2009.

Dallal, Ahmad. "The Origins and Objectives of Islamic Revivalist Thought, 1750–1850." *Journal of the American Oriental Society* 113:3 (July–September 1993): 341–59.

Delong-Bas, Natana. *Wahhabi Islam: From Revival and Reform to Global Jihad.* London: I.B. Tauris, 2007.

Diané, Kabiné. *Recueil des cinq piliers de l'Islam.* Imprimerie A. Diop, 1959.

Doi, A.R.I. "Education in Nigeria: Teaching of Islamic Studies as an Academic Subject." *Journal of the Muslim World League* (June 1978): 33–8.

Dudley, B.J. *Politics and Parties in Northern Nigeria.* London: Cass, 1968.

Dukawa, Yakubu Ahmad. "Makānat al-Lugha al-ʿArabiyya fī Wilāyat Kanu." M.A. thesis [in Arabic], Bayero University Kano, 1986.

Eickelman, Dale F. and James Piscastori, *Muslim Politics.* Second Edition. Princeton: Princeton University Press, 2004.

Esposito, John L. and John O. Voll. *Makers of Contemporary Islam.* Oxford; New York: Oxford University Press, 2001.

Farquhar, Michael. "The Islamic University of Medina since 1961: The Politics of Religious Mission and the Making of a Modern Salafi Pedagogy." In *Shaping Global Islamic Discourses: The Role of al-Azhar, al-Medina, and al-Mustafa*, edited by Masooda Bano and Keiko Sakurai, 21–40. Edinburgh: Edinburgh University Press, 2015.

Federal Republic of Nigeria. *2006 Population Census.*

Gaffney, Patrick. *The Prophet's Pulpit: Islamic Preaching in Contemporary Egypt.* Berkeley: University of California Press, 1994.

Galadanci, S. A. S. *Ḥarakat al-Lugha al-ʿArabiyya wa-Ādābuhā fī Nayjīriyā.* Second Edition. Cairo: Dār al-Maʿārif, 1993.

Gauvain, Richard. *Salafi Ritual Purity: In the Presence of God.* New York: Routledge, 2012.

Al-Ghāmidī, Aḥmad ibn ʿAṭīyya. *al-Kitāb al-Wathāʾiqī ʿan al-Jāmiʿa al-Islāmiyya bi-l-Madīna al-Munawwara.* Medina: al-Mamlaka al-ʿArabiyya al-Saʿūdiyya, Wizārat al-Taʿlīm al-ʿālī, al-Jāmiʿa al-Islāmiyya bi-l-Madīna al-Munawwara, 1998.

Graham, William. *Beyond the Written Word: Oral Aspects of Scripture in the History of Religion.* Cambridge: Cambridge University Press, 1987.

"Traditionalism in Islam: An Essay in Interpretation." *Journal of Interdisciplinary History* 23:3 (Winter 1993): 495–522.

Grendler, Paul. "Printing and Censorship." In *The Cambridge History of Renaissance Philosophy*, edited by C. B. Schmitt, Quentin Skinner, Eckhard Kessler, and Jill Kraye, 25–54. Cambridge: Cambridge University Press, 1988.

Gumi, Abubakar. *Al-ʿAqīda al-Ṣaḥīḥa bi-Muwāfaqat al-Sharīʿa.* Beirut: Dār al-ʿArabiyya, 1972.

Hadisai Arbain. Zaria: Gaskiya Corporation, 1959.

with Ismaila Tsiga. *Where I Stand.* Ibadan: Spectrum Books, 1992.

Gwarzo, Tahir. "Activities of Islamic Civic Associations in the Northwest of Nigeria: With Particular Reference to Kano State." *Africa Spectrum* 38:3 (2003): 289–318.

Al-Ḥabīshī, ʿAlī; ʿAbd al-Raḥmān Radmān. "Muqaddimat al-Muḥaqqiq." In Muḥammad ibn ʿAbd al-Wahhāb, *Kitāb al-Tawḥīd.* Dammāj, Yemen: Maktabat al-Imām al-Wādiʿī, 2009.

Ḥabūb, ʿUthmān ʿAbd Allāh. *Al-Imāma al-ʿUẓmā: Wājibāt wa-Ḥuqūq*. Al-Riyāḍ: Maktabat al-Rushd, 2012.

Hackett, Rosalind and Benjamin Soares, eds. *New Media and Religious Transformations in Africa*. Bloomington: Indiana University Press, 2015.

Hadiyyat Allāh, ʿAbd al-Rashīd. "Ḥaqāʾiq ʿan Nayjīrīyā." *Majallat al-Jāmiʿa al-Islāmiyya bi-l-Madīna* 6 (December 1969): 126–34.

Hall, Bruce and Charles Stewart. "The Historic 'Core Curriculum' and the Book Market in Islamic West Africa." In *The Trans-Saharan Book Trade: Manuscript Culture, Arabic Literacy and Intellectual History in Muslim Africa*, edited by Graziano Krätli and Ghislaine Lydon, 109–74. Leiden: Brill, 2011.

Hamid, Shadi. *Temptations of Power: Islamists and Illiberal Democracy in a New Middle East*. New York: Oxford University Press, 2014.

Harnischfeger, Johannes. *Democratization and Islamic Law: The Sharia Conflict in Nigeria*. Frankfurt: Campus, 2007.

Haykel, Bernard. "On the Nature of Salafi Thought and Action." In *Global Salafism: Islam's New Religious Movement*, edited by Roel Meijer, 33–57. New York: Columbia University Press, 2009.

Revival and Reform in Islam: The Legacy of Muhammad al-Shawkānī. Cambridge and New York: Cambridge University Press, 2003.

Heck, Paul. "'Jihad' Revisited." *Journal of Religious Ethics* 32:1 (Spring 2004): 95–128.

Hefner, Robert W., ed. *Remaking Muslim Politics: Pluralism, Contestation, Democratization*. Princeton: Princeton University Press, 2004.

and Muhammad Qasim Zaman, eds. *Schooling Islam: The Culture and Politics of Modern Muslim Education*. Princeton: Princeton University Press, 2006.

Hegghammer, Thomas. *Jihad in Saudi Arabia: Violence and Pan-Islamism since 1979*. Cambridge: Cambridge University Press, 2010.

"Jihadi-Salafis or Revolutionaries? On Religion and Politics in the Study of Militant Islamism." In *Global Salafism: Islam's New Religious Movement*, edited by Roel Meijer, 244–66. New York: Columbia University Press, 2009.

and Stéphane Lacroix, *The Meccan Rebellion: The Story of Juhayman al-ʿUtaybi Revisited*. Bristol: Amal Press, 2011.

and Stéphane Lacroix. "Rejectionist Islamism in Saudi Arabia: The Story of Juhayman al-ʿUtaybi Revisited." *International Journal of Middle East Studies* 39 (2007): 103–22.

Higazi, Adam. "The Jos Crisis: A Recurrent Nigerian Tragedy." Friedrich Ebert Stiftung, Discussion Paper 2 (January 2011).

"Mobilisation into and against Boko Haram in North-East Nigeria." In *Collective Mobilisations in Africa*, edited by Kadya Tall, Marie-Emmanuelle Pommerolle, and Michel Cahen, 305–58 (Leiden: Brill, 2015).

"Les origines et la transformation de l'insurrection de Boko Haram dans le nord du Nigeria." *Politique Africaine* 130:2 (2013): 137–64.

Hirschkind, Charles. *The Ethical Soundscape: Casette Sermons and Islamic Counterpublics*. New York: Columbia University Press, 2006.

Hiskett, Mervyn. "The Maitatsine Riots in Kano, 1980: An Assessment." *Journal of Religion in Africa* 17:3 (October 1987): 209–23.

The Sword of Truth: The Life and Times of the Shehu Usuman dan Fodio. New York: Oxford University Press, 1973.

Hodgkin, Elizabeth. "Islamism and Islamic Research in Africa." In *Islam et sociétiés au sud du Sahara* 4 (November 1990): 73–132.

Hodgson, Marshall. *The Venture of Islam: Conscience and History in a World Civilization*, Volumes 1–3. Chicago: University of Chicago Press, 1974.

Hoover, Jon. *Ibn Taymiyya's Theodicy of Perpetual Optimism*. Leiden: Brill, 2007.

Hoover, Stewart and Nadia Kaneva. "Fundamental Mediations: Religion, Meaning, and Identity in Global Context." In *Fundamentalisms and the Media*, edited by Stewart Hoover and Nadia Kaneva, 1–22. London and New York: Continuum, 2009.

Hourani, Albert. *Emergence of the Modern Middle East*. Berkeley: University of California Press, 1981.

Human Rights Watch. "Criminal Politics: Violence, 'Godfathers,' and Corruption in Nigeria." October 2007.

"Nigeria: Post-Election Violence Killed 800." May 16, 2011.

"Nigeria: Prosecute Killings by Security Forces." November 26, 2009.

"Spiraling Violence: Boko Haram Attacks and Security Force Abuses in Nigeria." October 2012.

Hunwick, John, compiler. *Arabic Literature of Africa, Volume II: Central Sudanic Africa*. Leiden; New York: E.J. Brill, 1995.

"Timbuktu: A Refuge of Scholarly and Righteous Folk." *Sudanic Africa* 14 (2003): 13–20.

Ibn Bāz, ʿAbd al-ʿAzīz. *Al-Shaykh Ibn Bāz wa-Mawāqifuhu al-Thābita*. Edited by Aḥmad ibn ʿAbd Allāh al-Farīḥ. Kuwait: Maktabat al-Rushd, 2000.

Ibn Ḥanbal, Aḥmad. *Kitāb al-Sunna*. Mecca: Al-Maṭbaʿ al-Salafiyya, 1930/1.

Ibn Taymiyya, Aḥmad. *Al-Wāsiṭa bayn al-Ḥaqq wa-l-Khalq*. Translated by Jaʿfar Maḥmūd Ādam. Kano: Al-Muntada al-Islāmī Trust, 1999.

Al-Waṣiyya al-Kubrā, edited by Muḥammad ʿAbd Allāh al-Nimr and ʿUthmān Jumʿa al-Ḍamīriyya. Al-Ṭāʾif: Maktabat al-Ṣiddīq, 1987.

Iddrisu, Abdulai. *Contesting Islam in Africa: Homegrown Wahhabism and Muslim Identity in Northern Ghana, 1920–2010*. Durham: Carolina Academic Press, 2013.

Al-Ifrīqī, ʿAbd al-Raḥmān. *Al-Anwār al-Raḥmāniyya li-Hidāyat al-Firqa al-Tijāniyya*. No publisher: 1937.

International Crisis Group. "Curbing Violence in Nigeria II: The Boko Haram Insurgency." 3 April 2014.

"Islamic Actors and Interfaith Relations in Northern Nigeria." Nigeria Research Network Policy Paper 1 (March 2013).

Islamic University of Medina. *Buḥūth Multaqā Khādim al-ḥaramayn al-Sharīfayn li-Khīrrijī al-Jāmiʿāt al-Saʿūdīyya min Ifrīqiyā, al-Awwal: al-Muqām bi-Nayjīriyā, Kānū taḥta Ishrāf al-Jāmiʿa al-Islāmiyya bi-l-Madīna al-Munawwara*. Medina: al Jāmiʿa al-Islāmiyya bi-l-Madīna al-Munawwara, 2003.

Jalal, Ayesha. *Partisans of Allah: Jihad in South Asia*. Cambridge, MA: Harvard University Press, 2010.

Al-Jāmī, Muḥammad Amān. *Majmūʿ Rasāʾil al-Jāmī fī al-ʿAqīda wa-l-Sunna*. Medina: Dār Ibn Rajab, 1993.

Al-Jazāʾirī, ʿAbd al-Mālik Ramaḍānī, compiler. *Fatāwā al-ʿUlamāʾ al-Akābir fīmā Uhdira min Dimāʾ fī al-Jazāʾir*. ʿAjmān: Maktabat al-Furqān, 2001/2.

Johnson, Boris and York Membery. "Homer to Plato: Boris Johnson on the Ten Greatest Ancient Greeks." *Daily Mail*, 25 June 2011.

Juergensmeyer, Mark. *Terror in the Mind of God: The Global Rise of Religious Violence*. Revised Edition. Berkeley: University of California Press, 2003.

Kaba, Lansiné. *The Wahhabiyya: Islamic Reform and Politics in French West Africa*. Evanston: Northwestern University Press, 1974.

Kane, Ousmane. *Muslim Modernity in Postcolonial Nigeria: A Study of the Society for the Removal of Innovation and Reinstatement of Tradition*. Boston: Brill, 2003.

Kawka, Rupert, ed. *From Bulamari to Yerwa to Metropolitan Maiduguri: Interdisciplinary Studies on the Capital of Borno State*, Nigeria. Köln: Rüdiger Köppe Verlag, 2002.

Kepel, Gilles. *Jihad: The Trail of Political Islam*. Translated by Anthony F. Roberts. Cambridge, MA: Harvard University Press, 2003.

Khān, Ṣiddīq Ḥasan. *An Interpreter of Wahabiism*. Bhopal: Ṣiddīq Ḥasan Khān, 1884.

Al-Rawḍa al-Nadiyya. Edited by Ḥilmī ibn Muḥammad Ismāʿīl al-Rushdī. Alexandria: Dār al-ʿAqīda, 2002.

Al-Tāj al-Mukallal min Jawāhir Maʾāthir al-Ṭirāz al-Ākhir wa-l-Awwal. Second Edition. Beirut: Dār Iqrāʾ, 1983.

Kippenberg, Hans. *Violence as Worship: Religious Wars in the Age of Globalization*. Translated by Brian McNeil. Palo Alto: Stanford University Press, 2011.

Kobo, Ousman. *Unveiling Modernity in Twentieth-Century West Africa Islamic Reforms*. Leiden; Boston: Brill, 2012.

Kramnick, Jonathan. *Making the English Canon: Print-Capitalism and the Cultural Past, 1700–1770*. Cambridge: Cambridge University Press, 1998.

Kresse, Kai. *Philosophising in Mombasa: Knowledge, Islam and Intellectual Practice on the Swahili Coast*. Edinburgh: Edinburgh University Press, 2007.

Kurzman, Charles. "Introduction: The Modernist Islamic Movement." In *Modernist Islam, 1840–1940: A Sourcebook*, edited by Charles Kurzman, 3–27. Oxford: Oxford University Press, 2002.

Lacroix, Stéphane. *Awakening Islam: The Politics of Religious Dissent in Contemporary Saudi Arabia*, translated by George Holoch. Cambridge, MA: Harvard University Press, 2011.

"Between Revolution and Apoliticism: Nasir al-Din al-Albani and his Impact on the Shaping of Contemporary Salafism." In *Global Salafism*, ed. Meijer, 58–80.

"Sheikhs and Politicians: Inside the New Egyptian Salafism." Brookings Institution, June 2012.

"Understanding Stability and Dissent in the Kingdom: The Double-Edged Role of the jamaʿat in Saudi Politics." In *Saudi Arabia in Transition: Insights on Social, Political, Economic and Religious Change*, edited by Bernard Haykel, Thomas Hegghamer, and Stéphane Lacroix, 167–80. Cambridge: Cambridge University Press, 2015.

Lacunza-Balda, Justo. "Translations of the Quran into Swahili, and Contemporary Islamic Revival in East Africa." In *African Islam and Islam in Africa: Encounters between Sufis and Islamists*, edited by Eva Rosander and David Westerlund, 95–126. Athens, OH: Ohio University Press, 1997.

Laitin, David. *Hegemony and Culture: Politics and Religious Change Among the Yoruba*. Chicago: University of Chicago Press, 1986.

Laoust, Henri. *Essai sur les doctrines sociales et politiques de Taḳī-d-Dīn Aḥmad b. Taimīya, Canoniste ḥanbalite né à Ḥarrān en 661/1262, mort à Damas en 728/1328*. Cairo: Imprimerie de l'Institut Français d'Archéologie Orientale, 1939.

Larkin, Brian. *Signal and Noise: Media, Infrastructure, and Urban Culture in Nigeria*. Durham: Duke University Press, 2008.

Last, Murray. "Muslims and Christians in Nigeria: An Economy of Political Panic." *The Round Table: The Commonwealth Journal of International Affairs* 96:392 (2007): 605–16.

"The Search for Security in Muslim Northern Nigeria." *Africa* 78:1 (February 2008): 41–63.

The Sokoto Caliphate. London: Longmans, Green and Co. Ltd., 1967.

Launay, Robert. *Beyond the Stream: Islam and Society in a West African Town*. Berkeley: University of California Press, 1992.

Lauzière, Henri. "The Construction of Salafiyya: Reconsidering Salafism from the Perspective of Conceptual History." *International Journal of Middle East Studies* 42:3 (2010): 369–89.

The Making of Salafism: Islamic Reform in the Twentieth Century. New York: Columbia University Press, 2015.

Lav, Daniel. *Radical Islam and the Revival of Medieval Theology*. Cambridge: Cambridge University Press, 2012.

LeVan, A. Carl. *Dictators and Democracy in African Development: The Political Economy of Good Governance in Nigeria*. New York: Cambridge University Press, 2014.

Leveau, Rémy. "Les mouvements islamiques." *Pouvoirs* 62 (September 1992): 45–58.

Lia, Brynjar. *Architect of Global Jihad: The Life of Al Qaeda Strategist Abu Mus'ab Al-Suri*. New York: Columbia University Press, 2008.

Lings, Martin. *What Is Sufism?* Berkeley: University of California Press, 1975.

Lister, Charles. "Profiling the Islamic State." Brookings Institution, December 2014.

Little, Donald. "Did Ibn Taymiyya Have a Screw Loose?" *Studia Islamica* 41 (1975): 93–111.

Lo, Muḥammad Aḥmad. *Taqdīs al-Ashkhāṣ fī al-Fikr al-Ṣūfī*. New Edition. Al-Dammām: Dār Ibn al-Qayyim li-l-Nashr wa-l-Tawzīʿ, 2002; Cairo: Dār Ibn ʿAffān, 2002.

Loimeier, Roman. *Between Social Skills and Marketable Skills: The Politics of Islamic Education in 20th Century Zanzibar*. Leiden: Brill, 2009.

Islamic Reform and Political Change in Northern Nigeria. Evanston: Northwestern University Press, 1997.

Muslim Societies in Africa: A Historical Anthropology. Bloomington: University of Indiana Press, 2013.

"Playing with Affiliations: Muslims in Northern Nigeria in the 20th Century." In *Entreprises religieuses transnationales en Afrique de l'Ouest*, edited by Laurent Fourchard, Andre Mary and René Otayek, 349–71. Paris: Karthala, 2005.

Lubeck, Paul. "Islamic Protest under Semi-Industrial Capitalism: 'Yan Tatsine Explained." *Africa: Journal of the International African Institute* 55:4 (1985): 369–89.

"Nigeria: Mapping a Sharīʿa Restorationist Movement." In *Sharīʿa Politics: Islamic Law and Society in the Modern World*, edited by Robert W. Hefner, 244–79. Bloomington: Indiana University Press, 2011.

Lucas, Scott. *Constructive Critics, Ḥadīth Literature, and the Articulation of Sunnī Islam: The Legacy of the Generation of Ibn Saʿd, Ibn Maʿīn, and Ibn Ḥanbal.* Leiden: Brill, 2004.

Luqmān, Akhtar Jamāl. *Al-Sayyid Ṣiddīq Ḥasan al-Qannūjī: Ārāʾuhu al-Iʿtiqādīyya wa-Mawqifuhu min ʿAqīdat al-Salaf.* Al-Riyāḍ: Dār al-Hijra, 1996.

Lynch, Marc. "Introduction." In *Rethinking Islamist Politics*, Project on Middle East Political Science Briefing 24, 3–6 (11 February 2014).

Al-Madkhalī, Rabīʿ ibn Hādī. *Aḍwāʾ Islāmiyya ʿalā ʿAqīdat Sayyid Quṭb wa-Fikrihi.* Al-Madīna: Maktabat al-Ghurabāʾ al-Atharīyya, 1993.

Mahmood, Saba. *Politics of Piety: The Islamic Revival and the Feminist Subject.* Princeton: Princeton University Press, 2005.

Maigari, Muḥammad Dahiru. *Al-Shaykh Ibrāhīm Inyās al-Sinighālī: Ḥayātuhu wa-Ārāʾuhu wa-Taʿlīmuhu.* Beirut: Dār al-ʿArabiyya, 1981.

Makdisi, George. "Ibn Taymiyya: A Sufi of the Qadiriya Order." *American Journal of Arabic Studies* 1 (1973): 118–29.

Al-Maqdisī, Abū; Muḥammad. *Hādhihi ʿAqīdatunā.* 1997.

Millat Ibrāhīm wa-Daʿwa al-Anbiyāʾ wa-l-Mursalīn. 1984.

Mandaville, Peter. *Transnational Muslim Politics: Reimaging the Umma.* London; New York: Routledge, 2001.

Marshall, Ruth. *Political Spiritualities: The Pentecostal Revolution in Nigeria.* Chicago: University of Chicago Press, 2009.

Martin, Richard C., Mark R. Woodward, and Dwi S. Atmaja. *Defenders of Reason in Islam: Muʿtazilism from Medieval School to Modern Symbol.* London: Oneworld, 1997.

Al-Mashʿabī, ʿAbd al-Majīd ibn ʿAbd Allāh. *Manhaj Ibn Taymiyya fī Masʾalat al-Takfīr.* Al-Riyāḍ: Maktabat Aḍwāʾ al-Salaf, 1997.

Masquelier, Adeline. *Women and Islamic Revival in a West African Town.* Bloomington: Indiana University Press, 2009.

McCain, Carmen. "The Politics of Exposure: Contested Cosmopolitanisms, Revelation of Secrets, and Intermedial Reflexivity in Hausa Popular Expression." Ph.D. dissertation, University of Wisconsin–Madison, 2014.

Meijer, Roel, ed. *Global Salafism: Islam's New Religious Movement.* New York: Columbia University Press, 2009.

"Politicizing al-Jarḥ wa-l-Taʿdīl: Rabi b. Hadi al-Madkhali and the Transnational Battle for Religious Authority." In *The Transmission and Dynamics of the Textual Sources of Islam: Essays in Honour of Harald Motzki*, edited by Nicolet Boekhoff-van der Voort, Kees Versteegh and Joas Wagemakers, 375–99. Leiden: Brill, 2011.

Melchert, Christopher. *Ahmad ibn Hanbal.* London: Oneworld, 2006.

Metcalf, Barbara. *Islamic Revival in British India: Deoband, 1860–1900.* Princeton: Princeton University Press, 1982.

Meyer, Birgit. "Impossible Representations: Pentecostalism, Vision, and Video Technology in Ghana." In *Religion, Media, and the Public Sphere*, edited by Birgit Meyer and Annelies Moors, 290–312. Bloomington: Indiana University Press, 2006.

Miles, William F. S. "Muslim Ethnopolitics and Presidential Elections in Nigeria." *Journal of Muslim Minority Affairs* 20 (2000): 229–41.

"West Africa Transformed: The New Mosque-State Relationship." In *Political Islam in West Africa: State-Society Relations Transformed*, edited by William F. S. Miles, 183–93. Boulder, CO; London: Lynne Rienner Publishers, 2007.

Mohammed, Kyari. "The Message and Methods of Boko Haram." In *Boko Haram: Islamism, Politics, Security and the State in Nigeria*, edited by Marc-Antoine Pérouse de Montclos, 9–32. Leiden: African Studies Centre, 2014.

Monteil, Vincent. "Un visionnaire musulman sénégalais (1946–1965)." *Archives de sociologie des religions* 19:19 (1965): 69–98.

Moosa, Ebrahim. "Shaykh Aḥmad Shākir and the Adoption of a Scientifically-Based Lunar Calendar." *Islamic Law and Society* 5:1 (1998): 57–89.

Mouline, Nabil. *The Clerics of Islam: Religious Authority and Political Power in Saudi Arabia*. Translated by Ethan Rundell. New Haven: Yale University Press, 2014.

Murtaḍa, Aḥmad. "Jamāʿat 'Boko Haram': Nashʾatuhā wa-Mabādiʾuhā wa-Aʿmāluhā fī Nayjīriyā." *Qirāʾāt Ifrīqiyya*, 13 November 2012.

Mustapha, Abdul Raufu, ed. *Sects & Social Disorder: Muslim Identities & Conflict in Northern Nigeria*. London: James Currey, 2014.

Nafi, Basheer. "The Rise of Islamic Reformist Thought and Its Challenge to Traditional Islam." In *Islamic Thought in the Twentieth Century*, edited by Suha Taji-Farouki and Basheer Nafi, 28–60. London and New York: I.B. Tauris, 2004, 40.

"Taṣawwuf and Reform in Pre-Modern Islamic Culture: In Search of Ibrāhīm al-Kūrānī." *Die Welt des Islams* 42:3 (2002): 307–55.

"A Teacher of Ibn ʿAbd al-Wahhāb: Muḥammad Ḥayāt al-Sindī and the Revival of Aṣḥāb al-Ḥadīth's Methodology." *Islamic Law and Society* 13:2 (2006): 208–41.

National Population Commission of Nigeria. "Nigeria 2008 Demographic and Health Survey: Key Findings." Abuja, 2009.

Al-Nawawī, Yaḥyā ibn Sharaf. *Al-Arbaʿuna Hadithan*. Translated and annotated by Sheikh Jaʿafar Mahmoud Adam, edited by Muhammad Rabi'u Umar Rijiyar Lemo and Muhammad Sani Umar R/Lemo. Second Edition. Kano: Sheikh Jaʿafar Islamic Documentation Centre, 2011.

Riyāḍ al-Ṣāliḥīn. Mecca: The Muslim World League, undated.

Newman, Paul. "The Etymology of Hausa *boko*." Mega-Chad Research Network, 2013.

Niandou-Souley, Abdoulaye. "Les 'licenciés du Caire' et l'État au Niger." In Le radicalisme islamique au sud du Sahara: daʿwa, arabisation et critique de l'Occident, edited by René Otayek, 213–28. Paris: Karthala, 1993.

Niasse, Ibrahim. *Ijābat al-Fatwā fī Tahāfut al-Ṣūfiyya*. Kano: Northern Maktabat Printing Press, 1964.

Nietzsche, Friedrich. *The Use and Abuse of History*. Translated by Adrian Collins. New York: Cosimo, 2010.

Nigeria Elections Coalition. "Nigeria Presidential Elections – 2011 (FINAL)."

O'Brien, Susan. "La charia contestée: Démocratie, débat et diversité musulmane dans les 'états Charia' du Nigeria." *Politique Africaine* 106 (2007): 46–68.

Ochonu, Moses. *Colonialism by Proxy: Hausa Imperial Agents and Middle Belt Consciousness in Nigeria*. Bloomington: Indiana University Press, 2014.

Olidort, Jacob. "The al-Nour Party: A Salafi Partner in the Fight against Terrorism?" Washington Institute for Near East Policy, 13 March 2015.

"The Politics of 'Quietist' Salafism." Brookings Institution, February 2015.

Onapajo, Hakeem and Abubakar Usman. "Fuelling the Flames: Boko Haram and Deteriorating Christian-Muslim Relations in Nigeria." *Journal of Muslim Minority Affairs* 35:1 (2015): 106–22.

Østebø, Terje. *Localising Salafism: Religious Change among Oromo Muslims in Bale*, Ethiopia. Leiden; Boston: Brill, 2012.

Ostien, Philip. "An Opportunity Missed by Nigeria's Christians: The 1976–78 Sharia Debate Revisited." In *Muslim-Christian Encounters in Africa*, edited by Benjamin Soares, 221–55. Leiden; Boston: Brill, 2006.

Ostien, Philip, ed. *Sharia Implementation in Northern Nigeria, 1999–2006: A Sourcebook*. Ibadan: Spectrum Books, 2007.

Otayek, René. "L'affirmation élitaire des arabisants au Burkina Faso: enjeux et contradictions." In *Le radicalisme islamique au sud du Sahara: da'wa, arabisation et critique de l'Occident*, edited by René Otayek, 229–52. Paris: Karthala, 1993.

and Benjamin Soares. "Introduction: Islam and Muslim Politics in Africa." In *Islam and Muslim Politics in Africa*, edited by Benjamin Soares and René Otayek, 1–24. New York: Palgrave Macmillan, 2007.

Paden, John. *Ahmadu Bello, Sardauna of Sokoto: Values and Leadership in Nigeria*. Zaria: Hudahuda Publishing Company, 1986.

Faith and Politics in Nigeria: Nigeria as a Pivotal State in the Muslim World. Washington, DC: United States Institute of Peace, 2007.

Religion and Political Culture in Kano. Berkeley: University of California Press, 1973.

Palmer, H. R. *The Bornu Sahara and Sudan*. London: John Murray, 1936.

Pearson, Elizabeth and Jacob Zenn. "How Nigerian Police Also Detained Women and Children as Weapon of War." *The Guardian*, 6 May 2014.

Peel, J. D. Y. *Religious Encounter and the Making of the Yoruba*. Bloomington: Indiana University Press, 2000.

Pérouse de Montclos, Marc-Antoine, ed. *Boko Haram: Islamism, Politics, Security and the State in Nigeria*. Leiden: African Studies Centre, 2014.

The Pew Forum on Religion and Public Life. "The Future of the Global Muslim Population," 2011.

Pierret, Thomas. *Religion and State in Syria: The Sunni Ulama from Coup to Revolution*. Cambridge: Cambridge University Press, 2013.

Pink, Johanna. "Where Does Modernity Begin? Muḥammad al-Shawkānī and the Tradition of Tafsīr." In *Tafsīr and Islamic Intellectual History: Exploring the Boundaries of a Tradition*, edited by Andreas Görke and Johanna Pink, 323–60. Oxford: Oxford University Press, 2014.

Psalidopoulos, Michalis, ed. *The Canon in the History of Economics: Critical Essays*. London and New York: Routledge, 2000.

Al-Qaḥṭānī, Sa'īd bin 'Alī bin Wahf. *Garkuwar Musulmi Ta Addu'o'i Daga Alkur'ani Da Sunna*. Translated by Bashir Aliyu Umar, edited by Muhammad Sani Umar and Abubakar Muhammad Sani. Riyadh: Ministry of Islamic Affairs, Endowments, Da'wa, and Guidance; Kano: al-Dar al-Salafiyya, second printing, 2000.

Al-Qayrawānī, Ibn Abī; Zayd. *Matn al-Risāla*. Beirut: Al-Maktaba al-Thaqāfiyya, undated.

Quṭb, Sayyid. *Fī Ẓilāl al-Qur'ān*. Beirut: Dār al-Shurūq, 1973–1974.

Rabil, Robert. *Salafism in Lebanon: From Apoliticism to Transnational Jihadism*. Washington, DC: Georgetown University Press, 2014.

Rapoport, Yossef and Shahab Ahmed, eds. *Ibn Taymiyya and His Times*. Oxford: Oxford University Press, 2010.

Renne, Elisha. "Educating Muslim Women and the Izala Movement in Zaria City, Nigeria." *Islamic Africa* 3:1 (2012): 55–86.

Reno, William. *Warlord Politics and African States*. Boulder, CO: Lynne Rienner, 1998.

Reynolds, Jonathan T. "Good and Bad Muslims: Islam and Indirect Rule in Northern Nigeria." In *The International Journal of African Historical Studies* 34:3 (2001): 601–18.

The Time of Politics (Zamanin Siyasa): Islam and the Politics of Legitimacy in Northern Nigeria, 1950–1966. San Francisco: International Scholars Publications, 1999.

Ricci, Ronit. *Islam Translated: Literature, Conversion, and the Arabic Cosmopolis of South and Southeast Asia*. Chicago: University of Chicago Press, 2011.

Riḍā, Muḥammad Rashīd. *Ḥuqūq al-Nisāʾ fī al-Islām*. Edited by Muḥammad Nāṣir al-Dīn al-Albānī. Beirut: al-Maktab al-Islāmī, 1984.

Al-Wahhābiyyūn wa-l-Ḥijāz. Cairo, 1925.

Riedl, Rachel. *Authoritarian Origins of Democratic Party Systems in Africa*. Cambridge: Cambridge University Press, 2014.

Rijiyar Lemo, Muḥammad al-Thānī ʿUmar Mūsā. *Ayyāmī maʿa Dāʿiyat al-Jīl wa-Mufassir al-Tanzīl*. Kano: Dar al-Ḥikma li-l-Kitāb al-Islāmī, 2011.

Bughyat al-Mishtāq fī Sharḥ Risālat Shaykh al-Islām Ibn Taymiyya ilā Ahl al-ʿIrāq. Kano: Al-Imamul Bukhari Centre for Research and Translation, 2011.

"Ḍawābiṭ al-Jarḥ wa-al-Taʿdīl ʿind al-Ḥāfiẓ al-Dhahabī min khilāl Kitābihi Siyar al-Aʿlām al-Nubalāʾ: Jamʿan wa-Dirāsatan." M.A. thesis, Islamic University of Medina, 1999.

"Al-Madrasa al-Ḥadīthiyya fī Makka wa-al-Madīna wa-Atharuhā fī al-Ḥadīth wa-ʿUlūmihi min Nashʾatihā ḥattā Nihāyat al-Qarn al-Thānī al-Hijrī." Ph.D. dissertation, Islamic University of Medina, 2005.

Rougier, Bernard. "Introduction." In *Qu'est-ce que le salafisme?*, edited by Bernard Rougier, 1–21. Paris: Presses Universitaires de France, 2008.

Sada, Ibrahim Naʾiya. "The Making of the Zamfara and Kano State Shariʿa Penal Codes." In *Sharia Implementation in Northern Nigeria, 1999–2006: A Sourcebook*, edited by Philip Ostien, 22–32. Ibadan: Spectrum Books, 2007.

Saeed, Abdullah. "Salafiya, Modernism, and Revival." In *The Oxford Handbook of Islam and Politics*, edited by John Esposito and Emad el-Din Shahin, 27–41. New York: Oxford University Press, 2013.

Saeedullah. *The Life and Works of Muhammad Siddiq Hasan Khan, Nawab of Bhopal*. Lahore: Published by Sh. Muhammad Ashraf, printed at Ashraf Press, 1973.

Salomon, Noah. "Evidence, Secrets, Truth: Debating Islamic Knowledge in Contemporary Sudan." *Journal of the American Academy of Religion* 81:3 (September 2013): 820–51.

"The Salafi Critique of Islamism: Doctrine, Difference and the Problem of Islamic Political Action in Contemporary Sudan." In *Global Salafism*, edited by Meijer, 143–68.

Al-Ṣanʿānī, Muḥammad ibn Ismāʻīl al-Amīr. *Rafʿ al-Astār li-Ibṭāl Adillat al-Qāʾilīn bi-Fanāʾ al-Nār*, edited by Muḥammad Nāṣir al-Dīn al-Albānī. Beirut: Maktab al-Islāmī, 1984.

Sani, Shehu. "Boko Haram: History, Ideas, Revolt," Parts 1–6. *Vanguard*, various issues, 2011.

Sanusi, Sanusi Lamido. "Identity, Political Ethics and Parochialism: Engagement with Jaʿfar Adam (1)." *Gamji*, 27 April 2005. Available at: www.gamji.com/sanusi/sanusi49.htm; accessed April 2013.

"Identity, Political Ethics and Parochialism: Engagement with Jaʿfar Adam (2)." *Gamji*, 3 May 2005. Available at: www.gamji.com/sanusi/sanusi50.htm; accessed April 2013.

"Politics and Shari'a in Northern Nigeria" in *Islam and Muslim Politics in Africa*, edited by Benjamin F. Soares and René Otayek, 177–188. New York: Palgrave Macmillan, 2007.

Al-Sawwāb, Muḥammad Maḥmud. "Shakhsiyyat al-Dāʿiya Hiya al-ʿĀmil al-Asāsī fī Najāḥihi." *Al-Rābiṭa* 29:34 (May 1990): 20–5.

Schulz, Dorothea. *Muslims and New Media in West Africa: Pathways to God*. Bloomington: Indiana University Press, 2012.

Schulze, Reinhard. *Islamischer Internationalismus im 20. Jahrhundert: Untersuchungen zur Geschichte der Islamischen Weltliga*. Leiden: Brill, 1990.

Seesemann, Rüdiger. *The Divine Flood: Ibrahim Niasse and the Roots of a Twentieth-Century Sufi Revival*. Oxford; New York: Oxford University Press, 2011.

"On the Cultural History of Islamic Knowledge and Its Contemporary Relevance." Religious Studies Faculty Colloquium, Northwestern University, 17 February 2010.

"The Quotidian Dimension of Islamic Reformism in Wadai (Chad)." In *L'islam politique au sud du Sahara: Identités, discours, et enjeux*, edited by Muriel Gomez-Perez, 327–46. Paris: Karthala, 2005.

"The Takfīr Debate: Sources for the Study of a Contemporary Dispute among African Sufis, Part One: The Nigerian Arena." *Sudanic Africa* 9 (1998): 39–70; and "Part Two: The Sudanese Arena," *Sudanic Africa* 10 (1999): 65–110.

Shākir, Aḥmad. *Ḥukm al-Jāhiliyya*. Cairo: Maktabat al-Sunna, 1992.

"Introduction." In Aḥmad Ibn Ḥanbal, *Al-Musnad*, Volume 1. Cairo: Dār al-Maʿarif, 1949.

El Shamsy, Ahmed. *The Canonization of Islamic Law: A Social and Intellectual History*. Cambridge: Cambridge University Press, 2013.

Shariff, Muhammad Ujdud. *Hisbah: Origin, Philosophy and Practice in Kano State*, Nigeria. Kano: Center for the Propagation of Shari'ah, 2011; printed and bound by Tellettes Consulting Company.

Al-Shawkānī, Muḥammad ibn ʿAlī. *Al-Fawāʾid al-Majmūʿa fī al-Aḥādīth al-Mawḍūʿa*, edited by 'Abd al-Raḥmān Yaḥyā al-Muʿallimī. Cairo: Maktabat al-Sunnah al-Muḥammadīyya, 1960.

Nayl al-Awṭār. Egypt: Muṣṭafā al-Bābī al-ḥalabī, 1952.

Shah, Ami. "The Urban Living Room: Space and Identity amongst Migrant Communities in Ibadan, Nigeria, and Ahmedabad, India." Ph.D. dissertation, University of Oxford, 2007.

Shaḥrūr, Muḥammad. *Al-Kitāb wa-l-Qurʾān: Qirāʾa Muʿāṣira*. Damascus: Al-Ahālī li-l-Ṭibāʿa wa-l-Nashr wa-l-Tawzīʿ, 1990.

Al-Shinqīṭī, Muḥammad al-Amīn. *Al-Qawl al-Sadīd fī Kashf Haqīqat al-Taqlīd.* Benares: Idārat al-Buḥūth al-Islāmiyya wa-l-Daʿwa wa-l-Iftāʾ, 1983.

Riḥlat al-Ḥajj ilā Bayt Allāh al-Ḥarām. Cairo: Dār Ibn Taymiyya, undated.

Sivan, Emmanuel. *Radical Islam: Medieval Theology and Modern Politics.* Second Edition. New Haven: Yale University Press, 1990.

Sklar, Richard. *Nigerian Political Parties: Power in an Emergent African Nation.* Princeton: Princeton University Press, 1963.

Smith, Daniel Jordan. "The Bakassi Boys: Vigilantism, Violence, and Political Imagination in Nigeria." *Cultural Anthropology* 19:3 (August 2004): 429–55.

A Culture of Corruption: Everyday Deception and Popular Discontent in Nigeria. Princeton: Princeton University Press, 2008.

Smith, Wilfred Cantwell. *The Meaning and End of Religion: A New Approach to the Religious Traditions of Mankind.* New York: Macmillan, 1963.

What Is Scripture? A Comparative Approach. Minneapolis: Fortress Press, 1993.

Soares, Benjamin F. "The Historiography of Islam in West Africa: An Anthropologist's View." *The Journal of African History* 55:1 (March 2014): 27–36.

Islam and the Prayer Economy: History and Authority in a Malian Town. Ann Arbor: University of Michigan Press, 2005.

"An Islamic Social Movement in Contemporary West Africa: NASFAT of Nigeria." In *Movers and Shakers: Social Movements in Africa*, edited by Stephen Ellis and Ineke van Kessel, 178–196. Leiden: Brill, 2009.

Sounaye, Abdoulaye. "La 'discothèque' islamique: CD et DVD au cœur de la réislamisation nigérienne." ethnographiques.org 22 (May 2011).

"Les héritiers du cheikh: Izala et ses appropriations d'Usman Dan Fodio au Niger." *Cahiers d'Études africaines* 206–207:2 (2012): 427–47.

"Irwo Sunnance yan-no! 1: Youth Claiming, Contesting and Transforming Salafism." *Islamic Africa* 6:1–2 (July 2015): 82–108.

"Speeches Delivered at the Historic Ceremony of the Opening of the Rebuilt 100,000 Sultan Bello Mosque on Friday, 5th July, 1963 at Sokoto." Zaria, Nigeria: Gaskiya Corporation, 1963.

Starrett, Gregory. *Putting Islam to Work: Education, Politics, and Religious Transformation in Egypt.* Berkeley and Los Angeles: University of California Press, 1998.

Stolow, Jeremy. "Religion and/as Media." *Theory, Culture, and Society* 22:4 (August 2005): 119–45.

Suleiman, Salisu. "Northern Traditional Institutions and the Crises of Legitimacy." *Nigerians Talk.* 24 September 2012.

Tahir, Ibrahim. "Scholars, Sufis, Saints and Capitalists in Kano, 1904–1974: The Pattern of Bourgeois Revolution in an Islamic Society." Ph.D. Thesis, University of Cambridge, 1975.

Tamari, Tal. "Islamic Higher Education in West Africa: Some Examples from Mali" in *Islam in Africa*, edited by Thomas Bierschenk and Georg Stauth, 91–128. Münster: Lit Verlag, 2002.

Al-Ṭawiyān, Abd al-ʿAzīz ibn Ṣāliḥ ibn Ibrāhīm. *Juhūd al-Shaykh Muḥammad al-Amīn al-Shinqīṭī fī Taqrīr ʿAqīdat al-Salaf.* Medina: The Islamic University, 1998.

Thomassen, Einar. "Some Notes on the Development of Christian Ideas about a Canon." In *Canon and Canonicity: The Formation and Use of Scripture*, edited by Einar Thomassen, 9–28. Copenhagen: Museum Tusculanum Press, 2010.

Thurston, Alex. "Coded Language among Muslim Activists: Salafis and the Prophet's Sermon of Necessity." Unpublished paper, under review.

"'The Disease Is Unbelief": Boko Haram's Religious and Political Worldview." Brookings Institution Project on U.S.-Muslim World Relations, November 2015.

"Muslim Politics and Shari'a in Kano, Nigeria." *African Affairs* 114:454 (January 2015): 28–51.

"Nigeria's Mainstream Salafis between Boko Haram and the State." *Islamic Africa* 6:1–2 (July 2015): 109–34.

Al-Tuwayjirī, Ḥamad ibn ʿAbd al-Muḥsin. "Editor's Introduction." In Taqī al-Dīn Ibn Taymiyya, *Al-Fatwā al-Ḥamawiyya al-Kubrā*. Al-Riyāḍ: Dār al-Ṣamīʿī, 2004.

Tweed, Thomas. *Crossing and Dwelling: A Theory of Religion.* Cambridge, MA: Harvard University Press, 2006.

ʿUmar, Bashīr ʿAlī. *Manhaj al-Imām Aḥmad fī Iʿlāl al-Ḥadīth.* Saudi Arabia: Waqf al-Salām 2005.

Umar, Muhammad Sani. "Changing Islamic Identity in Nigeria from the 1960s to the 1980s: From Sufism to Anti-Sufism." In *Muslim Identity and Social Change in Sub-Saharan Africa*, edited by Louis Brenner, 154–78. Bloomington: University of Indiana Press, 1993.

"Education and Islamic Trends in Northern Nigeria: 1970s to 1990s." *Africa Today* 48:2 (Summer 2001): 127–50.

Islam and Colonialism: Intellectual Responses of Muslims of Northern Nigeria to British Colonial Rule. Leiden: Brill, 2006.

Al-ʿUthaymīn, Muḥammad ibn Ṣāliḥ. *Akidar Ahlus-Sunna.* Translated by Shu'aib Abubakar Umar. Riyadh: Ministry of Islamic Affairs, Endowments, Daʿwa, and Guidance, 1999/2000.

ʿAqīdat Ahl al-Sunna wa-l-Jamāʿa. Al-Riyāḍ: Muʾassasat al-Shaykh Muḥammad Ṣāliḥ al-ʿUthaymīn al-Khayriyya, 2009.

Sharḥ al-ʿAqīda al-Wāsiṭiyya li-Shaykh al-Islām Ibn Taymiyya. ʿAyn Shams: Maktabat al-Hady al-Muḥammadī, 2011.

Vikør, Knut S. *Between God and the Sultan: A History of Islamic Law.* Oxford and New York: Oxford University Press, 2005.

Vogel, Frank. *Islamic Law and Legal System: Studies of Saudi Arabia.* Leiden: Brill, 2000.

Voll, John. "ʿAbdallah ibn Salim al-Basri and 18th Century Hadith Scholarship." *Die Welt des Islams* 42:3 (2002): 356–72.

"Linking Groups in the Networks of Eighteenth-Century Scholars." In *Eighteenth-Century Revival and Reform in Islam*, edited by Nehemiah Levtzion and John Voll, 69–92. Syracuse: Syracuse University Press, 1987.

de Vries, Hent. "In Media Res: Global Religion, Public Spheres, and the Task of Contemporary Comparative Religious Studies." In *Religion and Media*, edited by Hent de Vries and Samuel Weber, 3–42. Stanford: Stanford University Press.

Wagemakers, Joas. *A Quietist Jihadi: The Ideology and Influence of Abu Muhammad al-Maqdisi.* Cambridge: Cambridge University Press, 2012.

Wakili, Haruna. "Islam and the Political Arena in Nigeria: The Ulama and the 2007 Elections." Northwestern University Institute for the Study of Islamic Thought in Africa Working Paper 09–004, March 2009.

Walker, Andrew. "What Is Boko Haram?" Washington, DC: United States Institute of Peace, June 2012.
Ware, Rudolph. *The Walking Qur'an: Islamic Education, Embodied Knowledge, and History in West Africa*. Chapel Hill: University of North Carolina Press, 2014.
Wedeen, Lisa. *Peripheral Visions: Publics, Power, and Performance in Yemen*. Chicago: University of Chicago Press, 2008.
Weimann, Gunnar. *Islamic Criminal Law in Northern Nigeria: Politics, Religion, Judicial Practice*. Amsterdam: Amsterdam University Press, 2010.
Weismann, Itzchak. "Between Ṣūfī Reformism and Modernist Rationalism: A Reappraisal of the Origins of the Salafiyya from the Damascene Angle." *Die Welt des Islams* 41:2 (July 2001): 206–37.
Wheeler, Brannon. *Applying the Canon in Islam: The Authorization and Maintenance of Interpretive Reasoning in Ḥanafī Scholarship*. Albany: State University of New York Press, 1996.
Whitaker, C. S. Jr. *The Politics of Tradition: Continuity and Change in Northern Nigeria, 1946–1966*. Princeton: Princeton University Press, 1970.
Wiktorowicz, Quintan. "Anatomy of the Salafi Movement." *Studies in Conflict & Terrorism* 29 (2006): 207–39.
The Management of Islamic Activism: Salafis, the Muslim Brotherhood, and State Power in Jordan. Albany: State University of New York Press, 2001.
Wood, Graeme. "What ISIS Really Wants." *The Atlantic*, March 2015.
Yakubu, Mahmood. *An Aristocracy in Political Crisis*. Aldershot, UK: Avebury, 1996.
Yūsuf, Abū Yūsuf Muḥammad. *Hādhihi 'Aqīdatunā wa-Manhaj Da'watinā*. Maiduguri: Maktabat al-Ghurabā', likely 2009.
Yusuf, Shehu Tijjani. "Stealing from the Railways: Blacksmiths, Colonialism, and Innovation in Northern Nigeria." In *Transforming Innovations in Africa: Explorative Studies on Appropriation in African Societies*, edited by Jan-Bart Gewald, André Leliveld, and Iva Peša, 275–96. Leiden: Brill, 2012.
Zaman, Muhammad Qasim. *Religion and Politics under the Early 'Abbāsids: The Emergence of the Proto-Sunnī Elite*. Leiden: Brill, 1997.
Zenn, Jacob. "Cooperation or Competition: Boko Haram and Ansaru after the Mali Intervention." *CTC Sentinel* 6:3 (March 2013): 1–8.

INTERVIEWS

Abdallah, Shaykh Abdulwahhab. 5 October 2011, Kano.
Abdullah, Kabiru Umar. 16 November 2011, Kano.
Atiq, Dr. Lawi. 25 January 2012, Kano.
Galadanci, Professor Shehu. 16 November 2011, Kano.
17 December 2011, Kano.
Garangamawa, Shaykh Abdullahi. 16 June 2012, Kano. (Recorded interview by anonymous research assistant.)
Ibrahim, Shaykh Baba Uba. 1 December 2011 and 8 December 2011, Kano.
Ibrahim, Shaykh Kabiru Uba. 9 December 2011, Kano.
Inuwa, Shaykh Muhammad Nazifi. 12 October 2011, Kano.
Pakistan, Dr. Abdullahi Saleh. 22 October 2011, Kano.
Umar, Dr. Bashir Aliyu. 2 October 2011, Kano.
Uthman, Shaykh Bashir Tijjani. 13 December 2011, Kano.

ARCHIVAL SOURCES

BRITISH LIBRARY

Palmer, H. R. "Report on a Journey from Maidugari, Nigeria to Jedda in Arabia," 1919. IOR R20/A1236 No. 1/7.

NATIONAL ARCHIVES KADUNA (NAK)

GENS 425, "Saudi Arabian Study Grants."

LEAKED U.S. EMBASSY CABLES

U.S. Embassy Abuja. "Nigeria: 2009 Country Reports on Terrorism." December 11, 2009.
"Nigeria: Snapshot of Northern Gubernatorial Elections." April 17, 2003.
"Nigerian 'Taliban' Attacks Most Likely Not Tied to Taliban nor Al-Qaida." February 6, 2004.
"Politics of Nigeria's Northern Borno State." November 3, 2009.
"Terrorist Arrest Exaggerated." March 19, 2004.

RECORDED LECTURES (AUDIO AND/OR VIDEO)

Ādam, Jaʿfar Maḥmūd. "Gwagwarmaya Tsakanin Karya da Gaskiya." November 15, 2006, Kano.
"Kalubalen Shari'a." June 15/16, 2000, Kano.
Kitāb al-Tawḥīd, first lesson. September 6, 1997.
"Me Ya Sa Suke Cewa Boko Haram Ne?" 2007.
Riyāḍ al-Ṣāliḥīn, first lesson. February 28, 1999.
Riyāḍ al-Ṣāliḥīn, second lesson. March 6, 1999.
Riyāḍ al-Ṣāliḥīn, third lesson. March 13, 1999.
"Tarihin Rayuwata a Ilmi." No date, Kano.
"Siyasa a Nigeria." 2003, Kano.
Untitled. 16 August 2006, Kano.
Gumi, Aḥmad. "Al Aqidatul Wasidiyyah." April 19, 2012, likely Kaduna.
"Al Aqidatul Wasidiyyah," May 27, 2012, likely Kaduna.
"Ramadan Tafseer." July 17, 2013, Kaduna.
Kabara, Abduljabbar Nasir. "Garkuwar Mauludi (1/14)." June 17, 2006, likely Kano.
"Menene Sunnah? (Part One)," undated, likely Kano.
"Wajabcin Zikir (1/2)," undated, likely Kano.
Muṣṭafā, ʿAlī. "Fiqhul Aqida 1." October 2, 2013.
Nur, Muḥammad and Muḥammad Yūsuf. Untitled, 2009, Maiduguri.
Pantami, Isa 'Ali and Muḥammad Yusuf. Undated debate.
Rijiyar Lemo, Muḥammad Sani ʿUmar. "Kungiyoyin Jihadi (1)." April 2009, Maiduguri.
"Kungiyoyin Jihadi (2)." April 2009, Maiduguri.
"Musulunci a Jiya da Yau." September 2008, Kano.
"Shirin Freedom akan Maulidi." Recorded radio broadcast, Freedom Radio, March 2007, Kano.
al-Tuḥfa al-ʿIrāqiyya fī al-Aʿmāl al-Qalbiyya, first lesson, 13 May 2008.

Al-'Ubūdiyya, first lesson, December 2005.
Al-Waṣiyya al-Kubrā;, first lesson, 9 January 2007.
Al-Waṣiyya al-Kubrā;, twenty-first lesson, 17 July 2007.
Al-Waṣiyya al-Kubrā;, twenty-second lesson, 24 July 2007.
Shekau, Abubakar. "Abubakar Shekau Claims Responsibility on Barracks Attack," March 2014.
"Bay'at Jamā'at Ahl al-Sunna li-l-Da'wa wa-l-Jihad li-Khalīfat al-Muslimīn Abī Bakr al-Baghdādī," 7 March 2015.
"Boko Haram Declares a New Caliphate in North Eastern Nigeria," 24 August 2014.
"Message to Jonathan," 11 January 2012.
"A Message to the Leaders of the Disbelievers," February 2015.
"Message to the World on Baga," January 2015.
"Wannan ne Akidarmu," likely 2015.
Yūsuf, Muḥammad. Oral commentary on *Hādhihi 'Aqīdatunā*, circa 2009.
"Open Letter to the Government of Nigeria," 11 June 2009, Maiduguri.
"Warware Shubuhar Malamai," circa 2008.
Zaria, Muḥammad Awwal 'Albānī.' *Ṣaḥīḥ Muslim*, introduction, 10 October 2011.

NEWSPAPERS AND ONLINE NEWS SOURCES

Agence France Presse
BBC
Bloomberg
Daily Times
Daily Trust
Desert Herald
Forbes
The Guardian
IRIN
Al Jazeera
Vangurd
Xinhua

Index

9/11, 180, 241

Abacha, Sani, 176
Abbasid Caliphate, 31, 37, 42, 173
Abd al-Aziz, King of Saudi Arabia, 68
Abd al-Nasir, Gamal, 68, 79
Abdallahi, Kabiru Umar, 153, 156
Abduh, Muhammad, 53
Abdullah, Abdulwahhab, 4, 169, 229, 232, 234, 242
  behavior toward his students, 104
  life before Medina, 99
  return to Nigeria, 103
  writing on Hisbah, 188
Abu Zayd, Bakr, 209
Abuja, 205
activism, 1, 2, 4, 25
Ādam, Ja'far Mahmud, 4, 7, 15, 19, 91, 92, 119, 125, 136, 140, 143, 145, 160, 167, 168, 175, 177, 212, 222, 235, 242
  assassination of, 97, 194
  attitude toward al-Albani, 34
  attitude toward elections, 181
  attitude toward geopolitics, 180
  and Boko Haram, 231
  canonization of, 245
  and Freedom Radio, 153
  and Ibrahim Shekarau, 169
  life before Medina, 99
  and politics, 220
  preaching style of, 104, 117
  relationship with Izala, 87, 96, 111
  return to Nigeria, 103
  and the Sabuwar Gandu Mosque, 152
  and Sanusi Lamido Sanusi, 166
  teaching style with hadith, 130
advice, 135, 185
Afghanistan, 171, 180, 240
Africa, 1, 9
  Salafi attitude toward, 74
African Union, 197
ahl al-hadith, 5, 38
ahl al-sunna, 38
ahl-e hadith (India), 48, 52, 54
Ahlussunnah, 93, 95, 97, 103, 109, 172, 182
Ahmad, Muhammad, 148
Ahmadu Bello University, 98
A'isha, 127
Aji, Abba, 230
Al Jazeera, 150
Al-Abbad, Abd al-Muhsin, 35, 70, 102
Al-Afghani, Jamal al-Din, 53
Al-Albani, Muhammad Nasir al-Din, 9, 19, 40, 46, 56, 70, 72, 93, 100, 118, 123, 129, 130, 137, 214, 234, 244
  biography of, 61
  and Boko Haram, 209, 211, 230
  education of, 131
  followers in Nigeria, 110
  and jihadism, 195
  and Juhayman al-Utaybi, 210
  and legal schools, 155
  legacy online, 226
  reception in Nigeria, 137
  relationship with Islamic University of Medina, 17
  role in shaping Salafi canon, 35
  succession to, 224
  Sufi attitudes toward, 159
Al-Alusi, Nu'man Khayr al-Din, 55
Al-Ansari, Hammad, 72
Al-Asqalani, Ibn Hajar, 122
Al-Azhar University, 13, 17, 69, 78, 121
  and the Tijaniyya, 162
Al-Baghdadi, Abubakar, 218
Albani Zaria, Muhammad Awwal, 119, 129, 222
Albania, 15, 59, 159
Al-Banna, Hasan, 171
Al-Bukhari, Muhammad, 122, 125, 128, 137, 149, 243
Al-Buti, Sa'id Ramadan, 157
alcohol, 98
Al-Fiqqi, Muhammad Hamid, 58
Al-Furqan Mosque, 102, 105
Algeria, 197
Al-Ghazali, Abu Hamid, 59, 89

Ali, Yusuf, 152
Al-Ifriqi, Abd al-Rahman, 72, 77
Al-Jami, Muhammad Aman, 46, 67, 72, 79, 112
  attitude toward Africa, 76
  biography of, 36
al-Jāmī, Muḥammad Amān, 6
al-jarḥ wa-l-taʿdīl, 125
Al-Jilani, Abd al-Qadir, 134, 160
Alkali, Idris Kuliya, 148
All Nigeria People's Party, 200, 205
Allah. *See* God
Al-Madkhali, Rabi, 72, 129, 224
  and the Internet, 228
Al-Maʾmun, 37, 40
Al-Maqdisi, Abu Muhammad, 15, 218
  and Boko Haram, 212
  and the Internet, 226
Al-Muntada al-Islami Trust, 102, 105
Al-Nawawi, Yahya, 122, 125, 128, 184
  position within Salafi canon, 129, 135
Al-Nur Party (Egypt), 171, 221
Al-Qaʿida, 173, 214, 221
  in the Islamic Maghreb (AQIM), 198
Al-Sadat, Anwar, 172
Al-Sanʿani, Muhammad ibn Ismaʿil al-Amir, 47, 48, 49, 123, 137, 218
Al-Shabab, 198, 207
Al-Shawkani, Muhammad ibn Ali, 48, 54, 60, 71, 107, 137, 208
Al-Shinqiti, Muhammad al-Amin, 72, 76, 209
  role in Saudi Arabia, 74
Al-Utaybi, Juhayman, 214, 218
  and Boko Haram, 210
Al-Uthaymin, Muhammad
  death of, 223
Al-Wadii, Muqbil, 46, 71, 224
al-walāʾ wa-l-barāʾ, 214, 216, 218
Al-Ẓāhiriyya Library, 55, 60, 131
Al-Zakzaky, Ibrahim, 22, 199
Al-Zarqawi, Abu Musʿab, 214
Aminu Kano College of Islamic and Legal Studies, 104
Angel Gabriel, 150
Ansar al-Sunna al-Muhammadiyya, 5, 57, 67, 110, 226
anticanon, 12, 14
anticolonialism, 86
anti-Sufism, 94, 95, 100, 109, 111, 118, 170
Appiah, Kwame Anthony, 165
Arabic language, 108, 120, 143, 145, 146, 149, 225
Arabic Teachers' College in Gwale, 98
Ashʿariyya, 6, 8, 42, 47, 52, 92, 110, 128
assassination, 221, 222, 244
Atiq, Abubakar, 158, 161, 162
Atiq, Lawi, 163
audiences, 4, 9, 15, 19, 33, 58, 60, 64, 65, 66, 68, 77, 84, 88, 93, 95, 96, 103, 104, 108, 113, 117, 118, 119, 121, 123, 124, 125, 126, 127, 128, 130, 133, 135, 141, 142, 146, 152, 153, 154, 156, 158, 160, 166, 168, 180, 194, 195, 196, 214, 221, 225, 228, 230, 233, 234, 236, 239, 242, 244
authenticity, 244

Baba, Ahmad, 121
Baghdad, 4, 38, 42, 53, 54, 158
Basra, 38, 45
Bauchi, 202, 203, 205
Bauchi, Dahiru, 237
Bayero University Kano, 99, 103, 237, 238
Bayero, Ado, 140, 160
BBC, 201
BBC Hausa Service, 145
Bello, Ahmadu, 66, 78, 81, 83, 89, 90
  and Saudi Arabia, 79
Bello, Iysa Ade, 88
Bhopal, 50
bidʿa, 7, 39. *See* heresy
Bin Ladin, Osama, 173, 218
Bin Uthman, Muhammad, 106
Binji, Haliru, 122
blasphemy, 4
Boko Haram, 4, 17, 23, 26, 160, 189, 220, 239
  and al-Qaʿida affiliates, 198
  and mainstream Salafism, 222
  history of, 207
  overview of, 195
  Salafi refutations of, 234
bombings, 205, 207
British colonialism, 20, 50, 82, 86, 181
Buhari, Muhammadu, 205
  and Boko Haram, 207
Burkina Faso, 64, 83

Cairo, 42, 56, 57
Cameroon, 22, 207
canon, 25
  definition of, 1, 14, 31
canonization, 9, 31, 62
  Salafi process of, 35
census, 177
Central Bank of Nigeria, 93
Chad, 207
charisma, 94, 163
Chechnya, 179
Chedi, Yahaya Faruk, 185
Chibok, 206
Christianity, 75
  in Nigeria, 177, 203, 229, 238
  and Nigerian politics, 172

Christians
in Nigeria, 205
colonial schooling, 86
Committee of Senior Scholars (Saudi Arabia), 16
Companions of the Prophet Muhammad, 5, 18, 31, 54, 112, 127, 168, 218
conspiracy theories, 204
Constitution of Nigeria, 151, 172, 205, 212
corruption, 164, 169, 179, 207, 238
Côte d'Ivoire, 104
coup, 81, 84, 221
creed, 6, 33, 41, 52, 91, 94, 118, 120, 121, 133, 134, 168, 170, 178, 187, 211, 215, 234

Damascus, 41, 42, 54, 57, 60, 188
Dan Fodio, Uthman, 78, 83, 134, 155, 186, 217
Salafi views of, 80
Daura, 97
Daurawa, Aminu, 110, 170, 235
and anti-Sufism, 237
da'wa, 33, 74, 108, 109, 113, 132, 179, 214, 228, 231, 238
dawra tours, 89, 98
debates among Muslims, 133
democracy, 181, 216
democratization, 176
Dibal, Adamu, 203
divorce, 175, 236

education, 120, 124, 132, 135, 138, 144, 238, 241
hybrid, 161
and politics, 183
Egypt, 3, 5, 13, 15, 41, 60, 68, 79, 110, 121, 147, 158, 160, 161, 170, 174, 182, 221, 226, 237, 241
Egyptian Cultural Center (Kano), 99
elections, 23, 170, 181, 200, 205, 207, 236, 238
Salafi attitude toward, 127
elites, 182, 204
Emirate Council of Kano, 152
epistemology, 139, 142, 155, 163
ethics, 4
Ethiopia, 35, 64, 72, 152, 197
ethnicity, 177, 181
evidence, 8, 234, 242
exclusivism, 194, 208, 218, 219, 242
exegesis. *See* tafsir
extremism, 196, 240

Facebook, 25, 160, 226, 235, 237, 238
Fallata, Umar, 72
Faraj, Abd al-Salam, 172
Faysal, King of Saudi Arabia, 69
Federal Government of Nigeria, 146, 185, 194
federalism, 4
Federation of Muslim Women's Associations in Nigeria, 177
filmmakers, 150
Foi, Buji, 201
Fourth Republic Nigeria, 177, 200
Freedom Radio, 157, 187
Fulani, 166

Gadon Kaya, 102
Gaffney, Patrick, 174, 182
Gamji, 145, 164
Ganduje, Abdullahi, 170, 236
Garangamawa, Abdullahi, 109, 148
generic Islam, 170
geopolitics, 33
Ghana, 64, 83, 141
globalization, 24, 209
God
attributes of, 6, 170
Salafi attitude toward, 7
Gombe, Muhammad Kabiru, 231, 232
Graham, William, 124
Guinea, 69
Gulf War, 96, 99, 223
Gumi, 79
Gumi, Abubakar, 66, 70, 77, 90, 92, 93, 95, 144, 162, 231
and the Islamic University of Medina, 81
biography of, 86
Gumi, Ahmad, 96, 119, 235
and the 2015 elections, 238
and Boko Haram, 234
Gwoza, 207, 217

hadith (hadīth), 2, 22, 32, 40, 42, 45, 49, 56, 84, 101, 113, 118, 140, 149, 151, 158, 162, 168, 186, 208, 209, 218, 234, 238, 243
in northwest Africa, 121
Salafi attitude toward, 6, 8, 9, 13, 16, 17, 33, 34, 60, 119, 130
Hadiyyatullah, Abdurrasheed, 89
Hanbalism, 7, 18, 32, 36, 40, 41, 45, 54, 61, 71, 154
politics of, 37
Hausa, 20
language, 84, 108, 122, 123, 135, 145, 146, 186, 212, 238
people, non-Muslims among, 182
Haykel, Bernard, 169, 243
hereditary Muslim rulers, 1, 22, 149, 160, 164, 172, 173, 181, 199
heresy, 22, 37, 50, 77, 107, 113, 150, 168, 173

hip hop, 243
Hirschkind, Charles, 147
Hisbah, 97, 110, 170, 188, 210, 236
history, 33, 241
  Salafi attitude toward, 14, 25, 32, 33, 36, 41, 74, 128, 164, 175, 180, 184
human rights, 242
humor, 103

Ibn Abd al-Wahhab, Muhammad, 18, 33, 36, 39, 61, 84, 98, 118, 119, 121, 184, 223, 229
  biography of, 45
  canonization of, 46
  and politics, 173
  reception in Nigeria, 133
  and Uthman dan Fodio, 80
Ibn Atiq, Hamad, 211
Ibn Atiq, Saʿd, 61
Ibn Baz, Abd al-Aziz, 9, 17, 35, 61, 69, 70, 77, 89, 93, 99, 118, 130, 145, 168, 171, 186, 209, 210, 234
  and Boko Haram, 211, 230
  legacy online, 226
  relationship with Islamic University of Medina, 17
  succession to, 223
  teaching style of, 121
Ibn Hanbal, Ahmad, 36, 45, 101, 117, 186, 208
  and politics, 173
  biography of, 40
Ibn Ibrahim, Muhammad, 35, 59, 69
Ibn Kathir, Ismaʿil, 43, 84, 133, 208
Ibn Musafir, Adi, 134
Ibn Qayyim al-Jawziyya, 43, 58, 61, 128, 208, 217
Ibn Rushd, 89
Ibn Saʿud, Muhammad, 45
Ibn Taymiyya, Ahmad, 14, 18, 32, 33, 36, 39, 44, 45, 47, 48, 49, 52, 56, 57, 58, 59, 60, 71, 92, 101, 110, 118, 119, 121, 160, 165, 169, 174, 184, 195, 208, 210, 211, 214, 217, 230, 235, 239, 243
  biography of, 43
  canonization of, 44
  and Hisbah, 186
  Islamic revivalists' interest in, 56
  and Nigerian Salafis, 106
  and politics, 173
  reception in Nigeria, 134
  reception online, 225, 226
  and the refutation of Boko Haram, 233
  translations of, 136
Ibn Uthaymin, Muhammad, 10, 17, 61, 72, 93, 100, 110, 118, 130, 136, 186, 234
  and Boko Haram, 209, 229, 230
  legacy online, 226
  political attitude of, 62
ideals, 169, 242
  relationship to canons, 13
identity, 164, 177
ideology, 31, 194
idols, 212
Idris, Ismail, 86, 95, 96, 145
ijtihad, 32, 37, 41, 48, 50, 53, 55, 56, 234
India, 4, 8, 32, 34, 44, 46, 49, 64, 90
Indimi, Muhammad, 105, 198
infrastructure, 119, 144, 225, 235, 239
International University of Africa, 104, 164
Internet, 142, 143, 145, 152, 164, 235
  and Salafism, 228
Inuwa, Muhammad Nazifi, 100, 106, 125, 146, 148, 233
Iran, 22, 69
Iranian Revolution, 98, 199
Iraq, 96, 158, 171, 193
Iraq War, 173, 174, 184
ISIS. *See* Islamic State in Iraq and Syria (ISIS)
Islam in Africa, 3, 7, 240
Islamic Association of Niger, 177
Islamic Courts Union of Somalia, 197
Islamic modernism, 18, 53, 180
Islamic revivalism, 18, 32, 34, 57, 126, 180
Islamic State in Iraq and Syria (ISIS), 26, 193, 198, 210, 214, 218, 220, 243
Islamic Studies, 13, 238
Islamic University in Islamabad, 98
Islamic University of Medina, 4, 13, 17, 22, 25, 32, 34, 35, 60, 62, 63, 65, 66, 72, 79, 84, 88, 90, 105, 118, 134, 143, 169, 173, 194, 210, 225, 227, 229, 242
  and first Nigerian students, 80
  history of, 69
  Nigerian students life at, 102, 108
  role in Africa, 75
  role in canonization, 72
Islamism, 3, 174
  and Salafism, 173
Islamiyya schools, 161
Israel, 69
Izala, 92, 94, 97, 105, 117, 132, 162, 177, 199, 222
  and media, 145
  and Salafi unity, 233
  and the Sabuwar Gandu Mosque, 152
  history of, 88
  schisms within, 96

Jalingo, Ibrahim Jalo, 107, 135, 235
Jami movement, 36

jihadism, 10, 169, 172, 189, 193, 210, 214, 220, 239, 242
and the Internet, 228
and the Salafi canon, 195
in Africa, 198
Jingir, Sani Yahaya, 96, 231
Joint Task Force-Restore Order, 206
Jonathan, Goodluck, 164, 207, 215
and Boko Haram, 207
Jordan, 15, 60
Jos, 96, 107, 231
jurisprudence, 45, 49, 121, 161, 234

Kabara, Abd al-Jabbar, 160, 163
Kabara, Nasir, 104, 158, 160, 162, 231
Kabara, Qaribullah, 160
Kachalla, Mala, 200
Kaduna, 87, 107, 231
Kane, Ousmane, 165, 199
Kanem-Bornu, 21
Kannama, 201
Kannywood, 145, 150
Kano, 87, 95, 107, 112, 119, 130, 140, 143, 145, 177, 202, 203, 205, 236, 244
Medina graduates' lives in, 99
Kano, Aminu, 236
Kashmir, 179
Katsina, 97, 130, 238
Kenya, 197, 207
Khan, Siddiq Hasan, 47, 50, 54, 60, 71, 107, 129
canonization of, 52
relationship with Wahhabism, 52
role in canonization, 51
King Abdullah of Saudi Arabia, 99
King Fahd of Saudi Arabia, 99
King Faysal of Saudi Arabia, 186
Kitab al-Tawhid, 45, 84, 88, 98, 118, 130
knowledge, 128, 132, 142, 143
Kuwait, 96
Kwankwaso, Rabiu, 170, 178, 236

Lagos, 177, 205
Larkin, Brian, 144
Last, Murray, 199
Lau, Abdullahi Bala, 235
Lebanon, 56
legacy websites, 226
legal schools in Islam, 7, 13, 14, 18, 36, 45, 50, 56, 61, 85, 110, 123, 154, 155
liberalization, 143, 176
Libya, 162
literalism, 144
localization, 91, 114, 137, 139, 142, 152, 155

madhhab. *See* legal schools in Islam
Mahdi, 210
Maiduguri, 15, 21, 119, 201, 206, 207, 215, 230
and Boko Haram's emergence, 198
Maitatsine, 22, 162
Mali, 44, 197
Malian Association for the Unity and Progress of Islam, 177
Malikism, 64, 73, 82, 83, 85, 98, 120, 122, 159, 167, 183
Salafi attitude toward, 157
marriage, 31, 103, 109, 113, 175, 178, 236
Marwa, Muhammad. *See* Maitatsine
Mauritania, 69, 72, 78
mawlid, 157
Mecca, 45, 49, 58, 74, 97, 98, 136, 146, 186, 209
media, 24, 26, 139, 147, 153, 176, 180, 188, 225, 234, 235, 239, 241
in northern Nigeria, 147
and religious communities, 142
Medina, 33, 45, 49, 79, 95, 98, 121, 130, 178
memorization, 119, 124, 126
meritocracy, 142, 147, 148, 152, 153, 156, 242
metaphor, 174, 240
methodology, 11, 38, 58, 66, 84, 108, 113, 137, 151, 171, 186, 242
metonymy, 174, 244
micropolitics, 4
Mihna, 39
millenarianism, 83, 218
miracles, 160
modernity, 53, 181
Mongols, 42
monotheism, 38
morality, 185, 186, 236
Morocco, 69, 158
Mubarak, Hosni, 172
Muhammad al-Amin al-Kanimi, 21
Muslim Brotherhood, 3, 15, 173, 221, 227
influence in Saudi Arabia, 100
role at Islamic University of Medina, 71
Muslim ibn al-Hajjaj, 122, 125, 137, 149
Muslim Students' Society, 98
Muslim World League, 68, 72, 76, 77, 79, 84, 88, 90, 98, 111, 123
Mustafa, Ali, 232, 234
Mu'tazila, 37, 38, 41, 47, 53, 128

N'Djamena, 207
Nairobi, 197, 207
Najd, 44, 45
NASFAT (Naṣr Allāh al-Fātiḥ), 94
National Police Force of Nigeria, 185, 205
newspapers, 145

Niamey, 94
Niasse, Ibrahim, 77, 83, 160, 236
Niger, 94, 146, 207
Niger Delta, 177, 204
Nigeria, 1, 2, 76
  First Republic, 84
  history of, 25
  politics of, 4, 14, 25
  regional disparities in, 24
  Salafism in, 31
  southwestern, 88
Nigerian civil war, 22
northern Nigeria, 1
  relationship with Saudi Arabia, 66
Nyass, Abdul, 238

Obasanjo, Olusegun, 181, 204
oil, 23, 69, 78, 146, 240
Operation Flush, 202, 213
orality, 124
Organization of Islamic Cooperation, 180
Organization of Petroleum Exporting Countries, 78
Organization of the Islamic Conference, 69, 72
orthodoxy, 53, 113, 143, 172

Pakistan, 71, 90, 98
Pakistan, Abdallah Salih, 107, 108, 109, 149, 233
  life before Medina, 99
Palestine, 15, 171, 179
Pantami, Isa, 229
pedagogy, 126
Pentecostal Christianity, 141
People's Democracy Party (PDP), 177, 205
Pharaoh, 237
Philippines, 171
philosophy, 5, 6, 39, 40, 49, 89, 165
piety, 86, 95, 124, 216
pilgrimage, 49, 78, 98, 102
pluralism, 164, 173
polemics, 77
politicians, 185
politics, 147, 164, 167, 212, 239, 241
  and Boko Haram, 215
  Salafi attitude towards, 10, 151
Port Harcourt, 106
preaching, 94, 107, 189, 215
  Salafi styles of, 110, 113
progressive Muslims, 143, 166, 172
proof-texts, 142, 147, 149, 152, 155, 166
propaganda, 194, 214
Prophet Muḥammad, 2, 6, 31, 38, 93, 112, 120, 132, 153, 154, 168, 180, 184, 185
purity, 127, 173, 179, 180, 181, 187, 237

Qadi Iyad, 85, 121, 155
Qadiriyya, 78, 83, 104, 134, 152, 231
  and Salafism, 160
Qadiriyya Sufi order, 20
quietism, 39, 169, 173, 188, 220, 239
Qur'an, 2, 32, 36, 41, 53, 59, 61, 84, 109, 118, 119, 121, 126, 131, 149, 155, 178, 208, 243
  debates over, 37
  Salafi attitudes toward, 7, 9
  schooling, 97, 126
  translations of the meaning of, 89
Qur'anic recitation, 144, 161, 235
Qutb, Sayyid, 85, 100, 171, 210
  and the Internet, 228

Rabiu, Abdulsamad, 106
Rabiu, Isyaku, 106, 237
radicalization, 95, 241
radio, 84, 103, 106, 142, 144, 152, 153, 157, 235
Ramadan, 105, 119, 151, 180, 183, 198, 207, 232
recorded lectures, 119, 126, 130, 140, 142, 145, 147, 152, 235
religious authority, 5, 14, 64, 94, 96, 151, 160, 164, 186, 244
  fragmentation of, 2, 22, 199
  and university degrees, 162
religious marketplace, 199
religious studies, 11, 196
Rida, Muhammad Rashid, 18, 53, 56, 59, 60, 61, 71, 208
  canonization of, 56
  students of, 57
Rightly Guided Caliphs, 38, 54, 185
Rijiyar Lemo, Muhammad Sani Umar, 4, 17, 19, 119, 130, 135, 143, 145, 166, 212, 234, 242
  attitude towards history, 184
  attitude towards Islamism, 172
  and Boko Haram, 231
  commentary on Ibn Taymiyya, 137
  life before Medina, 99
  and mawlid broadcast, 157
  relationship with Izala, 96, 111
  return to Nigeria, 103
Ringim, Uba, 158
Riyad, 67, 70, 72
Roman Catholic Church, 13
Roosevelt, Franklin Delano, 68

Sabuwar Gandu Mosque, 152, 156, 161, 213
Sabuwar Gandu neighborhood, 105, 140, 142, 144
Sahara, 197
Sahel, 197

saints, 12, 50
Salafism, 1
  definition of, 2, 11, 32
  history of, 19
Salafiyya, 19, 53
Salih, Ali Abdullah, 221
Sanusi, Sanusi Lamido, 21, 166
Saudi Arabia, 1, 4, 7, 9, 13, 16, 33, 35, 42, 44, 46, 52, 54, 64, 83, 84, 90, 111, 121, 133, 162, 165, 171, 180, 196, 201, 210, 227, 241
  absorption of Islamic revivalists, 58
  Nigerian students' life in, 102
  outreach to Africa, 67, 90
  resources of, 66
scriptural literalism, 48
scripturalism, 18, 141
scripture, 2, 45, 119, 124, 142, 149, 189, 244
sectarianism, 22, 38, 94, 163, 171
secularism, 142, 146, 151, 198, 209, 212
security force abuses, 206, 215
Senegal, 64, 69, 77, 89, 104
Sermon of Necessity, 10, 11, 93, 126, 194, 208, 215
  and ISIS, 217
Shah Wali Allah, 49, 50, 54
Shakir, Ahmad, 59, 60, 186, 195, 214, 230
  and Boko Haram, 209
sharīʿa, 23, 103, 152, 160, 164, 170, 171, 182
  and Boko Haram, 201
  and Hisbah, 188
  implementation in northern Nigeria, 178
Shekarau, Ibrahim, 97, 103, 140, 148, 169, 171, 178
Shekau, Abubakar, 26, 194, 222, 241
  as leader of Boko Haram, 207
  jihadist discourses of, 218
Sheriff, Ali Modu, 203, 204
Shettima, Kashim, 205
Shīʿa, 37, 40, 92, 112, 199, 208
Shiʿism
  in Nigeria, 22
Shitu, Halima, 97
Smith, Wilfred Cantwell, 124
social contract, 151
Sokoto Caliphate, 20, 78
Somalia, 5, 197, 240
strangers, 168
Sudan, 5, 64, 78, 100, 104, 164, 170, 226
Sufism, 2, 5, 6, 7, 40, 45, 48, 50, 54, 56, 67, 77, 80, 82, 87, 90, 106, 120, 134, 142, 153, 181, 212, 217, 231
  and responses to Salafism, 163
  in Nigeria, 22
Sunna, 2, 53, 58, 61, 117, 131, 155, 172, 208
  Sufi understanding of, 159
syncretism, 241
Syria, 4, 15, 41, 56, 60, 157, 174, 193, 227, 228

tafsir, 43, 84, 85, 105, 119, 151, 183, 198, 231, 235
takfir, 109, 135, 211, 215
  and Ibn Taymiyya, 44
Taliban, 180, 240
television, 152
terrorism, 206, 242
Thailand, 5
theology, 5, 9, 17, 39, 84, 112, 170
Tijaniyya, 77, 83, 104, 112, 140, 158, 208, 236
  and Salafism, 163
  and the Sabuwar Gandu Mosque, 152
Timbuktu, 121
Togo, 97, 232
tombs, 212
Toronto, 89
translation, 120, 122, 123, 124, 126, 131, 135, 138, 146, 186, 212, 238, 244
truth, 159, 179
Tunisia, 3, 180
Turkey, 41
Twitter, 226, 234

Umar, Bashir Aliyu, 136
  life before Medina, 99
  return to Nigeria, 103
Umayyad Caliphate, 37
Umm al-Qura University, 97
United Nations, 205
Uthman bin Affan Group, 102, 175
Uthman dan Fodio, 20
Uthman, Tijjani, 158, 162

values, 34, 91, 172
vanguard, 112, 132, 157, 167, 182, 208, 213, 242
  as structuring ideal of Salafi politics, 175
vigilantes, 200, 206, 215, 229
violence, 163, 196, 200, 206, 214, 231, 233, 234, 236, 242
  against Muslim rulers, 208
  in Nigerian politics, 177

Wahhābism, 7, 18, 19, 35, 46, 56, 61, 65, 73, 80, 107, 118, 156, 165, 195, 218
  and Boko Haram, 212
  and Yemeni Traditionists, 48
war, 22, 38, 179
War on Terror, 221, 240
Western-style schools, 97, 122, 198, 208, 209
  and Boko Haram, 194, 212

women, 173
  and public morality, 187
  and Salafism, 97, 103, 126, 141, 182
  in Afghanistan, 179
World Assembly of Muslim Youth, 72

Yar'Adua, Umaru, 204
Yemen, 4, 32, 34, 46, 68, 90, 221, 224, 240
Yoruba, 78, 89, 94
youth, 94, 113, 117, 141, 157, 182
  Salafi appeal to, 103
YouTube, 226, 234
Yusuf, Muhammad, 26, 113, 199, 218, 219, 222, 241
  and mainstream Salafis, 231
  and Nigerian politics, 203
  relationship with Salafi canon, 209
  rhetorical deb to Ja'far Mahmud Adam, 194

Zamfara, 185
Zaria, 98

Titles in the Series

52. ALEXANDER THURSTON *Salafism in Nigeria: Islam, preaching, and politics*
51. ANDREW BANK *Pioneers of the Field: South Africa's women anthropologists*
50. MAXIM BOLT *Zimbabwe's Migrants and South Africa's Border Farms: The roots of impermanence*
49. MEERA VENKATACHALAM *Slavery, Memory and Religion in Southeastern Ghana, c.1850–Present*
48. DEREK PETERSON, KODZO GAVUA, and CIRAJ RASSOOL (eds.) *The Politics of Heritage in Africa: economies, histories and infrastructures*
47. ILANA VAN WYK *The Universal Church of the Kingdom of God in South Africa: a church of strangers*
46. JOEL CABRITA *Text and Authority in the South African Nazaretha Church*
45. MARLOES JANSON *Islam, Youth, and Modernity in the Gambia: the Tablighi Jama'at*
44. ANDREW BANK and LESLIE J. BANK (eds) *Inside African Anthropology: Monica Wilson and her interpreters*
43. ISAK NIEHAUS *Witchcraft and a Life in the New South Africa*
42. FRASER G. MCNEILL *AIDS, Politics, and Music in South Africa*
41. KRIJN PETERS *War and the Crisis of Youth in Sierra Leone*
40. INSA NOLTE *Obafemi Awolowo and the Making of Remo: the local politics of a Nigerian nationalist*
39. BEN JONES *Beyond the State in Rural Uganda*
38. RAMON SARRÓ *The Politics of Religious Change on the Upper Guinea Coast: iconoclasm done and undone*
37. CHARLES GORE *Art, Performance and Ritual in Benin City*
36. FERDINAND DE JONG *Masquerades of Modernity: power and secrecy in Casamance, Senegal*
35. KAI KRESSE *Philosophising in Mombasa: knowledge, Islam and intellectual practice on the Swahili coast*
34. DAVID PRATTEN *The Man-Leopard Murders: history and society in colonial Nigeria*
33. CAROLA LENTZ *Ethnicity and the Making of History in Northern Ghana*
32. BENJAMIN F. SOARES *Islam and the Prayer Economy: history and authority in a Malian town*
31. COLIN MURRAY and PETER SANDERS *Medicine Murder in Colonial Lesotho: the anatomy of a moral crisis*
30. R. M. DILLEY *Islamic and Caste Knowledge Practices among Haalpulaar'en in Senegal: between mosque and termite mound*
29. BELINDA BOZZOLI *Theatres of Struggle and the End of Apartheid*
28. ELISHA RENNE *Population and Progress in a Yoruba Town*
27. ANTHONY SIMPSON *"Half-London" in Zambia: contested identities in a Catholic mission school*
26. HARRI ENGLUND *From War to Peace on the Mozambique–Malawi Borderland*
25. T. C. MCCASKIE *Asante Identities: history and modernity in an African village 1850–1950*
24. JANET BUJRA *Serving Class: masculinity and the feminisation of domestic service in Tanzania*

23. CHRISTOPHER O. DAVIS *Death in Abeyance: illness and therapy among the Tabwa of Central Africa*
22. DEBORAH JAMES *Songs of the Women Migrants: performance and identity in South Africa*
21. BIRGIT MEYER *Translating the Devil: religion and modernity among the Ewe in Ghana*
20. DAVID MAXWELL *Christians and Chiefs in Zimbabwe: a social history of the Hwesa people c. 1870s–1990s*
19. FIONA D. MACKENZIE *Land, Ecology and Resistance in Kenya, 1880–1952*
18. JANE I. GUYER *An African Niche Economy: farming to feed Ibadan, 1968–88*
17. PHILIP BURNHAM *The Politics of Cultural Difference in Northern Cameroon*
16. GRAHAM FURNISS *Poetry, Prose and Popular Culture in Hausa*
15. C. BAWA YAMBA *Permanent Pilgrims: the role of pilgrimage in the lives of West African Muslims in Sudan*
14. TOM FORREST *The Advance of African Capital: the growth of Nigerian private enterprise*
13. MELISSA LEACH *Rainforest Relations: gender and resource use among the Mende of Gola, Sierra Leone*
12. ISAAC NCUBE MAZONDE *Ranching and Enterprise in Eastern Botswana: a case study of black and white farmers*
11. G. S. EADES *Strangers and Traders: Yoruba migrants, markets and the state in northern Ghana*
10. COLIN MURRAY *Black Mountain: land, class and power in the eastern Orange Free State, 1880s to 1980s*
9. RICHARD WERBNER *Tears of the Dead: the social biography of an African family*
8. RICHARD FARDON *Between God, the Dead and the Wild: Chamba interpretations of religion and ritual*
7. KARIN BARBER *I Could Speak Until Tomorrow:* oriki, *women and the past in a Yoruba town*
6. SUZETTE HEALD *Controlling Anger: the sociology of Gisu violence*
5. GUNTHER SCHLEE *Identities on the Move: clanship and pastoralism in northern Kenya*
4. JOHAN POTTIER *Migrants No More: settlement and survival in Mambwe villages, Zambia*
3. PAUL SPENCER *The Maasai of Matapato: a study of rituals of rebellion*
2. JANE I. GUYER (ed.) *Feeding African Cities: essays in social history*
1. SANDRA T. BARNES *Patrons and Power: creating a political community in metropolitan Lagos*